CASS SERIES: STUDIES IN INTELLIGENCE
(Series Editors: Christopher Andrew and Michael I. Handel)

FROM INFORMATION TO INTRIGUE

Also in this series

FROM INFORMATION TO INTRIGUE

Studies in Secret Service
Based on the Swedish Experience
1939–45

C.G. McKay

FRANK CASS

First published 1993 in Great Britain by
FRANK CASS & CO. LTD.
Gainsborough House, Gainsborough Road,
London E11 1RS, England

and in the United States of America by
FRANK CASS
c/o International Specialized Book Services, Inc.,
5804 N.E. Hassalo Street,
Portland, Oregon 97213-3644

British Library Cataloguing in Publication Data

McKay, C.G.
  From Information to Intrigue: Studies in
  Secret Service Based on the Swedish
  Experience, 1939–45. (Studies in
  Intelligence Series)
  I. Title II. Series
  327.12485

  ISBN 0-7146-3470-0

Library of Congress Cataloging-in-Publication Data

McKay, C.G., 1940–
  From information to intrigue: studies in secret service: based
  on the Swedish experience, 1939–45 / C.G. McKay.
      p.   cm. — (Cass series—studies in intelligence)
  Includes bibliographical references and index.
  ISBN 0-7146-3470-0
  1. World War, 1939–1945—Secret service—Sweden. 2. World War,
  1939-1945—Secret service—Great Britain. 3. World War, 1939–1945—
  Secret service—Germany. I. Title. II. Series.
  D810.S7M38 1993
  940.54'85—dc20   92-35249
                                                                        CIP

Typeset by Vitaset, Paddock Wood, Kent
Printed in Great Britain by
Antony Rowe Ltd, Chippenham

Contents

From the neatly purloined telegram to the nicely planted lie,
From information to intrigue,
The spectrum of the spy.

Felix Filosoff

Preface

Interesting themes require no lengthy introduction but kind people deserve thanks. Nor is my gratitude any less for being expressed collectively, rather than individually. Every writer on a historical topic is dependent on the information at their disposal, and the present monograph has only been made possible by the goodwill, kindness and co-operation of a great many people in several countries. I am indebted to those unsung heroes, the keepers of the archives who facilitated my search for relevant documents and courteously received my sometimes curious requests. I also have an obvious debt to other authors who have ploughed in neighbouring fields although it would be a trifle too polite to say that I have trustingly accepted what they have to relate. Through the years, former members of Stockholm's *corps diplomatique* and others – gamekeepers and poachers – with intimate knowledge of the events described have generously provided me with informal accounts that often usefully complement official records.

It is not for the author to decide how ingenious he has been in navigating the quicksands which infest this area of historical research. As the author of one fascinating book on the Oslo Report, based upon considerable research and much praised by the great and the good, was subsequently to discover, what is highly plausible is not always what is true. A certain humility is therefore in order. I have tried at any rate to make an unhurried and dispassionate analysis of a wide range of source material relevant to the subjects I address and can only hope that this will have saved me from straying too far from the firm ground of truth. A familiar *caveat* is in order: I do not claim to have said the last word on the topics mentioned in the text, far less to have covered all matters of potential interest.

The organisation of the book is straightforward. Chapter 1 begins by providing a conceptual framework for the theme of the book as a whole and then goes on to describe Swedish wartime legislation and those Swedish organisations most intimately concerned with matters of internal security and intelligence. Chapter 2 deals with the work of the British and certain other Allied special services while Chapter 3 is devoted to the German side of the equation. The appendices follow. The archival sources mentioned in the notes and a fairly extensive bibliography should assist those wishing to pursue the subject in more depth. Indeed even the general reader is recommended to browse through the notes. A subject like the present one does not lend itself easily to a linear presentation and the notes, apart from their role in giving chapter and verse, provide a limited but useful opportunity for supplementary observations, qualifications and speculations. British State Papers in the Public Record Office are Crown Copyright and are quoted by permission of the Controller of HM Stationery Office.

I am very grateful to Professor Wilhelm Carlgren and Sven Wäsström for casting their experienced eyes over initial drafts of this book.

It would be pleasant, of course, to disclaim the final responsibility for those errors – whether of fact or judgement – which remain, but I fear that in this instance I am compelled to echo Blinker Hall and say 'Alone I did it'.

London, July 1991

1

Gamekeeper's perspective

FIRST PRINCIPLES

Some states try to maintain their national security through military alliance; other states reckon that this aim is best served by avoiding such ties altogether, hoping in time of war, as neutrals, not only to ensure that their territory remains outside the field of conflict but also to preserve as far as possible their accustomed commercial and diplomatic ties with the belligerents, irrespective of side.

Neutral status presupposes both rights and obligations. However, the actual policies and behaviour of a neutral are in practice shaped by a host of factors relevant to the complex calculus of statecraft: its geographical position; the strategy and war aims of the belligerents; the neutral country's relative military and economic strength; its state of military preparedness; the morale and attitudes of its people; its economic ties; the strength of its ideological preferences; its historical links of language, culture, kinship and sentiment; and last but not least the expectation of its policy makers as regards the military outcome of the conflict. It is a calculus in which perceptions, as well as the facts they relate to, have to be taken into account.

At the beginning of the Second World War, there were no fewer than twenty neutral European states. By the end of 1944, only six remained: Sweden, Switzerland, Turkey, Spain, Portugal and the Irish Republic. How the neutral countries proposed to steer their course was one thing; but for the belligerent states themselves, absorbed by the calculations of war, the neutral countries were viewed in accordance with their own pragmatic ends. In varying degrees, the neutral states functioned as potential sources of supplies. In addition, they constituted useful listening posts and were to serve, in different ways, as support points for mounting a range of more or less clandestine activities: the collection of information by unauthorised means; the provision of courier facilities for underground movements and intelligence services; counter-espionage; economic warfare; the distribution of black propaganda; the spreading of rumour; exercises in deception; the extension and reception of peace feelers. This overspill of war in the form of clandestine activity in neutral countries – the chief concern of the present monograph – was nothing new. The First World War when in the north Sweden, Norway and Denmark all remained neutral, provided several illustrations of some of its characteristic features:

The former British Minister at Stockholm, Sir Esme Howard, recounts in his memoirs how Mr. Owen Philpots was sent from Britain to take charge of the special investigative work involved in blacklisting those individuals and companies in Sweden suspected of forwarding prohibited goods to Germany, after the consuls had shown a reluctance to become engaged in this work.[1]

On 9 October 1918, a former corporal in the Swedish armed forces was arrested and later charged with supplying, during 1917 and 1918, hundreds of reports regarding individuals and individual firms trading with the Central Powers and regarding the cargoes, arrivals and departures of vessels calling at Swedish ports, to the French Naval Attaché, Talpomba and the American Assistant Military Attaché, Thorling. The corporal was also charged with having engaged in military espionage against Germany.[2]

In 1917, the Germans established an information post in Gothenburg under the command of Captain Lassen, who had previously served at Antwerp. Its function was to collect intelligence about Entente vessels and trade as well as information about the position of minefields etc. When one of the members of the organisation was compromised and expelled, it continued to operate under commercial cover as the trading company 'Emptio'.[3]

In 1917, the French Naval Attaché, Talpomba, enlisted the help of certain youths, including a very junior member of the Swedish Telegraph Service, to provide him in due course with several hundred copies of official German, Austrian and Turkish

2

telegrams passing between the legations of these countries in Stockholm and their respective foreign offices.[4]

The first German spy arrested in Britain was Karl Lody. Lody was in correspondence with a merchant Adolf Burchard, Stockholm. Inside one of Lody' s letters was another envelope addressed to J. Stammer, Berlin.[5]

A member of the editorial staff of *Göteborgs Aftonblad* was given the task of recruiting people in Sweden to travel to England on espionage missions.[6]

In a Swedish memorandum of 31 October 1918 relating to a visa application by the Greek citizen, Lykiardopoulos, it was said that there were grounds for considering him the leader of a comprehensive military espionage organisation in Stockholm. At the beginning of the war, he had lived in Sweden under a false name. In May of 1916, the police had been instructed to keep him under surveillance after his return from a visit to Germany. Bruce Lockhart mentions in *Memoirs of a British Agent* that at the end of 1915 Lykiardopoulos, who was secretary of the Moscow Arts Theatre, 'had undertaken a hazardous mission on our behalf into Germany', travelling as a Greek tobacco merchant.[7]

In an attempt to repair the damage done to its system of overseas communications by the *Telconia*'s successful slicing of German underwater telegraph cables and to circumvent enemy monitoring activities, *Auswärtiges Amt* persuaded the Swedish Ministry for Foreign Affairs to allow it to make use of Swedish cables and the Swedish diplomatic pouch for its traffic between Berlin and Washington. In 1915, the British lodged a protest in Stockholm which led to a discontinuation of some of this traffic. However German traffic continued to use the Swedish communication channels to North America by means of a detour via South America.[8]

Fully conscious of the difficulties of waging a war on two fronts, Imperial Germany strove to split the alliance of their opponents. This could be accomplished in two basic ways. One was to appeal to influential groups in the enemy camp to work towards the conclusion of a separate peace. Several discreet attempts to probe possible Russian interest in such a peace, were made through Stockholm.[9]

When the various attempts to promote separate peace negotiations failed, Germany increasingly relied on the second method of weakening the enemy alliance, namely by fomenting disorder in the empires of its adversaries through the support of diverse movements for national independence or for socialist revolution (*Revolutionierungspolitik*). The neutral countries became havens for the representatives of such movements. Often sustained by German funds if not always responsive to German wishes, the representatives were able to organise conferences and issue propaganda likely to embarrass the common enemy. At the same time, links were maintained with secret sympathisers at home. Stockholm provided an important base for various groups working against Imperial Russia: Finns, Balts, Bolsheviks and others.[10]

In 1917, a certain Baron von Rautenfels, a courier in the service of the Kaiser, was detained by the police in Kristiania and his official baggage was opened to disclose a large amount of sabotage equipment, some part of which was believed to be intended for German-sponsored operations within Russia.[11]

The involvement of neutral countries in clandestine activities is not fortuitous: rather it is a consequence of the logic of neutrality and the totalisation of war.

First and most important, the neutral state enjoys the right of being able to maintain diplomatic and commercial relations with both belligerents. Neutral diplomats are able to report from the belligerent countries; merchant ships and commercial aircraft may travel between neutral countries and the belligerents. This fact immediately gives rise to the possibility of various types of *flow* whether they are flows from one belligerent B1 to the other belligerent B2 via the neutral N (*transit flows*) or simply flows which originate in N and end up in a belligerent B or vice-versa (*non-transit flows*). There are also transit flows which go from an area or country occupied by a belligerent B via N to another area or country occupied by B. In the case of transit flows, N functions as a *channel* or *connecting corridor*: in the case of non-transit flows between N and a belligerent B, N may in practical terms function as an *annex* to B. Transit flows involving a neutral N are in an obvious sense *roundabout* or *indirect*. It is this latter feature which often makes them of particular interest to a belligerent seeking a cloak for some activity since a well-established technique in all clandestine activity is precisely the use of indirect links.

The foregoing notion of flow is abstract and therefore usefully wide. There are flows of goods and services, of money, of men and of information. The flow of goods may be made up of a single piece of complex technical equipment, a crashed rocket, or tons of metallic ore. The flow of men may consist of trainloads of troops on leave or single civilian couriers. The individuals involved in the flow may be nationals belonging to one of the belligerent states or to a state occupied by a belligerent or they may be citizens of a neutral state. They may be senior diplomats, legation chauffeurs, international bankers or merchant seamen. The flow of money covers sackloads of dollars, gold, works of art and bank credits. The flow of information embraces the flow of military intelligence as well as newspapers, books, films, academic theses and radio transmissions. Rumour, propaganda and deception material also constitute flows of information, albeit of a special kind.

International law, which merely codifies certain agreements slowly arrived at by the representatives of sovereign states conferring together, already places certain restrictions on flows between neutral and belligerent states. Thus Article 2 of the Hague Convention (V) respecting the rights and duties of neutral powers and persons in case of war on land (1907) specifies that:

> Belligerents are forbidden to move troops or convoys of either munitions of war or supplies across the territory of a neutral Power.[12]

Article 5 ordains (by implication) that a neutral Power must not allow such a flow to take place. Prize law and the contraband list stipulate which items may or may not be carried on a neutral ship to a belligerent. Further restrictions may apply by reason of some particular treaty or agreement reached between the neutral state and a belligerent. Thus the 1939 War Trade Agreement between Sweden and Great Britain placed a ceiling on the amount of iron ore which could be annually supplied to Germany by Sweden. Lastly there are the specific restrictions introduced by a belligerent to control flows within its own territory. Thus in the case of the flow of men, while a company in a neutral country may be allowed to send a commercial representative to a branch factory in a belligerent state, the security service of the belligerent state may refuse to sanction the right to enter

5

of certain individuals or, having conceded it, may place restrictions on their movements within the country, certain regions being placed out of bounds.

Although laws, treaties and agreements have a normative role and provide to some extent standards which may be appealed to in a controversy, it is a commonplace of history that they are not always honoured to the full. Such regulatory codes cannot cover every contingency; the rapid dynamic of events may make them less relevant; ambiguities in their formulation may be exploited in unforeseen ways. An agreement may be reached between states but states are made up of individuals and individual companies and these do not always observe the niceties of government regulations. War places great pressures on both belligerents and neutrals and at the end of the day international law and indeed any prior paper commitment will tend to give way to what is conceived as a vital national interest or more generally as a vital interest of the alliance to which the nation is party. For this reason, irrespective of any formal agreements which may have been signed, a belligerent B cannot afford to ignore flows involving a neutral N. In practical terms, N may constitute a chink in its armour; alternatively it may constitute a chink in the enemy's armour, to be exploited to best advantage.

A second reason for the involvement of neutral territory in clandestine activities, is to be found in the principle of comparative advantage. A neutral country is often not to the same degree subject to the whole range of internal restrictions imposed by a belligerent. Even if certain practices are expressly forbidden by law, the penalty for defying the law may be significantly less than that which would be exacted in the territory of a belligerent. Espionage is a case in point, being often a capital offence in a state at war but a non-capital offence in a neutral country, if it is directed against a power other than the neutral country itself.

Lastly, a neutral state often forms a place of asylum for diverse refugees from territory controlled by the belligerent powers. They form a pool of knowledge regarding their homelands and countrymen and from their ranks can sometimes be recruited useful and willing foot-soldiers of clandestine warfare: agitators, cutouts, couriers and agents. Equally, *agents provocateurs*, spies and informers may be infiltrated as self-proclaimed refugees to work in secret against that power which, under a false flag, they claim to support. They identify hostile elements, reveal the structure of their covert and open

6

organisations; more actively they may attempt to neutralise these organisations by pursuing or advocating a course of action likely to compromise their standing and reputation with the host nation.

The imminence of war leads, in countries likely to be affected, to the introduction of regulations of all sorts, intended to safeguard national security. The movement of aliens within a country is subject to greater controls, the press may be subject to certain types of censorship and so on. The flow of fresh information passing via open channels, declines at a time when relevant information is at a premium. How far this shortfall in information can be made up via conventional diplomatic contacts and the confidential exchange of information between governments, is open to question. One element in helping to close a government's information gap is the intensification of effort by Secret or Special Services entrusted with the task of collecting information by unauthorised means. There are several sound operational reasons why such unauthorised collection of information is kept as secret as possible.

The collection of information is, however, only one of several activities which may from time to time require clandestine methods. Covert action (propaganda, sabotage) may be entrusted to a section of an intelligence service or it may be the concern of a separate service set up for that purpose. This applies also to counter-espionage. At the same time, it is clear that the study of clandestine activities cannot simply be restricted to the study of the activities of the Special Services since individuals and organisations outside the ranks of these services may also engage briefly or over a period of time in important secret activities which are of interest for the present study. Service attachés, for example, although by diplomatic convention barred from having any truck with spies and agents, may none the less under the pressure of war or some other pressure be disposed to cut corners in their quest for information. Increased use of diplomatic cover for personnel of the Special Services tends further to blur distinctions between what might be called the regular and irregular members of a mission. Diplomatic immunity may be a necessary requirement for certain members of an intelligence service but if they are compromised, their status may have unpalatable consequences for the head of the mission and his staff. It is not unusual for this circumstance to create tensions within a mission between the representatives of the Special Services and those who for one reason or another disapprove of their activities and who fear its possible repercussions. To the friction that often

7

exists between *bona fide* diplomats and the members of the clandestine services must be added the friction generated by rivalries between different arms of the clandestine services themselves.

The increase in clandestine activities brought about by a war, if unchecked, carries with it a threat to the internal stability of the host nation. No autonomous state will tolerate representatives of a foreign power conspiring to blow up commercial or military installations in its territory or acquiring, by some unauthorised means, knowledge of its most sensitive defence secrets. Nor can any state afford to turn a blind eye to attempts by a foreign power to mould internal opinion, whether covertly or otherwise.

In the case of neutral states, however, a further complication arises from the essentially triangular nature of neutrality: the activities of belligerent A, while not a *direct* threat or inconvenience to a neutral N, may nevertheless – if they are directed against belligerent B and simultaneously make use of N's neutrality – constitute an *indirect* threat or inconvenience, inasmuch that *if they become known to B*, they serve to discredit N's neutrality in B's eyes and may lead B to retaliate in a way injurious to N's own national interests. The italicised condition is worth noting for it also suggests why secret agreements of various kinds have a part to play in the diplomacy of neutral states themselves.

IN DEFENCE OF THE REALM

It is unclear how far the punishments meted out by criminal law are ever likely to deter individuals from espionage and related offences against the state. Diplomatic immunity may also place important restrictions on the effectiveness of law in this sphere. But legislation regarding such offences and the extraordinary powers conferred on the executive organs of control in time of crisis, provide a state with the formal instruments for the relatively unhampered monitoring of potentially subversive activity. Control is achieved not through one law, but by the combined effect of a number of laws working together. In the following sub-section, some of the more important wartime Swedish laws impinging on internal security are reviewed, and in the next sub-section a description is given of the principal Swedish authorities involved in the monitoring and control of clandestine activities. The third sub-section deals briefly with some of the methods employed.

Laws
Aliens. In the basic law relating to aliens[13] regulations were set forth covering such matters as passport, visa, residence and work permits, refusal of entry and expulsion. Thus according to Chapter 2, section 7 of this law, aliens intending to remain in the country for over 3 months were required to have a residence permit. The responsibility for the detailed implementation of these regulations fell upon a number of authorities: the National Social Welfare Board, the police, the passport authorities and the Ministry for Foreign Affairs. According to Chapter 8, section 54, the Crown retained the right to introduce, when necessary, special provisions regarding refusal of entry and expulsion. Fears about an uncontrolled immigration of Jewish refugees led soon after the *Anschluss*, to tighter control. By September 1938, however, various concerned authorities were expressing doubts about the adequacy of existing procedures. There was a demand for a census of aliens in the country and this was subsequently implemented in the period 10–18 February 1939. Another law introduced at the beginning of 1939 imposed restrictions on the presence and movement of aliens within certain militarily sensitive areas.[14] Section 3 of this law, *inter alia*, prohibited aliens from taking photographs within a prohibited area, drawing objects of importance to the defence of the realm or carrying out topographic or other measurements.

With the outbreak of war, a visa requirement was introduced for citizens outside the Nordic area and simultaneously the frontier control system was strengthened.[15] In a decree of 14 October 1939, it was announced that the National Social Welfare Board had the right to prohibit aliens from entering certain railway, harbour or factory areas or from photographing in such areas, if the situation required it. The invasion of Norway and Denmark led to this power being put into effect in the decree of 16 April 1940. A regulation introduced the day after placed the northernmost part of Sweden out of bounds for aliens other than Finns.[16] This was the first of a series of decrees restricting the movements of aliens within certain specific geographical regions.[17] Arrangements were made for the detention or internment of aliens in cases where it had not been possible to execute a refusal of entry or expulsion order and establishments for this purpose were set up.

The movements of foreigners within the country could also be monitored in other simple ways. Thus hotels and guest-houses were routinely required by law to provide the police with basic information regarding their guests, a requirement later extended to anyone

9

providing a foreigner with sleeping quarters.[18] Existing statutes variously attempted to limit foreign influence within the country in key sectors such as mining.

Espionage. According to Chapter II, Article 29 of the Hague Convention on Land Warfare, 1907, a person 'can only be considered a spy when, acting clandestinely or on false pretences, he obtains or endeavours to obtain information in the zone of operations of a belligerent, with the intention of communicating it to the hostile party', and in Article 30, it is laid down that 'a spy taken in the act shall not be punished without previous trial'.[19] Although Article 29 offers a definition of the spy in the classical sense – that is a collector of information 'acting clandestinely or on false pretences' in the service of another – it is plain that a state cannot ignore the activities of those who do not disguise their attempts to acquire certain types of sensitive information about it, on behalf of a foreign power. The fact that the collection of this information is undertaken on behalf of a foreign power is more important than the form (covert or otherwise) which the collection takes. Furthermore, the Hague Convention is concerned solely with the laws of warfare. But information-gathering activities prejudicial to national security occur in times of peace as well as in times of war and legislation must be framed to deal with such activities in all their various forms. The Swedish laws relating to espionage for the period under consideration were to be found in Chapter 8 of the Penal Code which dealt with treason and crimes prejudicial to the security of the realm. In addition to the paragraphs dealing with espionage, this chapter included laws covering rebellion and armed insurrection, diplomatic treason, the recruitment in the realm of men for service in the armies of foreign states, the spreading of rumour likely to endanger the security of the realm, the receipt of foreign financial or other support for propaganda activities within the country. Chapter 8 was to undergo several important revisions in the course of the Second World War and by way of orientation, it is useful to begin by looking at the legislation relating to espionage as set forth in the enactment of May 1940. The first section dealing with espionage was section 8. Its first sentence stipulated:

> Whosoever in war or when war threatens the realm, allows himself to be used by the enemy to obtain information about matters of fact which ought to be kept secret with respect to the

security of the realm or its provisioning, is to be sentenced for war espionage to hard labour for life or from six to ten years.[20]

Section 8 was restricted in its application by the condition 'in war or when war threatens the realm'. Less restricted in character were sections 9–12. Sections 9 and 10 dealt with the unauthorised collection and supply of secret information. Section 9 read as follows:

> Whosoever without authorisation places himself in possession of, or gathers information about some matter of fact which ought to be kept secret from a foreign power with respect to the realm's friendly relations with such a power or with respect to the defence of the realm or its provisioning in war and in the exceptional circumstances occasioned by war, is to be sentenced to a maximum of two years' hard labour. The same law applies where someone without authorisation has any dealings with writings, drawings or any other object involving information about a matter of fact of the aforementioned kind.[21]

If section 9 was aimed at the person who *collects* the information, section 10 dealt with the person who, without authorisation, *supplies* the information. Anyone guilty of such unauthorised supply of secret information could be sentenced to a maximum of two years' hard labour or prison with the possibility of a fine in cases where the danger to national security was minimal. If the offences covered in sections 9 and 10 were committed *with the intention of assisting a foreign power*, the charge became (according to section 11) one of espionage and a maximum sentence of six years could be imposed. In the case of someone in a particular position of trust who was found guilty of the unauthorised supply of information, the sentences could be increased to six years' hard labour or to six to ten years' hard labour or life, depending upon whether the charge was one of espionage or not.

Laws relating to the collection and supply of secret information and espionage in the sense of section 11 had been introduced first in 1913. Not so, however, section 14:

> Whosoever with the purpose of assisting a foreign power collects or allows to be collected information about matters concerning the realm or another power, the communication of which to a foreign power can injure the realm's friendly relations with a foreign power or its defence or also its provisioning in war and in the exceptional circumstances occasioned by war, or for the

11

aforesaid purpose has any dealings with such information, is to be sentenced, unless a heavier sentence is merited, for espionage to prison or hard labour for a maximum of two years.

The same law applies to anyone in the realm who otherwise on behalf of a foreign power carries out secret intelligence activity for a military or political purpose.[22]

This wide-ranging law prohibiting in certain circumstances the collection of *non-secret* information, was to be the source of much controversy and it is useful to review its development before 1940.

Non-secret information/unlawful intelligence activity. In 1932, there had been motions in both Chambers of the *Riksdag*, calling for new legislation against subversive activities but these motions failed to gain support. The next year another attempt was made and a committee of enquiry was set up to look into the matter. Its conclusions, however, were not unanimous. The deliberations of the committee eventually appeared in an official report.[23] Among the package of measures proposed was a new law (Chapter 8, section 21a) designed to make it a criminal offence for a Swedish citizen to collect or allow to be collected information, *not publicly accessible in print*, concerning the defence of the realm or matters influencing its defence capability, with the purpose of assisting a foreign power.

In suggesting such an extension of the espionage legislation to cover the collection of non-secret information, the report drew attention to the activities of the so-called Sillén Communists – that part of the fissiparous Swedish Communist movement which accepted the authority of the Comintern. At an anti-war conference in Stockholm on 22 September 1934, a unanimous resolution had been carried concerning the organisation of activities within the armed forces whereby one group was to deal with propaganda against militarism while the other was to be concerned with the establishment of an information service, involving the regular reporting on the political views of the troops, their quarters, their weaponry, their supplies of fuel and other materials. Although at least one military commander doubted the need or possibility of legislating against this type of information work, the report of the enquiry stated that it was desirable that those involved in such activities were dissuaded from the belief that there was nothing impermissible about supplying information to a foreign power. It was argued that the boundary

12

between the secret and the non-secret was constantly changing and there was therefore, by implication, a risk that such information collection could be extended imperceptibly to encompass increasingly sensitive material.

At the end of January 1936, the goverment presented its Bill dealing with subversive activities. But before it could come before the *Riksdag*, it had to be referred to the Standing Judicial Committee. In considering the proposed formulation of Chapter 8, section 21, this latter body rejected the assumption that an exception should be made for the collection of information already in print. Such material when put together could provide valuable assistance for a foreign intelligence service, which as often as not relied on the co-operation of a Swede for the actual business of collection. Furthermore the Freedom of the Press Act offered little protection for military secrets. For it to be punishable to collect information relating to defence under the proposed law, it was required that the collection was *a systematic enterprise undertaken on behalf of a foreign power*. This key provision afforded, in the view of the Standing Judicial Committee, a safeguard that the proposed exception for material already in print could be discarded without the risk that the new law would have too wide a sphere of application. The Committee noted that a comparable law recently introduced in Switzerland made no distinction between information in print and other types of information.

When Chapter 8, section 21 came before the *Riksdag*, it was the Standing Judicial Committee's formulation that was to win support. Among the dissenting voices was that of Östen Undén, a law professor who was no stranger to high office:

> I for my part as a government member, have had the opportunity of reading many of the reports from our military attachés abroad and I may say that it is very often the case that their information is based on newspaper articles in the foreign country concerned. These official government representatives have after all been given the task of acquiring information in some foreign country or other. That is why indeed they are placed in the different states. It seems to me under these circumstances that it would be a rather unreasonable illogicality for Sweden to criminalise in its Penal Code such collection of newspaper items, even allowing for the fact that this would not apply to foreigners, but only to Swedish citizens.[24]

Furthermore how would the law be applied? The Chinese Legation in Stockholm (Undén went on to muse) employed a Swedish secretary whose job was to keep track of articles in the Swedish press dealing with the Swedish Defence system. If this information were to come to the knowledge of the Chinese government, there was nothing to prevent it being handed on to other governments. Would the work of such a secretary therefore be in breach of the law? In general, Undén believed it was wrong to make a mystification of everything to do with defence installations. Their effectiveness did not depend primarily on secrecy and it was a sign of outmoded thinking to believe that it was necessary to surround them with a veil. Indeed paradoxically, the armaments industry was more than willing to supply its manufacturing secrets to prospective customers.

Placed on the Statute Book, the new law, Chapter 8, section 21a, read as follows:

> A Swede who with the purpose of assisting a foreign power collects or allows to be collected information about the armed forces of the realm or about other matters the communication of which to a foreign power can injure the defence of the realm or with the aforesaid purpose has any dealings with such collected information, is to be punished, where the offence does not merit a more severe punishment according to this chapter, with prison. If the circumstances are especially serious, the sentence may be increased to a maximum of two years' hard labour; if they are especially mitigating, fines may be imposed.[25]

Shortly after the outbreak of the Second World War, this law was recast, to give it a greatly increased sphere of application, with the declared intention of preventing the country becoming a base for the operations of foreign intelligence services.[26] First of all, the restriction to Swedish citizens was removed. Secondly, the potential range of injury to the State's interest, specified in the law was extended from *the defence* of the realm in the narrow military sense, to embrace in addition its *provisioning* and its *friendly relations with foreign powers*. Lastly the law applied not only to the collection of information about Sweden but significantly also to the collection of information *about another power* if it could be shown that the collection of such information was prejudicial to Swedish interests in the sense already defined. To be punishable according to section 21a, it was required, however, that the collector of information was *aware of the danger involved in what he was doing.*

In 1940, the new version of Chapter 8 of the Penal Code appeared.[27] The previous 21a was now incorporated in section 14 of the new law which has already been quoted. The second part of this paragraph made any kind of secret intelligence activity 'for a military or political purpose' on behalf of a foreign power, punishable within Swedish territory. Speaking in the debate in the First Chamber of the *Riksdag* on 15 May 1940, Georg Branting, the son of the former leader of the Swedish Social Democratic Party and later a vigorous critic of the Swedish wartime legislation on espionage and of the activities of the Security Service, doubted whether the new revised version of Chapter 8, while strengthening the country's defence on the legal front, did justice to the ability of hostile powers to find new ways of attacking peaceful, civilised societies.[28] The Standing Judicial Committee had pointed out the inadequacy of the existing legislation against sabotage. Branting for his part wondered whether there should not also be sharper measures against defeatist propaganda. Section 21 of Chapter 8 which punished the spreading of false rumour failed to cover more subtle ways of cultivating an attitude of defeat within the population. Branting, in calling upon the Chamber to support the proposals, concluded by emphasising that he viewed the proposed legislation of Chapter 8 as a regrettable temporary necessity brought about by the emergency the country found itself in.

Recapitulating, it may be said that the espionage laws of Chapter 8 (1940) consisted of two fundamental types: those (sections 8–13) involving secret information and those (section 14) involving non-secret material. In addition to these principal laws, Chapter 8 contained certain supplementary laws relating to espionage. Thus section 26 dealt with those who aided or abetted espionage while section 28 dealt with those having knowledge of the commission of this offence.

In the later course of the war, the espionage laws were altered in various ways. In 1942, the overall penalties for espionage were increased. Section 14 was redrafted in a way intended to allow a more discriminating treatment of offences involving non-secret material and now read as follows:

> Whosoever with the purpose of assisting a foreign power collects or allows to be collected information about matters concerning the realm or its relations with another power, the communication

of which to a foreign power can injure the realm's friendly relations with a foreign power or its defence or also its provisioning in war and in the exceptional circumstances occasioned by war, or for the aforesaid purpose has any dealings with such information, is to be sentenced, where a heavier sentence is not deserved for espionage, to prison or hard labour for a maximum of four years.[29]

There was also a new paragraph, section 14a, which introduced the new term *unlawful intelligence activity*:

Whosoever otherwise than previously stated carries out secret intelligence work in the realm on behalf of a foreign power for a military or political purpose, is to be sentenced for unlawful intelligence activity to prison or hard labour for a maximum of two years. If the circumstances are especially mitigating, fines may be imposed.[30]

Sections 26 and 28 were correspondingly recast to cover the changes introduced in section 14 and 14a. In the case of section 26, an additional clause was added:

Whosoever despite the fact that they have reasonable grounds to suppose that espionage or unlawful intelligence activity is being carried out by another, assists in its performance, is to be sentenced to prison or fined.[31]

In formulating this clause, it was argued that on several occasions in the past, people who had been charged with aiding and abetting espionage, had been acquitted because it could not be proved that they had been aware of the kind or aim of the activity in which they had participated. This had been especially the case where a spy had made use of another person's address for the purpose of receiving letters and other communications.

In the *Riksdag*, Östen Undén, although accepting the general need for the stiffer legislation that had been proposed, was unhappy about the scope of section 14a:

Intelligence activity carried out in Sweden and not directed against Sweden, is a criminal offence of a decidedly political chàracter. Hitherto we have been very careful about legislating against such political crimes where our own interests are not directly at stake. It is only in most recent years that the chapter

16

dealing with espionage has been extended generally to cover also these categories of action. With this extension, one has even gone as far as setting on a par in one and the same paragraph espionage offences directed against Sweden and those directed against a foreign country. This was obviously a mistake. It was designed to rub out the boundaries between offences involving espionage against Sweden and simultaneously the paragraph covered actions of very varying type as regards intelligence activity directed against a foreign country.

The Standing Judicial Committee has now in the matter of section 14 partially met the requirements of my Bill and has removed from this paragraph those offences which are directed against a foreign country. Thus there is one paragraph on its own dealing with espionage against Sweden and then other actions have been grouped under the heading 'unlawful intelligence activity'. Among those assigned to the latter are intelligence activities directed against a foreign country. I am grateful to the Standing Committee for introducing this change which as far as I can understand, is an improvement on the Government's Bill. However the Standing Committee has not found itself able to accept my other proposal that prosecution involving this type of offence should be discretionary.[32]

In Undén's view, the new term 'unlawful intelligence activity' appeared too indefinite in its application. He cited the example of a man arriving from a foreign country where he had made various observations about military matters which were of the greatest importance both to Sweden and to other countries. Suppose this man were to report quite idealistically these observations to some official representative of his country. Was such a person really to be put on a par with an espionage organisation involving paid agents?

The Minister of Justice (Westman) believed that Undén had missed the point and that his fears regarding the range of application of the new laws were unfounded. For an action to be punishable, it had to be shown that it was part of a *systematic activity* and this requirement, Westman maintained, was a sufficient safeguard against the type of case envisaged by Undén.

Despite Westman's reassurances, the practical implementation of section 14a, however, continued to arouse controversy. In 1944, Undén tried once more to bring about a change by proposing that the contentious paragraph should be replaced by one directed more restrictedly at those who carried on

> for payment or on behalf of a foreign power, activity in the realm, aimed at obtaining secret information regarding another foreign power's military situation.[33]

The Standing Judicial Committee, however, was unable to accept this proposal.

> Among other things, there are doubts about the suitability of restricting the offence to the obtaining of secret information regarding another foreign power's military situation. Irrespective of the fact that the total character which is characteristic of today's warfare, often makes it difficult to draw a line between military and political matters of fact, a secret intelligence activity of a primarily political kind, can be such that its toleration can place our country's friendly relations with foreign powers, at risk. There is no shortage of examples illustrating this point, among the cases of unlawful intelligence activity that have been brought before the court.[34]

The Committee believed that it would be necessary to undertake an overall revision of Chapter 8. But in the meantime, it considered the best solution would be to accept Undén's earlier proposal to allow discretionary powers, in deciding whether cases under section 14 a should be brought before the court. This proposal was accepted by the *Riksdag* and a law was introduced whereby the permission of the Crown had to be obtained before the Public Prosecutor was allowed to bring charges for offences under Chapter 8, section 14 a or the corresponding parts of sections 26 and 28.[35]

Information and opinion. The espionage laws dealt both with those who try to acquire certain sensitive information and those who supply it. The supply of information was itself subject to restrictions imposed in other laws. Thus section 4 of the Act relating to certain undertakings regarding the import and export of goods, etc., made it a punishable offence to disclose without authorisation, information to a foreign power about the import and export of goods.[36] An analogous law had been introduced during the First World War, primarily in response to the efforts of the *Entente* Powers to collect the trade information required for the drawing up of their Statutory List (Black

List) in the enforcement of the blockade. As far as publications in general were concerned, section 3:10 of the Freedom of the Press Act made certain reservations about the unauthorised publication of information concerning ongoing negotiations with foreign powers and about certain defence matters. In April 1940, a decree was issued specifying in much more detail areas of defence about which it was forbidden to publish information.[37] Different in character were those restrictions aimed at curbing the expression of certain types of opinion.

As far as the propaganda activities of foreign powers was concerned, section 22 of Chapter 8 of the Penal Code ruled that

> Whosoever receives from a foreign power money or some other thing for the purpose of attempting to influence public opinion about the government of the realm or about the running of its internal or external affairs, by the publication or distribution of writings or otherwise, is to be sentenced to prison.[38]

Control of other types of opinion, thought to be injurious to the national interest, was effected in two main ways. First of all, a dormant clause (section 3.9) of the Freedom of the Press Act was resurrected. This allowed the authorities without trial, to confiscate a publication which could generate misunderstanding with a foreign power. Secondly, a law was introduced allowing the Crown to prevent a periodical from making use of the post or public transport facilities for its distribution, where the periodical in question had on repeated occasions endangered the security of the realm, injured its relations with a foreign power, undermined military discipline and/or was intended to bring about the overthrow of the established order with the help of a foreign power or by violent means.[39] Before such a ban could be imposed, the matter had to be put before a special jury appointed for that purpose. The ban could only be imposed for a limited initial period (maximum of six months) but could be extended (by six monthly periods at a time). The application of this clause (section 3.9) and the transport prohibition remained highly controversial, the critics of official government policy maintaining that too often these instruments were primarily used to stifle opinions hostile to Hitler's New Order and therefore likely to elicit unwelcome protests from the German Legation.[40]

One of several tasks assigned to the National Information Board was to see that publications observed the restrictions imposed by the decree of 12 April 1940 regarding certain militarily sensitive types of information.[41] On 16 May 1941, the government decided to set up a 'coordination bureau for counterpropaganda'. Through the Postal Control Section of the Security Service, the Information Board was supplied with examples of foreign propaganda entering the country and its link to various groups within the country was noted. The Board then gave its opinion and recommended counter-measures.

Sabotage. The relevance of sabotage to modern warfare was made vivid for the Swedes with the arrest of Rickman in April 1940 and the ensuing revelations. At the close of the same year, a special sabotage law was introduced. Before this, acts of sabotage had been dealt with under section 6 of Chapter 8 of the Penal Code dealing with treason in time of war or under Chapter 19 dealing with wilful damage to property. However the provisions of this older legislation were considered inadequate and antiquated. Section 1 of the new law stipulated that

> Whosoever with the purpose of damaging the defence or provisioning of the people or of disrupting the administration or the public order,
>
> destroys or damages an establishment, institution or object which is of importance for defence, the provisioning of the people or the administration,
>
> or in the manufacture, delivery, storage or transportation of such an object, causes a defect in the object or brings about a delay in its delivery,
>
> or otherwise delays or impedes the use of an establishment, institution or object as here aforesaid,
>
> or does anything else thereby which is comparable to sabotage, is to be sentenced to hard labour for a maximum of ten years. Where the circumstances are particularly extenuating, a prison sentence may be imposed.[42]

Further clauses dealt with attempted sabotage and incitement to sabotage. Section 3 dealt with those who manufactured, acquired, stored or otherwise had dealings with explosives or other material to be used for the offence. The sabotage law was introduced for a limited period (up to 31 March 1942) but was thereafter successively renewed.

Radio transmitters, etc. Following the outbreak of war, a number of

20

restrictions were introduced regarding radio transmitters. Thus Swedish and foreign vessels in Swedish coastal waters, as well as aircraft in Swedish airspace, were prohibited from making unauthorised use of their transmitters.[43] In November, it became necessary to have official permission (which was granted for a limited period only) for the possession or right to use a transmitter and further special conditions were placed on the use of radio transmitters on foreign vessels and aircraft within Swedish territory.[44] The use of commercial codes or cipher systems in private telegrams was also stringently regulated.

Coercive means. Of great importance for the work of the security authorities, were the laws relating to Special Coercive Means which were introduced in October 1939.[45] These allowed for the interception of mail or telephone calls, in the investigation of offences under Chapters 8 and 19 (the latter containing certain older legislation relating to sabotage, see above) of the Penal Code or under the Act relating to certain undertakings regarding the import and export of goods, etc., which has already been noted. The implementation of these powers could be authorised by certain specified Crown representatives. As a safeguard, the representative was obliged immediately to notify the Justice Chancellor. If the Chancellor upon examination took exception to the measure, he was empowered to call it off.

The Special Coercive Means were further extended by the enactments of January 1940 which relaxed the requirements for interception, allowing in the defined emergency situation for this to be undertaken with a view to *preventing or bringing to light* offences under Chapters 8 and 19, which could injure the defence of the realm or its provisioning or its friendly relations with a foreign power.[46] Furthermore, it was no longer incumbent on the Crown representative authorising the interception to notify the Chancellor of his decision. This obligation however was introduced from 1 July 1943. In addition to the powers to intercept mail and telephone calls, the Special Coercive Measures Act also allowed, under the specified conditions, the rights of search and confiscation and the prohibition of the dispersal of effects.

An important further clause gave the authorities extended powers to hold persons. According to the practice normally adopted, a person apprehended by the police was required to be speedily confronted with the prosecutor who then had to decide whether to release them or to inform them that they were being formally held and that an application for their remand in custody would be made to the court. At most five days (and normally much less) were allowed to elapse between the initial arrest and the court proceedings to determine whether the individual should be remanded in custody or released. Taking the view that investigations into espionage and related offences were often time-consuming, it was now allowed that anyone suspected of offences under Chapters 8 and 19 could be held without court warrant for up to 30 days (and with the Chancellor's approval even longer but at most for an additional 30 days).

After the law had been in force for one year, it became clear that it normally took less than 30 days to bring the individual held under the new legislation before the court. When the law was extended for a further year, the period for which a suspect could be held without court warrant was therefore halved (to 15 days). Thereafter the suspect could be held for a further 45 days, provided the Chancellor's approval was sought after each lapse of 15 days.

During 1942, applications to the Chancellor for the detention of persons for more than 15 days, had been made with respect to 43 persons and in 1943, this fell to one. In the two years before July 1944, there was only one case in which a person had been detained without a court warrant for more than 30 days. It was therefore decided (from July 1944) to reduce the maximum period for detention without a court warrant to 30 days with the proviso that the Chancellor's permission was sought after 15 days.

With the introduction of the Sabotage Law, the Special Coercive Means Act of 1940 was further extended to cover offences under this law. Although introduced for a limited period of time, the Special Coercive Means Act was successively renewed during the course of the war and constituted an essential legal instrument for the work of the Security Service.

Powers to dissolve subversive organisations. In January 1940, during Finland's Winter War, there was widespread criticism of the Communists and in the *Riksdag* there was a call for the prohibition and dissolution of subversive parties. For a time, however, the government preferred to stall, placing its trust instead in the Special Coercive Means at its disposal. But by June 1940, Sweden's situation had become still more precarious and a new emergency Act – now aimed not simply at the Communists but also at the National Socialists – was placed on the statute book, giving the authorities the power to close down potentially dangerous organisations. According to this Act, any

> organisation whose activity aims to overthrow or change the government of the realm by violent means or with the help of a foreign power or whose activity is likely to place the security of the realm in jeopardy or to seriously disturb order in the country, may by the joint decision of King and *Riksdag* be declared dissolved.[47]

Despite vigorous calls in the summer and autumn of 1941 to invoke the Act in banning the Communist Party, it was never put into effect. The Act was subsequently successively renewed, remaining valid until 30 June 1944.

Organs of control and other departments

The day-to-day monitoring and control of clandestine activities in the country engaged the attention of a number of Swedish government departments.

The newly combined Swedish Defence Staff had come into being on 1 July 1937. Its Intelligence Department was headed by Colonel Carlos Adlercreutz who was to serve in that position until the reorganisation which took place in the autumn of 1942. Counter-espionage and related matters would form a not unimportant part of the duties of the new intelligence chief. Before Adlercreutz's appointment, Ernst Leche, a reserve officer with the requisite legal training who had been temporarily assigned in June to the Foreign Division of the General Staff had been given the task of working out the details of

> a proposal for the reconstruction of the secret police service which according to the two secret circulars of 1914-15 which were to be set up under the control of the County organisations in the event of war.[48]

After six weeks, the details of the proposed scheme were ready and it was then submitted to the heads of various government departments for comment. On 18 July 1937, two proposals were placed before Torsten Nothin and received his blessing.[49] It was suggested, first, that provision should be made for the establishment of a general or civilian

Security Service which would become operational in time of war or when there was an immediate danger of war, and second, that this service should be given special powers in law to carry out its work. In December 1937, a proposal regarding the setting up of a general Security Service and containing a provisional plan of organisation and a review of the rules which were to govern its activity, was submitted to the government by the Chief of the Defence Staff.[50]

The next step occurred on 10 June 1938 when a secret decree proclaimed the need for the establishment of a general Security Service intended to prevent in wartime (or when war was likely) the communication of various types of information to unauthorised persons.[51] According to the decree, the work of the Security Service was to embrace both the monitoring of communications and conventional police surveillance. It was to be headed by a security chief who would be directly answerable to the government and who would be assisted by a number of regional controllers. Other departments of government were obliged to place manpower at the disposal of the proposed service and to supply information when needed. It was stipulated that a member of the Security Service who was not a police officer, nevertheless enjoyed the protection and powers of such an officer in the exercise of his duties.

The decree of 10 June provided the green light for the establishment of a civilian Security Service in Sweden. In the months that followed, the organisation began to take more concrete form. Eric Hallgren, a senior police official with prior experience of counter-espionage work, was appointed Security Chief.[52] At a functional level, the work was distributed between Bureau 1 which dealt with the monitoring of communications, Bureau 2 which was devoted to police investigation, surveillance etc and Bureau 3 which took care of administration and finance. The country itself was divided into seven districts and regional controllers were appointed.

The most important region was Stockholm where Martin Lundqvist was regional controller. There was little or no fund of experience to draw upon and the core of the new organisation was formed by the members of the police force who were reassigned at short notice to Security Service duties. From April 1940, these duties were the main responsibility of the 6th Division. It comprised three sections and a registry. Bureau 1 (under Superintendent Lönn) concentrated on Soviet or Communist activity, Bureau 2 (under Superintendent Magnusson) on German or National Socialist activity and Bureau 3

24

(under Superintendent Fahlander) on British and other allied activity.[53] In 1944, a reorganisation took place. Bureau 3 now focused on sabotage; the surveillance of the Western Allied Special Services was reduced to a minimum while the surveillance of Soviet and Communist activities was correspondingly intensified. Bureau 2 continued to deal with German espionage as before. The relative strengths of these bureaux over the war years are shown in Table 1.

TABLE 1[54]

Date	B1	B2	B3	R	Total
1/7/40	14	24	15	22	75
1/7/41	26	15	16	18	75
1/7/42	31	23	27	16	97
1/7/43	33	24	27	15	99
1/7/44	28	30	25	15	98
1/1/45	50	31	4	15	100

The general Security Service was a civilian service which was the administratively incorporated within the Ministry for Social Affairs. It had come into being largely as the result of a military initiative. However there remained under Colonel Adlercreutz's own command, another important control organ in the shape of the Swedish or Home Section of the Intelligence Department of the Swedish Defence Staff. After the departure of Adlercreutz in 1942 and the ensuing reorganisation of the Intelligence Department, Major Thorwald Lindquist was appointed head of the Home Section. His reign lasted until October 1943 when he in turn was replaced by Lieutenant-Colonel Bonde who was to remain at the post for the rest of the war.[55]

The Home Section of the Intelligence department consisted of four units (1) the Mobilisation Unit (Mobd) which dealt with legal questions, orders, regulations, information and propaganda work (2) the Personnel Unit (Pd) which was in charge of the supervision and implementation of security measures within the armed forces and the granting of permission to foreigners or other unauthorised persons to visit military establishments, etc. (3) the Industrial Security Unit (Dd) which was concerned with industrial or economic espionage and sabotage and with combating activities directed against industrial targets and finally (4) the Counter-Espionage Unit (Ed) which dealt with the surveillance of suspected aliens, the monitoring of communications, the receipt and processing of information from home and abroad about certain aliens as well as the organisation of training courses for police and customs officials.[56]

The work of the Home Section formed an important complement to the work of the civilian Security Service and consisted in (i) the provision of information obtained by the Defence Staff about different methods of espionage and sabotage abroad and of the various countermeasures (ii) the provision of information about individuals (iii) direct participation in the surveillance and investigation work of the police in certain cases (iv) the provision of information about imminent military events and about fears regarding agent activity in certain areas or likely targets for sabotage and (v) the provision of official statements to courts of law and other authorities regarding the extent of military damage caused in cases where secret information had, in one way or another, been leaked.

A third organ of some importance, was the Aliens Bureau which had been set up within the Ministry for Social Affairs in January 1938 and in particular its so-called Control Section which was responsible for the maintenance of registers of aliens in general and more specifically for keeping an eye on those who for whatever reason were thought to be suspect. Its prior history is not without interest.

On the outbreak of the First World War, the Swedish General Staff had set up a special Police Bureau – known to initiates as Section 100 because of its internal telephone number – to fight espionage and to keep a watch on foreigners.[57] In 1918, it became a civilian agency and part of Stockholm's police and as the First World War faded into memory, its work became less concerned with counter-espionage in the strict sense. According to the Royal Letter of 2 December 1932, its task was to

receive, register and process the information concerning aliens which according to special instructions were to be deposited with the District Police Commissioner in Stockholm, and with the guidance of this information to check that the permitted length of stay in the realm was not exceeded etc., and further to carry out investigations of applications for an entry visa or for an extended period of residence in the realm where the investigation must take place outside Stockholm, in cases where such an investigation had been requested by the Ministry for Foreign Affairs.[58]

On 1 January 1938, the Police Bureau and its important collection of dossiers was incorporated within the Control Section. The nature of its work entailed regular liaison with representatives of the police (general Security Service) and the Home Section of the Defence Staff Intelligence Department and Robert Paulsson, who had been associated with the Police Bureau from its inception, was placed in charge of this part of the work.[59]

The work of the counter-espionage services was to be crucially assisted by the efforts of the cryptanalysts. Before the outbreak of war, radio monitoring and cryptanalysis had been assigned to different sections of the Defence Staff, with cryptanalysis incorporated within the Crypto Department which was also responsible for Swedish crypto-security. After the National Defence Radio Institute (FRA) had come into being on 1 July 1942, this new independent authority assumed responsibility for all military work in radio monitoring and cryptanalysis. Simultaneously with their attack upon Denmark and Norway on 9 April 1940, the Germans made certain demands upon Sweden, among them a request for permission to lease part of the Swedish cable system for their telephone and teleprinter communications. German use of Swedish cables was subsequently extended and included lines linking, for example, Stockholm–Berlin, Stockholm–Helsinki, Stockholm–Oslo, Berlin–Helsinki, Copenhagen–Oslo. The signals passed by these lines were open to physical interception by the Swedes. A large part of the teleprinter traffic was encrypted and sent by the so-called *Geheimschreiber*.[60] Already by the summer of 1940, however, the Swedes were in a position to begin reading this traffic. This fundamental breakthrough, which began to be exploited to the full in the autumn of 1940, gave invaluable insights both into German military operations and German foreign policy.

On the counter-espionage side, the Swedes were also able through this cryptanalytical breakthrough to obtain valuable information about *Abwehr* activities in the country. Arrivals and departures of agents, case officers and couriers, could be noted in advance. Although these might be identified in telegrams by cover-names or numbers, supplementary information (e.g., from intercepted telephone calls or surveillance) often ultimately allowed this cover to be pierced. Information collected by agents could be studied and possible sources could be identified. In short, a more detailed picture of German espionage efforts in Sweden began to

27

emerge. Not all German espionage traffic, however, was accessible to this mode of attack.[61]

Some time in the middle of 1942, a warning reached the Germans that the Swedes were reading their teleprinter traffic. Various steps were then successively introduced to guard against this. As a result, Swedish dividends from this information source declined in 1943. However important diplomatic traffic on the Berlin–Stockholm line continued to be read for some time thereafter.

In addition to reading various types of German traffic, the Swedes also succeeded during the war in reading the signal traffic of a number of other nations.[62] Some of this was of direct relevance to the work of the counter-espionage services in following, for example, the activities of the Czech and Polish intelligence services.

The activities of foreign intelligence services in Sweden involved the Swedish Ministry for Foreign Affairs in a number of ways. The Ministry was able to alert the control and surveillance authorities about individuals who might reasonably be suspected of having some clandestine assignment. Its missions abroad were in a position to gather useful information about the organisation and work of foreign intelligence services in other countries. In cases where a person had been held by the Security Service in connection with offences under Chapter 8 of the Penal Code or the Sabotage Law for example, a different type of problem often arose which required the attention of the Ministry. Where a foreign intelligence service could with reasonable certainty be assumed to be involved in the incident (perhaps with the compromising of a case officer enjoying diplomatic immunity) the normal procedure would be for the Head of the Security Service to notify the Foreign Minister of the facts of the case, at the same time perhaps recommending the recall of the diplomat involved. It was then up to the Ministry for Foreign Affairs to decide how to take up the matter with the mission involved. Here the legitimate desire of the Security Service to be rid of a particular malefactor had to be weighed against often complex considerations of foreign policy.

Hitherto the negative view of the neutral host nation to the work of foreign intelligence services in its midst has been stressed. From this perspective, these services are mainly seen as having a destabilising and subversive role. Yet in truth, the matter is more subtle than this. The activity of foreign intelligence services in its territory, gives the neutral country useful additional indices of likely developments in the foreign policy of the belligerents. More temptingly, it provides apparent opportunities for the neutral country to stimulate and initiate dialogue and thus to some extent, to influence the policies of the belligerents themselves.

Too brusque measures – rather than a calculated response of a different kind – against the unwelcome activities of a foreign diplomat may simply generate a tit-for-tat development which is to the ultimate disadvantage of the neutral state. It must bear in mind its own foreign intelligence requirements. These can be satisfied in a number of ways but principally through the reporting of diplomatic missions abroad and through the exchange of information with other foreign powers. This latter exchange may itself take a number of forms. One convenient device is for the maintenance of discreet channels of communication between the respective intelligence services. Whereas a host security service may attempt to establish contact with a foreign intelligence service as a way of infiltrating and controlling a potential opponent, the host intelligence service is primarily interested in accessing whatever store of information is available to the other service. This may sometimes be achieved better by authorised (but deniable) contacts with another service than by recourse to sur-reptitious (potentially embarrassing) methods.

The traditional core of Swedish military intelligence was formed by the reports of service attachés in various capitals abroad. In the course of the war, this traditional source was complemented by the flow of high-quality information from signals intelligence (Sigint). At the end of 1939, in response to the Finnish emergency, an unofficial or secret intelligence service (later known as C-Bureau) was set up under Major Carl Petersén. At first directly answerable to the Chief of the Defence Staff, it was later (from 1 October 1942) incorporated within Section II of the Defence Staff. Its sphere of operations covered routine (but valuable) tasks such as a border watch service and the debriefing of travellers, refugees or deserters entering Sweden as well as the dispatch of officers on special missions abroad and the running of agents in the field.[63] In the field of covert communications, C-Bureau received useful assistance from the Finnish Radio Intelligence unit under Colonel Hallamaa and in the course of the war, contact was established and maintained for longer or shorter periods with illegal stations in Norway, Denmark, Switzerland, Hungary and the Baltic States.[64] A special naval organisation was created to follow, on the one hand, possible German operations directed against Sweden and on the other Allied preparations for the invasion of Europe.[65] Various subsidiary enterprises were established by way of cover. In 1941, a press agency PANI came into being. Apart from its function as camouflage, it paved the way for contacts with journalists and was also used by the authorities for siphoning various articles to the press.[66]

In contrast to the security authorities, who tended for some time to treat the activities of, for example, Norwegian resistance groups operating in Sweden with a certain suspicion, C-Bureau – perhaps just because it was primarily an information gathering unit – found it natural at a much earlier stage to co-operate with these groups and where possible, to support their endeavours.

A central task was naturally the maintenance of covert links with other intelligence services. While Petersén was principally responsible for contacts with the Western Allies, his deputy Major Hellmuth Ternberg looked after liaison with Finland, Germany, Hungary, Turkey and Switzerland.[67] For the belligerents, these multifarious exchanges presented a familiar dilemma: how to make optimal use of them for information collection or deception while simultaneously ensuring that one's own operations were not put at risk by the unauthorised seepage of information.

Exchange of information with a foreign intelligence service offers a country a way of extending its own store of information. However, preparedness to exchange information and a willingness to turn a blind eye to the information-gathering activities of certain foreign services, may also provide useful bargaining counters. The irritation of belligerents, who feel themselves labouring under an explicit disadvantage, may be assuaged in part by the offer of some measure of discreet support for their intelligence efforts.

Finally by the encouragement of certain types of dialogue, the neutral country can hope to increase its own relative influence internationally. Its territory provides a convenient venue for such dialogue. The chosen instrument for this approach will normally be orthodox diplomacy but where the state finds it convenient to adopt a low profile, other devices such as the cultivation of contacts between informal representatives will also be pursued. In short, the activities of foreign intelligence services within its territory, may be viewed by a neutral country from more than one perspective. This difference in perspective also helps to explain the conflicts which can arise between security considerations on the one hand and foreign policy considerations on the other.

Methods

A principal concern of every Security Service is the careful maintenance of records. Thus the original registers of the Police Bureau were four in number: first, an in/out register noting when a given alien entered or left Sweden; second, a record giving the details relating to an alien's place of residence during his stay in the country; third, an employer's register and finally what was called a secret or confidential register in which were noted details relating to those aliens who had attracted the particular attention of the police or other authorities. In the period 1942–43, these registers were incorporated into a new set of six larger registers held by the Control Section. In addition, each alien was assigned a central dossier and if required, a confidential dossier.

For the Security Service, the so-called S-list (Black List) which was first drawn up in November 1939 and which covered those persons suspected of espionage or related activities, had a central role to play, allowing for example the postal and other authorities to exercise special vigilance in the case of certain specified individuals. In addition, the Security Service collected information about extremist political parties. As far as Communists were concerned, such registration long antedated the formation of the Security Service. In the period following the Russian revolution, a register of members of the Communist Party had been compiled by the police in Stockholm. With the rise of National Socialism in Germany, more attention began to be paid to its adherents and a similar register of National Socialists was drawn up.[68]

The outbreak of the Second World War led to new demands being made upon the Security Service. At the beginning of 1940, the Minister of Justice, K. G. Westman, who had already somewhat earlier stressed the importance of the Security Service's surveillance of extremist political parties, once more returned to this theme, enquiring of the security chief what steps had been taken and were planned in this direction. There then followed a discussion in which the security chief rather than the Minister of Justice appeared more alive to the danger of possible political icebergs adrift in the mists ahead. The task of the Security Service, said Hallgren, was according to the original decree to prevent the communication of intelligence to unauthorised persons and to detect those who participated in such activity. In Westman's view, this was entirely inadequate. A new fact of great importance that had to be taken into account was the danger which might arise from infiltration, especially by Communists and National Socialists, who because of their adherence to certain political and ideological beliefs might, in certain circumstances, be prepared to work on behalf of a foreign power. Hallgren, however, had certain reservations. If it was intended to use the Security Service for the surveillance of politically unreliable persons, it was desirable that the instructions given to it were explicitly altered. At the same time, it should be realised that such an extension of powers transformed the Security Service into a Russian *Ochrana* and this had not been originally envisaged.

As it transpired, a number of measures consistent with Westman's line of thought had already been put into effect by the Security Service. On 4 November 1939, the Regional Controllers were instructed to draw up with the help of the police, lists of the leading Communists and National Socialists within their area. Thereafter the Security Service on the basis of the regional information received, were able to compile a central register of Communists and National Socialists throughout the whole country. The initial registration suffered from a number of technical inadequacies and was later refined. Individuals registered were classified from A to D in terms of their level of political activity with A representing those holding key positions and enjoying to a high degree the confidence of the party and D those who were not known to be connected to the party but who had – for example, by the purchase of party literature – demonstrated an interest in its ideology or political programme.

While Communists and National Socialists formed the prime target for registration, certain pro-British groups also came in for their share of scrutiny, among them the so-called *Tuesday Group* and *Fighting Democracy* as well as the Syndicalists, who apart from a historical predilection for sabotage, had – according to the Security Chief – defended purely British interests in their morning newspaper *The Worker* even when these were opposed to Sweden's policy of neutrality.

Finally military security in the shape of the Home Section kept detailed files of possible security risk personnel within the armed forces. Among those considered politically active who were registered were numbered over 3000 Communists, 400 National Socialists and 50 British sympathisers. During the winter war in Finland, special Work

Companies were set up for Communist sympathisers and further such companies were established later on.

A highly important method of monitoring espionage and other forms of subversive activity, namely the interception and decoding of the official communications of other states, has already been mentioned. In addition to the work of the cryptographic department of the Defence Staff (later of the National Defence Radio Institute), a Radio Control Section, consisting of mobile and fixed units, was established within the general Security Service with the task of monitoring illegal radio traffic. In the case of private (press, commercial, etc.) telegrams, these were subject to the regulations of 17 September, which specified the types of commercial code which could be used and permitted ciphers only where the cipher system employed was supplied.[69] Certain supplementary rules ensured that the identity of the person sending the telegram could be established. On 13 January 1940, the employment of ciphers in private telegrams was forbidden altogether. Copies of official (foreign) state telegrams were automatically sent to The National Defence Radio Institute. The Institute was also given a copy of any private telegram in which a consulate or diplomatic mission was named or which was suspected of being a foreign official state telegram in disguised form. The languages allowed in private telegrams were limited. Several other authorities were also routinely consulted. Press telegrams were submitted to the Press Department of the Ministry for Foreign Affairs; those dealing with foreign trade to the Trade Section of the same Ministry; those dealing with military matters to the Home Section of the Defence Staff; those mentioning inventions to the Patent Office, etc. Telegrams to and from foreign countries remained the chief concern of Telegram Control although certain internal traffic was also monitored. The progress of the war had a number of important repercussions on telegram traffic between Sweden and abroad with radio links having a larger role to play.

Telephone monitoring was not a new feature brought about by the Second World War. It had already been practised, at least selectively, during the First World War, as the diary of Erik Palmstierna makes plain.[70] However, the Second World War witnessed a massive extension in this type of monitoring and Table 2 gives some idea of the figures involved.

In accordance with the provisions of the Special Coercive Powers Act, postal censorship was introduced on 5 January 1940, when the

33

mail to Finland via the northern town of Haparanda began to be monitored. From July 1940, all post to and from foreign countries abroad was systematically monitored. In addition, special provision was made for the censorship of mail from members of the Swedish armed forces. Postal control units were set up throughout the country under the general direction of the Postal Control Section of the Central Bureau of the Security Service in Stockholm. Eventually an average of over 200,000 items of mail (excluding parcels) were checked weekly. Special instructions to monitor the post of a particular person or organisation were issued on more than 16,000 occasions. The number of individuals or organisations checked was, however, lower since one and the same person or organisation might be the subject of special monitoring on a number of different occasions.

TABLE 2
CALLS MONITORED AND REPORTED BY THE SECURITY SERVICE[71]

Period	Foreign	Domestic	Total
1941	395,403	1,686,959	2,082,362
1942	420,840	2,412,231	2,833,071
1943	320,988	2,586,946	2,907,934
1944	320,108	2,999,922	2,620,030

The distribution of Security Service personnel employed in the different sectors of communications monitoring is given by Table 3.

TABLE 3

	1940	1941	1942	1943	1944	1945
Post	266	360	397	392	334	259
Telephone	162	265	305	289	217	157
Telegram	39	45	75	94	94	56
Total	505	710	816	807	677	484

Superficially the immense labour involved in telephone and letter monitoring brought meagre returns in the sense that relatively few espionage cases were brought to light by these means. In another way, however, these controls brought concrete gains:

34

In surveillance work, the controls – particularly telephone control – has provided good information about the meetings, journeys and other movements of the people being watched. Because of this, it has often been possible to concentrate shadowing and general surveillance to the times and places which were mentioned in a telephone conversation or in correspondence. In this way, it has been possible to use less intensive surveillance thus diminishing the risk that it will be detected. This has also led to a considerable saving in manpower. Because the number of cases of espionage which are cleared up is to some extent directly proportional to the number of police officers who are assigned to surveillance, the value of saving manpower can be appreciated.[73]

The most visible kind of control was of course that practised on persons entering the country. The goods traffic to and from the country was also subject to security checks. Records were kept of the detailed searches carried out and of persons or goods detained.

Last but not least, traditional methods of police work had their part to play in counter-espionage as well. Shadowing the movements of a suspect, allowed a network of possible relevant contacts of an agent to be determined. Information and tips came in diverse forms and for diverse reasons from members of the public. Now and again the Swedish counter-espionage authorities succeeded in recruiting or planting their own source in the ranks of a foreign intelligence service or in a foreign mission and new technology in the shape of hidden microphones – sometimes discovered and sometimes not – had their own clues to relay.[74]

CRITICISMS OF THE WARTIME SECURITY SERVICE

The secrecy surrounding both the existence and activities of the wartime security organs meant that for a time they were protected from public criticism. In 1941, however, there occurred an incident which was to have important repercussions for the secrecy of the civilian Security Service. On 28 April, three men – Martin, Lilliehöök and Lindberg – were detained by the police on suspicion that they were engaged in unlawful activities to British advantage but were later released. The reason for the police intervention was an anonymous letter sent to the Foreign Minister, which purported to describe a dinner in a Stockholm restaurant attended by a number of people known to be sympathetic to Britain, at which various opinions critical of Swedish policy had been expressed. The letter was forwarded by the Foreign Minister to Security Chief Hallgren who then authorised the detentions, pending enquiry. No great thought seems to have been given to the possibility that the letter was merely an unfounded provocation.

An action was brought against Hallgren for abuse of office and after the intervention of the Justice Ombudsman (JO), the matter went to the Supreme Court. The publicity generated by the case eventually forced the government to acknowledge publicly Hallgren's position as the head of the Security Service. In the First Chamber of the *Riksdag* on 10 February 1943, Östen Undén praised JO's intervention and offered the following reflection:

> The contents of the anonymous letter which gave rise to the action of the police are known to numerous people. If selections from it were to be read out here I am convinced that the chamber would have a good laugh.
>
> It is however a much more serious matter that well-known persons of irreproachable character have been treated as dangerous conspirators on the basis of such preposterous accusations. It is even more serious that this business has revealed that we have got a political police which is so utterly lacking in political common sense and knowledge of politics.[75]

The debate about the Security Service rumbled on and in May 1943 questions were raised in the *Riksdag* about its powers and their possible abuse.[76] In the Second Chamber, the Prime Minister conceded that the organisation was far from perfect. Much was simply due to staffing problems. Unlike the Great Powers, Sweden lacked such a Special Service 'in normal times' and there was consequently a general shortage of experienced people to man it. Those who had been appointed 'were no doubt competent policemen but their training was not designed to meet the demands made by their new tasks'.[77] It had therefore been necessary to recruit people with academic qualifications from other branches of the civil service or indeed from outside the civil service altogether.

But could everything be ascribed simply to staffing problems? Hagberg, the Communist member for the northern town of Luleå, took a very different view of the incidents which had occurred: behind them, he surmised, the long arm of the Finnish Security Police and the Gestapo had been at work pulling the strings.

Still more damaging for public confidence in the control organs was to be the flood of accusations which followed the revelation at the end of 1944 that there were strong grounds for believing that an official (Paulsson) attached to the Control Section of the Alien's Bureau had supplied the German Legation with certain confidential information in his possession. In response to the public outcry, the government decided to set up an official committee of enquiry to look into these and other associated allegations relating to the treatment of aliens and the work of the Security Service. It was headed by Rickard Sandler who had served not only as Foreign Minister but also as Prime Minister after the death of Hjalmar Branting. Its findings were published in three reports which appeared after the war. In the attendant discussion, the police and the civilian Security Service, now released from obscurity into a blaze of publicity, were often the principal targets of criticism. As executive organs charged with the day-to-day enforcement of often contentious legislation, they were not well placed to win prizes in any popularity stake.

Among the more politically embarrassing items contained in the reports was the revelation that direct contacts had taken place between the Gestapo and the Security Service. It transpired that with the approval of the Ministry for Foreign Affairs a trio of Swedish policemen had visited Heydrich in Berlin in March 1941 and that a certain exchange of information had taken place. Furthermore, as a follow up, several Gestapo officers had visited Stockholm in connection with enquiries into Soviet or Comintern espionage and sabotage activities.

It might be argued that in these contacts with the guardians of Hitler's Reich, the Swedes in fact gave relatively little away and helped simply to keep a potential aggressor sweet while working simultaneously to thwart his more sinister and wide-ranging ambitions. Was contact itself intrinsically wrong? Could it – superficial appearances to the contrary – be turned to good account? Could one not sup with the Devil provided one had a sufficiently long spoon?

Such arguments – inasmuch as they were heard at all – weighed little in the balance with outraged opinion. The contacts with the Gestapo were rather seen as symptomatic of an ambivalence in certain circles to Hitler's programme to bring order to the Reich. Critics were more concerned to dwell on the fact that the contacts had not simply come about owing to Sweden's weak bargaining position with respect to Germany in 1941, although that had undoubtedly been a major factor. The snares, it seemed, had been set long before the outbreak of the Second World War. In the circumstances, it was natural to ask how far these and other contacts with German sister services had conditioned – directly or indirectly – the practical implementation of Swedish internal security policy when the war got under way.

In examining the criticism that the Security Service had been more zealous in pursuit of Allied agents than their Axis counterparts, the Commission produced a number of statistics. For the period 1939–44, out of a recorded total of 1,837 persons held on suspicion of being involved in espionage or sabotage activities (as distinct from those whose cases actually went to court), 935 were entered as working for the Western Allies and the Soviet Union as against 284 for the Axis. Of the 935 agents of powers belonging to the Grand Alliance, 305 were entered as working specifically for the Soviet Union, the majority of whom (281 persons) had been arrested in the period from 1941 onwards. In Stockholm, among persons arrested, 224 were entered as working on behalf of Britain and the USA, 197 on behalf of the Soviet Union and 122 on behalf of Germany.

For the critics, these figures – and their year by year development – merely served to confirm their suspicions about the partiality of the police and the political direction of their efforts. The Commission report, however, drew attention to a number of general points which – it believed – had to be taken into consideration before any secure conclusions could be drawn from the arrest statistics that had been presented. Thus *inter alia* it was argued that the preponderance of arrests of Allied agents had to be seen in relation to the respective total efforts of the Allied and Axis services and their different character. In the judgement of the Security Service, the collective Allied covert activities in Sweden had quantitatively greatly exceeded those of their Axis counterparts. Furthermore it was pointed out that the Allied covert services had often fallen back on walk-in volunteers from the refugee community whose clandestine skills had not always matched their enthusiastic commitment.

That the figure for the Allied agents detected became surprisingly high at various times compared with the number of German agents has certainly not been because the Allied agents 'were hunted' with greater energy. The fact of the matter was that the Allies got a large number of patriots from the occupied countries as agents and these were in no way trained or particularly careful in their behaviour, with the result that the Swedish authorities had no choice in exposing them, because existing laws must be applied as soon as a crime became known to the authorities. In fact, those in charge could not steer the work assignments, but rather the work assignments steered them. Through the various controls, e.g., postal censorship, a large number of minor agents came to light and legal process against them obviously must go ahead, since it was clear that they had committed a criminal offence. But many times one felt that the major offenders got by undetected.[78]

If the Western covert services and their friends – in particular the representatives of Norwegian underground organisations – hoped for a sympathetic Swedish blind eye to some of their more flagrant indiscretions, their prayers were by no means always automatically answered. There were influential factions within the Security Service and elsewhere who resolutely opposed any bending of the rules in their favour. In the Tranmael case, the minister who presided over the Security Service took the unusual – and constitutionally controversial – step of personally intervening in the judicial process.

Martin Tranmael, born in 1879, was something of a grand old man among Norwegian socialists and in 1905 – the year of Norway's separation from Sweden – he had participated in the foundation of IWW (International Workers of the World) in Chicago. Critical of Moscow's attempts to interfere in the internal affairs of the parties affiliated to the Comintern, he became a leading member of the reconstituted Norwegian *Arbeiderparti* and the chief editor of its principal organ, *Arbeiderbladet*.

After the German occupation of Norway, Tranmael came to Stockholm where he employed his long-standing contacts with Swedish social democrats in his country's struggle against the invaders. At the end of 1941, his activities attracted the attention of the Swedish Security Service and it was noted after more careful investigation that Tranmael was receiving information about German military dispositions in Norway at a variety of cover addresses. Voices within the security organs were now raised calling for a stop to

Tranmael's work and for him to be brought to trial for his unauthorised intelligence activities. However, at the express intervention of Gustav Möller, to whose ministry the Security Service was attached, an instruction was issued forbidding any such action.[79]

The handling of the Tranmael case, although doubtless pointing to an important underlying political divergence of view about Security Service priorities, did not signal a dramatic shift in the field of internal security. As late as July 1943, it is interesting to note that the number of personnel of the general Security Service involved in the investigation of Allied but non-Soviet activities (Bureau 3) was still somewhat greater than the comparable figure for those engaged in the investigation of German activities (Bureau 2). The decisive reduction of Bureau 3 enters first with the final figures of 1 January 1945. However, already by 1943, winds of change had begun to blow: co-operation with the representatives of the exiled Norwegian authorities in Sweden improved and smoother routines were evolved;[80] the British and Swedish authorities began to exchange information in the area of counter-espionage;[81] and Major Lindquist, a stalwart of the hidden world who was regarded with less than enthusiasm by the Allies, vanished from the Home Section.[82] Although the war was by no means over, the end was in sight. It was time for Sweden to prepare for the post-war world.

2

Poacher's perspective – 1

BRITISH POLICY: THE BROADER PICTURE

At the cost perhaps of a certain oversimplification, it is possible to see British policy towards Sweden during the Second World War, as consisting of three different phases. First of all, there was the initial period of the Phoney or Twilight War in which Sweden enjoyed to some extent an abnormally prominent place in British calculations owing to the significance attributed to the supply of Swedish iron ore to Germany. By denying Hitler's war machine this supply, it was hoped to strike a blow which would contribute decisively to the prevention of a further escalation of the conflict. The Norwegian débacle and the collapse of France rolled the British back into their island. The iron ore question on which so many words had been lavished, retreated from the world of high strategy to the familiar confines of the Ministry of Economic Warfare and Sweden itself, inasmuch as it entered British strategic calculations at all, became a place of at most peripheral interest. As a neutral island in Scandinavia, its prospects in the late summer of 1940 – seen from the British horizon – were bleak: an accelerating slide into the New Order seemed all too likely. Britain's diplomatic appeals could not be backed by military force that was needed elsewhere. Should Sweden therefore be written off entirely and every economic concession withheld or was it despite everything better to support Sweden in its strivings to maintain some measure of independence? Despite the arguments of those who advocated the more abrasive approach and despite those dissenting voices which continued to be heard – sometimes loudly – at various moments of crisis later on, it was the latter alternative that was to form the basis of the second phase of British policy towards the neutral in the north. As long as Sweden

41

possessed a fair degree of autonomy, it provided a corridor to Britain's friends in occupied Europe and indeed in Germany itself. Propaganda could be distributed from Sweden; information and intelligence could, it was hoped be fed back via Sweden; it offered a useful line of communication with Russia. Moreover the Swedish contribution to Britain's own war industry had to be considered.

In the period 1940–42, Swedish official policy followed the line least likely to bring about open confrontation with the powerful architects of *Neuropa*. An agreement of 8 July 1940 allowed the *Wehrmacht* to use the Swedish railways for the transit of troops and material between Norway and Germany. By the time the agreement was finally revoked, over two million troops and 100,000 wagon loads of materials had been transported. When Hitler launched 'Operation Barbarossa' on 22 June 1941, the Swedes were asked to allow the transit of a German division from the Oslo area to Finland's Eastern Front. Three days later, approval was granted and the transport of some 15,000 German troops got under way. Swedish and German mine barriers complemented one another in the Baltic. German troop transports were given Swedish escort through Swedish territorial waters. So-called German courier aircraft traversed Swedish airspace.

After the occupation of Norway, ten Norwegian vessels were detained in Swedish waters and their fate and that of their cargoes were soon the prize in a long-lasting prestige tug of war between the belligerents. On 15 January 1943, the Swedish government yielded to Allied pressure and grudgingly gave its permission for two of the remaining vessels, *Lionel* and *Dicto*, which had already been involved in an unsuccessful break-out attempt, to make a run for it to England. As it happened, the British decided that the risks involved in such a dash were too great and the operation ('Cabaret') was called off soon after being launched. For the Swedes the episode led to a temporary closing of their trans-oceanic trade route from Gothenburg to the West at German insistence. In crude terms, it seemed that the Allies had gained little apart from the diversion of German naval forces. But in terms of bargaining psychology, the effectiveness of British and American pressure in extracting a Swedish concession to their demands, boded well for their efforts in the future.

On 29 July 1943, the Swedish Transit Agreement with Germany was revoked. The War Trade Agreement initialled on 23 September committed Sweden to a major reduction in its overall exports to Germany and countries occupied or associated with Germany, the prompt repayment of all debts due to Sweden by these countries and a freeze on further credits. Iron ore exports were to be reduced to 7.5 million tons. The export of all ferro-alloys (except ferro-silicon which was subject to limitations) was prohibited. Chemicals, wood and wood products, machinery and instruments were to be pegged at 75 per cent of the export figure for 1942. Further limits were imposed on some 40 other groups of materials including special steels, machine tools and ball bearings. These reductions underlined the fact that a new third phase in Sweden's relations with the Western Allied Powers had begun, in which the latter would be able to exert increasing pressure on the northern neutral.

Just as iron ore had dominated Anglo-Swedish relations during the Phoney War, so ball bearings were to become a bone of contention between Sweden and the Allies (particularly the United States) in 1944. According to the agreement of 23 September 1943, the Swedes agreed to limit their export of ball and roller bearings to the Axis, to 29 million crowns in 1944. (The corresponding figures for 1942 and 1943 were 51 million and 60 million crowns respectively.) By the end of the year, it was believed in Allied circles that enemy production of ball bearings was running at about 70 per cent of the level prior to the Schweinfurt raid of October 1943 and it seemed therefore logical to pressure German supply still further by reducing foreign supplies as much as possible. According to an American report of January 1944, Sweden had been able to provide 70 per cent of German demand for certain important types of ball bearings for the aircraft industry and had answered for some 25 per cent of Germany's overall requirements. This was deemed unacceptable. The earlier agreement was judged to be too generous. An attempt was made to induce the Swedes to reduce substantially their export of ball bearings to Germany by offering them Spitfires but this was turned down on the ground that it would involve a breach of prior agreements. Germany was too significant a customer for its wishes to be ignored; in addition the German subsidiaries of the Swedish SKF company accounted for 55–60 per cent of the total German production and formed a vital part of the SKF industrial empire. In April 1944, the Americans who had consistently advocated a much tougher line on the ball bearing question than the British, called for a complete cessation of all exports of ball and roller bearings, machinery and special steels to Germany, for the ensuing three months and intimated that in pursuit of a satisfactory settlement along these lines, serious consideration would be given to 'all measures at the disposal of the US government'. A direct approach was made to the SKF company and the Allies were eventually able to extract further concessions.

This turnabout on the economic front – a reflection of the belligerents' changed fortunes of war – had its political counterpart. Swedish support for resistance to German rule in Scandinavia became bolder and the deviations from neutrality which occurred were now in favour of the other side. 1943 closed with the go-ahead having been given to the training in Sweden of thinly disguised Norwegian and Danish paramilitary forces. In December 1944, detachments of the so-called Norwegian Police Troops were flown by American military aircraft from Västerås in Sweden to Kirkenes in northern Norway, as the German withdrawal from Finnmark got under way. The closing months of the war also witnessed active Swedish involvement in the supply and infiltration of weapons to groups inside Denmark.

As the end of the war loomed in sight, the Norwegian exile government in London appealed to the Swedes to mobilise on their behalf, as a way of signalling to German troops remaining in Norway after a German collapse, that any further resistance was pointless. But while various contingency mobilisation plans were prepared, the Swedish government saw no need for such intervention. Meanwhile, their representative Count Bernadotte was engaged in negotiations with Himmler. In April 1945, the latter asked Bernadotte to transmit an offer of a German capitulation on the Western Front, which was promptly turned down by the Western Allies. Bernadotte, however, at the request of the Swedish government, continued negotiations with Himmler with a view to reaching a settlement for a peaceful withdrawal of German forces from Norway and Denmark. Agreement was reached in principle whereby Sweden would have been required to intern several hundred thousand German troops within its borders. Simultaneously, the Western Allies made their one and only formal appeal to Sweden to enter the war on their side. However Germany's capitulation on all fronts on 8 May 1945 rendered both these questions otiose.

SPECIAL OPERATIONS AND ECONOMIC WARFARE

The iron ore war: Rickman's organisation
In March 1931, the British government created an office for the study

of 'industrial mobilisation'. Its task was to explore the economic factor in modern warfare and to investigate the state of preparation of potential foes. Heading this Industrial Intelligence Centre (IIC), as it was to be called, was Major Desmond Morton, a man with useful contacts not only in the army, business and politics but also in the Special (or Secret) Intelligence Service (SIS) with which he had served.[1] At first entirely covert, IIC's secrecy was found to be counterproductive and steps were taken to make it an open department, administratively attached to the Department of Overseas Trade but receiving its instructions from the Committee of Imperial Defence. Upon the outbreak of the Second World War, the Ministry of Economic Warfare came formally into existence and IIC staff were duly absorbed there with Morton becoming head of the Intelligence Branch. During the Phoney War, two problems in particular – Rumanian oil and Swedish iron ore – greatly exercised the minds of the economic warriors, for Hitler's war machine was judged to be critically dependent on both. By stemming the supply of these commodities to Germany, it was argued with increasing fervour, the Führer could be stopped in his tracks before the war had a chance to escalate further.

The significance of iron ore for the German war economy had been stressed some years before in Consett's book *The Triumph of Unarmed Forces* in which he had summed up his views on blockade warfare in the light of his experience as British naval attaché in Scandinavia during the First World War. After noting Ludendorff's endorsement of the importance of Swedish iron ore imports for German submarine construction, Consett concluded:

> Germany took from 4,000,000 to 5,000,000 tons a year of iron ore from Sweden; this represents a quantity of metal for which a far larger quantity of ore in Germany would have had to be mined, varying with the rates of the German to the Swedish percentage of iron contained. Germany, to obtain the equivalent value of Sweden's ore, would have had to employ two or three times the number of men employed by Sweden: hence the value of Sweden to Germany.
>
> The haulage of ore from the mines to the coast was carried out to a large extent by the Swedish railways with British coal; its further transport by steamer across the Baltic sea also (certainly for the first two years) effected by British coal. Nothing would

have hastened the end of the war more effectively than the sinking of ships trading in ore between Sweden or Germany in the Baltic, or by economic pressure brought to bear on the Swedish ore industry.[2]

Consett's book appeared first in 1923. Sixteen years later, Swedish iron ore was once again the focus of attention but in the interval, Britain's ability to exert military and economic pressure in the area had significantly declined: the Anglo-German Naval Agreement of 1936 had underwritten Germany's claim to be the undisputed master of the Baltic. Hydro-electrification and the British General Strike had reduced the significance of British coal imports to Sweden. None the less Britain's ability to put pressure, if need be, upon Sweden's transoceanic provisioning from the West, constituted an important British counter in diplomatic negotiations between the two countries and one which the Swedes from their experience in the First World War were well aware of.

Diplomatic negotiation, economic pressure, pre-emption, the deployment of military force – these were some of the ways by which the supply of critical commodities might be denied the Reich. As the European situation deteriorated, the British government also began to give some thought to various types of special operation intended to contribute to the accomplishment of this end.

In 1938, Section D had been set up within the SIS. Headed by the Major Laurence Grand of the Royal Engineers, Section D was concerned with 'attacking potential enemies by means other than the operation of military forces'. Its prime task was sabotage. Unlike a kindred organisation, MI R at the War Office which also had sabotage on its agenda, the personnel of Section D were expected to operate covertly as civilians. Its recruits, hardly surprisingly, were to prove a motley band.

In the late summer of 1938, one of their number, A. F. Rickman, was sent to Scandinavia.[3] Armed with a letter of introduction from the Grängesberg Company's London office, Rickman toured iron ore fields and ports, gathering information about the industry apparently intended for a book which he was writing on the subject. Indeed this book duly appeared in the autumn of the following year. Impressively scholarly in tone for an author whose prior acquaintance with the matters described was minimal and whose tour of inspection was so brief, it contained not only a sketch of the historical development of

46

the orefields and of the composition of Swedish ore export markets but also a detailed description of the latest mechanical loading equipment at the various ports. At Oxelösund, the author noted the new bridge crane, then under construction by the German Demag company.[4]

In July 1939, Rickman returned to Sweden but this time on a more permanent basis. Commercial cover had been arranged for him in the shape of two small companies, specialising in dental materials and tinned goods respectively. Various contingency plans for sabotage operations in Sweden had been considered and were to be evolved in London. But these were measures of last resort which it was hoped, would not be required. Rickman spent the first few months making contacts and forming his team in Stockholm. And there, for the time being, he can be left.

Not long after the outbreak of war, a top level Swedish delegation consisting of Erik Boheman the Under-secretary of State at the Swedish Ministry for Foreign Affairs, Marcus Wallenberg, a banker, and Gunnar Carlsson, a shipping expert, arrived in London to negotiate with the British government a possible trade agreement. A principal subject on the agenda was naturally the export of iron ore to Germany. The Swedes insisted that there could be no question of any promise that the deliveries of iron ore to Germany would be less than the average of the last four years. What they were prepared to offer the British government was the assurance that they would allow no capital improvements that would increase the amount exported and that they were willing to try to obstruct the German trade by 'various technical manoeuvres'. In addition, to show that everything was above board, they were prepared to supply in secret to the British government all relevant statistics regarding the export of iron ore so that the British authorities could follow developments for themselves.[5]

Despite Boheman's assurance that an informal agreement along these lines would be more satisfactory from Britain's point of view than appeared at first sight, the British negotiators were disappointed by the Swedish proposal. But while they pressed for a reduction in the amount of ore being shipped to Germany there were, at the backs of their minds, other factors to be taken into account. The Admiralty – in other respects no friend of uncooperative neutrals – was keen to have a swift agreement about the chartering of Swedish tonnage. The Ministry of Supply was eager to have the Swedish special castings,

47

ferro-chrome and charcoal pig-iron deemed vital to the British armaments industry. On balance therefore, the British negotiators decided that it was better – with the German–Swedish trade negotiations looming up – to content themselves with the kind of gentlemen's agreement floated by Boheman and his friends than to have no agreement at all. On 19 October, Boheman was able to send a telegram to Stockholm with the soothing news that the only formal restriction demanded by the British was that the export of ore to Germany had to be kept to the level of 1938. With the iron ore question out of the way and with simultaneous progress in the shipping negotiations, the path was cleared for reaching a war trade agreement. It was finally signed on 7 December and came into effect on the 20th of the same month.

The Swedes could feel well satisfied with the result of the London agreement on iron ore. According to their interpretation, they were permitted to export 9 million tons to Germany plus a further 1.5 million tons to German-occupied Poland and Czechoslovakia. This 10.5 million tons gave them some leeway in their negotiations in Berlin. Thinking to employ iron ore as a weapon against various German infringements of their neutrality – the sinking of their merchant vessels and the dispute over the four-mile limit to their territorial waters – the Swedes began by offering to supply the Reich 7 million tons of ore. This ploy, however, cut no ice. They were told bluntly that no war trade agreement would be signed unless they increased their bid and more ominously on 25 November, the German navy mined the Sound to within three miles of the Swedish coast. By the end of the month, the Russians had begun their offensive against the Finns. With the deteriorating situation on their Eastern flank, the Swedes decided that they had no cause for embroiling themselves in a dispute over iron ore with Germany. By 6 December, they had upped their bid to 10 million tons and this was the figure that was finally accepted in the Swedish–German agreement.

Not everyone at the Ministry of Economic Warfare in London had been happy with the drift of negotiations leading up to the Anglo–Swedish agreement. Had perhaps the British negotiators been too soft? Morton, for one, thought so. On 26 October, he summarised his own views on the subject. First of all, he was sceptical about the apparent assumption that the Swedes had laid in sufficient stocks; if indeed they had not, they were vulnerable to harder bargaining and hard bargaining was what was needed. Otherwise there was a risk that the Germans were going to get what they wanted without having to lift a finger:

> Again, should Germany invade Sweden, would she really obtain much more supplies than she will apparently get under the proposed agreement without any exhaustion of her military potential?[6]

Compared with military intimidation, noble ends, rational arguments and economic threats counted for very little.

> Although the Swedish Delegation are honourable gentlemen, in sympathy with our cause, they, and the whole of their country are terrified of the Germans and not the least afraid of us. This is not because we are powerless to do hurt to Sweden, but because they believe we will not use that power, and, anyhow, because the pressure we can bring to bear is only in the economic field, the effect of which cannot rapidly be felt, while Germany is able to take immediate military action.[7]

Furthermore, if too generous an agreement were to be signed, it would create a bad precedent for Britain's negotiations with other neutral states.

Meanwhile the thoughts of a much more powerful political figure had already begun to stray northwards. Churchill's interest stemmed in part from an accelerating concern with the iron ore question, then much discussed, but also, one suspects, from considerations of strategy. From the moment that he had sent out his telegram announcing that 'Winston was back', the First Lord of the Admiralty was tossing out ideas and initiating schemes. Among them was Operation Catherine which envisaged sending a British naval force to break into the Baltic. It was to include two battleships armed with 15½-inch guns that could outrange their rivals, *Scharnhorst* and *Gneisenau*. Their decks were to be strengthened against air attack and they were to be insulated from mines by an accompanying protective force of 'mine-bumpers' with specially devised bows. The object of this operation was fourfold: to isolate Germany from Sweden and Norway (thus automatically cutting off the iron ore supply lines from the North); to persuade the Scandinavian countries to enter the war on the side of the Allies; to intimidate the enemy; and to impress Russia (whence the name of the operation). This was stirring stuff, but was it feasible? Until this was decided, Churchill found himself having to grapple with a second, more specialised ancillary problem – the iron ore traffic from the Norwegian port of Narvik.

During the First World War, the Admiralty had been made aware of the naval significance of Norway's 800-mile-long, indented coastline with its protective fringe of islands. By hugging this and remaining within Norwegian territorial waters, it was possible for German warships and submarines to evade the vigilant Home Fleet and reach the open waters of the North Atlantic. Now in the Second World War, the Leads – as this protected waterway was called – offered, it seemed, a safe corridor for vessels carrying Swedish iron ore from Narvik. The matter was taken up at a meeting of senior Admiralty officials which took place on 18 September. The need to prevent the flow of iron ore to Germany was stressed but it was agreed that diplomacy should be tried first. If this failed, force in some form or other would have to be used. The next day, the First Lord returned to the subject. If (he said) the Norwegian government could not be persuaded by diplomatic means to put a stop to the iron ore traffic from Narvik, the navy should go ahead and mine Norwegian waters with a view to forcing the ore ships out onto the open sea.

In pursuing the goal of cutting off supplies of iron ore to Germany, it soon became clear to Churchill that action against Narvik alone would not suffice. There was a danger that the ore exports could be shipped through the Baltic ports (Luleå and Oxelösund) instead. If Catherine were to be implemented successfully, that difficulty would be resolved. But it was far from certain that the professional mariners in the Admiralty were prepared to back the First Lord's favourite scheme. Something therefore had to be done about the Baltic ports. Luleå – the most important of these ore ports – would soon be closed for the winter. But what of Oxelösund farther south? A new problem began to crystallise. The First Lord returned to the Narvik question in a memorandum which was discussed at a Cabinet meeting on 5 October. But the Cabinet was in no hurry to act. The matter, it was decided, was not sufficently urgent.

Weeks went by and changed circumstances served to reawaken Churchill's interest in action against the ore traffic. Most importantly, the trade negotiations with the Swedes on limiting their export of iron ore had yielded apparently little. In addition a disquieting rumour had been passed on to the Ministry of Economic Warfare (MEW) from Sweden that the Germans were planning to increase considerably their shipments from Narvik.

Churchill immediately set in motion an investigation at the Admiralty into the problems involved in stopping the Narvik iron ore traffic. On 12 December, the MEW delivered their report on the pros and cons of such a stoppage. In their view, it would cause Germany acute industrial embarrassment but at the same time they noted that action against Luleå would be required when it reopened in the spring. Various other government departments were more critical. The Foreign Office, always nervous of opinion abroad, did not like the scheme because it involved the infringement of the rights of a neutral state. The Ministries of Supply and Trade thought the scheme had been oversold and warned about the detrimental effects of possible Norwegian retaliation.

In any case, developments in the North soon threw the calculations of the strategists into confusion. On 30 November, the Red Army began its onslaught on Finland and, with the Winter War, a new range of possible scenarios presented itself. For some, the conflict seemed to offer a chance of opening a new front; for others, it was a way of directing the attention of the German High Command away from their own doorsteps; some saw it as an opportunity to lead a crusade against bolshevism; more devious minds saw intervention as a convenient pretext for gaining control over the output of the northern Swedish orefields. This subject was to dominate the fourth meeting of the Supreme War Council in Paris on 19 December.

It was also at this Paris meeting that another figure was to enter the debate about the iron ore question. On 2 September, Fritz Thyssen, a disenchanted Ruhr steel baron, had taken up residence in Switzerland. There he had made contact with the French intelligence service.[8] His message to these gentlemen, was simple: 'Coupez la route du fer et vous verrez Hitler obligé de capituler.' Whatever Thyssen's credentials as a technical expert, the magic of his name was potent. In the month that followed, discussions about the importance of Swedish iron ore invariably included some deferential reference to his opinion.

Alarmed at the way the wind was blowing, the Swedes took various steps to put forward their side of the matter. The magazine *Le Nord* which was sponsored by the Foreign Ministries of the Nordic countries and which served as a vehicle for the wider discussion of Scandinavian opinions and issues, published in one of its numbers at the close of 1939, an article in English by the ironmaster, Gerard de Geer, entitled 'The importance of Sweden's iron-ore in the present war'. According to de Geer, Anglo-French discussions of the question had tended to ignore certain elementary but crucial facts: the relative importance of ore in iron and steel manufacture had declined owing to the use of scrap iron; the Germans had built up considerable reserves of scrap iron; in addition they had improved their domestic ore position through the Four Year Plan and to a lesser extent by the incorporation of Austria into the Reich. Lastly, it was not true (although widely believed) that the armaments industry consumed a great deal of iron. In fact purely peacetime requirements predominated to such an extent that if they were effectively reduced there would be plenty of room for war requirements even under conditions of reduced ore supplies.

De Geer's article was duly studied at MEW in London:

Mr. De Geer's argument is plausible and the majority of the facts on which he bases it are accurate. On the other hand his argument is entirely vitiated by Germany's obvious desire to get as much Swedish iron ore as she possibly can. Swedish iron ore is vitally important to Germany. The Allies know it and so does Germany. If Germany did not believe it then she would not browbeat the Swedes for five months in order to increase the quota etc., nor would she suggest adopting special methods to keep Luleå icefree or to improve the railway facilities to that port. The fact is that Germany needs Swedish iron ore badly and if the Swedes won't recognise the fact then it is no more than wishful thinking on their part.[9]

The crux of the matter was German scrap production and in the view of the MEW critic, the situation was very much tighter than De Geer had suggested. In addition, as Morton was to confide to Laurence Collier, Head of the Northern Department, a rumour about the author and his article had reached London:

I have just learned from a Mr. William Stephenson of my acquaintance, who travels frequently to Sweden and has considerable interests in the country, that the author of this article, Mr. De Geer, has confessed to certain Swedish friends of Mr. Stephenson that the article is all nonsense and was written to the order of the Swedish Foreign Minister, who is starting a considerable propaganda to try and divert Allied attention from the iron ore.[10]

As shall be seen, the mention of Stephenson in this context was no mere coincidence.

By the second half of December, feverish attention was being paid to the Swedish iron ore question in London. At the fourth meeting of the Supreme War Council in Paris on the 19th, it had been decided to make a diplomatic approach to the Norwegian and Swedish governments on the matter of assistance to Finland. Looking beyond the soft and alluring overture of diplomacy, the Chiefs of Staff were set to work evaluating the implications of various military schemes to commandeer the orefields. At the Admiralty, Churchill continued to press for action against Narvik.

Apart from the consideration of plans for some kind of larger-scale military or naval intervention in Scandinavia, thought was also being given to special operations. On 16 December, Churchill had recommended that the export of ore from Oxelösund had to be prevented 'by methods which will be neither diplomatic nor military'. What these methods consisted of, was spelled out by the Chiefs of Staff in their report of 31 December when they noted that the port could be put out of action either by blocking the harbour (thus encouraging the formation of ice) or by the destruction of the mechanical loading apparatus on the docks. This latter project was considered promising and it was calculated that if it were successfully executed, the flow of iron from the port might be interrupted for six months or more. It is time to return to Rickman in Stockholm.

He was now the effective owner of a small company in the Swedish capital, dealing in dental materials. This had been acquired with the help of a loan from Walter 'Freckles' Wren, a British businessman involved with SIS.[11] After the purchase, Wren appears to have dropped out of the picture to be replaced by Ingram Fraser as Rickman's operational boss in Section D. Both Wren and Fraser were later members of William Stephenson's British Security Coordination organisation in the Americas and it is noteworthy that in the period between the summer of 1939 and January of 1940, all three men – Wren, Stephenson and Fraser – visited Sweden, the latter two on several occasions, their stays neatly complementing one another.[12] Both Wren and Fraser had direct contacts with Rickman during their visits. There is no record, however, of any encounter between Stephenson and Rickman taking place on Swedish soil. None the less while the Canadian businessman may have had other intelligence matters to attend to in Scandinavia, the pattern of his visits, his circle of acquaintances and the Official History of SOE in Scandinavia, certainly suggests that he was 'in the picture' as regards Section D's plans in Sweden.

By October 1939, Rickman had built up the nucleus of his team. One of his first contacts was with Ernest Biggs, a British advertising man who had been based in Stockholm since 1931 and who knew the Swedish scene well. Another helpmate as regards things Swedish, was Elsa Johansson, Rickman's secretary. Key assistance of another kind was to come from the ranks of German refugees in Stockholm.

Rickman's initial task concerned propaganda rather than sabotage and consisted of organising the distribution of black propaganda within Germany. London-inspired texts were enclosed in envelopes, bearing counterfeit stamps and infiltrated into the Reich by merchant seamen and other sympathetic travellers. Thereafter they were disseminated throughout the country by means of the ordinary postal system. The list of addresses of possible targets for this campaign was subsequently greatly augmented with the help of customer lists from the exiled publisher Gottfried Berman Fischer, who assisted in Rickman's German propaganda in other ways as well.[13] A central figure in Rickman's group was Arno Behrisch from Dresden, who combined the useful skill of printer with substantial experience of covert political activities in Germany and Czechoslovakia. In 1933, he had been tipped off that the Gestapo were looking for him and he decided to get out of Germany as quickly as possible. Eventually he settled in Czechoslovakia where *Sozialistische Arbeiter Partei* (SAP) – a numerically small, but lively left-wing splinter group party to which he belonged – had built up an émigré organisation which was able to support the activities of members still within Germany.[14] In order to carry out such support work, a special frontier post was set up on the border between Czechoslovakia and the Reich, first near Bodenach and later near Teplitz, which had a threefold function: to keep in close contact with the outlawed organisation in Dresden; to pass on/receive various types of information, usually – for security's sake – by word of mouth; and to look after the infiltration of banned political material such as the SAP's *Neue Front* and *Banner des revolutionären Marxismus*. The latter was printed in miniature form on thin paper and could be folded up and hidden in a matchbox. The whole operation was run on a shoestring and the people involved had to make out as best they could by their own exertions. Behrisch began by helping to run the post and when the acting head was forced to move with his family to Prague, Behrisch assumed joint responsibility for the work until 1939, when the worsening situation forced him to leave. Travelling by way of Poland and Latvia, he reached Sweden in August and after being granted a work permit, he was able to resume his trade at the Workers' Press in Stockholm.

Before its dissolution in the middle of April 1940, it was estimated that Rickman's organisation had managed to distribute some 30,000 pre-addressed propaganda letters within Germany. In the beginning, Rickman received the leaflets, envelopes and stamps, with the envelopes already addressed, directly from England. The only thing required was to smuggle them into Germany. Later, more and more work was carried out in Stockholm itself.

In addition to this German-language propaganda campaign directed at the German public, the Rickman group was also involved in January 1940 in preparing a *sub-rosa* scheme to influence Swedish opinion. Its object was to mobilise support for the transit of Allied troops to Finland through Sweden and to draw attention to the role of Swedish iron ore in the German war economy. Appropriate leaflets and booklets with such titles as *Wake up Sweden!*, *Germany – Ruler of Europe* and *Nazism calls itself Socialism* were produced, purporting to have been written by Swedes and to represent popular Swedish opinion, but in reality composed by certain of Rickman's associates.

At the end of November 1939, perhaps in response to information alleging increasing stockpiling of ore at Oxelösund, an important development in British contingency planning for sabotage in Scandinavia took place with an initial major transfer of various explosive devices to the Swedish capital where they were eventually stored in a cellar, rented by Rickman from the Windsor Tea Company. No permission, however, had been given at this stage by Section D – far less by the British government – to proceed with any act of sabotage. Nor had the precise target or method to be used at Oxelösund been fixed.

Throughout the following month, as has been noted, the iron ore question was dissected in London again and again. Irked by the lack of action, Churchill jumped the gun on 2 January 1940 by instructing Section D to go ahead with the sabotage at Oxelösund, only to find his order being countermanded the following day by the Prime Minister. None the less approval was given for further reconnaissance of the port.

At the end of January, Fraser and Stephenson were simultaneously in Stockholm. In a report to London, they advocated prompt action. The harbour was frozen, no work was going on and security was minimal. However, the War Cabinet continued to dither and Stephenson was recalled for further consultation. Fraser remained in Stockholm to brief Rickman and his friends. At one meeting, a map of Oxelösund was produced. On the back of it, nine key points were listed:

1. Are these machines used at present: a) traverse b) German crane c) American crane?
2. Are there always vessels at the quay?
3. Loading equpment under repair? Which?
4. Description of illumination at night and if possible, the location of the main lights and their power.
5. Are the ships' lanterns sufficiently strong to light up both fore and aft?
6. Are the vessels lit up also on the seaward side?
7. What kind of energy (electricity or steam) is supplied to the traverse and loading cranes?
8. Photographs of the loading cranes, quay, etc.
9. Where is the barbed wire? How many armed guards on the quays etc? Where are their posts?[15]

The situation had crystallised. The dock cranes were now specifically mentioned as the targets. Alternative schemes for preventing the flow of ore from Oxelösund had proved incapable of implementation or were laid aside for other reasons.

Around 6 February, Rickman and Elsa Johansson drove to Oxelösund for a prelimary reconnaissance and a couple of days later Rickman, Behrisch, Bonnevie – a Norwegian associate of Rickman – and an unidentified acquaintance of Behrisch (presumably the same individual designated in British official papers by the codename Dago) were back there again but this time with the necessary explosive devices at hand. The prospective operation, however, was called off because the cranes were being used. A second attempt a fortnight later was also ditched because work was in progress. Interestingly enough, these attempts appear to have been carried out without the full authorisation of the British government which was first granted on 8 March after Churchill's agitation.

After receiving an instruction to carry out the sabotage as soon as possible, Rickman sent Elsa Johansson to Oxelösund to determine what work was going on at the port. Upon her return, he then got in touch with Behrisch about having another go. But by now Behrisch and Dago had had second thoughts and withdrew from the scheme. A new crisis arose about who was to replace them.

On 5 April, Ingram Fraser passed through Stockholm and conferred yet again with Rickman and Biggs about sabotage at Oxelösund. Rickman's secretary was dispatched once more to the port to check on developments on the spot. Plans were also afoot to recruit suitable people for the sabotage work. The pace of events began to quicken.

When the Germans occupied Copenhagen on the 9th, Ingram Fraser fell into their net.[16] By virtue of his courier's pass, he was subsequently repatriated four days later with the rest of the British legation staff. In the meantime his deputy at the Scandinavian section of Section D, Gerald Holdsworth, flew at short notice to Stockholm in anticipation of a further German strike against Sweden and upon arrival set about trying to breathe new life into Rickman's organisation.[17]

Contact had been made with some young English flight mechanics in transit from Finland where they had served as volunteers during the Winter War.[18] Three of these were now recruited for the sabotage project. By the 10th, Rickman was ready. He telegraphed the London HQ for authorisation. Grand's reply came the following day: *For D. 1. from D. Reference your telegram April 10. Go ahead. Good luck.*

On the evening of Friday 12 April, having fixed up petrol for the car journey down to Oxelösund with the help of the local BP representative, Rickman set off with the three flight mechanics on what appears to have been a preparatory run to acquaint them with the layout of the place. However they discovered when they got there that security at the docks had been significantly strengthened. Rickman reported back to Holdsworth the next day and it was agreed to call off the sabotage attempt. At the same time it was decided, in case there was a German attack on Sweden to disperse the sabotage equipment for alternative deployment. Before this could be done, however, the Swedish police intervened. On 19 April at 7.15 in the evening, Rickman, described as an English company director, was detained pending further enquiries. The reason for his detention was clear enough from the inventory of items unearthed in his Stockholm flat:

6 suitcases, each containing 4 wooden boxes, holding in toto 53. 6 kilos of gelignite.

2 electrical timing devices with 2 clocks in each.

11 electrical detonators.

2 chisels.

1 box containing nails and screws.

1 case containing 28,285 crowns in Swedish notes, 1,750 crowns in Norwegian notes and 35 crowns in Danish notes.

3 modern pistols with several rounds of ammunition.

1 map of Oxelösund, along with three picture postcards of the port.

3 Swedish passports, printed in 1938 and suitably endorsed.

1 official police stamp used for the endorsement of passports and other documents.

1 specification and description of explosives and sabotage material.

miscellaneous correspondence about explosives, sabotage material and propaganda.

1 small black book with various notes.[19]

His office, which was searched at the same time, yielded much less: four empty boxes and a collection of propaganda leaflets. The next day the search was extended to the 'Windsor Tea Company' cellar. There a new surprise awaited the police in the shape of a large number of boxes containing a further 33.5 kilos of gelignite, 57.3 kilos of another explosive (hexogen) disguised as modelling clay, 8 limpet mines and a whole range of other equipment intended for sabotage.[20]

One by one, the other members of Rickman's group were picked up by the police. Only Holdsworth, among the principals on the spot, avoided detailed interrogation but it was a narrow escape. What then had led the Swedish police to become interested in Rickman?[21] Initially – perhaps in January 1940 – the Englishman had attracted some attention through the routine surveillance of various other people, among them Ernest Biggs, but initially no particular measure appears to have been taken. Increased police interest in him came about as a byproduct of another investigation into German espionage.[22]

At the end of 1939, Biggs and Rickman had contacted an émigré journalist, 'Kant', with the intention of eliciting his help in preparing the black propaganda for Germany but to no avail. The journalist, however, continued to keep an eye on what Rickman and his associates were up to, and in February 1940, he sent a letter to a post box address in Berlin which read as follows:

> Dear Herr Kutzner,
> I am very grateful for the 'Tintenkuli' which Horst brought with him from you. I am making use of it for the first time and hope that you will be pleased with the result. Contact with my Uncle Richard whom you have heard about, has hitherto been of little value though I feel that it is promising for the future. The old chap is very suspicious and as far as he is concerned, has little to gain from his contact with me but I hope to come into closer contact with his family and thus be able to win his trust as well. Although at present, he does not possess a command of Swedish, he feels quite at home here and it is always interesting to see a man like him practising his profession, from which one can only derive benefit. As far as I can make out, he is engaged in commerce and has nothing to do with the authorities, only with private individuals, but nonetheless he has enjoyed a certain beginner's luck. Of course, the war causes much disruption in this branch too, but these just have to be surmounted.
> From a material point of view, things are not going well for me as in the beginning, because I must spend a great deal of time on secondary matters simply to get at the real original sources but this is probably only temporary. Naturally the poor postal services are something of a trial: apart from disruption due to the war, there are delays due to the weather conditions etc. I would be very interested to hear if and when this letter reaches you, I hope in any case to hear from you. Every word from home is precious and doubly so at present. What is your opinion of my possible transfer plans? I still do not know if they are practical, but your advice would be greatly valued.[23]

This communication was intercepted on 8 February by Swedish Post Control and when submitted to various tests, it was found to contain a further message, written in invisible ink:

> After sustained effort, I have succeeded in determining the various members of the 'Secret Service' here. I managed to do so by getting in touch with a former acquaintance who is now in

London. My supposition that he had made similar contacts in England proved quite correct. I came into contact with him through an [English] courier and eventually was put in touch with a Mr. Rickman who has made a study of Swedish iron ore and has written a book on that subject. This man was subordinate to a Mr. Wilson, whose acquaintance I have not been able to make. He divides his time between here and Norway and is in charge of an organisation for English propaganda directed against the Reich. He stamps the material here with German stamps for subsequent distribution within the Reich. Judging from the various samples, the quality is wretched. I have an acquaintance who is involved in this business and through whom I am able to gain some insight into what is going on. Rickman is afraid of the Swedish authorities and camouflages everything. At present, his interest is focused on Malmö. In my accounts about him in the future, I shall call him Uncle Richard. Perhaps through him and his associates, I shall have a chance to go to England, where I am now mobilizing other acquaintances (the Press, Foreign Office). You will receive further information about this.[24]

On 8 March 1940, Kant had a new titbit about 'Richard' for his friends in Berlin.[25] After outlining the opinions of Lambert, the Stockholm correspondent of the *Manchester Guardian*, about British policy regarding Norway and Sweden, his report continued:

The opinions put forward in the most intimate circle grouped around the English confidential agent [*Vertrauensmann*] here whom I called 'Richard' are quite otherwise. He has informed his friends here that the next months – he mentioned again and again May – could be pretty turbulent ones in Sweden and Norway. A propos of this, he also maintains that the German Reich would no longer be able to obtain economic advantages as hitherto. Still less are the Allies interested in allowing their opponent to quietly enjoy this state of affairs. Intermezzos like that with the 'Altmark' could be repeated. There would be no harm done if thereby the Germans were forced 'to extend their Front'. From a British standpoint there was little to lose and much to gain. These statements would suggest that provocations in this direction on the part of the English are to be expected and it may be assumed that this agent would be informed about such intentions and might even have a certain role to play in them.[26]

Meanwhile the Swedish Security Service had begun to take a closer look at Rickman himself. It was recalled that during his 1938 tour of ports and installations, the Englishman had exhibited great interest in many details relating to the Swedish mining industry, allegedly so that his forthcoming book would be as complete as possible. The book had duly appeared and Rickman had sent a copy of that work to the Social Board in connection with his latest application for a residence permit. It displayed great knowledge of the subject in hand and it was therefore all the more puzzling that Rickman, the expert on iron ore, should now be involved in a quite different area of commercial enterprise. On 23 February 1940, a request was made to place Rickman's post and telephone under surveillance.[27]

The next major development was the arrest of Kant on Saturday 13 April. Through his confession, the true scope of Rickman's propaganda activities became for the first time clear to the police and it was this that prompted their call on Rickman the following Friday. The discovery of the store of explosives and sabotage equipment, however, apparently constituted a genuine surprise.

With Rickman's arrest, a great deal of compromising material fell into the hands of the Swedish security authorities. His testimony and that of the other accused and the material seized by the police in their search, revealed the British government's involvement in the conspiracy. The military attaché, Sutton-Pratt, had functioned as a mailbox between Rickman and London. One of his staff had helped to transfer the explosives. There was a letter of 5 April from Rickman to Fraser, which tied Sutton-Pratt still closer: 'It ought to be pointed out,' Rickman complained, 'that many of our visits have turned out unsuccessful because of YM's (= Sutton-Pratt's) absence for one reason or another' and later on in the same letter, he took up YM's trip to Finland to get suitable people, noting that 'YM has naturally no intention of revealing his true purpose'. Commander Martin, the local Passport Control Officer, was also involved. He had functioned in part as Rickman's banker, taking charge of certain funds to be used by Rickman for propaganda and other purposes. The PCO in Oslo had performed a similar service. There were several unequivocal pointers to Section D and its personnel. Rickman was D/1 (or possibly D/I) and Fraser most certainly D/G. A 'Section D' was explicitly mentioned in correspondence carelessly preserved and Fraser's attachment to this section was also explicitly noted therein. The sabotage equipment told its own story, some of it bearing the name of its English manufacturer.

As a result of a map found in Rickman's possession and their knowledge of Rickman's trips to Norway and of the Norwegian Bonnevie's association with Rickman, the Swedish police suspected that Oxelösund was perhaps only one intended target among several. Security was therefore immediately tightened both at that port and other key installations. On the basis of the equipment seized and its accompanying instructions for use, an information leaflet was drafted and circulated to the appropriate regional Swedish authorities so that the significance of the latest methods of sabotage could be better understood and guarded against.

Rickman was sentenced to eight years' hard labour for his part in the conspiracy while his collaborators received sentences from one year (after reduction) to three and a half years. The operation had miscarried hopelessly. The whole thing was astonishing in its amateurishness. Rickman was involved in too many diverse schemes; his two-fold cover – first as the author of a book on iron ore and later as an businessman dabbling in dental materials and preserves – served simply to attract further attention; papers and materials which should have been destroyed, were hoarded religiously, etc.

Yet if Section D's antics were to be as unsuccessful in Sweden as they were elsewhere during the Phoney War – a catalogue of bangs that failed to materialise – the operational failure could not be attributed simply to Grand and his men in the field. Beset by moral scruples on the one hand and inspired on the other by a vague hope that the war might somehow blow over, the British government procrastinated. Uncomfortable with the prospect of full-scale military action, it preferred to theorise over the efficacy of economic pressure, direct and indirect, upon the enemy. From indirect economic warfare to schemes neither diplomatic nor military, the step was short. But called upon to implement such schemes, the government relapsed into indecision. That hesitation was to be a major factor, in ensuring that Operation Lumps at Oxelösund, came to naught.

The activities of Rickman and his group provided – in their failure and exposure – a fruitful subject for the propaganda efforts of Britain's adversaries. More seriously, it led quite naturally to a heightened surveillance of members of the British community by the Swedish Security Service and the task of the British Special Services became correspondingly more difficult.

From special operations to support for resistance

The German occupation of Denmark and Norway isolated Sweden from the West. For a time its maritime trade through its principal port of Gothenburg on the west coast ceased completely and goods had to be shipped via Petsamo in northern Finland. As long as hostilities continued in Norway, the British could still toy with ideas of cutting off supplies of Swedish ore by military force and of opening a northern front against Germany. By the autumn of 1940, the situation looked very different and the principal goal of British policy towards Sweden became now one of sustaining it in its attempts to assert its independence *vis-à-vis* Germany. In keeping with this policy, the British therefore sanctioned the introduction of a 'safe route' through their blockade lines for approved ships passing between Sweden and the West. Somewhat paradoxically, the Germans gave approval in February 1941 for this Westbound traffic, based on *their* calculation that such traffic assisted Swedish industry to maintain production levels of export goods then largely destined for Germany and those countries under its control while at the same time diminishing Sweden's dependence on German supplies of oil. The British and Germans had done their sums and, fortunately for the Swedes, had arrived at different answers.

If the introduction of a maritime safe route was of primary importance to Sweden, a functioning air service between the two countries was essential to Britain if swift courier lines with Scandinavia were to be maintained. Before the invasion of Denmark and Norway, there had been indirect air services linking Stockholm and Britain. On 30 April 1940, BOAC was given permission by the Swedish authorities to fly directly between Stockholm and Britain at their own risk. At first conceived mainly as a link for conveying key personnel in and out of the country, the service from February 1942 onwards was also used to transport critical war materials (in the main, ball bearings) from Sweden to Britain. The American Air Transport Service introduced a parallel service in 1944 while the Swedish company, ABA, having obtained both German and British authorisation, commenced their courier service between the two countries in February 1942.

Another important consequence of the German invasion of Denmark and Norway was the cessation of the cable traffic between Sweden and Britain on 13 May 1940, when the second of the two lines operated by the Great Northern Telegraph Co. Ltd, was cut; the first had been cut a month earlier. All signal traffic between Britain and Sweden thereafter went by radio.[28] The bulk of this was sent via 'Gothenburg radio', a transmitter operated by the Swedish authorities. This handled not simply commercial and press telegrams but also the enciphered communications of the British legation.

As far as British special operations in Sweden during the second phase were concerned, the main emphasis was now placed in strengthening resistance both within the country and in contiguous parts of occupied Europe. The task was complicated by the general trend of events, the climate of opinion in the country, the vigilance of the Security Service, the repercussions of the Rickman affair and the unsympathetic attitude of the British minister who tended to regard unorthodox active measures as a threat to his own approach of quiet persuasion.

An important role in liaison with groups sympathetic to the British cause in Sweden, was played by the press attaché, Peter Tennant, who in the autumn of 1940 was made formally responsible for Special Operations Executive (SOE) work there.[29] As a former Cambridge don with a specialist knowledge and love of Scandinavia, he was well qualified linguistically and temperamentally to win the support of Swedes from many walks of life. Among his friends was Amalie Posse. A member of a distinguished Swedish family, she had married a Czech and had experienced Hitler's methods at first hand. An ardent anti-Nazi, she became the champion of the Czech cause in Sweden and something of a thorn in the side of Swedish officialdom. Through her initiative, the Tuesday Club came into being, which brought together influential Swedes for informal discussions about topics of the moment and the progress of the war. At the same time, a secret section of the club busied itself with wireless telegraphy and other tools of resistance. Another independent group concerned with these latter matters and with whom Tennant also was in touch, was made up of Syndicalists, many of whom had served in the Spanish Civil War.[30] In addition to these activities, Tennant's position as press attaché provided him with a broad spectrum of contacts and he was often therefore well placed to act both as a channel for intelligence and as a cut-out for other colleagues in the British Special Services who preferred to maintain a lower profile. On the propaganda front, mindful of the Rickman muddle, his main energies went into getting the British view of things across, in a variety of open, rather than covert ways and most conspicuously by means of a weekly, *Nyheter från Storbritannien* (News from Great Britain), which eventually attained an impressive circulation.

According to the Chiefs of Staff formal directive of July 1942, the task of SOE in Sweden was to build up a contingency organisation in the event that the country was invaded by the Germans.[31] Sweden was divided into ten districts from north to south and regional organisers were appointed with the job of preserving radio communication with Britain. At the same time, a provisional list of post-occupation sabotage targets was drawn up. In October, Captain T. F. O'Reilly arrived to put the final touches to these contingency plans. His initial impression of morale in the country was unusually positive and he felt that there was now both will and ability on the part of the Swedes to resist any German invader. From this point onwards, SOE's projected role in purely Swedish affairs became increasingly more limited. Active measures became more a question of training W/T operators rather than of recruiting potential saboteurs. In due course, even SOE's radio network in Sweden was to be deemed superfluous and by November 1943, it was time to close the account.

Although after Rickman, British sabotage activities within Sweden were deliberately soft-pedalled, this did not rule out using the country as a base for striking at the enemy outside its borders. On 27 January 1942, Henry Threlfall, who was attached to the German Section of SOE, arrived in Stockholm and was given cover as a secretary to the naval attaché.[32] Cover notwithstanding, Swedish suspicions had almost immediately been aroused by the interception of a Czech telegram to London which announced the arrival of Threlfall 'from the I[ntelligence] S[ervice]' and described him as having 'a special German assigment'.[33] Thereafter Threlfall was the object of close surveillance. On 17 February the Security Service registered that a meeting between Threlfall, the British naval attaché and the Dutch Consul General had taken place, at which *inter alia* the possibility of interrupting the traffic through the Kiel Canal by sabotage was discussed.[34] On 23 February, it was observed that during a stroll in Stockholm, Threlfall had dropped a number of envelopes in different letter-boxes.[35] One of these was found to contain a letter in German, addressed to a certain Herr Morlion in Portugal, purportedly from a member of the German Association in Stockholm, which took up a rumour about the possibility of marking a submarine with an invisible layer of some phosphorescent substance which later on made the vessel detectable from the air and thus vulnerable to attack. Had not several German submarines already been lost off the Portuguese coast, due to some such method? The letter concluded by stating that the atmosphere in Sweden was now so thoroughly anti-German that the writer had no intention of becoming involved in anything that would lay the country open to the charge of espionage.

During February, the Swedish Postal Control Section had noted the occurrence of a number of letters sent to Germany and Portugal containing rumours intended to chip away at German morale: it was claimed that two German Alpine regiments, half mad with cold, hunger and the darkness had decided to return to Germany from the Murmansk front but that only three men had made it; typhoid fever was said to have broken out in Germany and a submarine which had left Bremen with the illness on board, had arrived back with a third of its crew dead and another third in a hopeless condition. These rumours were attributed to Swedish seamen, Swedish newspapers and Finnish journalists. After a while, the rumours had changed. Now it was claimed that mortality on the Eastern Front was 20 per cent higher than usual because the extreme cold hindered blood transfusions and that the German population was declining due to a reduction in male potency. The British, it was said, had apparently managed to sink submarines by sabotage carried out in Germany. Submarines marked by some phosphorescent substance became visible from above after a few days in the water. In seven letters, there was a rumour that the Pope planned to leave Rome and that Mussolini had asked Roosevelt if Rome would be spared from bombing.

Threlfall's undoing was to come about through his association with a dubious character called Blackman.[36] The latter served as a steward on Swedish vessels plying the German ports and had, after offering his services to the British legation, been passed on to Threlfall. Various schemes were now proposed with Blackman as Threlfall's paid operative in the field: (i) the use of Swedish vessels to infiltrate propaganda; (ii) sabotage against German shipping; (iii) the collection of information about German vessels in Gothenburg; (iv) espionage and sabotage directed against German transit traffic through Sweden to Norway and Finland; (v) the interruption of traffic through the Kiel Canal by sabotage. In due course, Blackman enquired if a friend of his – a ship's cook, Lindström – might also participate in the work and after Blackman had vouched for the man's reliability, this was agreed. Money and explosives changed hands.

In truth neither Blackman nor his friend was to be trusted. On 30

July 1942, a telegram went to the counter-espionage section of the *Abwehr* in Berlin notifying them that a seaman called 'Windström' had written to the German Consul in Gothenburg informing him that a new British 'espionage organisation' was in process of formation in Sweden.[37] With the help of pro-British seamen, it hoped to bring on board a German iron ore vessel in Luleå, a large quantity of explosives equipped with a timing device. As the vessel passed through the Kiel Canal, the explosives would be dropped overboard at an opportune moment, to explode 24 hours later. Berlin was notified at the same time that this information would be passed to the Swedish counter-espionage authorities and it was hoped that the informant could be found so that more could be learned about the proposed operation.

On the same day (30 July) Blackman and Lindström were picked up by the Swedish police. They were later tried, found guilty for their part in the affair and received stiff sentences. As for Threlfall, he was flown out at short notice ten days after the arrest of his unreliable assistants. Suspicions did not disappear quite so easily and on the debit side, the British naval attaché, as the SOE man's nominal superior, was now wrongly identified as an *éminence grise* in the planning of British sabotage in Sweden.[38]

If the sabotage of German supplies was one aim of British economic warfare and special operations, the positive facilitation of British provisioning was another. A conspicuous example of this side of things was the work of George Binney.[39] Binney had arrived in Sweden in December 1939 as a representative for British Iron and Steel Control with the task of ensuring that British industry was supplied with key materials, such as ball bearings, machine tools and special steels. After the occupation of Denmark and Norway, a small amount of goods was shipped through Petsamo in Northern Finland and other consignments went by rail through Russia but eventually the only possibility left was to defy the German blockade of the Skagerrak. Binney hit upon the scheme of loading up certain Norwegian ships shored up in Swedish ports and of making a dash for it across the North Sea. So began a train of ideas that was to lead to Operation Rubble. Many problems remained to be solved. Apart from keeping things hidden as far as possible from the eyes of the enemy intelligence service, the doubts of the Legation, the Foreign Office and the Admiralty concerning the viability of the scheme, had to be overcome. When this was done and having joined forces with William Waring, a chartered accountant then employed in the cipher department of the British legation, the two men were given cover positions as assistants to the Commercial Counsellor, and could devote themselves, with the assistance of a small back-up team, to the detailed planning of the operation. Rubble was successfully carried out in January 1941 and resulted in the transfer of over a million pounds worth of valuable cargo to Britain as well as a useful increment to British merchant tonnage.

Rubble having gone so smoothly, Binney (now Sir George) returned to Sweden to continue with Waring the planning of a repeat performance. The Germans, however, were not slow with countermeasures, on the one hand calling into question the legal ownership of the remaining Norwegian vessels in Sweden and on the other threatening to withdraw their permission for the Swedish safe conduct traffic. Delay upon delay followed and when finally in March 1942 the operation, codenamed Performance, was ready to be implemented, the circumstances, exacerbated by what the British considered to be intentional obstruction by the Swedes, fearful of German recrimination, were far from propitious. As the expedition got under way, at the last minute an attempt was made to call off the breakout, but the signal was not received. Two of the vessels involved, the *Lionel* and *Dicto*, managed to return to Gothenburg. Of the remaining fleet, only two vessels reached Britain. In April, when it became openly known that the vessels in the fleet had been carrying arms, in breach of Swedish neutrality, there was a vigorous German protest to the Swedes and the upshot was that Binney was declared *persona non grata*. The Foreign Office resisted, however, the recall of Waring who was left to take charge of the on-the-spot planning of future operations in Binney's absence.

Attention now focused on *Lionel* and *Dicto*. The Germans were under the impression that the Swedes would in no circumstances permit these two vessels to leave. The British now decided (Operation Cabaret) to try a new breakout with them and the triangular tussle involving Britain, Germany and Sweden resumed. But now a fourth factor entered the game in the shape of the Americans who took a much more abrasive line towards neutrals in matters of economic warfare than the British. When Boheman, the Under-Secretary of State at the Swedish Ministry for Foreign Affairs, went to America for negotiations, he found that if satisfactory terms were to be reached, then the Swedes would have to give way on *Lionel* and *Dicto*. These obtained formal clearance on 11 January and a few days later moved down river, awaiting instructions from the Admiralty. The attitude of the Swedish naval authorities, however, continued to cause problems and after various delays, the operation was finally called off. Meanwhile the granting of formal clearance to the two Norwegian vessels had led Berlin to withdraw its permission for the Swedish safe conduct traffic on 15 January, and this traffic was first resumed again on 6 May.

As the general military position of the Allies improved, Swedish opposition to these British special supply operations slowly diminished. At the same time British tactics changed. The *Lionel* and the *Dicto* were moved from Gothenburg to the small port of Lysekil which offered more protection from the attention of the enemy intelligence service. Here their cargoes were transferred to specially equipped motor gun boats (MGBs) which were now brought into use as blockade busters. Between the end of 1943 and March 1944 (Operation Bridford) several successful round trips were made. Success was very much dependent on the supply both of meteorological information and of intelligence supplied by the Admiralty Operational Intelligence Centre regarding the dispositions of enemy vessels in the Skagerrak.

A final action (Operation Moonshine, January–February, 1945) involving these MGBs had more significance for resistance activities than for British economic supply and consisted in ferrying a quantity of arms to Sweden for subsequent transfer to Denmark.

Binney's dramatic blockade-busting attempts were concerned to assure the continuance of British supplies rather than to interdict German supplies. Another example of an operation with the same object but quite different in character, was the following.[40] The A6 Wild machine which was made in Switzerland, was an important instrument in the interpretation of the results of photo reconnaissance. In order to facilitate and cloak the purchase of this instrument, an order for it was placed by a company based in Sweden and the dismantled machine was later flown to Britain from Stockholm.

Navicerts and the Statutory List: while the sabotage preparations of Section D (and later of SOE) and the blockade-running activities of Binney formed constituents of economic warfare, more typical of the latter was the Navicert system and the Statutory List, both of which entailed considerable routine investigation and control of flows.

The Navicert system was intended to facilitate the passage of approved neutral goods through British-controlled waters, by allowing a merchant in a neutral country to apply for prior but provisional clearance from the local British consular authorities. A certificate of origin or interest duly signed by a consular official, after the receipt of invoices or other trustworthy documents, declared that the designated merchandise being shipped from X to Y 'has not been grown, produced or manufactured in enemy territory, that no person who is an enemy, or with whom trading is prohibited under any law or proclamation for the time being in force relating to trading with the enemy or relating to trading with persons of enemy nationality or associations, has any interest in such merchandise.'[41]

The Statutory List (or Proclaimed List as the Americans called it), was drawn up by the appropriate departments in London and Washington on the advice of the legation and consular staff in the country concerned.[42] It sought to deprive firms in neutral countries thought to be directly or indirectly under enemy control or serving enemy interests, of their commercial ties in Allied countries and more generally to exercise pressure upon them.[43] In the case of British economic warfare policy, the following categories of firms risked being listed:

1. Firms controlled from enemy or enemy-occupied territory
2. Firms whose sole or main activity was that of acting as agent for a particular enemy firm or group of firms, of pushing the sales of a particular enemy product, i.e., their sole or main function consisted in rendering economic assistance of special value to the enemy, and they qualified for listing on grounds of close enemy association.
3. Firms which knowingly transacted business with Statutory List firms outside of Sweden.
4. Firms which acted as cloaks for delivery of goods to or from Statutory Listed firms.
5. Firms which acted as intermediaries for transactions between a neutral country and enemy or enemy occupied territory.
6. Firms which acted as cloaks for enemy financial transactions such as the nominal transfer of enemy shares to a Swedish holder.
7. Firms which tried to evade controls, in any way not specified.
8. Firms whose trade with the enemy had increased abnormally since the outbreak of war.

70

9. Firms or individuals who were politically active on behalf of the enemy.
10. Firms or individuals who furnished specially useful economic assistance to the enemy.
11. Individuals who became members of the Board of a Statutory Listed firm.

By May 1945, the number of listed companies or persons in Sweden amounted to 530, of whom more than half had been put on the list in the preceding two years.[44] Although this number was still small compared to the list of companies and individuals in, for example, Spain, the operation of the list caused predictable resentment.[45] At an official level, it was maintained by the Swedes that the practice of listing accorded ill with the spirit of the War Trade Agreement.[46] Furthermore the commercial detective work which listing presupposed, brought it into potential conflict with Swedish law.[47] In Swedish business circles, listing was often felt to be arbitrary or ill-conceived. Smaller firms, it was said, were placed under the microscope while larger firms with international reputations could sail close to the wind with impunity.[48]

These criticisms were certainly not without foundation, but in the eyes of the Allied economic warfare departments, charged with exerting every pressure at their disposal on the German War Economy and its suppliers, they did not cut much ice. In the end, a decision had to be made and the last word could not be left to the government of the neutral state itself, far less to the representatives of aggrieved firms or individuals.[49]

In some cases – as for example with DNB, the German information service – the reason for statutory listing was fairly obvious. But on other occasions, matters were less simple. Such was the case with Birger Dahlerus, a businessman well known to the British Foreign Office for his peace-broking exertions on the eve of war. In a report of 13 May 1942, it was reported that a firm which Dahlerus was intimately associated with, was trying to work up a trade in Germany in sundry small engineering equipment. However at this stage, the Minister and the Foreign Office were both opposed to listing. Soon, however, a divergence of opinion arose between the Commercial Department and Chancery about the Swede.

The view of the Chancery is that it would definitely be inadvisable

71

to place either Dahlerus or Bolinders on the Statutory List, as Dahlerus, who is on very friendly terms with certain members of the Legation, has at times in the past been useful for intelligence purposes and may very well be useful in the future. While declaring his dislike of the Nazi regime and his belief that Germany will be defeated, he makes no attempt to conceal from us the fact that he retains his personal contacts with Goering, as he believes that this contact may have its uses not only to himself and the Swedes but also to us. The Chancery also feel that Dahlerus is one of their most useful channels through which certain information can be 'planted' on German officials.[50]

The Commercial Department took a different, more mundane view.

Bolinders are working very closely with Germany and have sold between 5000 and 6000 gas generators units to that country. This is business which cannot be said to be normal trade on the basis of the figures for 1938. Moreover it can be classified as giving especially valuable economic and even military assistance to the enemy and therefore, to justify inclusion in the Statutory List.[51]

In the autumn of 1943, the Commercial Department view finally triumphed and the company was placed on the List.

The newspaper *Dagsposten*, about whose ideological allegiance few were in doubt, avoided being placed on the list until the end of 1944 when its covert funding by the Germans had become a matter of public record. *Dagsposten*, however, had a relatively small circulation and preached largely to the converted. Much more worrying to the Allies in fact was the line taken by Torsten Kreuger's *Aftonbladet*. On 22 January 1942, the Commercial Counsellor at the British Legation took up one aspect of the matter with the Ministry for Foreign Affairs.

Referring to our discussion at the last meeting of the Joint Standing Commission about *Aftonbladet* and Mr. Torsten Kreuger, I now suggest that before we reply to London about the question of the Statutory List (and incidentally the Proclaimed List) we should give you an opportunity of discussing the matter, if you so wish, with the parties concerned. Perhaps if you drop them a hint that the Americans and ourselves are contemplating certain action, they may decide to modify their journalistic policy and adopt a more neutral line. Otherwise *Aftonbladet* would probably find it very inconvenient to be cut off from their regular connections with such American concerns as King Features Inc., and other syndicates and new organizations.[52]

With the end of war in sight, there was an upsurge in the flow of German-controlled assets seeking a safe haven in neutral countries, a fact also noted by the Swedish postal censorship authorities.[53] Thus on 21 September 1944, a German-born lawyer who had become a Swedish citizen, offered his services for cloaking purposes, stating that it was 'only a matter of writing over all German shares to neutral firms or persons who undertake to sell them back at a later date and at an agreed price'.[54] Among more specific plans was a scheme to channel back German payments for the delivery of certain locomotives and wagons to Turkey via the Iberian Peninsula and Sweden, where the proceeds of sale (less commission to the Swedish cloaking consortium) would be credited to the German company. Rumours of loot in transport began to filter through to London, among them a report from an (evidently non-British) source in Stockholm concerning certain pictures.

In Stockholm last summer, there were some men from Berlin who were curious to know the possibilities of picture restoration, and one of them stated that it concerned pictures from private German collections damaged during air raids. After a short time the mentioned agent left Sweden without solving this question but in the Free Harbour here, there are some big cases from Germany, which give the impression of containing some carefully packed pictures. Because of the Free Harbour, however, the Swedish police have no authority to interfere.[55]

Not surprisingly, the theme of fleeing capital was gratefully seized upon by Allied political warfare departments who were only too pleased to write about rats leaving the Reich's sinking ship. The fake German forces newspaper *Nachrichten für die Truppe* of which between 250,000 and 750,000 were dropped daily by US aircraft, carried juicy exposures about the lifestyle and manipulations of Dr Paul Schmidt, the head of *Auswärtiges Amts* Press Department, in Sweden.[56] On 15 November 1944, the newsheet moved on to a new target alleging that a member of *Reichskommissariat Ostland* had, via intermediaries, deposited gold and jewels in a Swedish bank and in January 1945 there were similar stories about the Swedish nest-eggs of certain Nazi officials in Denmark.[57]

RESISTANCE IN OTHER COUNTRIES

Norway

As a neutral island in northern Europe, Sweden provided geographically a convenient platform for supporting the resistance movements in German occupied territories, most notably in Norway and Demark. In the period 1940–42, however, the attitude of the Swedish government, concerned not to rock the carefully balanced boat in which they were sitting, made the conditions for such activities far from ideal. The redrawing of the power map of Europe from 1938 onwards had repercussions upon the diplomatic representation of victim nations and governments. In Stockholm, the Czechoslovak, Estonian, Latvian and Lithuanian legations disappeared altogether and there was increasing German pressure to limit the activities of the Norwegian and Polish legations. An interesting test-case, illustrative of prevailing attitudes, was to arise with the death of the Norwegian Minister, J. H. Wollebaek on 24 October 1940 and the question of the appointment of his successor. Five days later the Swedish Minister in Berlin informed the Ministry for Foreign Affairs that the Assistant Secretary of State at *Auswärtiges Amt*, Woermann, had 'expressed the hope that the question of the appointment of a new Norwegian Minister in Stockholm would not need to arise'.[58] However, the question *did* arise. Jens Bull, Counsellor at the Norwegian Legation, in due course intimated that he was going to be appointed Minister by the Norwegian government in London. The Ministry for Foreign Affairs now sent its instruction to Prytz, the Swedish Minister in London:

> Request the Norwegian Foreign Minister as a matter of our common interest, that Bull continues as *chargé d'affaires* which will not make the slightest difference to his position. It may be recalled that Erkko, after having been Foreign Minister, served in Stockholm as *chargé d'affaires* during the Finnish–Russian war. It has been reported that the German government at the time informed the Swiss government that it would recall their Minister if a new Polish Minister was accredited. Try to get Koht to understand the situation.[59]

Koht, however, was in no mood for soothing precedents. Prytz reported that the Norwegian Foreign Minister was 'very distressed over this new proof of the Swedish government's antipathy towards Norway'.[60]

During the visit of the German diplomat von Grundherr to Stockholm, the matter of the diplomatic missions representing occupied countries came up for discussion. The Swedish Foreign Minister asked his visitor to do what he could in Berlin to prevent Sweden being requested to close down the Norwegian, Dutch, Belgian and Polish legations. The Swedes were prepared, as in the case of Wollebaek, to refuse the appointment of any new minister in the event that any of the present ministers were for some reason to leave their post but, the Foreign Minister emphasised, they could not go any further. The question was particularly sensitive in regard to Norway.[61]

The issue of ministerial recognition, which the Swedes insisted was more symbolic than practical in nature, continued to infect Swedish–Norwegian diplomatic relations for a period ahead. It also influenced British perceptions as well. As Sir Charles Hambro told Prytz:

> . . . there is one most important point which I have taken up with Marc Wallenberg and which I have not mentioned to you, that is the question of the status of the Norwegian legation in Stockholm. The attitude taken by the Swedish Government towards this matter has I must say caused surprise and indignation in this country and never fails to spoil the atmosphere when any question of Swedish concessions arises . . . Cannot something be done to make it possible for the unfortunate attachés to be recognised and better still, a *chargé d'affaires* to the Norwegian Government here . . .?[62]

This plea was passed on to the Ministry for Foreign Affairs in Stockholm. There it was felt that there was some British mis-understanding of the situation. Prytz was instructed by Stockholm to make Hambro aware of the true facts. Thus, whereas previously the Norwegian legation had consisted of at most a Minister and one other official, it now (December 1941) had a staff of 50, including several highly qualified diplomats. It was too much to expect Sweden, which had resolutely opposed German pressure regarding the missions of the occupied territories, to take a symbolic step that did not accord with practical needs. Lastly it had to be pointed out that Sweden was supplying comprehensive humanitarian assistance to Norway and that thousands of Norwegians had been granted asylum in the country.

While the recognition question generated irritation at the diplomatic level, the flames of fraternal inter-Nordic dispute were also fanned by the attitude of the Swedish authorities on occasions to the activities of certain patriotic but indiscreet Norwegians in their midst who had run foul of the Swedish espionage laws. Two examples may be cited.[63]

On 30 October 1940, a Norwegian journalist had been arrested in Stockholm and later sentenced to four months' imprisonment for an offence under Chapter 8, Sections 9, 10 and 11 of the Penal Code. The basis of the charge was that he had contacted the British Legation and had informed them, *inter alia*, that the airfield at Fornebu was out of action but that the Germans had arranged for an emergency landing place at Linderud near Oslo.[64]

On 1 April 1942, a law student was sentenced to four months imprisonment under Chapter 8 Section 14a. His offence was that in September 1941 he had arranged with two Swedish citizens to use their addresses for the receipt of communications from Norway which were then to be passed on to the Norwegian Legation. The communications received included plans of military installations at Alstahaugfjord and Vefsnfjord, a report about the military situation at various places in Norway and a list of NS members in Helgeland.[65]

Cross border activities were rigorously controlled and Swedes offering to assist practically in the maintenance of courier lines between the Norwegian resistance in Stockholm and its people at home, faced arrest if discovered unless they could induce the local police to turn a blind eye, perhaps by an appeal to a higher protective authority.[66]

As far as British SOE help to Norway was concerned, the Stockholm-based section began its work with more enthusiasm than with either diplomatic caution or conspiratorial finesse and soon found itself in hot water with the Swedish authorities.

On 9 June 1940, the British Minister in Stockholm, Mallet notified the Swedish Ministry for Foreign Affairs of the appointment of Captain Malcolm Munthe to the position of assistant military attaché. Munthe had been one of the original recruits to MI R, the sister organisation to Section D. Shortly before the German invasion, he had been sent to Stavanger to make preparations for the landing of a British expeditionary force and after an adventurous journey, had made his way to Sweden. There he was expected 'to establish communication links with Norway to support the resistance there, and to provide intelligence for SIS'.[67] It did not take long, however, before he was compromised by the arrest of some of his associates. As a consequence, the Security Chief wrote on 28 January 1941 to the Foreign Minister asking for Munthe's expulsion.[68] The next day, the Under-Secretary brought the matter up with the British Minister: Munthe had to cease his unlawful activities and had to return to England as soon as possible.[69]

By now, however, Munthe was involved in a new scheme (Barbara).[70] This was to send a team into Norway to sabotage the railway line from Trondheim to Storlien. At the beginning of February the team set off and a month later, in accordance with the plan, the would-be saboteurs were picked up by the British special covert ferry service, the Shetland Bus, and spirited across the sea to Scotland where they were given a lightning course of instruction in their chosen expertise. Meanwhile two of the team were left behind to prepare for the return of their comrades. By 10 April, the saboteurs were back and ready to move into position. The plan had been to sabotage the line on three different stretches but due to work in progress on the line, in fact only the sabotage at Gudaa was attempted but with minimal result. When the team crossed over the border to Sweden, they were arrested by the Swedish police. William Millar, one of Munthe's main assistants in the operation had been arrested earlier after being compromised.[71] Barbara had ended badly. In an instruction to Prytz in London, the Swedish Ministry for Foreign Affairs, summed up its view of things:

> The activities of the British Assistant Military Attaché, Major Munthe, in Stockholm have for a long time constituted a source of irritation because we have clear proof that from here he has organised an intelligence service relating to Norway by sending Norwegian and Swedish agents there. Several of these helpers are now imprisoned or detained. Already a couple of months ago the Under-Secretary of State discussed the matter with Mallet. The latter became highly indignant, initially denied Munthe's involvement, threatened with reprisals and pointed out all our sins in the eyes of the British. The matter was dropped after Mallet had given his word of honour that Munthe would not engage in anything outside a diplomat's permitted sphere. When further indications were obtained that notwithstanding this

Munthe had continued with his former activities, the Foreign Minister several days ago once more took the matter up with Mallet. Also on this occasion Mallet seemed much excited by the point at issue and the Foreign Minister contented himself finally with a further assurance from Mallet.[72]

Despite this assurance, Munthe was back in business again. The facts of the matter pertaining to Barbara, as they had become known to the Swedes, were then summarised. Because of this, Mallet had been told that the Swedes had decided to declare Munthe *persona non grata*. He should be recalled as soon as possible. If Mallet did not see to it himself, then there would be no alternative left save to instruct Prytz to make an official request to the British government to withdraw Munthe immediately and it 'was not certain that publicity could be avoided'.[73]

Two months later, Munthe – despite having been declared *persona non grata* – was still in Sweden because – according to Mallet – there was no place available on a courier plane.[74] The patience of the Swedish Ministry for Foreign Affairs began to run out. If Munthe was not recalled, his diplomatic status would be withdrawn and he ran the risk of being put on trial.

Finally on 19 July 1941, the controversial attaché took off for Britain. He was lucky to arrive there in one piece. The day before his departure Söderblom, an official at the Ministry for Foreign Affairs, had reported with unconcealed pleasure to the Swedish Minister in Berlin:

The Assistant Military Attaché Munthe at the British Legation departs any day now for London and will not be returning. It is not a day to soon. On being asked, I have informed Counsellor Dankwort [German Legation] about this.[75]

Thus alerted, the Germans did not waste time. On the day of Munthe's flight, Section III of the *Abwehr* sent a telegram to the *Abwehr* Station in Norway, announcing that a British aircraft had landed at 2.30 at Bromma airport, Stockholm, the day before. On the return flight to Britain, there would be an important British intelligence officer on board, and Section III 'had great interest in seeing that the British plane was forced down.'[76]

Among later, more successful special operations in Norway there were several which at the same time illustrated the importance of neutral Sweden as an escape route.[77] Thus in Operation Redshank directed against the Orkla Mines in April 1942, the three saboteurs involved were put ashore in Norway by the Shetland Bus and having carried out their mission, managed to slip over the border, after their cover story had been accepted by Swedish frontier officials. Similarly in Operation Gunnerside, mounted in February 1943, six men were dropped by parachute with the task of attacking the hydrogen electrolysis plant at Vemork, which was important for the German supply of 'heavy water'. Key plant and 3,000 lb. of heavy water were destroyed and afterwards five of the party arrived safely in Sweden.

While the Norwegians for some time had to tread very carefully to avoid falling foul of the Swedish Security authorities, the response of the Swedish Secret Intelligence Service, C-Bureau, was for understandable reasons more supportive. Charged with the task of keeping track by unofficial and covert means, of what was going on in neighbouring territories, it was soon realised that one obvious way of finding out about developments in Norway, was to plug into the information-gathering capabilities of the Norwegian resistance organisations. This began initially in the early months of 1941 with the joint debriefing of Norwegian refugees in camps in Sweden and gradually extended to more active measures designed to support the Norwegian courier activities over the frontier.[78] At the same time, C-Bureau found itself called upon to use its good offices to intercede on behalf of Norwegians who fell into the Security Service's net. In January 1942, Carl Petersén, the Head of C-Bureau, was asked to obtain the release of two Norwegians who had been arrested for unauthorised intelligence activities. In May 1943, a Swedish company director held on a similar charge, was set free, after coming to an agreement with Petersén whereby the radio transmitters he supplied to the Norwegian Resistance, would in future go via C-Bureau.[79] In the course of 1943, the border crossings into Sweden gradually became less problematic and the police and provincial authorities were more and more willing to turn a blind eye to those Norwegian couriers whose journeys had been approved by C-Bureau and the Norwegian Resistance authorities in Stockholm. At the same time, the intelligence coming from these Norwegian sources was relatively more valuable since the prime source of Swedish intelligence – decrypted German signal traffic – had begun to dry up after mid 1942.[80]

In Stockholm, a growing staff of people serviced the activities of the resistance in Norway.[81] Before 9 April 1940, the Norwegian Legation in Stockholm consisted of four persons; by the end of the war, the Legation and its ancillary offices employed around 1200. In the Military Office, where a certain division of labour became formalised around mid 1943, Section II under Ørnulf Dahl took charge of military intelligence while Section IV under Heyerdahl-Larsen was responsible for the interests of the Norwegian underground military organisation MILORG. There were also other departments with intelligence assigments, such as the Press Office and the innocently named 'Sports Office'. The latter had come into existence on 10 May 1942 with Harald Gram as overall head. Consisting of people who had been active in the civilian home front in Norway before coming to Sweden, it provided a courier service prized among others by the Norwegian naval attaché, Hans Peder Henriksen, in his contacts with the members of the naval intelligence service RMO in Norway. Security matters were the responsibility of Section II of the Legal Office. A further investigation unit, the Security Service, administratively attached to the Legal Office, came into existence in June 1944 and was concerned with collecting information of importance for the security of the resistance movement in Norway. In addition to these specifically Norwegian covert organisations, there were other sections of the Allied Special Services (such as SOE and OSS) in Stockholm which were specifically concerned with Norwegian affairs.

Denmark

Whereas the occupation of Norway had resulted in the emigration of the monarch and the establishment of a government in exile in London, the situation in Denmark was quite different. In what was intended as a showpiece protectorate, things on the surface continued superficially as before with King, *Rigsdag*, a military leadership and a lawful Communist party in Copenhagen. The Stauning-Scavenius government embarked on a consciously conciliatory policy towards the German invaders. But where might such a policy lead? Not all Danes were happy with the prospect before them and some were concerned to ensure that contact with England was not completely severed. Stockholm became a focal point for these endeavours in which the journalist Ebbe Munck was to play an important role.

In the summer of 1940, he had talked over the situation with a number of friends in Danish military intelligence, notably Colonel

E. Nordentoft, Major H. Lunding and Captain V. Gyth. In October, Munck took up residence in Stockholm, having persuaded his newspaper *Berlingske Tidende* to appoint him its correspondent in the Swedish capital, thus providing the necessary cover for his clandestine task of acting as a liaison officer between the 'Princes', as the leaders of Danish military intelligence became known, and the British Legation. Munck was soon in operation and a first report carefully surveying the various German organisations in Denmark and detailing the occupation forces in the country and the transport links between Denmark and Norway, was handed over to the British Legation for forward transmission to London.

Not long after Munck had got down to business in Stockholm, an important visitor arrived from London. This was Sir Charles Hambro, then much involved with the organisation of SOE and in particular with the work of its Scandinavian Section. In his meeting with Munck, Hambro explained:

> how it was the opinion of my government that it would be most helpful to the Allied cause if those Danes . . . who were prepared to fight for their country's freedom, would start to form an Underground Organisation trained to conduct sabotage against the Germans. I made it clear at that time that it would not be in the interests of Denmark or Great Britain if uncoordinated sabotage was to break out in Denmark at the moment.[82]

For the time being, the priorities were to be: intelligence gathering; an extended news service for the BBC; and sabotage. In order to smooth contacts between SOE in London and the work in Denmark, Ronald Turnbull, who before the German invasion had served as press attaché in Copenhagen, was assigned to the British Legation in Stockholm, arriving there in March 1941.

The flow of information from Denmark to Sweden whether transmitted by W/T or by courier-borne microfilm continued. But as time went on, there was increasing British pressure for more active measures. In June 1941, the Danish section of SOE had begun training people for sabotage assignments ('Table'). At the same time, related organisations bearing such codenames as 'Chair', 'Dresser', 'Settee', 'Divan' and 'Chest' were set up to cope with other aspects of resistance from propaganda to covert funding. But Table got off to an unlucky start and its initial performance in the field was far from impressive, although the situation improved markedly after

Flemming Muus was parachuted in, in March 1943. The Princes, for their part, remained unreceptive to British suggestions about the direction resistance in the country should take. At a meeting with Turnbull in Stockholm in March 1942, Major Lunding had laid stress on the Danish Army's own capability to build up a secret force, ready to strike when the moment was ripe: in his view, there was no need for SOE to build up a duplicate organisation in the country. As for sabotage, its effect was deemed to be almost entirely counter-productive. These were views which would be reiterated at later Princes–SOE meetings in Stockholm. For a time, the British deferred to the judgement of the Princes. Certain projected sabotage schemes like the one to put out of action the Copenhagen–Malmö train ferry (Barholm) were dropped. But by the end of September, the tone changed and Turnbull was telling the Princes:

> London . . . insists . . . that Denmark must fall into line with their comrades in other countries, and contribute something real now to breaking down the German system of communication and transport.[83]

But were they likely to alter their policy? The SOE leadership remained sceptical of the motives of the Danish military leadership. As Gubbins was to confess:

> My reading of the position is that they [the Princes] wish to keep their country absolutely free of any sabotage or anti-German action until the Germans break up altogether and begin to leave the country and then in point of fact we shall not need them.[84]

A year later, the Danish picture had altered dramatically. The ground was collapsing under the feet of the proponents of the policy of negotiation. The more subtle conciliatory approach favoured by the German plenipotentiary, Dr Best, yielded to the hard line of General von Hanneken. Faced with a rapidly deteriorating internal situation in the summer of 1943 with its wave of strikes and sabotage, Berlin decided that the time had come to call a halt. On 28 August, the Danish government was asked to give its immediate assent to a battery of draconian emergency measures. When objections were raised to this, the occupiers took matters into their own hands. The next day, von Hanneken proclaimed a military state of emergency and baldly announced that it was he who now exercised power in the land. Round the country the Danish armed forces were disarmed, their officers temporarily interned and their weapons confiscated. In the wake of these developments, the Princes were thrown into disarray with Nordentoft and Gyth escaping to Sweden and Lunding falling into German hands. Provision had been made, however, for the continued supply of intelligence.

The polarisation of the situation in Denmark further broke down psychological opposition among the people at large to the pursuance of a vigorous policy of active measures by the various resistance groups and at the same time helped to cement the efforts of those groups. On 16 September 1943, the Freedom Council with representatives from the major resistance organisations, including the Communists, was set up as a central co-ordinating and directing organ for the Danish resistance as a whole. During 1944, acts of sabotage increased with railways a particular target. In the first half of that year, there were 56 attacks and in the second, 272. Vessels under construction in Danish shipyards and German ships moored in Danish harbours, were also priority targets.

The events of 29 August 1943 and their follow-up led in the ensuing period to a notable increase in the number of Danes seeking refuge in Sweden. Among those to flee over the Sound were some 7,000 members of Denmark's Jewish community threatened with deportation to concentration camps. In addition to the social and humanitarian issues which arose, the influx of people entailed practical problems for the Danish resistance organisations working in Sweden. Some of those who came, had been involved in underground work and wished to continue. Others who came, were suspected of working for the occupiers. The need arose for an organisation in Sweden which would look after the interests of the Freedom Council. In response to this need, the so-called Contact Committee was set up in Stockholm, holding its first meeting on 30 March 1944.[85] Among its members were included not only the representatives of the various active Danish resistance organisations, but also a representative of Danish Military Intelligence, Captain N. B. Schou. The day-to-day business of the Committee was dealt with by its executive secretariat, the Cuttings Office. This name arose from the fact that part of its duties was to supply resistance groups inside Denmark with books, photographs and cuttings of newspaper articles from the Swedish and Allied press. This outgoing flow of information was matched by an incoming flow of reports from Denmark.

A matter of some importance was the supervision of persons

travelling between Denmark and Sweden. After the events of 29 August, it had been necessary to arrange a number of 'illegal routes' between the two countries thus evading German control. One such route was that established in Malmö by the 'Danish–Swedish Refugee Service' on the initiative of the Jewish Community in Stockholm. Its purpose was to convey people whose life was in danger from Denmark to Sweden. A boat was acquired and the more tricky problem of fuel was solved.[86] In Malmö, Leif Hendil was placed in charge. Although the Danish resistance organisations had by now good relations with several members of Swedish Security serving in Hälsingborg and Malmö, it was necessary to obtain the approval of the Swedish government. On 15 October 1943, the go-ahead came through. The next day the Danish–Swedish Refugee Service had its own berth in Malmö harbour, conveniently screened from prying eyes. While Hendil had stressed the humanitarian aspect of the route in his appeal to the Swedish authorities, it soon took on another character as a communication channel between the Freedom Council in Denmark and Ebbe Munck which allowed the forwarding of post by special courier.

Hendil's route was one of several that came into existence and it was essential that their security was protected. This meant that people returning to Denmark via them had to be screened to ensure that they were reliable and that their journey was really motivated. But who was to have a say in this matter? Apart from the Contact Committee, the Danish Legation which saw itself as the legitimate representative of official Denmark, believed that it also had a right to be consulted. At a meeting in Stockholm on 28 June 1944, an attempt was made to try to iron out some of the differences which had arisen regarding this question and certain other administrative matters. It was agreed that the final decision about journeys home should rest with the Contact Committee. Procedural routines were clarified so that the Legation was responsible for looking after contacts with the Swedish police authorities. A decision was also taken to limit the number of journeys home as far as possible. Despite this agreement, however, disputes about route policy would continue to flare up until the end of the war.

Another function taken over by the Cuttings Office was anti-infiltration work. This was carried out in concert with Danish Military Intelligence whose representative Captain Schou, it will be recalled, was a member of the Contact Committee. The starting point of this work was a card index supplied by Military Intelligence of over 2,400 persons. Originally it was assumed that this side of things would involve close co-operation with the Legation's police section. However, the latter were not sympathetic to the idea of collaborating with – in their eyes – the amateurs in the Cuttings Office. Despite these elements of friction, Schou was able to establish a fruitful liaison at an informal level with the police officer Christian Andersen, who from July 1944, served on the Contact Committee. Schou's involvement in counter-espionage also led naturally to co-operation with both the Swedish Security Service and the British Special Services.

In the last months of the war, the Swedish government no longer sought to disguise its support for the Norwegian and Danish resistance.[87] During the summer of 1944, 3,000 submachine guns had been purchased by the Danes in Sweden for the equipping of groups in Denmark. From August 1944, these were wafted over the water by the special Danish maritime transport service which had been set up in Sweden with Commander Bangsbøll in charge. In Denmark, Captain Schjødt-Eriksen was responsible for their receipt and distribution.[88] Further consignments were to follow. In all it has been calculated that just over 100 tons of Swedish weapons and ammunition were infiltrated into Denmark via the maritime transport service between August 1944 and the beginning of May 1945, thus providing a complement to the weapons dropped by the Allies or brought in by Operation Moonshine.

While kinship of language and traditions and geographical proximity made Sweden a natural base for the operations of the underground groups of the Scandinavian countries, it was not only the Norwegian and Danish resistance movements (or for that matter the Finns) which found it convenient to establish support organisations in Sweden: the Poles and Czechs also had reason to make use of the Swedish corridor for contacts between their underground networks and their governments-in-exile in London, as the following illustrations show.

Poland

Less than a fortnight after the Russian attack on Finland on 30 November 1939, the British envoy in Riga, proposed that some 4,000 Polish regular troops, including frontier guards and an airforce regiment, who had escaped to Latvia and were interned there, should be sent to Finland. Although it was cold-shouldered by the Foreign

Office, the idea of deploying the Poles who were marooned in the Baltic countries, in Finland, lingered on a little longer in other quarters. General Sikorski dispatched a trusted representative, Lieutenant-Colonel Tadeusz Rudnicki, to undertake secret negotiations about the matter in Finland.[89] Like many other schemes mooted during the Phoney War, this one was to come to nothing. Rudnicki, however, stayed on in Scandinavia, attached to the Polish Legation in Stockholm. Placed in command of Station Anna as it would be called, his main task became one of establishing contact by courier with the Home Army detachments in Poland, more particularly those in the Wilno area.[90] This proved easier said than done and it was first in July 1940 that the link was made.

The Polish Legation in Stockholm had its own radio transmitter. But a courier service was important for a number of reasons. For a start it was more than simply a means of conveying information. Not everything (e.g. money, certain cipher materials, radio parts, etc.) could be sent by radio. Transmitters or skilled radio operators were not always available. Even when they were, there were constraints on the amount of information that could be sent in encrypted form over the air. Radio transmissions in an occupied area were kept short for fear of detection and longer and less urgent reports were therefore best sent by courier. At the beginning of December 1939, the Poles had begun to establish bases abroad – in Hungary (Nr. 1 Station), Rumania (Nr. 2) and Lithuania (Nr. 3) with the explicit intention of maintaining lines of communication between Poland and the Government in Exile. New stations were to be established as and when required. When Kaunas (Kowno) as the site for Nr. 3 fell out of the reckoning, Stockholm took its place. The importance of the Stockholm base in the Home Army's system of external communications increased relative to the others, with the progress of the war: the Government-in-exile pulled back from France to Britain; conditions in Hungary and Rumania became increasingly unfavourable and the main Continental routes more circuitous.

Rudnicki's own diplomatic standing, however, soon came under pressure. Before 1939, the Swedish authorities had learned that a Polish citizen named Tadeusz Rudnicki 'was associated with the Polish Intelligence Service'.[91] In the course of 1940, it was noted that the diplomat had travelled on at least two occasions with a visa made out in the name of Vinci. In November 1940, a certain Ignacy Arnold had been arrested by the police. Arnold was a Pole and had been the

Swedish representative of the Polish State Coal Mines. After the German occupation of his country, Arnold found himself without a job but was eventually installed in the Polish Legation in Stockholm, collecting and compiling items of interest which appeared in newspapers and other open sources. When he was arrested, however, a piece of paper was found which disclosed that Arnold had obtained from a visiting German businessman information relating to changes in the railway network around Berlin. The fact that the information had been acquired in this manner, was taken as proof that the Pole had engaged in espionage. Commenting on the case, the military security expert consulted by the court, observed that

> . . . the Defence Staff will merely add that the fact that the information can be obtained from accessible press sources, is irrelevant. Even in a carefully controlled press, items of military interest can creep in, in a variety of forms, and they are often of the very type to be found in the case of Arnold. Although such items may perhaps be quite valueless taken by themselves, they become significant when they are placed in their proper context and for that reason, military intelligence services methodically search them out either with the help of official representatives like military attachés or through agents who have been commissioned on a temporary basis.[92]

This view was accepted by the court and Arnold was sentenced to four months' hard labour for offences under Chapter 8, Sections 9, 11 and 14 of the Penal Code. It was known that Arnold had worked for Rudnicki at the Polish Legation and his arrest therefore compromised the diplomat in the eyes of the Security Service. In addition, further investigations into the activities of quite independent Polish clandestine organisations, where Rudnicki was perhaps only marginally involved, tended to increase the Security Service's suspicions against him.

At the end of May 1941, Boheman at the Ministry for Foreign Affairs informed the Polish Minister that a number of Poles, including Rudnicki, could no longer be considered as members of the Polish Legation and that 'while awaiting their departure for England, they would be considered as diplomats in transit, respectively Polish citizens expecting to travel on'.[93] Behind the scenes, the Germans were agitating strongly for the complete closure of the Polish Legation.

Steps, however, had been taken to ensure the continuation of Anna's courier activities after Rudnicki's departure. In May 1941, his successor Colonel Edmund Piotrowski arrived in Stockholm. Apart from initiating his own courier lines, Piotrowski co-operated with other Polish groups, already active in Sweden, among them that associated with the engineer Mieczyslaw Thugutt.

The Polish Minister of Home Affairs, Professor Stanislaw Kot had been keen to have his own civilian communications system for keeping in touch with developments at home. Kot therefore decided to set up a network of six bases, situated in neutral countries. In the spring of 1941, overtures were made to the Polish leader Stanislaw Thugutt, then in exile in Sweden, in the hope of getting him to accept responsibility for the Stockholm base. But Thugutt was too ill and it was left to his son Mieczyslaw to step in and fill the breach. Rudnicki and Thugutt found that they could co-operate well and when the former finally left Sweden, he passed on many of his contacts to Thugutt.

The principal problem was naturally the selection of reliable couriers. One idea had been to use Swedish seamen with the help of the ITF network (see pp. 119–25). Another was to make use of Swedish mercantile contacts with Poland. With the help of the Polish honorary consul, Stanislaw Kocan and the businessman Zygmunt Brodaty, Mieczyslaw Thugutt was put in touch with various Swedish businessmen who had permission to travel in Germany and the occupied regions.

The 1920s had witnessed a lively increase in Swedish–Polish trade. One consequence of the 1926 General Strike in Britain, was that the Poles were able to gain an important foothold in the export of coal to Sweden. At about the same time, a number of Swedish commercial and industrial concerns began to extend their activities to Poland. Best known – not to say notorious – were the manipulations of Ivar Kreuger, whose Swedish Match Company in 1925 was granted a state monopoly in the production of safety matches in Poland, in return for a loan of six million dollars. In order to cope with his complex financial transactions, Kreuger also founded a special bank – the Polish–American Bank – which was to survive the subsequent crash of the match king's empire.

In 1928, Carl Herslow was appointed managing director of Swedish Match in Poland. Herslow's background was not at all commercial but he had other merits. He was a talented linguist, he was used to command and he had a sound knowledge of Eastern Europe. Before this, his career had been in the army and he had served with distinction as military attaché in Moscow and Berlin. Although the Kreuger concern, because of its peculiar position in Poland, had many opponents, its managing director was well liked and respected. In due course, Herslow became the Swedish Consul-General.[94]

A second Swedish company which opened a sales office in Poland in 1925, was the electrical engineering firm ASEA, in which the Wallenbergs had a controlling interest. Placed in charge of the Polish operation was Sven Norrman. He was well suited to his new task. He had been ASEA's representative in Russia, before the Revolution. With a knack for Slavonic languages, he soon mastered Polish and made new friends and business contacts. In 1937, the company moved from sales into production in Poland by taking over the Polish Electric Corporation, PTE.

L. M. Ericsson, the well-known Swedish telephone company, was also established in Poland with two subsidiary enterprises in which a number of Swedes were employed.

After the invasion of Poland, the German authorities permitted the Swedes to resume their business activities. Appalled by the brutality of the new rulers, several businessmen undertook to assist their Polish friends in their hour of need, by acting as couriers. In the desperate circumstances which prevailed, they felt that it was the least that they could do. Among those volunteering their services were Carl Herslow, Tore Widén and Einar Gerge of the Match Monopoly, Sven Norrman and Carl Gösta Gustafsson of ASEA, Sigfrid Häggberg and Nils Berglind from Ericsson and Harald Axell from the Polish–American Bank.

The importance of the Swedish couriers can be glimpsed in surviving records of the Home Army.

Communications with Anna via Swedes especially valuable for us. Most Swedes well informed whom they are serving. Please order special protection for this route and isolation from all private consignments.[95]

The Swedes, although very irregular, provide a quick and reliable route: moreover they can be trusted with bulk mail. We cannot permit them to be exposed.[96]

In the main, their function was to carry money from Stockholm to

Warsaw and to carry microfilmed reports in the opposite direction. The actual amount of money carried to the underground in this way is unkown but Himmler's later estimate of 25,000 dollars corresponds only to a fraction of the amount sent. The reports, irrespective of any items valuable for military intelligence they contained, provided indispensable sources of information about life in the occupied areas, spelling out in great detail the martyrdom of the civil population and the terrible afflictions of the Jews. Films and photographs from the Ghetto were smuggled out, as well as information relating to the first mass executions.

The work of the Swedish businessmen couriers continued until the summer of 1942. Then the German security authorities pounced. They were already well aware of Sweden's potential as a northern corridor between the occupied territories of Central and Eastern Europe and the governments-in-exile in London from other cases.

The Swedish Crypto Department had first broken the Polish signal traffic between Stockholm and London in 1942.[97] But what the Swedes could do, might not the Germans do also? In the summer, Hellmuth Ternberg, Petersén's deputy, travelled to Warsaw in the guise of the businessman Robert Bross, in an attempt to warn his countrymen of the danger they were in.[98] By then, it was too late.

Nils Berglind of Ericsson, was arrested on 10 July after the plane he was on, was forced back to Tempelhof airport in Berlin. This was the first of several waves of arrests which led to the detention of seven of the 'Warsaw Swedes' and of a still greater number of Poles. On 1 August, the Head of *Abwehr* in Stockholm was told in confidence by the Head of the Counter-espionage Branch that recent messages from London and Stockholm had revealed that the courier route Warsaw–Stockholm was now at a standstill due to the arrest of the Swedes.[99] As will be seen, the imprisoned Swedes were to become important counters in German attempts to apply pressure upon Sweden.

The arrest of the Warsaw Swedes had consequences in Stockholm. On Monday 31 August 1942, eight Poles – including Thugutt, Kocan and the journalist Maurycy Karniol – were detained for questioning by the Swedish police. Karniol was later released conditionally while Thugutt was flown to Britain on 6 September. Also swept away by the crisis, was the Polish Minister himself. Monsieur Potworowski was reminded that at the time of the expulsion of Rudnicki and certain members of the Polish intelligence Service from Sweden in 1941, he had promised the Foreign Minister that the

Legation would only concern itself with ordinary diplomatic or humanitarian business. Because this promise had not been honoured, he could no longer be considered *persona grata*. The Swedish government, however, did not wish to break off diplomatic relations with Poland and would be ready to accept the present counsellor as *chargé d'affaires*. At the end of August, the Polish Minister was called to the Ministry for Foreign Affairs for a talk with Söderblom who wished to make the Swedish position clear. He was told that it was important for the continuance of diplomatic relations between their governments if his departure and that of other Poles who had been compromised, could be arranged as quickly as possible. The best solution would be to leave only a skeleton staff of perhaps three people to take care of ordinary business. There was no need for more. The sooner matters were settled, the easier it would be to ease the hard lot of Herslow and the other Warsaw Swedes. The interview ended with Söderblom assuring Potworowski that 'the Germans had in no way intervened but difficulties from that quarter could certainly expected on account of what had transpired'.[100]

As it happened, a change of view was to occur within the German security *apparat* about the best way of tackling the problems raised by the activities of the personnel of the Polish Legation in Stockholm. This was to be made clear in a Himmler memorandum at the end of 1942. In it, the *Reichsführer-SS* noted that there was nothing to be won by insisting on the total closure of the Polish Legation. It sufficed if known intelligence officers were removed from the country and that no newcomers took their place. In line with this policy, Potworowski's recall must have appeared something of a German triumph, for the Germans themselves (mistakenly as it happened) attributed to the Minister a leading role in the direction of Polish clandestine resistance activities in Stockholm. In some of their other demands, most notably for the deliverance into their hands of 'one of the most dangerous members of the Polish intelligence service' who was installed in the Japanese military attaché's office, they failed entirely. Indeed, all appearances to the contrary, a nucleus of Polish intelligence officers remained in place in Stockholm after the crisis of the summer of 1942.

There was no doubt, however, about the blow that had been delivered to Anna's courier service. In the spring of 1943, Jan Nowak who was active in Polish black propaganda activities against the Germans (Action N) conceived the idea of making direct contacts with his British opposite numbers.[101] He was then put in touch with

'Zaloga', a clandestine cell responsible for the maintenance of courier communications with the Polish military authorities in London. Nowak was informed of the current state of Home Army communications and of how the quick northern route over Sweden, previously traversed by Swedish businessmen, had been blocked. The alternative route through France was too slow. It was suggested that Novak should try to re-establish a route to Sweden in both directions via Gdynia or Gdansk and organise a regular courier service with Anna. On 20 April, buried beneath a cargo of coal on a Swedish ship, Nowak sailed off on his mission and eventually reached Stockholm around 5 May. With him he carried, apart from material illustrating the work of Action N, microfilmed intelligence reports artfully concealed. Once arrived in the Swedish capital, Nowak set about carrying out his prescribed tasks. With Colonel Piotrowski, he prepared a detailed route for a regular courier service between Warsaw and Stockholm. At the same time, contact was made with British black propaganda and desired material was microfilmed for the return journey back to Poland.

This was not to be Jan Nowak's last trip from Poland via the Swedish corridor. Although that summer in a series of arrests, the Gestapo managed to liquidate the entire organisation on the coast, he was back in Stockholm again in November 1943 and his memoir makes it clear that it was planned for other couriers to traverse the same route after him. The Gestapo nevertheless continued to be highly active. A severe blow was struck in March 1944 when Zaloga was betrayed and 22 members and their families were arrested. As a result the northern corridor was put out of commission for a long time to come. When at the end of 1944, plans were made for Nowak to undertake a third trip from Poland to England, two possible routes were discussed: one via Denmark and Sweden and another via Switzerland to liberated France, but the former turned out to be impossible.

Czechoslovakia

Unlike the Poles, the supporters of President Benes' Czech government in exile in London, had after the events of 1938, no legation to call their own in Stockholm. Deprived of diplomatic representation, it was inevitable that former members of the Czech Legation who opposed German rule, would sooner or later run foul of the Swedish espionage laws in their efforts to maintain contact with their homeland and London. In 1942, Dr Vladimir Vanek, a former Counsellor at the Czech Legation was sentenced to three and a half years' hard labour under Chapter 8 of the Penal Code. The Vanek case provides an insight into the use of the Swedish corridor by the Czech Resistance.

The Czech Intelligence Service had established a number of strategically placed branch offices, initially in Paris, Warsaw, Stockholm, Belgrade, Zurich and the Hague.[102] In Stockholm various convenience addresses for the forwarding of agents' reports were acquired and just before the outbreak of the war, Vanek acquired a radio transmitter. With it, he was expected to listen at certain scheduled times to Czech transmissions from Warsaw which he would then transmit to London. All this came very soon to the attention of the Swedish counter-espionage services. The transmitter was confiscated but no other action was taken. Perhaps as a consequence of the transmitter affair, an arrangement was eventually made whereby Vanek was allowed to send his reports via the British Legation, making use of the British diplomatic bag. He also obtained assistance in sending coded telegrams to a telegraphic address, MINIMISE, in London, making use, however, of the Czech intelligence service's own cipher.

Like the Poles, the Czechs had need for a courier service. Here again commercial ties were the key. Businessmen in Czechoslovakia who obtained German permission to visit Sweden, were recruited. So too Swedes visiting the Protectorate. In September 1941, a friend of Amelie Posse, Anna Sjöholm, obtained a visa to allow her to attend the Leipzig Fair and she had also been permitted to pay a visit to Prague at the same time. Announcing her impending arrival in Prague, Vanek sent a signal to London: 'The stones have been sent, packed as samples.'[103]

Whatever it was that Miss Sjöholm was delivering – possibly quartz crystals for a radio transmitter – they remained undetected and the trip passed off smoothly. On 22 September, Vanek reported to London:

> Sjöholm searched only by the Swedes . . . The Germans did not search the trunks. There was no special control-procedure at the Czech border.[104]

In December, Major Miloslaw Dolezel, one of Vanek's close collaborators, contacted another friend of Countess Posse about performing a similar service. Before this journey, Maria Kockum received an innocent-looking belt which she was asked to pass over to a contact in Prague. Its probable contents was made clear in the signal to London which Vanek despatched on 7 January 1942: 'Courier M. K. carried out all assignments in Prague. She handed over photo copies and orders.'[105] This time, however, the visit was to lead to the intervention of the Swedish police. Dolezel was detained in Stockholm after arrival from Malmö where he had met his returning courier and although he was released, it was a warning shot across the bows of the Czechs. Vanek destroyed the cipher materials in his house. On 8 January, he informed London: 'They released D. They got to know nothing. He said nothing.'[106] Dolezel attributed his detention to co-operation between the Swedish police and the Gestapo. In fact the Swedes already had exact knowledge about Vanek and his associates from a very different source. The Czech telegram traffic with London had been broken in October 1941. The purpose of Maria Kockum's visit had been known in advance and telephone control had provided other bits of the puzzle. This was why Dolezel had been detained. When Vanek was finally arrested on 27 March 1942, he was confronted with the Minimise telegram traffic.

Germany

German opposition to Hitler was heterogeneous rather than simple; the political views and motives which inspired it, the methods it employed and the experiences which shaped it, varied widely. Those belonging to its ranks, who dreamed of removing the tyrant from office by an internal *coup d'état*, were to be disappointed in their aim. In the end it was external military power and that alone which swept away the Führer.

Before the outbreak of war, there had been contacts between German circles opposed to Hitler and the Foreign Office in London. Efforts were made to resume them in the course of the conflict, in several cases through Stockholm. One Swedish channel of communication ran through the Wallenberg family, with whom Carl Goerdeler, a former mayor of Leipzig and a prominent figure in the civilian, conservative wing of resistance, had been in touch since 1934.[107] Through their banking interests, the Wallenbergs had an unrivalled position in Swedish economic life. During the war, the two brothers served their country as top-level negotiators; while Jakob took care of the German side of the equation, Marcus applied himself to the Anglo-American side. In 1940, Goerdeler had discussed the possibility of a *coup d'état* in Germany with Jakob Wallenberg, but had admitted that Hitler's military successes made the military support necessary for such a coup unlikely. By 1942, however, the situation had altered. Resentment among certain senior officers had increased and Goerdeler was more optimistic about the possibilities of a coup. On a visit to Stockholm in April 1942, he asked the Wallenbergs to get in touch with Churchill with a view to obtaining in advance an assurance of peace from the Allies in the event that the conspirators succeeded in deposing Hitler. A year later he was back in the Swedish capital and once again asking the Wallenbergs to contact the British Prime Minister. A memorandum in which Goerdeler outlined the positions to be adopted on various issues by the post-Hitler government, was drawn up at Jacob Wallenberg's request and according to the latter the information in it along with Goerdeler's plea for the Allies to discontinue bombing German cities as soon as the coup occurred, was passed on to the British via Marcus.

A somewhat different German resistance group (the Kreisau Circle) made up largely by much younger people than those belonging to the Goerdeler–Beck circle, was that which gathered round Helmuth von Moltke. The latter, a lawyer by profession, was the scion of the distinguished Prussian military family. His mother was the daughter of a South African judge and he had strong ties with England. His opposition to Hitlerism was the product of religious and moral convictions. Upon the outbreak of war, he joined the *Abwehr* which brought him into contact with anti-Nazi officers like Colonel Oster. His aim became that of knitting together the various disparate strands of resistance in military, foreign service and political circles in the country. His position as an intelligence officer allowed Moltke a useful freedom of movement and in March 1943, he visited Scandinavia. During his visit to Sweden, he made use of the opportunity to forward a report on the internal German situation to his friend Lionel Curtis in Oxford. After setting forth his view of the facts, Moltke made a plea

for a stable connection between the German opposition and Great Britain and a connection not based on secret service relations, not used mainly to extract information but a political connection.[108]

The object of this connection, Moltke wrote, was not to discuss peace terms or the post-war world. It was rather to assist in the internal war against Hitler, whereby a common strategy of how best to exploit various events that had occurred, could be discussed. In order to do this, it was desirable

> to have a man in Stockholm who knows Central Europe and who, working under the general guidance of the ambassador would have special functions to keep in touch with the various underground movements in Europe, especially in Germany and would have to deal with them on a basis of political discussion and cooperation.[109]

In the interest of security, such a man should

> be free from all entanglements of secret service work. As far as I can make out the channels of all secret services of the various nations are the same, and most agents will work for at least two parties. Therefore whatever you put into the secret service of one country will in due course be known to the secret services of all other countries. As a result the secret services of all countries are secret to everybody but its opponent.[110]

Moltke's plea for a political connection, however, fell on deaf ears in London.

Links between Moltke's circle and the British were maintained by other channels as well. A German transport officer in Norway, Major Theodor Steltzer, who belonged to the circle, maintained close contacts with the Norwegian Resistance and proved his good faith by providing them with useful inside information and timely warnings.[111] On 15 July 1944, he notified his friends of the impending coup and the names of those designated for office in the post-Hitler government. The leader of Milorg, Jens Chr. Hauge, then on the point of flying to England, planned to take a letter addressed to Curtis at Oxford dealing with these matters, but due to the prevailing flight schedule from Stockholm, he did not reach London until after the attempt on Hitler's life had taken place.

Another important intermediary in contact with Moltke's group was Adam von Trott, who in the war years was attached to the German Foreign Ministry. Trott had been a Rhodes Scholar at Oxford and had a number of close friends in England. Between 1942 and July 1944, he was to undertake some 16 journeys abroad – to Switzerland, Sweden, the Low Countries and Turkey – acting as a secret courier and spokesman for the 'other Germany'. When he heard that from his friends in Switzerland that George Bell, the Bishop of Chichester, would be going to Sweden in May 1942 for discussions with Swedish churchmen, he arranged for a German pastor, Hans Schoenfeld, Director of the Research Department of the World Council of Churches, to go there to speak to him. Later Schoenfeld was joined by another German pastor, Dieter Bonhoeffer, an old friend of Bell. The Germans assured the Englishmen that there existed a strong opposition in Germany, apparently drawing its support from present and former members of the administration, trades unionists, high Army officers, members of the police and church leaders and this message was duly passed on by Bell first to the British Minister in Stockholm and later directly to the Foreign Office itself. The Foreign Office, however, was not impressed and thought it all rather exaggerated:

> What would be interesting would be to see what any group of this kind can *do*. We are not going to negotiate with any Government in Germany that has not thoroughly purged its soul and we must have some convincing of that and we have got to be convinced first. Total defeat and disarmament is probably the only possible answer.[112]

In the meantime, a crucial phrase had crept into the formulation of Allied Policy towards Germany at the meeting between Roosevelt and Churchill at Casablanca where they declared

> the firm intention of the United States and the British Empire to continue the war relentlessly until they have brought about the unconditional surrender of Germany and Japan.

In the eyes of the German Opposition, the notion of unconditional surrender merely eroded their own position by placing an excellent instrument of propaganda in the hands of Dr Goebbels and by strengthening, rather than weakening support for Hitler's leadership.

Despite a lack of encouragement from the Foreign Office, Trott continued in his peripatetic efforts to establish contacts with the British, visiting Sweden personally in September 1942 and again in October 1943 when with the help of a Swedish intermediary, Fru Inga Almström, he was able covertly to meet with Roger Hinks and James Knapp-Fisher of the British Legation, confiding in them the secret of the proposed Operation Valkyrie designed to remove Hitler from the scene. At the same time, Trott was keen to learn how far the British were committed to the policy of unconditional surrender and how far they would be prepared to modify their bombing offensive in the event that a revolt took place. In a view that would be repeated elsewhere and at other times, the German emissary suggested that the emphasis of British–American policy on air raids and unconditional surrender, simply strengthened the Communist and thereby Soviet hand.

In March 1944, Trott was once more back in Stockholm, apparently instructed by his friends not to press the subject of unconditional surrender. In conversation with Ivar Anderson, a respected Swedish newspaper editor, Trott brought up once more the effect of the air raids on national morale, arguing that it had led to a removal of differences between party and people. More and more people (he maintained) considered that the only solution open to Germany was a separate peace with Russia and both men concluded that despite everything, it might not be surprising if Stalin and Hitler were to end up once more in fond embrace.

Trott's last visit to Sweden took place in the second half of June 1944, when he was asked to come to Stockholm for further conversations with a British representative. Hinks and his partner were this time replaced, at Trott's own request, by David MacEwen, a member of SIS, who had served in Germany. The meeting took place in the flat of another Swedish lady, Fru Kempe. According to her, MacEwen began by saying that the Allies had intended to launch an intensive bombing campaign against the great industrial centres in Western Germany. Before they began with this, they wished to know the strength of the German resistance. If it were sufficently strong to help the Allies swiftly end the war, the bombing raids could be avoided. Trott then answered that he was prepared to give the required information only on condition that the Allies were prepared to give up their policy of unconditional surrender. Since MacEwen was in no position to give such an assurance, the meeting ended with Trott supplying a memorandum setting out his views.

Steltzer's warning of 15 July 1944 about the impending coup in Germany has already been noted. It was not to be the only one from a reliable source indicating that some decisive action was afoot which reached Stockholm. Colonel Juhlin-Dannfelt, the Swedish military attaché in Berlin, met Admiral Canaris several times during March and April 1944 at the home of their mutual friend Vladimir, Baron

Kaulbars. Canaris, who had been discharged from his position as the Head of the *Abwehr*, now spoke quite openly to the Swede of the criminality of Hitler and the leading Nazis. Some time after this, Canaris forwarded a message through Kaulbars asking

> if the Swedish Legation would be prepared to relay a message from the new government to a West Allied Legation in Stockholm, were a fundamental political change to occur in Germany.[113]

The Swedish Ministry for Foreign Affairs answered to the effect that *if* such a fundamental change were to take place, then it would be prepared to do this. It is not known whether this hint – or still less if a more concrete message – from Canaris that something was in progress, was passed on to the British Legation.

With the benefit of hindsight, British coldness to overtures from the German opposition has seemed unnecessarily harsh and inflexible. Yet at the time, the issue facing the Foreign Office was not an easy one.[114] Confronted with these signals, there were four basic questions to be answered. First, were they given in good faith? Second, supposing them to be given in good faith, could it be assumed that those putting them forward were in a position to implement their aims in reality? Third, how far should Britain be prepared to enter into any commitment to such an opposition prior to the actual removal of the dictator? Lastly, what political consequences would follow the implementation of their aims? Each of these questions raised legitimate doubts, not insuperable in themselves but which taken collectively urged caution.

THE LISTENING POST: THE QUEST FOR INFORMATION

High level official sources and co-operation

In his memoir, *På Vakt*, the former Under-Secretary of State at the Swedish Ministry for Foreign Affairs, described a meeting with Mallet where the indiscretions of the British Assistant Military Attaché (Munthe) were taken up:

> I said to him [Mallet] that if one wanted to find out more about what we were doing as regards Germany, it was much better if he confined himself to asking me. I had no intention of hiding

99

anything and he received much more reliable intelligence. If the British wished to find out what the Germans were doing, it was perhaps natural and in any case difficult or impossible to prevent. But could one not then employ somewhat more competent agents, so that a string of Swedes, most of whom were inspired by commendable motives, did not end up being arrested?[115]

The belligerents were of course well aware of the advantages of the front door over the back door. That option, however, was not always available.[116] Nor could the pronouncements of Swedish official representatives – no matter how charming and confiding – be accepted without some independent checking.[117] None the less it remained broadly true that information obtainable in this way often had a high carat value. For the time being, three examples of the potential importance of high-level official sources and covert (official) co-operation will be given; further examples relevant to this theme follow in the ensuing subsections. Appropriately, the first example involves Boheman himself as a high-level source.

(1) In the middle of June 1941, Sir Stafford Cripps, the British ambassador in Moscow, passed through Stockholm *en route* for London. In the Swedish capital, he met Boheman at a dinner party.[118] Cripps put forward the view (a) that a German attack on Russia would *not* take place (b) that the threatening German posture was intended to extract Russian concessions and (c) that Stalin was prepared to make whatever concessions were necessary to avoid attack. By this time, on the basis of the intelligence they had received (particularly intercepted signal traffic to German forces in Norway and Finland and elsewhere) the Swedes had reached the conclusion that a German attack on Russia was imminent. Boheman therefore informed the British visitor (without revealing his sources) that he for his part was quite convinced that Cripps' assumption (a) was mistaken and that the date for the attack lay somewhere between 10 and 25 June.

(2) The second example deals with high-level covert co-operation in the exchange of military intelligence. On 4 November 1944, the British military attaché in Stockholm, Sutton-Pratt, sent a telegram to London in which he referred to a conversation with Colonel Curt Kempff, the then head of the Foreign Section of the Defence Staff and a key figure in the Swedish intelligence Community:

Personality No. 39 [Kempff] asked me to call upon him today.

Cooperation from Swedish General Staff in past has been perhaps 25% but he admits that he had now been given signal for full cooperation by Personality 34 [Major General Ehrenswärd, Head of the Defence Staff] and evidently intended trying to satisfy us. I spent an hour firing questions at him and he flung open his files for me and gave me what they contained.[119]

An interesting initial estimate of the value of this intelligence was given in a submission, of 9 November 1944, of the Joint Intelligence Committee to the Strategic Planning Section, where it is noted that:

The Swedish General Staff have recently been passing intelligence to us, but it is not always accurate. The Swedish Foreign Ministry have occasionally given us some useful intelligence.[120]

This somewhat critical standpoint, however, would be subsequently revised and on 6 March 1945 the Swedish military attaché in London was able to report that

In a conversation recently with the chief of the British intelligence department [Major-General Sinclair] he said that they now were receiving very reliable and regular intelligence from Stockholm for which they were very grateful.[121]

(3) The third example deals with co-operation in the field of counter-espionage. In the summer of 1943, Martin Lundqvist of the civilian Security Service contacted a representative of the British Secret Service who proposed the exchange of information on German activities.[122] This proposal was then submitted on the recommendation of the Security Chief to the Minister of Justice who gave the go-ahead for the exchange subject to certain conditions. Information about German citizens suspected of subversive activity could be handed over without restriction. Information about Swedish nationals could be supplied only if they had been found guilty of espionage or there were substantial grounds for suspecting them to be guilty of subversive activity.

Open sources: the Press Reading Bureau

It is often objected that the German and occupied press contains nothing of interest, as it is subjected to the strictest possible censorship and would not be exported if it contained anything of

101

any use to the enemy. Experience has proved the opposite. While revelations of great significance are seldom to be found, the sum total of material available provides a remarkably revealing and coherent picture of conditions in the occupied territories. Moreover the press of the few surviving neutral states, especially those whose frontiers are contiguous with Germany, often contains most useful indications of the trend of opinion in Germany itself.

But this picture can only be complete and undistorted if the papers are scientifically read on an adequate scale. It presupposes some kind of coordinated form of press reading whereby everything of political, social, economic and military interest is extracted and distributed to the Government departments involved. In particular, it demands a far reaching and exhaustive study of the local press, which offers a far more productive field than the normal press of the capitals and large towns.[123]

During the Second World War, there were special British facilities for the detailed study of the enemy and occupied press at Berne, Istanbul, Lisbon and Madrid. The largest unit was, however, the Press Reading Bureau in Stockholm. Founded on 24 September 1940 and placed under the direction of Cecil (later Sir Cecil) Parrot, the Bureau or 'Parrot House' as it became known, was set up partly as a contingency measure to guarantee at short notice the continued reading of the German press in the event that Switzerland were invaded and partly as a centre in its own right for the reading of Norwegian, Danish, Swedish, Czech (Protectorate), Polish, Soviet, Dutch and Belgian newspapers.[124] The information thus collected was used for general intelligence and propaganda purposes. The duties of the Stockholm Bureau were to be successively widened, both geographically and in kind.

On 6 November, it was instructed by the Foreign Office to take over two tasks, previously entrusted to Berne. These were the reading of well-known German medical and chemical periodicals for information regarding health and of the leading and minor provincial German press from Emden to Danzig, but not including the Berlin, Hanover and Frankfurt papers. Later the Finnish press and more surprisingly that of the Balkan countries became part of Stockholm's sweep. On 8 November Parrot was instructed to undertake the drafting of telegrams and memoranda based on information regarding political events in Germany and the occupied countries from private sources in Stockholm. Simultaneously he was asked by the commercial and service attachés to look out for economic and military information of interest. This latter aspect of the work of the Press Reading Bureau was subsequently (21 February 1941) to be the subject of a telegram from the Ministry of Information, approving the proper establishment of sections of the Bureau specifically concerned with economic and service matters.

By the middle of October 1941, the staff of the Bureau consisted of 31 whole or part-time employees including editors, readers, archivists, typists and messengers. After the newspapers had arrived at the Bureau, they were distributed to the various readers according to the country or countries they dealt with. The readers then extracted and typed out all items likely to interest London from the viewpoint of propaganda or as an indication of political or economic conditions in the country concerned. Their typed sheets were then passed to an editor (British, for language reasons) who chose what to transmit and put it into telegraphese. Doubtful points were referred to Parrot or his deputy but in time the readers became so expert in their selection of worthwhile material that little was omitted from their output. The edited versions were then typed on telegram forms and sent off to London the same evening.[125]

Collection of information is one thing, its efficient circulation and effective use quite another. This old truth was to become clear, when Parrot visited London in August 1941 to do a tour of the consumers of information, of whom the two principal ones were the Political Intelligence Department (PID) of the Foreign Office which used it for their general political summary and PID (Electra House) which was responsible for Black Propaganda. The response from these to the material received from Stockholm was in general positive, and indeed in some cases enthusiastic: Bruce Lockhart found the material on Czechoslovakia invaluable; the best material on the Balkans came from Stockholm, not Istanbul. Parrot was to report with evident pride: 'In almost all cases, the regional specialists concerned seemed to depend very largely for their information on our work.'[126]

The reception at the War Office was similarly laudatory where Major Hirsch spoke 'very warmly' of the work of the Stockholm Bureau's Polish reader (Mr Waskiewicz) and said that the intelligence material which he had provided regarding the eastern area of

Germany had been invaluable. In the view of another officer, the War Office would have been much worse off, had it not received the Stockholm information.

At the Admiralty and the Air Ministry, it was a very different story. The Deputy Director of Naval Intelligence had not seen any of the material and the same was true of Squadron Leader Dennys at the Air Ministry.

On his return to Stockholm, Parrot reported his findings to the Minister who sent a detailed critique to the Foreign Office. In the autumn of 1940, said Mallet, when the PRB was founded, the Legation had been assured that the Political Intelligence Department had been reorganised and that one of its functions was to co-ordinate and distribute incoming information. Parrot had therefore avoided passing his material directly to other departments. Thus information of some urgency for the three service departments had been forwarded to the PID. However, it became clear during Parrot's visit to London that the PID had in fact failed to copy any of the information and took no responsibility for distributing it to other departments. After receiving instructions in November 1940 on the importance of reading and reporting on German medical/chemical periodicals, highly qualified readers had been engaged. None the less their reports had lain idle at PID for eight months. In the Minister's view, the root cause of this inadequate state of affairs was the lack of a department whose primary duty was to ascertain what type of information was required by the different government departments: the Bureau for the Coordination of Military Intelligence, then in existence, was concerned solely with technical questions. Mallet ended by stressing the wider importance of the listening post under his command:

> But the fact remains that Stockholm is a centre at which a great many reports and rumours of varying importance and accuracy can be picked up, and, rather than transmit these in the form of official despatches, I have been in the habit of arranging for the Press Reading Bureau to turn the reports into Political Intelligence Department Memoranda, as the staff are naturally well informed about developments in Germany and occupied countries . . .[127]

There was little doubt that the PRB would employ some unusually well-informed people among its readers, such as Willi

Böhm, a former Minister of War in the Hungarian Bolshevik government under Bela Kun. Of Böhm, it would be later said that he had rendered the Foreign Office

> invaluable service both in his reading and interpretation of the Hungarian press and in supplying us with political intelligence from Hungary itself.[128]

Despite the initial co-ordination troubles, the PRB continued to grow. By 4 August 1943, the staff had risen to 59 and numbered some 15 nationalities or so. Indeed doubts had been raised about Parrot's little empire. When he applied for two extra German readers in February 1942, a sceptical voice had wondered

> if Parrot is trying a little too hard to build up a bloated organization. If ever the M of I or the Treasury get that suspicion, I hope PWE will not be accused of having encouraged him.[129]

The PRB and its activities raised doubts in other quarters as well. For a time (according to Parrot) the Swedish authorities appeared to have entertained suspicions that the Bureau had other less-advertised concerns than the mere reading of newspapers, but after the appointment of a Swedish reader, it was noted that surveillance was relaxed appreciably. By the end of 1943, a more dynamic approach to the collection of 'hot news' in Stockholm was being advocated by PWE. What was needed, was

> a man who would wander round the streets and buttonhole people as they got off the boat or train – the equivalent of a Daily Express Special Correspondent. Whereas a year ago, the Swedes might well have objected to such a person, I should expect the situation to have changed by now.[130]

At the same time, the PRB continued to cater to the assorted needs of the Political Intelligence Department. A shopping list of press cuttings required by its German and Austrian section, included any articles on the history of a whole province or parts of it, or on party organisation, any articles of topographical features and climate, articles on local customs, traditions, statistics. There was a standing need for the addresses of all government and municipal offices, fire stations, police stations, power stations, banks, big garages and radio dealers. Information was required about town councils, law courts of all descriptions, police activities, civil defence, etc.

Before the United States of America had entered the war, the State Department had occasionally been supplied with PRB material. In February 1942, Parrot reported to the Ministry of Information that the Americans had set up their own PRB – despite British suggestions about making common cause – with a staff of 15, concentrating on the press of Denmark, Norway, Sweden, the Baltic States and occupied Russia. The Soviet Legation also had its PRB with a staff of 25, but it was not known how many countries it covered.

Military Intelligence: the British Naval Attaché

When in the summer of 1940 Captain Henry Denham reached Stockholm, where he was to serve as British naval attaché, he could not have arrived at a less propitious time. The apparently unstoppable German military machine had made a deep impression in Sweden, not least among the officer classes; the publicity surrounding the Rickman affair served in a localised way to draw attention to British ineptitude and to increase suspicions about British intentions towards Sweden; and more importantly not long after Denham's arrival, the British seizure at Churchill's behest of four Swedish destroyers *en route* from Italy, only helped to fan the flames of anti-British sentiment within the Swedish Navy. Despite this unfavourable atmosphere, Denham, his second-in-command Dan Gibson Harris and their staff, were in time able to provide the Admiralty in London with a stream of valuable intelligence.[131]

Apart from his official contact (Admiral Giron) with the Swedish Defence Ministry, which gave virtually nothing in the way of intelligence, Denham was soon in touch with well-disposed legation and consular sources which promised to be more fruitful. Important links were established with the Dutch (Rijckevorsel and De Jong), the Poles (Morgenstern) and the Danes (Ebbe Munck). In the latter part of 1940, the first detailed reports about German coastal defences in Norway and Denmark were obtained. Perhaps Denham's most crucial initial contact, however, was with Alfred Roscher Lund, an officer who, Churchill himself would note,

> has been of great service to the British Intelligence organization in Sweden, and his presence there is of special value to His Majesty's Government, and to the Allied cause as a whole.[132]

In the mid 1930s, Roscher Lund had been one of the younger driving forces behind the creation of a Norwegian codes and cipher

106

bureau.[133] Such a bureau, with Roscher Lund as head, came into existence first in the autumn of 1939, its tasks including cryptanalysis, cryptosecurity and radio monitoring. On 17 May 1940, Roscher Lund received instructions to go to Stockholm, where he was to be responsible for organising Norwegian cipher communications from the Swedish capital. Once there, his work rapidly expanded and he was involved in developing contacts both with various resistance groups in Norway and with British and other intelligence representatives. Thoroughly familiar with the 'Who's Who' of the Swedish intelligence establishment, Roscher Lund was in a position both to supply Denham with high-grade information and to introduce him in due course to important Swedish intelligence officers.

Among Roscher Lund's Swedish contacts was Major Petersén of C Bureau. Whatever the exact conditions regulating their association, Roscher Lund was thereby enabled in effect to operate as a high-level cut out between a branch of Swedish intelligence and the British. Documents were brought to Denham from Petersén's office on a fortnightly basis and appropriate abstractions made.

One of the 'scoops' arising from this connection occurred on 20 May 1941 when Denham was able to alert London that the German warships *Bismarck* and *Prinz Eugen* had passed northward into the Kattegat, escorted by a number of destroyers and aircraft.[134] The Germans, however, were almost immediately aware of Denham's provision of this vital piece of intelligence.[135] As a result, they quickly brought pressure to bear on the Swedes to intensify their surveillance of the British naval attaché. The Swedish naval attaché in Berlin, in a most secret despatch to Adlercreutz, underlined German suspicions about the occurrence of British espionage in Sweden. This resulted in a circular from the Chief of the Civilian Security Service to his regional deputies on 16 June 1941, setting forth the German viewpoint.[136] According to this, a careful analysis of the possible ways in which the British had acquired knowledge of the movements of *Bismarck* and *Prinz Eugen* had shown that the warning must have come from Sweden. All British talk to the effect that they had found out via aerial reconnaissance off Bergen was false and was spread merely to conceal the real channel of communication. In German circles, it was known that the British naval attaché in Stockholm had at his disposal a highly effective agent network composed of skilled observers, forever on the move and consequently hard to detect. Indeed Sweden had become a veritable playground for spies. Behind these observations from Berlin lurked an imprecise threat of counter-measures if Sweden failed to put its own house in order. Security Chief Hallgren concluded by urging his men to spare no effort in seeing that those involved in such espionage were brought to book. Ironically, however, on this particular occasion, Denham's information – as we have seen – came not from the ship-watching service described by the Germans but from a member of Sweden's own intelligence service.

In late March 1941, at a meeting between Roscher Lund, Dahl, Denham and Gibson Harris, a shopping list of intelligence requirements respecting German naval and shipping activities had been drawn up for submission to Petersén and his associates. At the same time, the latter were encouraged to adopt the British system of grading.

C Bureau shared the result of their systematic interviews with returning Swedish ship captains about matters of interest (warship movements, U-boat and ship construction, concentrations of shipping for troop movements etc) in return for selected information extracted from the daily or weekly naval telegrams (NATELs) and the results of aerial photo-reconnaissance units (PRUs) over the principal German cities. In this way the British were furnished with material dealing with German preparations for the attack on Russia which was used in briefing Sir Stafford Cripps on likely naval and military scenarios on his visit to Stockholm in the early summer of 1941.

While Roscher Lund's contacts with C Bureau proved an invaluable source of naval information, other kinds of contacts also bore fruit. Up to the spring of 1944, Dutch merchant skippers and escapees were regularly interviewed at the Dutch Consul-General's office and provided information about shipping movements, German routes and minesweeping. Certain other individual informants in touch with the British naval attaché's office returned consistently high-grade information, among them a Swedish merchant captain (graded A) and a Dane (graded B).

Reports about U-boat construction – the number of hulls on the stocks and the number fitting out at yards in Hamburg, Bremen, Emden, Stettin and Danzig – could be cross-checked in London with the results from aerial reconnaissance and the ground reports were found to be generally accurate. Early in 1944, the Germans erected screens around the seaward side of their yards to make observation more difficult. Information relating to the movement of capital ships from ground sources, although often three to four days old, was none the less useful in helping to form a pattern of German intentions.

For some time, contacts between Denham's office and C Bureau went entirely through Roscher Lund who remained in Sweden until the autumn of 1941 when he was transferred to London at the insistence of the Norwegian Prime Minister and despite a last-minute plea by Churchill.[137] Eventually more direct exchanges were able to take place. Yet the connection remained throughout a limited and deniable one. Indeed to the British, it remained unclear how far Petersén was acting on his own initiative and how far he was carefully following instructions. When in April 1941, Denham had tried to couple a British export credit relating to petroleum to Sweden with a secret *quid pro quo* whereby the Swedish Defence Staff handed over all information about Germany and German activities, this proposal was turned down.

Useful as the Petersén contact was, C Bureau was not in a position to deliver information coming in from Swedish cryptanalysis. This lacuna was filled after the spring of 1942 when delicate contacts were spun between Denham and the Chief of the Foreign Section of Swedish military intelligence, Count Björnstjerna. By this means, the British authorities were able to obtain information of the highest grade (such as intercepted signals between the German Naval High Command and their Admiral in Norway) and of great value concerning German intentions and movements in Norway, especially regarding prospective actions against the northern convoys to Russia.[138] In return, the Swede was provided with situation reports compiled by Denham.

It did not take long for the link between Björnstjerna and Denham to be brought to the attention of the Supreme Commander of the Armed Forces who took a very different view of his subordinate's co-operation with the British.[139] The matter, however, was evidently played down and Björnstjerna was allowed to resign discreetly in the autumn of 1942. Round about the same time, Colonel Carlos Adlercreutz left his position as overall chief of Intelligence to become military attaché in Helsinki. Suddenly it was all change among the intelligencers at the Swedish Defence Staff.

Although Björnstjerna's removal from the scene presumably interrupted the flow of high-grade information reaching the British, Denham was able in due course to establish cordial and fruitful relations with Commander Daniel Landquist, the new Swedish Intelligence Chief.[140] Within six months of his appointment as successor to Adlercreutz (albeit with reorganised responsibilities), Landquist was invited to London for conversations with Commodore Rushbrooke, the DNI. These took up *inter alia* the all-important question of the exchange of information. In his agreement with his British counterpart, Landquist, however, went beyond what could be accepted and acknowledged in Stockholm as consistent with Swedish neutrality and a code provided by the British for the proposed exchange of information was later pointedly returned – an about-turn hardly likely to endear the Swedes to an already critical Admiralty. Behind the scenes, however, it may be surmised that the amicable relations between Landquist and Denham continued.

Ever since Denham's arrival in Stockholm had been notified to the Swedish authorities on 14 June 1940, his activities had been been an object of evidently intensifying interest for the Security Services and by January 1943, he had earned a number of black marks in their books. His association with Threlfall had led (wrongly) to suspicions that he was actively involved in sabotage work. In another case, a Swedish skipper, who was to be sentenced under Chapter 8 Sections 14, 29a of the Penal Code, to ten months' hard labour for unlawful intelligence activity, had admitted that he had provided Denham with miscellaneous information on a number of occasions: about safeways through German minefields in the Baltic, bomb damage at Rostock, the conveyance of Swedish iron ore to Germany, units of the German fleet spotted in German ports, etc. There was also the businessman Walter (arrested by the police on 30 November 1942), whose wallet had disclosed a list of probing questions from the British naval attaché, about the Italian Navy.[141]

The Admiralty view of the matter was very different. It saw behind the anti-Denham campaign inspired by Major Lindquist and certain of his assistants in Military Security, which it took to be the devil of the piece, certain German intrigues and it would not rest until it had the Major removed. While the Security Chief was complaining to the Ministry for Foreign Affairs in January 1943 'that Denham had been involved in espionage which has led and can in the future lead to imprisonment for Swedish citizens'[142] the British naval attaché had somewhat earlier routinely reported another matter which would soon succeed in ruffling still more Swedish feathers. The DNI had been informed by his man in Stockholm that there were grounds for believing that certain ships being built in Sweden for the Germans, ostensibly as fishing vessels, were in fact intended to be used as

110

minesweepers. The matter was passed on to the Foreign Office who quoted the requisite scripture of international law and its own analysis of the rights and wrongs of the case:

> The relevant provisions of international law are the following:
> *Hague Convention XIII, Article 6*
> The supply, in any manner, directly or indirectly, by a neutral Power to a belligerent Power, of war-ships, ammunition, or war material of any kind whatever, is forbidden.
> *Article 7*
> A neutral Power is not bound to prevent the export or transit, on behalf of either belligerent, of arms, munitions or war, or, in general, of anything which could be of use to any navy or fleet.
> *Article 8*
> A neutral Government is bound to employ the means at its disposal to prevent the fitting out or arming of any vessel within its jurisdiction which it has reason to believe, is intended to cruise, or engage in hostile operations, against a Power with which that Government is at peace. It is also bound to display the same vigilance to prevent the departure from its jurisdiction of any vessel intended to cruise or engage in hostile operations, which has been adapted in whole or in part within the said jurisdiction to warlike use.[143]

In the view of the Foreign Office, the question whether the building of the trawlers and their supply to a German firm, amounted to a breach of international law depended largely upon the facts. The essential distinction was that between a neutral person selling armed ships to a belligerent on the one hand and a neutral person building them *to the order of a belligerent* on the other.

On the face of it, the transaction reported by Denham, did not appear to be in breach of international law, were it not for the fact that the trawlers were being specifically constructed with special features to the order of the German firm concerned, the presumption being that the special features would enable them to be used as minesweepers. The fact that the order from Germany had been placed through a German firm and was not a direct order from the German government, was irrelevant, since it could be presumed to be the case that the German firm was merely acting as an agent for the German government. At the same time, it was noted that the Swedish

111

government might attempt to rely on this fact in claiming that the vessels were not warships, since normally an order for warships would be placed by a government.

> It may also be argued that in order to comply with this ruling the vessels must at any rate in part be built for war purposes and not merely used for such purposes by the enemy after handing over. Alternatively, the constructors must be aware of the use to which the enemy intends to put the vessels. If, however, these vessels have special constructional features unnecessary to trawlers to act as minesweepers the case would appear to fall within the 'Washington Rule' arising out of the Alabama decision, which has been enacted almost word for word in the latter part of Article 8 of Hague Convention XIII already quoted.[144]

In the view of the Foreign Office, Denham's report had provided good reasons for believing that the trawlers were intended for use as minesweepers and a submission from the Admiralty regarding the technical alterations envisaged for the vessels, strengthened his case. Mallet was therefore instructed by the Foreign Office (unless he had some strong objection) to address a note to the Swedish government to the effect that

> His Majesty's Government are of the opinion that the action of the Swedish Government in permitting the building in Sweden of such ships to the order of the Germans is an unneutral act, of which His Majesty's Government have taken note and against which they desire to enter a firm protest.[145]

Before this was done, further investigation into the disputed trawlers took place in Sweden with a visit of the assistant naval attaché to the yard where the vessels were being built. The technical features he noted showed that the vessels were to be specially reinforced in various ways and the owner of the yard had expressed the opinion that he was certain that they were intended as minesweepers and not fishing vessels. On 15 February 1943 Mallet handed his note of protest to Boheman at the Ministry for Foreign Affairs. Boheman claimed he had never heard of the case but promised to look into it.

The story about the fishing vessels/minesweepers soon escaped from the confines of diplomacy. On 25 February, a question had been raised in the House of Commons about ships for Germany being built in Sweden. On 10 March, it was time for the Second Chamber of the

112

Riksdag to hear Foreign Minister Günther's view of the matter. He began by reading out the text of the Swedish answer to the British note of complaint from which it transpired that the original permission for the yard involved to build 45 fishing vessels for Hugo Stinnes GmbH, Mülheim-Ruhr had been given on 28 March 1942. The order had been placed on condition that the German company supply the yard with any material needed for the construction of the vessels, which was in scarce supply in Sweden. Before the appropriate body (the Transport Commission) approved the order, the designs for the fishing vessels had been carefully examined. Nothing unusual had come to light and the Swedish authorities had no reason to suppose that Stinnes were acting on behalf of the German government in this matter. As a result of the British note, the Ministry of Foreign Affairs had ordered a new professional examination of the fishing vessels to be made.

> This investigation had shown that there was nothing about the vessels, whether in respect to their form, design or lay-out or in any other way, which suggests that they are intended for anything other than fishing. Indeed they appear in every respect well adapted for this purpose.[146]

Indeed there were technical features which tended to point *against* their use as minesweepers – they were much lower-powered than Swedish equivalents, their construction contained iron as well as wood, which made them vulnerable to magnetic mines, etc. The Minister for Foreign Affairs ended by reassuring the Chamber that there was no support for the charge that the Swedish government, in granting permission for the building of these vessels, had acted in contravention of the Hague Convention: the British government's protest was groundless.

But was the Swedish government being entirely above-board in this matter? The monitoring of German postal communications had in fact already provided an insight into the true state of affairs, as a postal censorship report at the beginning of 1942 was to make clear:

> Germany's increased need of tonnage finds frequent expression in the correspondence. Inter alia, the German Naval High Command has ordered 80 fishing boats, which are to be built in two series at Swedish yards. Regarding this order, a German representative has said that the whole order is outside the usual clearing agreement and therefore not all the details are known to

the *Reichswirtschaftsministerium*. In fact, neither Germany's shipping experts here in the country or Germany's Chamber of Commerce have been briefed about the project and the conclusion can therefore be drawn that the boats are primarily to be used for military purposes.[147]

If the fishing boat transaction was hardly a major issue, it was perhaps also something more than a prestige matter of little significance, as Boheman tended to dismiss it. There will be reason to return to it briefly again in the next chapter. From December 1943 onwards, the Ministry of Economic Affairs in London received a number of reports that the 'fishing boats' were being used by the Germans as escort vessels in convoys on the stretch Stavanger–Bergen and later as gun-mounts for anti-aircraft defences in German harbours.[148]

When in due course, the British government called for the withdrawal of the Swedish naval attaché in London, in connection with the Krämer affair, Denham's various misdemeanours in the eyes of the Swedes, were brought up anew. An attempt was made to have him recalled in 1944 but the Foreign Office was in no mood to listen. By then the relative standing of the belligerents was very different and eventually the matter was quietly dropped.

Secret intelligence: the SIS

Given the importance attached to the flows of iron ore (and later of ball bearings) from Sweden to Germany in Allied economic warfare thinking, it was natural to monitor them by a variety of methods, including those which were properly described as covert and which in Britain could be assigned to the SIS.

As the first volume of the official history of British intelligence in the Second World War makes plain, the passport control organisation provided official cover for the SIS HQ's representatives abroad. It may be reasonably assumed that the potential intelligence function of British PCOs was very much an open secret as far as the police or security authorities of several European countries were concerned. The role of British Military Control Officers/PCOs had become clear in Scandinavia quite soon from their activities in connection with the attempt to erect a *cordon sanitaire* around Bolshevik Russia and from various British efforts to initiate co-operation between Britain's own control agencies and those of the Scandinavian powers regarding this question. Thereafter routine scandals and exposures together with indiscreet memoirs helped to fill in the picture a little more: what was known in one country, soon spread to others through the exchange of information between their respective intelligence or security agencies.

If the PCOs provided convenient letterboxes, financial back-up and a chain of communication for servicing the agent in the field, the actual work of espionage was usually carried out by others. Perhaps typical of one type of interwar-years informant was O'Brien-Ffrench.[149] A personal friend of Stewart Menzies, later to become the wartime 'C', O'Brien-Ffrench had served as assistant military attaché in Stockholm and Helsinki during the First World War. In 1935, while holidaying at a hotel near the the Norwegian–Swedish Border, his attention had been drawn to the number of iron-ore trains travelling between the mines at Kiruna and Narvik. Boarding one of these trains, he had travelled to the Norwegian port to continue his enquiries. The findings of this trip were subsequently communicated directly to Menzies and led to O'Brien-Ffrench being involved in some further follow-up work on the spot, corroborating details of Swedish iron ore exports to Germany.

At the outbreak of the Second World War, the Stockholm PCO was Commander John Martin, who had arrived in Sweden on 20 June 1938. Throughout 1939, he travelled frequently to Norway – a fact duly noted by the resident security authorities.[150] Martin's role in the Rickman affair has already been mentioned but even before this case surfaced, Martin had already been compromised in connection with a monitoring operation involving *inter alia* Oxelösund which was to be the focus of Rickman's endeavours.[151]

In October 1939, discreetly screening himself with the help of intermediaries, one of whom was an advertising executive with Sunlight soap, Martin had begun to set up a special ship-watching network to cover certain Swedish ports. In Oxelösund, a local shipbroker agreed to collect the requisite information. His main task was to monitor the iron ore trade with Germany and he carried it out by returning a series of fortnightly reports. A report list from January 1940 told of the *Sabine Howald*, Flensburg, which had departed on the 4th of that month with a cargo of around 8,000 tons of ore; of the *Niedenfels* from Bremen, which left the day after with another 8,000 tons and of the *Ostpreussen* from Königsberg which departed on 8 January with still another identical cargo. On 9 January, the *Possehl* from Lübeck and the *Welheim* from Hamburg set off with 3,000 and 7,100 tons of iron ore respectively. The following day, the *Pylades* from Bremen had arrived with a mixed cargo of 700 tons and departed again with 700 tons of crushed ore. Sometimes the shipbroker was actually able to board the vessel, which made it easier to estimate the size of the cargo; in other cases, he simply estimated it roughly according to the size of the vessel.

The above network was broken up early in 1940 with the arrest of Martin's main agent on 13 January and of the advertising man on 1 February and they were subsequently sentenced under Section 21a of Chapter 8 of the Penal Code. The case was mentioned routinely in the Swedish press and naturally did not escape the Nazi propaganda machine in Germany.[152]

On 1 December 1942, Cyril Cheshire took over the reins as Head of Passport Control in Stockholm and around the same time Victor Hampton, who was to be particularly concerned with Denmark and Germany, arrived in the Swedish capital. The year before, the SIS contingent had been strengthened by the addition of the former members of the Finnish station under the command of Harry Carr.[153] Working links with colleagues from friendly services were fostered and agent networks expanded. Various links and enterprises involving SIS will be mentioned later. For the present it is useful to turn briefly to look at examples of SIS networks working within Germany, which communicated through Sweden.

In January 1944 a British agent, the Danish businessman Andreasen (R34), was captured by the Germans and provided them with a very detailed account of his work on behalf of the British intelligence service in Stockholm.[154] Although R34's account cannot be accepted uncritically, it nevertheless provides a knowledgeable insight into the range of activities being mounted from the Swedish listening post. According to R34, the SIS had succeeded in establishing important groups in Berlin, Hamburg, Bonn, Königsberg and Vienna. Berlin was said to contain three or four Intelligence nets reporting to Hampton and with a transmitter at their disposal. In Hamburg, it was claimed that Hampton had a network of 80 people, among them some technically well qualified, who were able to supply a stream of information and drawings dealing with U-boats and other matters of interest. Lines of communications to this network went via Kiel, Schleswig, Wärnemunde, Sylt and Emden. For the relaying of information to Hampton, use was made *inter alia* of a Hamburg export firm able to conceal microfilms among the goods sent to Sweden. In Bonn, which formed a centre for British intelligence activities in south-west Germany, a group consisting predominantly of foreign workers was active with two radio transmitters at their disposal. Before the occupation of Belgium and Holland, the information from Bonn had gone via these countries. After their occupation, new routes were developed via Sweden and Switzerland. For information routed through Sweden, the Bonn organisation had the assistance of the agents in Hamburg. In Königsberg, Hampton's organisation under a certain 'Steph' was said to number some eight to ten persons and to be militarily well informed, with good contacts with the armaments industry and the *Wehrmacht*. In Vienna, Hampton was in touch with an intelligence organisation with links to similar groups in Rumania and Bulgaria. In April 1943, a Danish agent (R101) had been sent to Vienna and had successfully made contact with an underground group there. Staying on until the beginning of September 1943, R101 had helped to secure the line of communication to Stockholm and to make preparations for the reception of agents dropped by parachute. In September 1943, three parachutists were dropped in the region of Vienna along with a consignment of small arms, ammunition, explosives and two transmitters. The Vienna organisation was said to dispose over a large quantity of money, originating in part from British sources.

In his account, R34 singled out a number of SIS agents in Germany for special mention. The garrulous and bibulous Hampton had for example indiscreetly confided to him that the most important agent in Germany was a woman who had a close personal relationship with one of the most prominent ministers or political figures in Germany. This Mata Hari was said to have delivered to the British Secret Service a steady stream of top-level diplomatic and strategic information, including it was claimed, advance notification of Barbarossa. It was significant perhaps that a meeting between her and Cheshire had taken place at the American Embassy in Berlin when the Englishman had lived in the German capital, apparently posing as an American. But R34 was less sure that her information was actually channelled through Stockholm, conjecturing instead that it went via the Swiss corridor. On the other hand, an agent who certainly *was* controlled from Stockholm, was R82. This agent had an impressive knowledge of military and technical subjects and had in addition to excellent reports and drawings delivered 600–800 photographs. R82 was not in the habit of sending reports frequently. It was more a question of once or twice a year (unless some piece of information was of urgent importance) and the link to Hampton in Sweden was maintained partly through personal contact and partly by courier. Among other agents earning a special mention were two working within the Messerschmitt Works in Augsburg and a foreign ballistics expert, employed by the *Wehrmacht*, who was privy to valuable technical information about weaponry.[155]

The acquisition of information from agents was one task of SIS. Another was that of handling those contacts with emissaries of enemy nationality which for one reason or another orthodox diplomatists preferred to have nothing to do with. MacEwen's contact with Trott has already been noted and the same member of SIS was also involved with various other German visitors.[156]

Another important function assigned to this service was counter-espionage and specialist officers attached to Section V were assigned to Stockholm for the purpose of keeping track of the more important German agents known to be active in Sweden.[157] A typical day in the life of one of them, was summed up as follows:

I was in the Passport Office from 9 a.m. to 6 p.m, (with 1 hour off for lunch 1 to 2 p.m.) and, on average, about 1 hour in the afternoon when I visited the Legation either to see Chancery or one of the Attachés about Passport work, or to visit Harry Carr. In the Passport Office, the order of work and the time allotted to the different jobs depended on priorities. The first priority was MM; translations of his previous day's messages into English for encoding by my secretary and immediate despatch by telegram to London. Comments, unless urgent, were prepared later in the day and sent by letter. Total time for MM varied from 1 to 4 hours a day. Second priority was Passport work. Visa applications were circulated to appropriate sections of the Legation, and combined comments, including my security comments, if any, were forwarded to London. This together with telephone calls to U.D, etc., occupied on average two and a half hours per day. No regular lists of Air passengers were obtained, but if information about these was needed, it was obtained from the Assistant Air Attaché. The only list arriving daily was of visitors to the Grand Hotel. I glanced through this and marked it for my secretary for carding. The remainder of the day was spent in preparing reports from the Norwegians and our other sources. Contacting these was done after dinner at night, visits varying in length from about 2 to 4 hours.[158]

Linguistic difficulties alone limited the extent to which British born personnel could be deployed in the field as agents, couriers and cutouts. This obstacle could, however, be overcome with the co-operation of political opponents of Nazism, the assistance of other allied intelligence services and indeed of other intelligence services – whether allied or not – which were prepared to supply information on acceptable terms. William Casey has drawn attention to the importance of such intelligence-sharing agreements to the efforts of the OSS Stockholm station, which was thereby able to draw on the resources of the intelligence services of *inter alia* the Baltic countries, Belgium, the Netherlands, Hungary and Poland.[159] Undoubtedly similar agreements were of importance to the British.

German resistance revisited

In November 1939, Herman Knüfken, an important figure in the underground work of ITF – the International Transport Federation – was arrested in Stockholm.[160] Knüfken's colourful career and great natural charm had made him something of a legend within the German labour movement. Originally active within *Profintern*-sponsored trade union activities among seamen, he eventually came under suspicion as a deviationist. At some time in the 1930s Knüfken transferred his allegiance to ITF and began to co-operate actively with its General Secretary, the Dutchman Edo Fimmen, in establishing an anti-Nazi underground trades union movement in Europe. Working from Belgium and Holland, Knüfken was in a position to contact and interview well-disposed German seamen and bargees who called at Antwerp, Rotterdam and elsewhere and to build up a system of communication designed to service illegal networks within Germany itself. These illegal networks produced leaflets and other propaganda designed to stiffen morale in the struggle against Nazism and to expose its oppression. At the same time, they provided a stream of reports on what going on in German ports, naval dockyards, armaments factories, etc. The small German radical socialist party SAP, which was well-versed in the covert struggle against Nazism, maintained close links with ITF.

In view of this information-collection capability and because of the strong British influence in ITF, it was hardly surprising if in the darkening days after the *Anschluss*, the British Secret Service and the underground union organisation had certain interests in common. With union assistance before the outbreak of war, Section D was able to infiltrate black propaganda via the North German Ports.[161] After the removal of the HQ of ITF from Amsterdam to England in the autumn of 1939, the ties were naturally strengthened and the bulk of the information which was passed to the HQ from the illegal networks on the Continent presumably became available, one way or another, to the British intelligence authorities. Trusted representatives of ITF in Sweden were also well placed to set up a courier service on ships sailing between Sweden and Germany.

In October 1939, Knüfken – later to be identified by the Gestapo as agent 101B of the SIS – arrived in Stockholm on a Danish passport (No. 276/35) made out in the name of engineer Carl Knudsen.[162] Once in the Swedish capital, Knüfken set about meeting Charles Lindley, the grand old man of ITF in Sweden and he also interviewed a number of German seamen who had jumped ship in Sweden. A report giving information from one of the latter was scheduled to be given to the Passport Control Office in Stockholm but ended up as part of the police evidence against Knüfken. It contained references to the movements of the *Scharnhorst, Gneisenau, Admiral Hipper* and *Seydlitz*, specified the location of certain underground hangars at Anklam, where there were 1,000 aircraft, and spoke of a factory on the River Peene which produced aircraft frames and wings for light fighters. Among the other items held by the police as evidence of Knüfken's intelligence task were postcards of Swedish iron ore ports.

On 13 December 1939, Knüfken was sentenced to five months' hard labour for entering the country on a false passport, unlawfully collecting information and for a breach of hotel regulations. Knüfken's sentence was due to end on 16 May 1940 and on 25 April the German Legation submitted a request for his extradition under the German–Swedish treaty of 1878, on the grounds that he had been involved in the sabotage of some ten merchant ships in 1938. While Knüfken remained in the penitentiary at Falun, the German submission was considered by the courts.

The evidence offered by the German authorities for Knüfken's involvement in the alleged ship sabotage was extremely thin; on the other hand for extradition under the treaty of 1878, which remained in force, it was not required for one of the parties to the treaty to prove their case to the legal satisfaction of the other. It was sufficient that a detention order had been issued by a competent authority in the country applying for extradition, and this the Germans claimed to have provided in the shape of a detention order issued by the Prosecutor's Office in Bremen. After a lengthy consideration of the issues involved, the Supreme Court ruled on 16 September 1940 that there was no formal legal obstacle to the extradition. The Swedish authorities, however, were well aware of the issue at stake and also of Knüfken's probable fate if he were to be delivered into German hands. In addition, ITF's Swedish representative, Charles Lindley, who had watched with some apprehension the legal developments of the case, was in touch with the British Legation in Stockholm. On 18 September, the British Minister visited the Ministry for Foreign Affairs where he took up the matter with the Under-Secretary of State:

> Mr. Mallet explained that some time ago he had received a visit from the representative of the Transport Workers, Mr. Charles Lindley, who had requested British intervention on Knüfken's behalf. Afterwards he had written to London and received the instruction to try to prevent Knüfken's extradition. Mr. Bevin had taken a special interest in the matter and Mallet feared that an extradition would cause a scandal. He wondered whether it was not possible for the man to escape abroad; perhaps a place in a British courier plane could be placed at his disposal.[163]

Meanwhile, after the ruling of the Supreme Court, Knüfken's case had been referred to two legal experts for a further opinion. One of these experts, Johan Hellner, held that the Supreme Court's interpretation of the treaty of 1878 in regard to Knüfken could not be a matter for further debate by the King in Council and that the only alternative left was to examine whether there might be *other* legal obstacles to the extradition. Östen Undén, on the other hand, drew attention to the fact that the treaty explicitly excluded the extradition of 'persons who have been guilty of some political offence' and he argued that inasmuch as Knüfken was involved in the crimes with which he had been charged by the German court – and the evidence was very weak that he had been so involved – his offence was a political one and for that reason the extradition treaty was not applicable.

At the beginning of 1941, the matter was still undecided. A

121

German note of 3 January, enquiring when the Swedish government could be expected to reach a decision about Knüfken's extradition remained unanswered. In February the British Minister took up the question with the Swedish Under-Secretary of State:

> Boheman said he didn't sympathise particularly with Knüfken who was a Communist agitator. The Supreme Court had ruled that it was in the Swedish Government's power to agree to the German request for extradition. The Swedish Government had managed so far to stall off the demand and that was as far as they were prepared to go. In these circumstances there was no likelihood of his being released or allowed to escape in order that we might waft him to England to continue his activities against the Nazi government.[164]

On 15 March 1941, the German Legation returned with the question that it had raised in January and was told that Knüfken's state of health had required his transfer to a prison hospital and that this in turn meant that the whole question of extradition had to be postponed for the time being. Three days before, Knüfken had been transferred to the psychiatric wing of Långholmen prison in Stockholm. Naturally, Knüfken's state of mental health was simply a ruse as the Under-Secretary of State confided to Mallet in July 1941 when his name cropped up during a conversation about Wollweber, also held in Sweden, and also the subject of a German extradition order for his part in sabotage activities:

> I took the opportunity to say that I imagined that he [Wollweber] was in quite a different category from Knüfken, regarding whom I had once before spoken to Monsieur Boheman. I was told that this was true and that Knüfken, although the Germans accused him also of sabotage, was not the same desperate type of character and had moreover many respectable friends, both in Swedish and British trade union circles. Knüfken could not of course be set free, especially as the High Court had also ruled that he was extraditable, but the Swedish Government wished to avoid giving in to the German demand in his case and they were trying, Monsieur Boheman said with a wink, to get him pronounced 'insane'. To my suggestion that I could answer for his safe removal from Sweden, Monsieur Boheman replied that this solution was out of the question as it would be far too dangerous for Sweden's relations with Germany.[165]

Despite further German requests, Knüfken remained in safe isolation and in conditions of great secrecy, in Långholmen until 4 February 1944, when he was granted more freedom of movement. He finally flew to England on 11 October 1944.

Another case which indicated ITF's potential role as an information service, was that of Ludwig Lewy, who was sentenced to eight months' hard labour under Section 21a of Chapter 8 of the Penal Code during the first year of the war.[166] Lewy was a Jew and a socialist and had worked in a bank in Berlin. At some stage in his career, he had met Edo Fimmen in Amsterdam, and after his emigration to Sweden Lewy continued to keep in touch with the union leader, informing him about political developments in Sweden and elsewhere, sending him articles and information which could be used by ITF directly or by newspapers sympathetic to the Federation's viewpoint. Several of Lewy's articles in England were channelled into *Reynolds News*, the old Co-operative and ILP newspaper. When Lewy was arrested by the Swedish police, he maintained that his efforts to collect information about the internal situation in Germany, were simply part and parcel of normal journalistic practice. The prosecution argued on the other hand that this was only partly true. Lewy had been extremely careful to carry on his correspondence with Fimmen through a cover address. Secondly, certain parts of that correspondence suggested that Levy's role went beyond that of mere journalism. Most incriminating was a letter of 15 June 1939:

> As I told you, I would like to give you some advice for your correspondents. Here it is:
> 1. Speed in transmitting the message is of great importance. The faster we're informed, the better.
> 2. A lot of your information loses in value because it is not precise. It is general and vague and therefore less useful. However I would make an exception for some of your information about factories.
> As far as we're concerned (and exactly the same holds for the other information) a full piece of intelligence should give an answer to the following four questions
> Who? When? Where? How?[167]

Fimmen – or whoever was behind these competent words of advice – then went on to illustrate these points in detail. In the case of vehicles for example, it was important to characterise these as light, medium, heavy, very heavy and to give the number involved. As far as artillery was concerned, the calibre and the number of pieces had to be supplied. Troops were to be identified as exactly as possible by looking out for badges, epaulettes, numbers and other distinguishing marks. When reporting on factories, it was important to give the real number of people employed, the shift system in operation, the arrangements made in the event of a general mobilisation, as well as exact details of the items manufactured.

Lewy's informants were refugees who had just arrived from Germany, German visitors to Sweden and after the outbreak of war, various Swedes (businessmen and others) who had visited the Reich. Typical of the information being relayed in this way were the two following snippets:

Magdeburg
Bramag, a subsidiary of I. G. Farben. This new installation between Magdeburg–Neustadt and Rothensee, is used exclusively for the production of poison gas.
Metallverken Polte. This factory situated between Sudenburg and Wilhelmstadt has been completely altered for the production of ammunition.

Heinsberg (near Freital, Saxony)
Aron's cycle factory. After 'aryanization', this factory was temporarily closed down. For a time, it was concerned with the manufacture of a timing device for grenades. Since 1936, production has swung over to manufacturing anti-aircraft guns of light calibre. Workforce: 4000.[168]

Lewy's information was not, however, purely industrial. Several of his reports dealt exclusively with military matters, such as the identification of various officers at certain bases, details of equipment and so on. Nor was his attention confined to Germany. In the summer of 1938, he heard from a German acquaintance who worked for a certain Swedish armaments company, that it had set up an experimental unit for hand-grenades in a little toy factory in Stockholm.[169] The hand-grenade was said to produce a blast effect 20 times the normal and had been tried out at Travemünde. Two German engineers were in charge of the research work and a new factory to produce this grenade was planned in Gothenburg. This rumour was quickly dispatched to London along with another about a

Stockholm engineering company, which had installed modern equipment for the production of ammunition. According to Lewy's source, the plant had been visited by officers from the technical section of the German General staff and preparations had been made so that in the event of war, it could be converted into an ammunition factory within the space of 12 hours.

In Stockholm, important work on behalf of ITF was carried out by the couple August and Irmgard Enderle, who were also highly active in SAP.[170] They had arrived in Sweden with false passports in March 1934, travelling via Belgium and Norway. August Enderle had known Edo Fimmen since 1922 and once established in Stockholm, he and his wife were able during the second half of the 1930s to participate in ITF's underground activities among seamen. A courier system was organised and contacts were made with underground ITF representatives in Bremen, Hamburg, Lübeck and other ports. Some at least of these communication lines appear to have remained intact throughout the war. German-speaking refugees in their political struggle against Hitler were of assistance to British intelligence in Stockholm in other ways as well. The activities of Karl Pulz and his friends may serve as an example.[171]

In November 1939, an organisation under the chairmanship of Josef Ladig, a former First Secretary of the Metalworkers' Union in Czechoslovakia, was set up in Stockholm to serve the interests of all Social Democratic trade union members of Sudeten German origins who had fled to Scandinavia as refugees. Karl Pulz was appointed as the Norwegian representative of the organisation. After the German occupation of Norway, Pulz came over to Sweden where he managed to obtain a residence permit and find work with the help of Siegfried Taub, the former Deputy Speaker of the Czech Parliament. In 1942, Pulz became friendly with Kurt Englich, a fellow political refugee from Berlin and the two men resolved to do what they could in active opposition against Hitler and his Reich.

With the encouragement of Vilmos Böhm and Dr Paul Lindner of the Press Reading Bureau of the British Legation, Pulz and Englich became involved in the infiltration and distribution of black propaganda within Germany. The leaflets which were prepared in England, were of a familar type. Hints were given to German soldiers on how to feign various complaints while other leaflets were devised to create organisational confusion.

When Pulz learned that some reliable person was about to undertake a trip in Germany or one of the occupied territories, he reported back to his contacts in the Press Reading Bureau. They then forwarded a packet of propaganda material to Pulz who then in turn saw that it was safely handed over to the prospective courier. Two other obvious target groups for this propaganda offensive were German troops in transit through Sweden and German seamen on ships calling at Swedish ports. Gradually a working field organisation was built up and Englich was later to speak of having some 30 or so helpers at his disposal.

Pulz and Englich also played a part in the infiltration of German circles in Stockholm. From the outbreak of the war, the British had a well-placed source within the German Legation.[172] This facilitated in various ways the monitoring of German espionage activities, among them those of Dr Krämer. Later, a new way of following some of Krämer's activities became available due to the conspiratorial efforts of Pulz and Englich.

Through a female contact at the German School in Stockholm, Englich made the acquaintance of a person with access to the German Air Attaché's Office. Arrangements were now made for telegrams to be copied surreptitiously. A sample copy was passed on to the British and finally ended up with Ewan Butler, the SOE man with special responsibility for Germany. He in turn passed it on to an SIS colleague for his opinion. The authenticity of the telegram having been checked, the British declared their interest in maintaining the contact and a useful inflow of telegrams could now be channelled directly from the Air Attaché's Office via Pulz and Englich. Englich looked after the link with the source while Pulz was responsible for dropping the telegrams at a convenience address in Valhallavägen, used by Butler. This monitoring activity was gradually extended to other German offices in Stockholm, among them that of the military attaché.

The British were not, however, the only ones to make use of the Pulz–Englich net. Englich and his source were also delivering material to a control in the Swedish Defence Staff Security Section while Pulz regularly passed on material to an independent Czech source.

Allied intelligence services

Some Danish activities. In Stockholm, as has already been seen, following the German occupation of Denmark, Ebba Munck functioned as an intermediary between the British Special Services and E-section of the Danish General Staff. E-section, which remained legally in place until the German intervention of 29 August 1943, set about collecting information about the forces of occupation for forwarding to Stockholm.[173] The task of processing the incoming material was placed in the hands of Volmer Gyth who from April 1941 was assisted by Per Winkel. The material for Stockholm was written down clearly and then photographed in a little room above the Section office. The film was then sent by courier to Munck in Stockholm. In February 1941, Ronald Turnbull arrived there to take up his duties as SOE Danish representative, functioning as Munck's principal British talking partner on the spot. As the flow of high-grade intelligence via this channel increased, it was decided around the middle of that year that SOE should act on behalf of SIS in Denmark. This arrangement however was not observed to the letter, as the mission in September 1941 of Thomas Sneum and his radio operator was to reveal.[174] After the arrival of Hampton in Stockholm at the end of 1942, SIS appears to have started recruiting its own Danish agents independently of SOE and further contacts between Danish intelligence and SIS were spun after the arrival of senior members of the Danish service in Sweden.

The events of August 1943 had a direct repercussion upon the lines of communication between Denmark and Sweden. Before that date, use had been made of couriers travelling on legitimate business. Now controls were tightened. In due course, new courier routes would be set up but in the interval, there was a pressing need to improve the flow of information by other means.

At the end of 1943, discussions took place with Major Petersén of C-Bureau and agreement was reached whereby the Danes would establish with Swedish help a network of radio transmitters. But this proposal was apparently not carried through partly due to other developments and partly to doubts about the vulnerability of the network to German monitoring.[175] 1944 witnessed notable strides in Danish covert radio communications, thanks not least to the contribution of the engineer, Duus Hansen. A direct contact was established with England to ensure the transmission of top-priority material, in particular naval intelligence, without delay. Changes in operating routines and the development of high speed transmission reduced time on the air and thus the risk of detection by the enemy. A new S-Phone link (Minestrone) was set up between Helsingør in Denmark and Hälsingborg in Sweden.

127

The primary purpose of these developments was to speed up communications between Denmark and London via Sweden rather than between Denmark and Sweden as such.[176] But there was also a pressing need for the Princes in Stockholm to have at their disposal other lines of communication to Svend Truelsen, the new covert chief of intelligence in Denmark. At the end of April 1944, they notified Truelsen that they were keen to establish a cable link over the Sound. The matter had been discussed with the Swedish authorities and the various possibilities examined. Now it was the task of Truelsen and his team to attend to matters at his end. In July 1944, the first cable link was opened, to be followed by a further cable link at the end of the year.

After the arrival of the Princes in Stockholm, the Swedes – anxious to continue their own co-operation with Danish intelligence – helped their colleagues to find suitable premises and a processing centre for incoming intelligence from Denmark was established. After being appropriately graded, it was then distributed to the various interested parties – Turnbull, the Swedes, Denham, as the case might be. A certain delicate diplomacy regulated the terms of this distribution. Somewhat earlier, in June 1943, it had come to the attention of the British that certain information which had come via Denham from the Swedes coincided with material which had been received from the Danes. When the matter was taken up with the latter, the Danes told the British not to spill the beans to the Swedes.

The Danes were to earn several tributes for the quality of the intelligence they delivered. A British communication of 8 September 1944 read as follows:

> The following telegram has been received this morning from H.Q.: 'Many thanks for German Battle Order dated August 29th. High authorities impressed with excellent work. I am sure you will be glad to have this little personal message to confirm what you already know that London is deeply grateful and appreciative of the very high standard of the intelligence which you are sending'.[177]

A further casualty of the events of August 1943 had been the flow of naval intelligence. The urgency of reactivating this service was duly emphasised for Truelsen and by the beginning of 1944, a new organisation responsible for collecting naval intelligence, had been set up. In Stockholm, P. A. Mørch had taken over from Ebbe Munck as

Denham's liaison. On 3 May 1944, in a letter to Mørch, Denham observed:

I felt you would like to know how very helpful your recent efforts have been in providing intelligence from Denmark. I therefore want to thank you warmly and to add a word of praise for your staff who must also have been instrumental in developing your reports so much, both in quality and quantity.[178]

At the same time, Denham tactfully took up another aspect of the matter:

There is only one small point where I would suggest an improvement on the recent quality, if that is possible, and that is the speed with which reports on matters of vital operational nature might be accelerated; but no doubt you are looking into this.[179]

Urgency, however, sometimes had to yield to practical constraints or matters of security. In accordance with the then prevailing procedure, for example, the observation of a lighthouse-keeper of the passage of a German ship through the Great Belt, was telephoned first to Copenhagen where (from April 1944) it could be radioed to England. But coding of messages took time and radio operators within Denmark had to be circumspect. The whole process from the initial sighting to the radio transmission was composed of a number of steps where delays of one type or another could occur. The introduction of the cable links over the Sound in the summer of 1944 allowed naval intelligence to be brought more rapidly to Denham in Stockholm who was then able to radio the Admiralty without delay.

In an interesting 'Personal – Most Secret' reply to Mørch in June 1944, Denham tried to convey to his colleague something both of the wider perspective and of the labyrinth of intelligence in which it was so easy for pieces of important information to go astray.

There are perhaps nearly a dozen sources or centres which in varying degree feed naval information to me. Your contribution until January this year amounted to 16% but now this has increased to nearly 20. You may think that with your increased output this percentage should be higher, but other sources have also increased so your proportion does not show the high figure one might expect. Naturally, being the only British naval officer in Northern Europe I have most naval intelligence to handle. This intelligence must be handled differently from any other, because to be of value, it must be not only accurate and rich in detail, but sometimes swift in transmission to our Admiralty where action may be taken sometimes at once. I could give you examples brought about successfully because of this. It is sometimes possible to forestall an enemy move when one knows from our side what he is anticipating or what new device he may be developing. I mention these as examples to show you how important it is to know at once any reliable report on what Dönitz may have believed in, or on any new U-boat invention. Any other organisation which may handle naval intelligence certainly gets it to London where eventually it is sorted out and made use of by the Service departments. There is, however, a great deal of difference between its usefulness when dealt with in this way as opposed to its being passed through our Naval Intelligence Organisation. As an example – I recollect an occasion when one of your reports did not reach me, but was sent to London the usual way. It happened to be a matter of considerable importance and a week later I had a telegram asking my views. One must of course have been at Admiralty to understand how these matters are actually dealt with at home.[180]

Some Norwegian activities.[181]   On 1 January 1941, Captain Finn Nagell was appointed to head the Norwegian Defence Department's Intelligence Bureau FD/E in London.[182] Among its tasks was liaison with the British Special Services (SIS, SOE and MI5) on behalf of the Norwegian authorities. In addition, it was expected to gather, process and distribute political and military intelligence about Norway and in addition to maintain contact with resistance groups at home.

After Russia and America had joined the Allied camp, the Norwegians found it expedient to re-establish an integrated supreme command (FO) for their armed forces.[183] It came into being on 6 February 1942 and consisted of a number of sections or bureaux, the second of which – (FO II) headed by Roscher Lund – was responsible for intelligence.

FD/E was not immediately absorbed within the new structure. That was to come first in July 1944 when FD/E was merged with FO II with Nagell becoming deputy to Roscher-Lund. There was, however, a re-allocation of tasks. FO IV took over liaison with SOE and Milorg.

In accordance with the instruction of 9 April 1942, FD/E was split into five sections of which Section V was responsible for liaison with SIS. More broadly, FD/E was given the task of collecting the information and (in conjunction with SIS) training agents while FO II was responsible for processing the intelligence collected. By March 1942, FO II had begun distributing intelligence surveys to other Allied departments on a regular basis. Initially, the numbers involved in the work of FO II were small, amounting to some 38 persons of whom 8 were British secretarial staff. The professional staff included 5 area specialists and a number of subject specialists to deal with questions of roads, railways, telecommunications, etc. A year later, the staff had risen to 83 with 53 Norwegians and 30 British secretaries. Liaison officers from the British and American armed forces were appointed and conversely FO II personnel served in other allied departments. January 1943 also saw the establishment of a special section dealing with XU, the home-based secret intelligence organisation.

In Stockholm there were also organisational problems to be overcome. In the aftermath of the German invasion, small groups dedicated to resistance sprang up in Norway, often independently of one another. It would take time before their efforts became more co-ordinated just as it would also take time to co-ordinate the efforts of the various people in Stockholm receiving the information supplied. Within the Norwegian Legation itself, the Military Attaché's Office (sometimes called simply the Military Office), the Naval Attaché's Office, the Legal Office, the Press Office and the so-called 'Sports Office' were all involved in the business of intelligence collection and jealously guarded their prerogatives in the matter.[184] At the same time the Legal Office tended to look somewhat askance at the 'Sports Office' while the Naval Attaché's Office was reluctant to hand over its own channels of information to the Military Office.

In 1943, a number of changes occurred. Among other things, FO's London structure was reproduced in Stockholm where the Military Office was divided – as has been mentioned earlier – into two sections: MI II under Ørnulf Dahl which dealt with intelligence and MI IV under Heyerdahl-Larsen dealing with Milorg and SOE liaison. At the same time, MI II was given overall responsibility for all *military* intelligence – a recommendation, however, which was not to be instantaneously implemented. Co-operation between British and Norwegian intelligence in Stockholm was strengthened by the secondment of John Turner (masquerading as Major Jon

Lauritz Pettersen) of SIS.

An indication of the respective roles of London and Stockholm offices regarding collecting information from Norway is given in an agreement between FO II, FD/E and SIS reached in the first quarter of 1943:

1. The aim of this cooperation is to set up a securely based independent secret intelligence service with respect to Norway. The responsibility for this service will be shared alike by the British, FO II and FD/E and its task is to collect secret intelligence material in Norway and forward it to the appropriate authorities in Great Britain.

2. The intelligence material which is collected, is to be sent in one of the following distinct ways: (a) by courier post which for the time being will almost without exception go via Sweden and (b) over radio stations which are in direct contact with Great Britain.

3. All matters of operational interest, wherever possible are to be reported over the radio stations and similarly all statistical information is to be sent with courier via Stockholm. The aim behind the establishment of this dual service is to release the radio stations for essential operational traffic.

4. All questions of importance regarding politics and planning are to be discussed and agreed upon by the British, FO II and FD/E. before any action is taken.

The tasks of the British Secret Intelligence Service will be:

1. Together with FD/E and FO II to choose suitable agents for the radio service.

2. Together with FO II to arrange travel possibilities for agents and recruits from Sweden to Great Britain.

3. Together with FD/E to train agents.

4. Together with FD/E and FO II to train suitable couriers.

5. To furnish agents with radio and other equipment.

6. To transport agents from Great Britain to their area of operation by sea or air.

132

7. To maintain and man radio stations with agents in their area of operation.

The tasks of FO II will be:

1. To arrange and carry out courier service from Norway to Sweden and from Sweden to Norway.

2. To organise together with the British travel possibilities from Sweden to England for recruits to the intelligence service.

3. To provide for FD/E and the British possible suitable candidates for this service.

4. To obtain and provide for FD/E and the British appropriate contacts for agents travelling to Norway.

5. To provide and assist FD/E and the British with the establishment and maintenace of radio stations in Norway.

6. To provide and arrange together with the British suitable and advantageous places and reception committees in Norway to receive agents and supplies which have arrived by sea or air.

7. To obtain certain types of supplies for agents and couriers.

The tasks of FD/E will be:

1. Together with the British and FO II to select agents for this service.

2. Together with the British to train these agents in Great Britain.

3. To be responsible for the security consciousness of the agents within Great Britain.

4. To ensure that the agents before they leave Great Britain have received the latest information regarding German counter-espionage activities in the agents' area of operation.[185]

When the OSS began to play a more active role from the beginning of 1944, the above agreement was extended to make the American service responsible for supplying instructors and various types of equipment, while allowing it to receive copies of all agents' reports other than those dealing with naval or shipping matters.[186] It is now time to look at some of the work of the various information-collecting bodies in the field and their use of the Swedish link.

Top priority for British intelligence efforts in Norway was the establishment of a coast-watching service equipped with W/T which would be able to report swiftly and directly to London on the movements of capital ships of the German fleet. It would provide an invaluable complement to the information obtained from Enigma.[187] On the same day that Norwegian forces capitulated to the Germans, contact was established between the SIS Home Station and the station Hardware in Haugesund. The Hardware group had instructions to build up a coast-watching service between Stavanger and Bergen. People were recruited and some 80 messages had been dispatched to the Home Station when disaster struck suddenly on 8 August 1940. The *Abwehr* had managed to penetrate an associated organisation and as a result eighteen members belonging to the Hardware group were arrested.[188]

Hardware's pioneer contribution was to be followed by many others as the SIS strove to build up and maintain its network of radio stations in Norway. Men and equipment were infiltrated into the country by sea, air and (from Sweden) by land. The year-by-year development of SIS operations into Norway is given by Table 4[189] which shows the increasing importance of the Swedish back door in the later stages of the war.

TABLE 4

	Sea	Air	Land	Annual total
1940	4	–	–	4
1941	10	1	1	12
1942	13	8	7	28
1943	13	18	6	37
1944	25	24	25	74
1945	11	10	14	35
Total	76	61	53	190

On 14 January 1942 the *Tirpitz* – the much-feared sister ship to the *Bismarck* – left Wilhelmshaven and for a time the Admiralty in London had no idea where it was until a message came in from the SIS station Theta in Bergen intimating that she lay in Trondheim's fjord.

At that time there was no SIS radio station in Trondheim itself and efforts were now made to repair this gap. In the course of 1942, no fewer than five stations were placed in the Trondheim area and managed to make contact with the Home Station but by the end of the year only one was still operational. This was Scorpion which had been sent in from Stockholm and which managed to maintain contact between 16 May 1942 and May 1943 when it lapsed into silence owing to radio malfunction.[190]

Nearly all Norwegian SIS-operations from Stockholm in the period 1941–42 went to/via Trondheim. Thus in 1942, two transmitters were sent from Stockholm to Trondheim by courier. They were intended for the establishment of two stations, Lyra and Taurus in Northern Norway – another prime target area. Taurus failed to become operational because of technical difficulties but Lyra eventually became part of a chain of seven key coast-watching stations between Lofoten and Alta. Contact was first made with the Home Station on 2 July 1943 and was maintained until 14 June 1944.[191] German signal monitoring, however, managed to get a 'fix' on Lyra and succeeded in capturing the station intact with disastrous consequences for other stations as well. Thereafter an (unsuccessful) attempt was made to make use of Lyra in a *Funkspiel* with the British.

A special mention should be made of the northern station Brunhild which was set up in the last quarter of 1943, conveniently and ambiguously placed on the Norwegian–Swedish frontier, near a spot used as a base (Kari) for courier traffic between Northern Norway and Sweden. The initiative for this station apparently came from the XU organisation which, under the direction of MI II in Stockholm, was busily developing its networks in the Troms region. Intended as a relay station between the northernmost part of Norway and London, no great use of it was made until the summer of 1944. It was then asked to help in the identification of German units being moved from northern Norway to the continent and later after the Soviet–Finnish Armistice, it was called upon to monitor the German evacuation. It was also employed to relay regular weather reports and to carry traffic on behalf of an adjacent SOE base.

An illustration of the very different work undertaken by another secret intelligence group in Norway whose reports were relayed to Stockholm, is to be found in the activities of XU Pan.[192] XU Pan – also known as the 'German group' because its members operated under

135

deep (strong pro-German) cover – was based in Halden near the Swedish border

In the autumn of 1940, the chief of XU Pan, Harry Bjerkebaek got in touch with the printing firm of Harald Haraldssøn in Oslo. Haraldssøn had been approached earlier that summer by a director for *Heidelberger-Gutenberg Druckerei*, which specialised in printing for the German Armed forces with a proposal for co-operation which had been accepted. Haraldssøn was given exclusive rights to printing *Heidelberger-Gutenberg Druckerei* material in Norway. At the same time the firm took charge of the storing of certain confidential matter too sensitive to be actually printed in Norway and which was sent from Germany. As a precaution, special security procedures were introduced at the firm.

These, however, could be surmounted. After discussions with Bjerkebaek, Haraldssøn agreed to supply copies of key material about the German forces to XU Pan which in turn then ensured that the material was forwarded to the Mil II in Stockholm. From there, it was passed to London. The first three or four hundred schedules and forms thus obtained, were of secondary interest but in due course material which was able to supply important clues to military intelligence experts was also obtained. Typical was a German directive dealing with the sea rescue service. At a first glance, this seemed totally unpromising but it was accompanied by a number of sketches showing the territorial organisation of the service. This coincided with the territorial organisation of naval defence. It was therefore concluded that the three services – Army, Navy and Air Force – were divided into the same zones and co-ordinated under one command.

The undramatic piece-by-piece nature of much crucial intelligence work was summed up by Alfred Roscher Lund in commenting on the importance of the Naval Catalogue which came in from Haraldssøn via XU Pan:

> Finding out the strength of the enemy, which is one of the greatest tasks of intelligence, is a gigantic jigsaw puzzle. But in this case, one got to know a considerable amount about the structure of the naval staff, more or less for free. The strength could be found out partly by direct computation and partly by studying the organisation of the enemy. Regarding this point, there was also help forthcoming. Fighting strength can also be

calculated by seeing which people are placed in various positions. Shipyard and workshop capacity is one of the crucial determinants of fighting strength and this could be partly ascertained through the catalogue. One has to know the whole organism in order to fight rationally against it: the Staff is its nerve system. Once one had all the addresses, the nerve system was mapped. In addition the function of the offices could be derived from the catalogue. The Naval Catalogue aroused admiration in British intelligence circles. It became a textbook example to which all who worked with these things, returned.[193]

XU Pan was not solely concerned with the link to the printer's. It gathered material from all over the Østfold province which it then dispatched to the MI-II office in Stockholm. Reports were photographed on 35 mm film and sent undeveloped so that any information on it would be destroyed if opened carelessly by prying eyes. At the end of the war, microdots were used. R34 provided an example of how a Dane with permission to travel to and fro between the Reich and Sweden, was able to act as an agent for Allied intelligence. Norwegians were also able to assist in this way as the assignment of Sverre Bergh shows.

Bergh was a young Norwegian studying at the Technical High School in Dresden. After his uncle, Theo Findahl, who was a newspaper correspondent in Berlin, had drawn his attention to the ball bearing factories in Schweinfurt, Bergh decided to make an on-the-spot investigation and subsequently a report was written on the basis of his findings. When he returned to Norway, Bergh gave his report to a friend who saw to it that it reached Øistein Strømnaes of XU for forwarding to London. Pleased with the efforts of the young man, Strømnaes persuaded him to return to Germany as an agent for the Allied intelligence services.

On his way back to Germany, Bergh stopped off in Gothenburg in Sweden where he was briefed by an SIS representative about his mission. His task was to make contact with the physicist Dr Paul Rosbaud in Berlin.[194] When finally the scheduled meeting took place, Rosbaud told the young Norwegian of the work being done at Peenemunde on rocket research. Although the German physicist knew a great deal about the research there, supplementary information was needed about the exact positioning of buildings at the research site and Bergh was sent to Peenemunde to acquire it. When he returned to Berlin, a joint report was prepared. One of Theo Findahl's friends who was serving at the Swedish Legation in Berlin, agreed to forward the report via the diplomatic bag to Stockholm where it was then handed over to Bergh's SIS contact.

An example of a clandestine network operating inside Norway independently of the XU organisation and sending its reports to the Norwegian authorities in Sweden, is provided by RMO. This network was set up by Andreas Rygg in the spring of 1942 at the suggestion of Hans Peder Henriksen, the Norwegian naval attaché in Stockholm.[195] Its job was to provide a naval and harbour reporting service and an experienced council of people in Norway was appointed to advise and oversee the work of the group. Like XU, RMO consisted of a number of district sections which reported to a centre in Oslo. The organisation had its own courier services.

In addition to reports specially collected in Norway by special secret organisations, another important source of intelligence available to the Norwegian authorities in Sweden was provided by the interrogation of Norwegian refugees arriving in the country. The annual number of Norwegians seeking refuge in Sweden is given in Table 5.[196]

TABLE 5

Year	Refugees arriving from Norway
1941	2,981
1942	7,626
1943	9,267
1944	16,088
1945	10,222

In order to cope with this influx, the Swedes set up reception centres, first at Öreryd and later at Kjesäter. From the summer of 1941, both the Norwegian Military and Press Offices gained Swedish permission for their representatives to attend interrogations at Öreryd.

Another quite separate problem posed by the new arrivals was the possible infiltration of enemy informers and agents of the German secret services. The task of screening was the responsibility of the Legal Office in collaboration with the Swedish authorities. Suspects had their Norwegian passports withdrawn. Their residence in Sweden was liable to certain restrictions and they could be held in detention centres for varying lengths of time. However, in some instances, rather than risk a dangerous infiltrator escaping from Sweden and informing the German authorities in Norway, it was preferred to send the person to Britain where they could be interned and more safely put out of harm's way.

Some Czech activities. It is interesting to note that a number of reports emanating from A54, the Czech Intelligence Service's star source within the *Abwehr*, were relayed to London via Stockholm.[197] The activities of the Vanek group also throw light on the type of information being passed to General Moravec, the head of the Czech service. Some of this was of the routine type:

> Northwest Prostejov between Stkovicka Prehada and Kostelec. Airfield. 7 hectares. 400 aircraft. Training place. Bombers and Messerschmitts. Flight group 4. Generaloberst Loesch. Usually flies to Russia.
> 2 kilometres from Vsetin (direction Cab . . .) ammunition factory hidden in valley. 1,200 workers. 2 shifts. Grenades. Mines.[198]

Other reports contained interesting evaluations of the general situation:

> In the investigation of the mood of the labour force it is impossible to ignore the fact that the new régime has provided it with considerable advantages: unemployment has decreased, the worker enjoys greater security in relation to his employer than before and every employer now negotiates with the workers in a more cautious and considerate fashion than was the case during the Republic. (March 1942)[199]

and it was noted in a telegram of 9 March 1942:

> Exhortations to sabotage are unnecessary. No one can undertake it. Particularly the workers. Only one thing is required: to bomb. People are annoyed because they have not done so. The Skoda works are weakly defended. Best time from Saturday to Sunday.[200]

In the same month, a telegram was sent claiming that glass bombs filled with gas were being transported to Riga. This was passed on to the British:

I have given the message about gas in Riga to the brothers and someone has carried it over. Now they are anxious to publicise it and need to communicate something. I have said: only via me. Let me have your view.[201]

The use of some of the material collected by the Czechs for Psychological Warfare purposes was also illustrated in Threlfall's activities. Certain information picked up by the Czechs and passed over to Threlfall by Walter Taub, eventually found its way into the letters circulated by the SOE operative. (See p. 65.)

Among the Vanek group's telegrams, there were also reports about miscellaneous Swedish matters and reports originating from Swedish sources. A telegram of 25 November 1941, spoke of an agreement whereby 200 lorries would be placed at Finland's disposal for the delivery of wooden barracks and goods purchased in Sweden; a telegram around the same time noted that the German General Staff planned to take Leningrad in January 1942 and cited as its ultimate source for this information, the 'Swedish military attaché in Berlin'; a telegram dated 26 January 1942, observed that Prince Eugen had confirmed that the Germans were exerting pressure to get rid of the Social Democrats in the government and replace them with Governor Nothin and General Thörnell; on 16 September 1941, it was reported that the Swedes were negotiating with the British about a possible common action in the event of a British landing in Norway. There were also telegrams which took up more delicate matters such as a proposed operation together with the British to suborn a member of the German Legation staff in Stockholm.

Some Polish activities.[202]   It will be recalled that Colonel Rudnicki, a confidant of General Sikorski, had been assigned the task in Stockholm of setting up an underground channel of communication between the Home Army and the government-in-exile in London. But in addition certain quite independent covert operations were mounted from the Swedish capital.

In pre-war Poland, military intelligence work was the responsibility of the Second Section of the General Staff. It consisted of six departments, one of which was devoted to secret service. This latter department had in turn two sub-departments, R under Captain Niezbrzycki directed against Soviet Russia and Z under Major Switkowski, directed against Germany. Among the officers attached to Z was Cavalry Captain Waclaw Gilewicz. He had been asked by Henryk Zychon, the head of Sector III O of the Intelligence Service in Poznan to take over the running of a highly important Polish agent within Germany. This was Wiktor Katlewski (codename Victor), who was employed in the *Marinewaffenamt*. Working through a cutout, 'Sontag', productive contact was successfully maintained with Victor. When, however, the Germans marched into Warsaw in 1939, documents which should have been destroyed fell into their hands and Victor was executed on 19 August 1940 at Lichtenberg.

Another agent inherited by Gilewicz from Zychon was 'Marcz'. He had been born in Berlin and had trained as an advocate. After certain financial improprieties, he was given the alternative of serving a term in prison or working for Zychon and chose the latter. He was duly furnished with false papers and sent to Germany where he was installed in a commision dealing with German–Polish currency questions. When in 1937, 2,000 Marks went missing, a German police investigation was mounted and suspicions fell on Marcz. Pressure was now put on him to work for the German security authorities and he was asked to name key Polish intelligence personnel in Germany. Marcz, however, managed to warn Gilewicz who made his escape back to Warsaw via Czechoslovakia.

It was now decided to send Gilewicz to Denmark. One of his first contacts there was the journalist Sven Dalhof-Nielsen, who had published articles on Poland. Through Dalhof-Nielsen, Gilewicz was put in touch with Hans Lunding, who had a leading role in Danish Intelligence.[203] The Danish and Polish services exchanged information about Germany on a regular basis. On 29 August 1939, Gilewicz was notified by Lunding of the imminent German attack on Poland. This warning came from a Danish officer serving in Germany.

At the same time as enjoying cordial relations with the host intelligence service, Gilewicz developed other sources of his own. One of these was a citizen of Danzig called Gunther Prey, who was involved in the arms business in several countries of Europe.[204] Prey was then living in Denmark. When the Germans refused to renew his passport, Prey was threatened with becoming stateless and having to leave the country. The Poles now provided him with a passport and in return Prey supplied Gilewicz every four weeks with information about German shipping in Scandinavia. At the same time Prey was able to act as an intermediary for Gilewicz. In this way contact was made with a Norwegian employed in a shipyard in Germany, where submarines were built. The Norwegian turned out to be a useful source and led to a combined covert operation involving the Danish, Polish and French secret services. Captain Mørch of Danish intelligence devised an appropriate questionnaire and the French agreed to contribute to the funding of the operation.

After the defeat of Poland, Gilewicz was called to Paris where he was ordered to take over the running of the Stockholm Station in succession to Captain Firla. In Sweden he would have the special task of co-operating with the Japanese. Gilewicz was then presented to the Japanese resident in Paris and furnished with the requisite introduction to Colonel Toshio Nishimura, the Japanese military attaché in Stockholm.

Various contacts between the Japanese and Polish intelligence services already existed based on a mutual interest in Russia. Thus Captain Alfons Jakubaniec and Lieutenant Daskiewicz who belonged to the Polish counter-espionage department in Kaunas in Lithuania, co-operated with the Japanese Consul General, Sugihara, in collecting information about Soviet garrisons near the German border. Later Jakubaniec and Daskiewicz would form important members of the Polish intelligence network within Germany itself, with Daskiewicz ('Perz') based in Königsberg and Jakubaniec ('Kuncewicz') in Berlin.

At the beginning of 1940, Gilewicz arrived in the Swedish capital with diplomatic cover as Second Secretary at the Polish Legation. Contact was made with the Japanese military attaché, Nishimura, who proved to be much cooler towards the Nazis than some of his Berlin colleagues and it was agreed to extend their exchange agreement to cover intelligence about Germany. Nishimura also provided valuable information about German military and diplomatic personnel in Stockholm and about iron ore shipments from Sweden to Germany.

The Polish–Japanese link was to be further strengthened with the arrival in Stockholm in 1940 of Major Michal Rybikowski ('Piotr Iwanow'). The original intention had been for Rybikowski to take charge of intelligence activities in the Baltic States and for this purpose, with the backing of the Japanese resident in Riga, Colonel Onouchi, he had acquired cover in the form of a Manchuko pass made out in the name of Piotr Iwanow, ostensibly a White Russian and suitably endorsed by the Finnish police. With the Russians poised to enter Riga, Rybikowski alias Iwanow withdrew across the Baltic to Stockholm.

In the summer of 1940, Nishimura travelled to Berlin where he managed to persuade the ambassador to employ Jakubaniec. The latter was given his own room and more importantly had the possibility of sending his reports by diplomatic bag to the Japanese Legation in Stockholm. At the same time, Jakubianec was told to be extra careful in Berlin and to avoid any type of intelligence work until it was certain that the German security authorities had bought his story: there were to be no contacts with the Polish Resistance movement.

No sooner had this Polish covert channel of communication, Berlin–Stockholm, been set up than it was announced that Colonel Nishimura was to be transferred to Manchuria. His place as the Japanese military attaché was to be taken by General Makoto Onodera, who had served in Riga and was on friendly terms with Major Feliks Brzeskwinski, the Polish military attaché who had been stationed in Latvia at the same time Although Nishimura had warned the Poles about saying too much to the new Japanese Resident about their intelligence work against the Germans, co-operation continued harmoniously after the change. Piotr Iwanow was duly installed as instructor and interpreter to the Japanese Minister and as such enjoyed diplomatic immunity as 'the Japanese Minister's servant as by law established'.

In addition to co-operating with the Japanese, the Stockholm Station also established an intelligence network drawing its reports via the Polish consulates in the major Swedish ports. Thus the task in Malmö was mainly to observe German ship movement through the Sound. Communications between Stockholm and Malmö were maintained either via courier or by the use of the ordinary post and telephone service where a special code was employed in the hope of foxing unintended listeners or readers.[205]

After the fall of France, co-operation with the SIS via one of its Stockholm representatives, Sidney Smith, became close and the British were responsible for the funding of part of the Polish network.[206] Individual agents, with specialised tasks different from those of the shipping groups, also reported to Gilewicz and Rybikowski.

While the full range of the activities of the Stockholm Station was only partially known to the Swedish security authorities, its leading officers, despite their attempts at cover, were systematically identified and their movements and contacts were watched. As early as 1938, the

Swedes had learned that a Polish intelligence officer calling himself Michailsky had tried to recruit a Swedish agent of Polish descent for work in Germany. At the end of 1939, it was reported that this Michailsky had been recognised in the street in Stockholm and eventually it was suspected that Piotr Iwanow, Michailsky and Michal were one and the same person. Similarly, the police received a tip in the spring of 1940 that a man called Walter Gürtler was the head of Polish intelligence in Stockholm. Further investigation led to the conclusion that Walter Gürtler was none other than Gilewicz.

One consequence of the intensified surveillance was the arrest in the summer of three Polish citizens, who were subsequently sentenced on a charge of espionage. At the time of the arrest, there were grounds for believing that one of those convicted was on the way to a meeting with Gilewicz. A further important break for the Security Service occurred in the autumn of 1940 when certain draft copies of a number of intelligence reports emanating from the Polish consulate in Malmö intended for Gilewicz, came into the hands of the police. These contained information dealing both with Sweden and with, practically speaking, every contingent territory. Telephone and postal control was now sharpened: certain coded telephone conversations and letters were disentangled and further evidence of information-gathering activities contrary to the stipulations of Chapter 8 of the Penal Code was obtained.

It became clear that Gilewicz was in regular contact with Ziembiewicz at the Polish Consulate in Malmö. The latter in turn controlled a number of agents. On 13 March 1941, two seamen belonging to the group were detained by the police in Malmö and a couple of days later a third agent was also arrested in Trelleborg upon his return from a trip to Germany. Further investigation revealed that this third man had been recruited in 1939 and that he had been given the task of infiltrating National Socialist circles and for this purpose had joined a local party organisation in Malmö. After the outbreak of war, he had undertaken a number of trips to Germany where he collected information of military interest. He had also received instruction in the use of invisible ink. His later work had concentrated on the collection of information about German vessels passing Öresund. He was subsequently sentenced to hard labour for one year and six months. As a result of this and other cases, the Swedish authorities withdrew the compromised Gilewicz's diplomatic immunity and he was flown to Britain.

The year 1941 also witnessed a severe blow to the efforts of Polish intelligence in Germany and the occupied areas. Despite the danger involved, Kuncewicz in Berlin had been activated. It was arranged for a Polish courier with a German national passport to travel several times to Berlin where contact was made with the cook, Janina Lapinska, at the Manchuko Legation. She in turn passed the material received to the Japanese attaché Yamada's secretary, Kuncewicz, who then forwarded it to Piotr Iwanow at Onodera's office in Stockholm. At the beginning of July, German intelligence became aware of this link, when over 100 microfilms containing detailed maps and encrypted information about German military forces in the general *gouvernement*, were seized. The principals involved were watched and on 6 July 1941, Kuncewicz was arrested. His true identity as the Polish intelligence officer, Jakubianiec, his contact with Iwanow via the Japanese and Stockholm's function as a collection point for Polish intelligence became clear.[207]

It remained for the German authorities to put a stop to Iwanow's activities in Stockholm. Some thought was given to exchanging Widén and Lagerberg, two of the Warsaw Swedes held by the Germans, for Iwanow, but without result. At the same time pressure was put on Onodera to get rid of his Polish assistant. From time to time Dr Wagner, the chief of *Abwehr* in Stockholm, tried to persuade his Japanese colleague to hand over Iwanow to the Germans and representations also came from Oshima in Berlin. But Onodera refused to budge: he valued Iwanow too highly as a source of information about Russia and Germany to dispense with his services. Thus at the conference of Japanese military attachés in Berlin in February 1941, Onodera – according his own later statement – was the only member present to insist that the next German target would be to the East, not England. His view regarding this matter, he declared, had been based upon the information received from Iwanow, in particular his accurate description of the disposition of German Army units in Poland and the enormous numbers of coffins which had been accumulated there.

Despite the fact that Poland and Japan were allied with opposing belligerents, co-operation in intelligence matters continued.[208] How far the Poles went behind the backs of their Japanese colleagues to gain information about Germany and how far the Japanese themselves simply turned a blind eye to these activities, remains unclear.

In Stockholm, Iwanow remained in Onodera's service until January 1944, supplying information to the Western Allies through Major Brzeskwinski, the Polish military attaché. His departure for Britain was brought about by the arrest of one of his agents in Stockholm.[209] This was a German Jewish girl who had been dismissed from her secretarial position in Stockholm after German pressure. Eventually she acquired a new post in the office of a company engaged in shipping ore. But before this, she had met Iwanow through a Polish acquaintance. This agent was able to assist Iwanow in a number of ways. First of all, she supplied regular reports concerning the shipment of various types of ore (zinc, lead, iron) to Germany and the occupied territories from Sweden; second she picked up through her friends and contacts various bits of information which were useful for political warfare purposes; and lastly, she was able to introduce Iwanow to other potential agents. In this way, Iwanow made the acquaintance of a member of the Cultural Department of the German Legation who provided much miscellaneous inside information, including a list of Germans who in the event of an Allied Victory would pretend never to have been Nazis.

1944 was also to see the departure of another Polish intelligence officer, Colonel Edmund Piotrowski, who, it will be recalled, had become head of station Anna in 1941. With a principal responsibility for the collection of political intelligence, Piotrowski made adroit use of various humanitarian activities as a covert channel of communication. In addition, he was able to recruit a number of seamen employed on the Baltic run for diverse courier services and general reporting. One such contact was to be his undoing.[210]

After the interception of a letter from the port of Luleå on the Gulf of Bothnia to a poste restante address in Stockholm, a cutout employed by Piotrowski was apprehended by the Swedish police. Soon other people were pulled in, including one of Piotrowski's principal agents. On 20 June it was the turn of Piotrowski himself. After making his statement, he was released and was flown to England the same evening.

Intelligence collected by various branches of the Allied intelligence services: further miscellaneous examples

Economic intelligence. The covert collection of information, which in Britain was the traditional prerogative of SIS, was in the United States of America entrusted to the newly formed OSS. In the autumn of 1943, a major air offensive against the German ball-bearing industry had started with raids on Schweinfurt in August and October. At the same time, the OSS in Sweden began to monitor the export of ball bearings from SKF to Germany.[211] For this purpose, contact was made through a cutout with a man working in the office of the company in Gothenburg. It was explained that information was required about SKF's production: the number of crated goods dispatched, the weight of the crates, the type of ball bearing involved, the destination and the delivery route. The man who had been approached agreed to help and with the assistance of another person at SKF was able to deliver a first report.

The main burden of these enquiries was to try to discover if various loopholes had occurred.[212] Thus it was suggested that although Sweden had agreed to reduce ball-bearing deliveries to Germany, one could still suspect that SKF within the agreed quotas were able to vary the type and dimensions according to German wishes and needs. The important thing was not so much the *quantities* of goods shipped but rather their *qualitative* features. At the same time, a watch was kept on the dispatch of machine tools (e.g. special lathes). This confidential reporting from inside sources within the company continued until 27 May 1944 when the principals involved were arrested by the police.

Weapon intelligence. At an early stage of the war, British Intelligence had received important clues about German work on rockets. After an apparent lull, the question of the German rocket programme acquired new urgency at the end of 1942, when a telegram from the SIS in Stockholm spoke of a rocket containing five tons of explosive with a maximum range of 200 kilometres and capable of inflicting damage over an area of 10 square kilometres. Whereas in the majority of cases involving SIS, the exact mechanics of the collection of a significant piece of information remain obscure or wholly unknown, the origin of this particular important telegram can be reconstructed with a reliable degree of accuracy.[213]

In the spring of 1941, the Dane Andreasen (R34) who has been mentioned above and who had business interests in industrial chemicals, met a Hungarian engineer called Szenasy at the Vienna Trade Fair. The two men got on well together and as a consequence their business and personal ties were gradually strengthened. At the time of this first meeting, Szenasy was working as a technical journalist. Later in 1942, he became the German representative of various Hungarian firms, with an office at Hektorstrasse 7 in Berlin-Hallensee and it was in Berlin that Andreasen again met him at the end of 1942 during a business trip. During one of their conversations, Szenasy mentioned to the Dane that the Germans were developing a weapon which could be decisive for the outcome of the war: it was a rocket of devastating effect with a range of 200 kilometres.

Shortly after his meeting with Szenasy in Berlin, Andreasen travelled to Stockholm where he was cross-examined by Cheshire and Hampton about his conversation with the Hungarian. The Dane now agreed to try to ensure that the link to Szenasy was maintained. As a result, Szenasy was able to supply two further reports enlarging on what he knew about the rocket, its construction, guidance and destructive potential. At the same time, the Hungarian's reliability as an agent was checked by asking him to supply information about production at the Messerschmitt factory at Augsburg. Szenasy apparently continued to supply information to the SIS in Stockholm until the end of 1943.

On 22 August 1943, an experimental V-1 rocket fell on Bornholm, the Danish island in the Baltic. The local Danish Naval Officer-in-Charge, Lieutenant Commander Hasager Christiansen was quickly on the spot and managed to sketch and note down the details of the rocket, before the Germans had a chance to seal the place off. His report was sent to Commodore Paul Mørch, the senior naval representative of Danish Intelligence. A microfilmed version was now prepared in Copenhagen and copies were dispatched to Ebbe Munck in Stockholm by two different routes, one via Helsingør-Hälsingborg, the other via Malmö. On the Helsingør route, things went wrong. The courier was subjected to a search. The microfilm was discovered and developed, when the importance of its contents became clear. As a result of this discovery, Commander Christiansen was interrogated and tortured. However the other copy of the report reached Munck in Stockholm safely.

In the summer of 1944, stray missiles from Peenemünde which crashed in Sweden itself, were to prove of great interest to British scientific intelligence, engaged in charting the progress of German technology in this field. On 16 April, an important first report of a V-1 rocket in flight came from the British naval attaché in Stockholm. The data in this report and its successors was to become clear, however, only after British investigators at the end of May had been given permission by the Swedish authorities to examine the wreckage of two pilotless aircraft which had crashed in the country.

On 14 June, the British air attaché in Stockholm sent a telegram to London with information that a rocket had crashed in Sweden, making a crater several metres wide and one and a half metres deep. More interestingly a week later, he was noting that it was furnished with a 'turbo-compressor' and different from other weapons that had previously landed there. Alerted to the fact that a new type of weapon was involved, two officers from Air Technical Intelligence were dispatched to Sweden. The weapon turned out to be a wingless rocket, much larger than a V-1. It was directionally controlled by vanes and by radio and was estimated to carry a warhead of not less than five tons. The various remains from the crashed rocket, after agreement with the Swedes, were flown to Britain for further analysis at Farnborough.

Another area of scientific research, which was covertly monitored by the British in Stockholm, was German work on nuclear fission. One of the pioneers in that sphere, Lise Meitner, formerly of the Kaiser Wilhelm Institute in Berlin, had been compelled to leave Germany as a non-Aryan and had found a position at Professor Manne Siegbahn's Institute of Physics in Stockholm. With Meitner in Stockholm and Bohr in Copenhagen and with the maintenance of contacts between scientists in Sweden and their opposite numbers in German controlled Europe, Sweden offered a valuable flow of information about German developments which remained to be tapped. In September 1941, a young Norwegian scientist called Njål Hole had escaped to Sweden. There he was approached by Professor Leif Tronstad, who persuaded him to get a position at a Swedish research institute where he would be in a position to keep track of what was going on.[214] Because of his previous experience, Hole managed to obtain a post with the cyclotron group in Siegbahn's laboratory. This brought him into daily contact with Meitner. Any information that Hole picked up, was channelled through Major Ørnulf Dahl of Norwegian Intelligence, to London. According to the official history, the SIS was still receiving Hole's reports in 1943.

A worrying security aspect of the race for the atom bomb was Niels Bohr's continued presence in Copenhagen. In the autumn of 1941, two leading German physicists, Werner Heisenberg and C. F. von Weizsäcker, had visited Copenhagen. In private conversation with Bohr, Heisenberg had brought up the question of the military application of atomic energy. In January 1943, the British authorities decided to try to persuade the Danish scientist to leave, and a microfilmed message concealed in a bunch of keys was sent via Stockholm to Bohr, inviting the Danish scientist to come to Britain. Although Bohr dragged his heels for a few months, he eventually accepted the invitation. The details of his flight were arranged by Svend Truelson of Danish Intelligence and after a relatively smooth crossing on a fishing boat, he managed to arrive safely in Sweden before the Gestapo had begun their operation against the Danish Jews on the night of 1/2 October 1943.

Signals intelligence. In 1940, Polish servicemen in a Swedish internment camp, were provided with the requisite equipment and instructed to monitor German military radio traffic from stations in Norway and the Baltic States. Not all these stations could be intercepted in England. This Sigint operation resulted in a series of monthly and fortnightly reports which were transmitted to England in cipher until the middle of 1943 when it was discontinued after the intervention of the Swedish authorities.[215]

DECEPTION

The Norwegian feint

The transmission of information and rumour designed to mislead the enemy is also part of the war of wits. In Britain, the overall responsibility for the framing of strategic deception schemes lay with the London Controlling Section (LCS). In the course of its career, LCS was to toy with a number of schemes designed to get the Germans to believe that a large-scale British operation against Norway was imminent. In 1944, Graffham was put into effect with the intention of getting the Swedish authorities to swallow this idea in the hope that this would in turn cause suitable perturbations in intelligence evaluations in Berlin. To this end, the British Minister in Stockholm, Mallet, was expected on his return to Sweden at the end of March 1944 after having been briefed in London, to approach the Swedish government with various requests designed to strengthen the view that Norway had been targetted. The requests were for: (a) the right to refuel aircraft which had made emergency landings after operating over enemy territory; (b) facilities for minor repairs of damaged aircraft (maximum time allowed 48 hours); (c) permission for PRUs (photographic reconnaissance units) to operate over Sweden; and (d) permission to send transport experts to confer with their Swedish counterparts regarding transport of supplies to Sweden and Norway in the event of a German withdrawal. Requests (c) and (d) were put to the Ministry for Foreign Affairs on 4 April 1944. However it was decided to delay pressing (a) and (b), and owing to an alteration in the Swedish regulations regarding the emergency landing of foreign military aircraft, it was eventually decided to drop them altogether.

The requests presented by Mallet were buttressed by various other manoeuvres: the visit of a former British Air Attaché at the Stockholm Legation, now suitably elevated to Air-Vice-Marshal, to give the impression that something was under way;[216] the rigging of Norwegian securities; and at the right moment an orchestrated increase in signal traffic between Stockholm and London. Nor did the play-acting cease when Overlord was finally launched on 6 June.[217] Graffham continued to trundle on, provoking some headscratching at the Ministry for Foreign Affairs in Stockholm where the older pieces of the puzzle were fetched out to see if they could be fitted together to form the total picture. On 8 June, the British and American Ministers had visited Boheman to elicit his personal assurance that Sweden would refuse any German demand to allow the transit of their troops in the event of an Allied invasion of Norway. Sven Grafström, the Deputy Head of the Political Department of the Ministry, noted in his diary:

> Boheman gave unhesitatingly such a promise. He interpreted the peculiar démarche as a warning about an imminent attack on the Germans in Norway and I believe that he is right. There is undeniably a whole host of factors which indicate that one of the further invasion operations expected will be aimed in that direction.[218]

And what were these factors according to Grafström? There was the curious British submission of 4 April, later supported by the Americans and the Russians; there was Brigadier Menton, the transport expert; there was Thornton's mysterious appearance on the scene: 'No one could fully understand the purpose behind his "tourist trip" to Sweden.'[219] There was also a final factor. There had been many personal letters from the Swedish Legation in Berlin indicating alarm at the prospect of Allied operations against Norway or Denmark. 'The Legation had been informed that the German authorities would not hesitate to attack Sweden if they were faced with an imminent Allied operation, especially against Norway.'[220]

Opinions about the concrete success of Graffham differ, as they do about other other operations such as Solo 1 and Fortitude North.[221] It is clear that the professionals at *Fremde Heere West* were not taken in by the Scandinavian red herring. At the same time, Hitler himself constantly worried about an attack on his northern flank and if the 'Norwegian Feint' deception operations did not specifically raise the level of apprehension above its normally heightened state, they certainly in a general sense helped to keep the pot boiling. So too at the agent level, did the use of SIBS as the following example illustrates.

On 7 May 1942, Dr Wagner, Head of the *Abwehr* in Sweden, reported to his superiors that he had been informed by a source 'working in English propaganda' that the press attaché at the British Legation, Tennant, had returned to Stockholm after a four-week visit to England with a general plan for British propaganda in Sweden to pave the way for a possible invasion of Norway.[222] During May and until 15 June, every method was to be employed to emphasise the frightfulness of the situation in Norway. Bit by bit, reference would be made to a possible British invasion as a means of assisting the Norwegians. If such an invasion involved the infringement of Swedish territory, this was to be explained away as an inevitable consequence of German military operations. At the same time, Swedish assistance to Germany, it was to be stressed, was dependent on the fact that Germany bought so much iron ore and after 15 June it should be advocated quite openly that the British ought actively to intervene to put an end to unneutral Swedish transport. If by 15 June, a British invasion of Northern Norway had taken place, the press were to support it by every possible means so that people would be ready to accept the transit of troops through Northern Sweden in order to attack German forces in Finland.

Dr Wagner's informant noted that the British press attaché had brought back with him a large number of photographs purporting to show British troops in action in different places in Northern Norway. In the event of an invasion, these photographs were to be distributed in the Swedish press.

Deception in the service of economic warfare

In order to determine German petrol and oil production, a bogus plan for building an oil refinery in Sweden was evolved by OSS with the object of attracting the interest of influential Germans. In October 1944, E. S. Erickson, an American–Swedish businessman who was in touch with Walter Surrey of the American Legation in Stockholm, undertook an eleven-day trip throughout Germany, purportedly for the purpose of engaging in negotiations about the proposed refinery. This allowed a first-hand survey to be made of the entire German synthetic oil industry. Upon Erickson's return, he provided Surrey with detailed reports concerning German petrol production, the places where aeroplane fuel was produced, the location of new plants for the manufacture of synthetic fuel, and the effects of Allied bombing on the petrol factories. These reports provided the Allies with innumerable bombing targets.[223]

Naval deception

In the war in the Pacific – particularly in the early stages – it was desirable to persuade the Japanese that certain warships had been concentrated at a particular base, even though in fact they might still be in service elsewhere. The use of dummy ships, a device used against the Germans in Europe, was not a practical proposition and other ways of deceiving the Japanese had to be found. The Director of Naval Intelligence decided that Stockholm should be one of the places to mount such a deception campaign and the services of Iwanow were enlisted for this purpose.[224] The deception scheme was judged to be a success. Iwanow was able to supply photographic proof that the desired messages had been passed from Stockholm to Tokyo and this could be independently confirmed by the Admiralty in another way. Later it became known to the Admiralty that the enemy had also acted on the information received and in this way Japanese aircraft carriers were on occasions contained in a certain area on the (false) assumption that an opposing force was preparing to threaten them.

Poacher's perspective – 2

CONTINGENCY PLANNING AND COAST WATCHING

In 1935, German military intelligence – the *Abwehr* – sounded out various foreign services about possible spheres of co-operation in the acquisition of information about the Soviet Union. To this end, the new head of the service, Admiral Canaris, visited Hungary in April of that year and in the summer, a Hungarian officer went to Berlin to continue discussions.[1] By the autumn, potentially useful contacts had also been established with two other services. The head of Estonian intelligence approached Canaris with an offer of co-operation on Russia in return for German financial and technical support and in October, the Japanese military attaché in Berlin, Major-General Hiroshi Oshima, joined the list of those willing to pool resources in collecting intelligence about the Soviet Union.[2]

As a Baltic power, Sweden had also an obvious interest in peering behind the Russian veil. During a visit to Berlin in the autumn of 1936, Lieutenant-Colonel Helge Jung, the Head of the Foreign Section of the Swedish General Staff, had discussions with Canaris which paved the way for German–Swedish intelligence co-operation regarding the sharing of information about Eastern Europe in general and about the Baltic states in particular.[3] In the spring of the following year, this co-operation was confirmed by the visit of the future head of Swedish Military Intelligence, Colonel Adlercreutz, to Canaris in Berlin.[4] At the same time, permission was obtained for a Swedish officer to study *Abwehr* techniques in Germany and Major Thorwald Lindquist, who was subsequently to head Swedish military counter-espionage, was selected for the task.[5]

At the spring meeting with Adlercreutz, Canaris had been at pains to insist that there would be no German agent activity directed against Sweden itself. This was perhaps easier said than done. Nor indeed would this polite assurance be relevant from the viewpoint of later Swedish espionage legislation.[6]

The German Intelligence Service was busy with contingency planning in other parts of Scandinavia as well. In July 1937, Captain Benecke was dispatched to Norway to spy out what the British and Russians were up to in that part of the world and in the Autumn of the following year, he was appointed head of *Abwehr* in Norway with cover as an assistant commercial attaché.[7] In June 1938, another counter-espionage officer also paid a short visit to Norway and Sweden. His task was to recruit people in Norway and Sweden willing to forward agent reports sent from enemy countries to Germany.[8]

Meanwhile a coast-watching service had been set up in Denmark, keeping an eye on visitors and vessels and ready to switch to more intensive activity in the event of war.[9] It was directed by Captain Pflug-Hartung, a former German naval officer with a chequered career. In the autumn of 1919, he had fled from Germany to Sweden in fear of his life, widely suspected of having had a part in the murder of Karl Liebknecht.[10] In 1931, after his involvement in the supply of arms to an ultra-right defence corps became public, he was forced to leave Sweden, going first to Norway, where his presence in the country caused a protest from the Norwegian Labour Party and thence to Denmark.[11] In Copenhagen, making use of a commercial front, he scooped up reports from the coast watchers and at the same time collected information about German refugees in the Danish capital.[12]

While coastal nets were being formed in Denmark (and as will be seen elsewhere) a book appeared which although certainly designed to serve a propaganda purpose, also provided a glimpse into German perceptions about possible scenarios in the Scandinavian peninsula. This was Vitalis Pantenburg's *Rußlands Griff um Nordeuropa*. Treading a path already to some extent prepared by Sven Hedin's pre-First World War pamphlet *Ett varningsord* and much influenced by geopolitics, Pantenburg emphasised the threat posed to Scandinavia by an expansive Russia's need to have access to the oceans. This need had stimulated interest in the further exploitation of the ice-free conditions in the Murmansk area and had thereby generated a new field of force in the North which put at risk the security of neighbouring Scandinavian territories. According to Pantenburg, Murmansk and the immediately adjacent coast was insufficient for

Russian needs. From this, in his view, there arose a natural Russian drive towards Norway's Atlantic coastline. It was this increased interest which explained Soviet espionage in northern Norway and the ominous flight of unidentified aircraft over these northern regions.[13] The Communist sympathies of the local population in addition made the area an easy prey for the professional agitators of the Comintern. At the same time, Norwegian defence was in a poor state. Pantenburg did not forget to observe that any Soviet advance would have other consequences as well: the northern iron ore supplies would fall to the aggressor and the caption to an illustration of Narvik which appeared in the book, noted that in a future war the port would undoubtedly play a significant role.[14]

The Danish authorities intervened against Pflug-Hartung and his associates at the end of 1938. However, important coastal nets were busy elsewhere in Scandinavia. A crucial part in co-ordinating their work was played by Admiral Steffan, the German naval attaché in Stockholm.[15]

Steffan had come to the notice of the Swedish Security Authorities in October 1939, when a shipping agent in Sundsvall, the Swedish port on the Gulf of Bothnia, reported that he had been asked by the attaché whether in the event of a war between Germany and Russia, he would be prepared to supply information about Soviet vessels visiting the port. In December, an employee of a merchant house in Gothenburg was detained and later confessed to collecting on behalf of Germany information about cargoes destined for England. In addition he had made enquiries about the manufacture and export of goods from Bofors and had also recruited other agents. For these offences, he was sentenced to one year and four months' hard labour. Gradually it became clear that it was Steffan who was responsible for directing the work of the group.

Steffan was, however, far from being concerned only with the running of agents within Sweden. It was also in October 1939 that a Swedish skipper had been arrested in Kristianssand in Norway and had confessed to being an agent of Steffan, charged with keeping a watch on the movements of British ships to and from Norwegian ports. Working closely together, the Norwegian and Swedish security authorities were able to identify other main participants in the coast-watching groups.

One of Steffan's sources was Karl Müller, a graduate engineer resident in Narvik. Müller represented the ore purchasing division of one of the large German steel combines and was able to come and go on the ore quays of the Norwegian port without drawing attention to himself. He had come to Narvik from Luleå and it was in this Swedish port that he had first encountered Steffan in 1934 at a supper party given by the German Consul. At that time, the naval attaché seemed mainly concerned with the possibility of a conflict between Germany and the Soviet Union and was anxious to recruit someone to keep an eye on things in that part of the world and to monitor the activities of local Communists. Thus began Müller's career as an intelligence volunteer. In April 1939, he moved to Narvik and here his instructions from Steffan were to note the arrival and departure of ore boats bound for England. After the outbreak of war, additional precautions were taken to ensure the security and efficiency of their lines of communication. Müller found himself being supplied with two bottles of invisible ink and special paper for his reports. On 14 October, he was called to a meeting at the Strand Hotel in Stockholm, where he was informed of a simple code which he could use. The reports themselves were sent to various confidants of Steffan in Stockholm, among them the physician to the German Legation. More urgent messages were to be cabled directly to the Legation.

These coast-watching activities had also another side to them. On 13 December 1939, the *Deptford* (4,030 tons) which was under charter to the British government, was torpedoed without warning off the Norwegian coast.[16] The ship sank immediately and only five out of a crew of thirty were saved. It was later established that on 8 December – the day the *Deptford* left Narvik – engineer Müller had sent a coded telegram to the Legation in Stockholm, noting the departure of a number of vessels for England, including the *Deptford*.

On 7 March, Security Chief Hallgren summed up the situation for the Swedish Foreign Minister: 'Steffan is undoubtedly the leader and chief for German espionage in Sweden and Norway. This espionage covers *inter alia* Swedish and Norwegian commerce and shipping as well as military matters.'[17]

Steffan's principal assistant in Sweden was said to be the German foreign correspondent, Herman Bolte, who was well informed about economic and trade matters in the Nordic countries.[18] At the beginning of April, Hallgren filled out the picture a little more: 'Steffan and Bolte have to a considerable extent brought disaster upon those citizens involved in their espionage activities and have caused Sweden's trade and shipping great losses. It would also appear that the aforesaid activities have led to the death of many seamen.'[19]

A demand was made for Steffan's recall and he left the country around the middle of May 1940, the 'Order of the Boot', however, being diplomatically softened by a congenial farewell breakfast and the conferment of the Swedish *Svärdsorder* on the departing attaché.[20] In the course of the investigation, a number of less favoured reporters not enjoying diplomatic protection connected with Steffan's groups in Norway and Sweden were sentenced to varying terms of imprisonment although those in Norway were later released after the occupation of the country. An immediate organisational consequence of the Steffan affair was a decision by the German authorities to ensure that Steffan's successor as German naval attaché, Paul von Wahlert, was distanced from *Abwehr* activities in Sweden.[21]

INTERMEZZOS: FLECK AND VON SCHOELER

Canaris had promised Adlercreutz that there would be no intelligence activities directed against Sweden itself. But where did neutral Sweden's interests end and those of the enemy belligerent begin? Did not the work of Steffan and Bolte spotlight this delicate philosophical distinction? Two further incidents occurred which served to expose another weakness in the Canaris assurance: the *Abwehr* was far from having a monopoly of German information-collecting activities in the field.

Before the war, a young German journalist, K. F. R. Fleck, had attracted the attention of the Swedish police because of his many journeys about the country and in April 1938, he was cross-examined about them.[22] In September 1939, the police received a tip-off that Fleck had mentioned that he had a special assignment in Sweden – that of keeping an eye on the Swedish newspapers – and this was why he had not been called up for military service. The next development occurred in 1940 when a letter from Fleck to Berlin, containing various political rumours, was intercepted. Orders were then given that Fleck's post was to be specially monitored. Later that month, police in Northern Sweden drew attention to Fleck's travels there. Information from his correspondence allowed his movements within the country to be shadowed. At the same time, his telephone conversations were monitored. During one such conversation between Fleck and Schurek, a member of the German Legation, on 17 April,

Fleck explained that he had a few brief notes still to write up. When Schurek said that the matter was urgent and that he would come up to Fleck's apartment, the Swedish authorities decided to intervene. During a search of Fleck's apartment, detailed notes on various Swedish defence installations were discovered. Subsequently Fleck was sentenced to a long term of imprisonment for espionage.

While there was enthusiasm in certain Swedish quarters[23] over the fact that an apparently dangerous German spy had been rounded up, for the German intelligence professionals the matter was something of an embarrassment and Fleck's abilities in the art of military reporting were judged very differently. The *Abwehr* duly reported to *Auswärtiges Amt* that Fleck had never received any assignment from them.[24] All that was known, was that he had once submitted to the Stockholm Legation a report about the shipbuilding plans of the Swedish navy, but because the man lacked all knowledge of military and naval matters, it had been quite worthless. Fleck was not their man.[25]

Could the same to be said of Eberhard von Schoeler, perceived by the Swedish police, as Fleck's successor?[26] In April, he had travelled to Luleå and had taken a trip on the iron ore railway

and could confirm that in every respect one is ready and in a position to ward off an Allied attack from the north. The reports of Norwegian refugees suggest that the English probably prepared such an attack. The mood up here is far from friendly, which is understandable given the situation in Narvik and the dangers which it might give rise to. In no way did I note any hint of a reduced state of readiness to meet an English attack. In my view, the Allies would encounter insuperable opposition in northern Sweden since moreover their own forces are not strong enough as the reports of Norwegian refugees bear out.[27]

In the middle of May, von Schoeler returned to Sweden to undertake yet another similar journey. He too, like Fleck, was picked up by the Swedish security authorities who had been keeping an eye on him and on 26 July 1940 he was given a one-year sentence (later increased to three and a half years by a higher court) for having studied Swedish defence preparations and the morale of the people and for having taken some 50 photographs of railways and harbours in northern Sweden.

BUREAU WAGNER TAKES SHAPE

While the activities of Fleck and von Schoeler occupied attention on stage to the embarrassment of the *Abwehr*, moves were soon afoot behind the scenes for the organisation of its real work in Sweden.

On 4 September, Canaris gave instructions for an urgent telegram to be sent to the German Legation in Bucharest, announcing that Major Dr Wagner was being assigned to other important duties abroad.[28] In fact, Dr Wagner had been selected to spearhead the *Abwehr*'s activities in Sweden. A week later, Canaris travelled north to Stockholm for discussions with the chiefs of the Finnish and Swedish intelligence services.[29] It was now necessary to finalise arrangements for the appointment under diplomatic cover of key personnel in these two countries and to sound out his colleagues about possible co-operation.

The proposal that Major Wagner, representing Section III F (Counter-espionage) of the *Abwehr* should be stationed in Stockholm as liaison officer, was approved by the Swedes.[30] Adlercreutz, for his part, was anxious to ensure that information from Swedish intelligence networks in Estonia could be passed back via Germany to Sweden with the assistance of the Canaris organisation.[31] Arrangements were also made for a Swedish counter-intelligence officer to be sent on a short-term posting to Berlin.[32]

With the decks cleared, things could now move quickly forward. On 27 September, Wagner put in an appearance in Stockholm. On 19 October the German military attaché was instructed to obtain a visa for him as a civilian assistant and he was officially attached to the Legation in November. Wagner's main tasks and his relation to Lieutenant-Commander Alexander Cellarius, who had been chosen to head the *Abwehr* in Finland, were regulated by the service instructions for the *Abwehr* liaison officer, Stockholm, dated 15 November.[33]

The duties of the officer (who was to be presented to the Swedish authorities as Dr rather than Major Wagner) lay firmly within the field of counter-espionage, an order of priority that would remain in force until the middle of 1944. The importance in Wagner's counter-espionage work of co-operating with Swedish military counter-espionage in the neutralisation (*Unschädlichmachung*) of hostile intelligence services working on Swedish territory, was explicitly stressed. Wagner ('Hans Schneider') was expected to work closely with

Cellarius (Corell) but at the same time, he was formally under the command neither of the latter nor of the military attaché in Stockholm. Although he had a duty to keep these colleagues informed in general terms about his activities, they had no right to question him about specific details of organisation and about their methods and finance. The instructions of 15 November also summarised the arrangements for courier, cable and telephone communications between Colonel Rohleder (Axel), the head of Section III F and his man in Stockholm.

In addition to the above instructions about the specific duties of the Stockholm representative, relations between the *Abwehr* and the German Foreign Office were regulated by other more general instructions.[34] Before an *Abwehr* officer could be installed in a Mission under diplomatic cover, the permission of *Auswärtiges Amt* had to be obtained. Not unexpectedly, disputes sometimes arose between the latter and the *Abwehr* about the desirability of boosting the numbers of such quasi-diplomats or about the wisdom of a particular appointment. The specific tasks assigned to an *Abwehr* officer were determined by the *Abwehr* central office, *Amt Ausland/Abwehr* but the officer had an obligation, on request, to give his Head of Mission an account – at least in general terms – of the assignment he had been given. In an attempt to demarcate the respective areas of intelligence collection falling to *Auswärtiges Amt* and the *Abwehr* respectively, the latter was specifically enjoined to concentrate on military, non-political intelligence. Military intelligence was to be sent directly to *OKW-Amt Ausland/Abwehr*, whereas reports which contained additional items of political interest, were to be made known to the Head of Mission and sent to *Amt/Ausland Abwehr* via *Auswärtiges Amt*.

In purely numerical terms, the *Abwehr* staff resident in Sweden was small in comparison with that maintained in Spain, Portugal and Switzerland and was firmly centred on Stockholm.[35] Initially Dr Wagner disposed over office space in the main building of the German Legation at Hovslagaregatan 2 but on 19 October 1942, his abode switched to Nybrogatan 27, where the additional presence of Colonel Theodor Macht, a supply officer attached to the Military Attaché's office, offered a convenient front.[36] Wagner personally took charge of certain key agents. Captain Albert Utermark, Dr Wagner's deputy whose cool head and organisational skills made him in the eyes of the staff a more feared and effective figure than his all too trusting and benevolent chief, was also allowed to deal with these more important sources.[37]

According to information reaching the Swedish authorities in 1944, Bureau Wagner was in the habit of receiving around 60,000 crowns per month to finance its activities.[38] The same source also provided a useful summary of what these activities were. Of central importance was the collection of information for counter-espionage purposes; the identification of possible Allied agents; Communist activities within Sweden; Norwegian refugees, their contacts with Norway and their possible involvement in sabotage there; the same for Danes; the names and addresses of German refugees and what they were up to; the courier air service between Sweden and Britain; people active in politics in Sweden, etc. The kernel of the system was formed by two sets of cards.[39] There was a set of some 200 blue cards, each with a codename and a number, covering Wagner's own V-men. For the more important of these, a dossier was kept, containing the V-man's reports and copies of telegrams and correspondence with Berlin. Money was paid out to agents against receipts signed with their codename. These receipts were then kept in a special safe. In addition to the blue cards, there was a much larger set (approximately 2,000) of red cards, devoted to persons suspected of working for enemy services or who had in some way aroused suspicions.

Although Dr Wagner did not always gain the respect of his subordinates, neither did he incur the wrath of his superiors in Berlin. Among his more important merits was held to be that he had succeeded in establishing a smooth working relationship with his Swedish counterparts. When in July 1942, Wagner reported the impending departure of Adlercreutz from his post as Swedish intelligence chief, he was simultaneously able to reassure Berlin that another friend (Lindquist) was tipped to take over as head of Military Counter-espionage.[40] Soon Wagner was reporting to Berlin that 'the new head of the Swedish *Abwehr*' was prepared to co-operate closely and it was noted 'There is no doubt that those of the agents in our service who in their assignments have not worked against Sweden, have been left in peace by the Swedes.'[41]

This harmonious view of things was again reiterated in a report by Himmler at the end of 1942 which spoke of 'the German military *Abwehr* and the Swedish military *Abwehr* working well together'.[42]

If the *SS Reichsführer* was content with the apparent rapport between Wagner and his Swedish colleagues, senior German diplomats in Stockholm were not always equally happy with *Abwehr* activities on their doorstep. In March 1942, the Minister had felt obliged to object to the *Abwehr*'s request to make use of a certain member of the Legation Staff for its own purposes, on the grounds that Dr Wagner had been informed by the head of the Swedish intelligence service that the man had long ago been 'blown'.[43] The fear of compromising the Legation was also uppermost in the Minister's mind when in the same year, it became desirable to establish a resident *Abwehr* presence outside Stockholm.

In 1942 *Amt Ausland/Abwehr* approached *Auswärtiges Amt* about the appointment of an officer in Gothenburg. The German Minister (Wied) in Stockholm was less than enthusiastic at the prospect, fearing diplomatic pitfalls ahead.[44] He pointed out that the activities of certain German agents in Gothenburg had resulted in their arrest in 1941. As a consequence, a close watch was being kept on the German Consulate by the Swedish authorities and it was entirely likely that the new officer, despite his cover, would be soon compromised. Gothenburg was too small a place for such a person to pass unnoticed. The *Abwehr* stood firm, insisting that the West Coast port had become a centre for enemy intelligence activities. It was claimed that enemy services disposed over a considerable staff of officers and a still greater network of agents, involved in collecting information from Denmark, Norway and elsewhere. To deal with the situation, a well-trained *Abwehr* man was absolutely essential there. It was therefore proposed that *Sonderführer* Schrott, who spoke fluent Norwegian and Swedish, should be installed in the Consulate in Gothenburg.

Schrott was duly sent off to Switzerland for a short spell to give a little more substance to his diplomatic cover and finally on 1 February 1943, he took up his new position as Vice-Consul in Gothenburg. Schrott (codename Gunnar) was responsible for the German counter-espionage effort, not only in Gothenburg but also for an area that ranged over Southern Sweden to the Norwegian border. Apart from leading a general offensive against resident Allied intelligence personnel in that area, he was expected to work closely with his III F counterparts in Denmark and Norway in preventing sabotage attempts against German targets in these countries and in hindering the flight of young Norwegians and Danes to Sweden. Schrott was formally under the command of Dr Wagner, and his reports went via the Stockholm station.

Wied's earlier fears, however, proved well founded, as his successor Thomsen was subsequently to explain to *Auswärtiges Amt*.[45] A Norwegian informant, 'Asbjörn', had been apprehended by the Swedish police in the course of a conspiratorial meeting with Schrott in Halmstad and a receipt and a letter to a certain Dr Feuer in Oslo, had fallen into their hands. In addition, yet another agent, 'Balduin', had fallen foul of the law on account of black-market manipulations. As a result, Schrott was being watched day and night and his intelligence work had been rendered impossible.

By 1944, Thomsen was complaining that there were far too many intelligence staff at the Legation and that they were interfering with the proper work of the Mission, namely diplomacy.[46] It was necessary to get rid of dead wood and concentrate on a nucleus of competent intelligence officers.[47] This was doubtless sound medicine but how far was the minister prepared to sip every drop of it? In July when Berlin decided that the time had come to dislodge Dr Wagner from his web and set an officer then serving in Denmark in his place, Thomsen was not impressed.

> In my opinion, a change in the post of Head of *Abwehr* in Sweden at the present moment, would be most inopportune. I would remind you that the present Head of *Abwehr*, Colonel Wagner, has only after some time been able to win the Swedish *Abwehr*'s trust, which was completely lacking when he took office because his predecessor Admiral Steffan, had to be recalled at the request of the Swedish government. It is known to me that Colonel Wagner maintains good and rewarding relations with the leading personalities of the Swedish *Abwehr*, Commander Landquist, Lieutenant-Colonel Count Bonde and Major Petersén. An 'accident in the course of work' like the sentencing of the employee Günther has changed nothing with regard to these important facts.[48]

If a change was necessary, Thomsen was against bringing in the man from Denmark. He would be unable to acquire the same standing and position of trust: 'But this relation of trust is essential for the special work of the *Abwehr* since its range of activities – at least in Sweden – is more or less confined to co-operating with the Swedish *Abwehr*.'[49] As Wagner's successor, Thomsen proposed instead Major Abshagen, who was said to be already acquainted with the Swedish situation.[50]

The matter was chewed over in Berlin. On 19 July, *Auswärtiges*

Amt reported back to Thomsen and began by recalling some of the underlying points. The proposal for a change in the post of Head of *Abwehr* in Sweden had come about for two reasons: first because of an internal difference of opinion and secondly because of the urgent need for a change in priorities in intelligence work in Sweden so that the active collection of intelligence, particularly about Russia (something for which Sweden was well placed) took precedence over counter-espionage. At the same time, the ban on the collection of intelligence about Sweden itself remained in force. The basic disadvantage with Wagner was that he was pre-eminently a counter-espionage man and lacked the necessary skills for directing the new activities in a way that would avoid disaster.

In an attempt to strike a compromise, *Auswärtiges Amt* suggested retaining Wagner but simultaneously strengthening active intelligence collection by the appointment of a new man to take charge of this side of things. Although the accepted trend had been to reduce *Abwehr* staff in Sweden, no other solution was possible. The new man who had been the head of the Scandinavian division of I. G. Farben for many years and had a great number of friends in Sweden, had the requisite qualifications for the job.[51] In another change, Major Busch who represented the Air Intelligence Section (I Luft) of the *Abwehr* in Stockholm, was to be replaced by Major Wenzlau. The latter was described as a very able *Abwehr* officer who had previously served in the office of the Air Attaché in Lisbon. On 26 July, Thomsen replied that provided no change was made in the post of Head of *Abwehr*, Sweden, he would be prepared to accept the assignment of the two new officers to the Legation.[52]

From the summer of 1941 onwards, evidence had been accumulating which showed Wagner's involvement in a number of espionage cases. However it was not until the end of 1944, when the Paulsson–Lönnegren scandal broke, that the Swedes finally found it opportune to demand his recall and he and Utermark left the country on 23 February 1945.[53]

ABWEHR

Counter-espionage

Routine work. 1. A certain salesman, RR, was sentenced to six months' imprisonment in April 1941 for offences under Chapter 8,

Section 9 of the Penal Code. When he was released, he got in touch with both the German and British Legations. In February 1942, RR overheard a conversation about a Swede who was going to Norway to collect information covertly. RR brought the matter to the attention of the German Legation and in this way was put in touch with Dr Wagner. Wagner had heard that the SIS was intending to organise sabotage activities with the intention of putting the blame on the Germans. RR was told to cultivate the SIS member thought to be responsible for the organisation of this scheme and also a British assistant military attaché.[54]

2. On 9 July 1942, Wagner was informed by his chief, Axel, that a certain Swedish official in Ireland who was sympathetic to the German cause, would be visiting Stockholm. This person was thought to be worth cultivating and Wagner was instructed to try to make contact.[55]

3. A week later Axel told Dr Wagner that two of the arrested 'Warsaw Swedes' had, during interrogation, provided the names of certain Polish contacts in Stockholm. Wagner was asked to check up on these people.[56]

4. On 27 November 1942, Axel asked Dr Wagner if a certain named cipher clerk was attached to the Soviet Legation in Stockholm.[57]

5. In June 1942 three Swedish citizens, a steward, a secretary at the Brazilian consulate and a customs official, were held by the police in Gothenburg, suspected of working for the German intelligence service. Upon interrogation, the following facts emerged. During a visit to Oslo at the end of 1940, the steward had met a German agent who had recruited him. Upon his return to Sweden, he had made contact with Dr Wagner who asked him to assist in unveiling enemy espionage and sabotage and also to discover the anticipated date for the departure of the Norwegian ships in Gothenburg. The steward agreed, established himself in Gothenburg in September 1941 and thereafter provided monthly reports against payment. To help him in his task, the steward in turn recruited the secretary and the customs official. On 25 March 1942, the customs official passed on the information that the ships' papers were now in order and that they could leave at any time. The vessels in fact left on the evening of 31 March.[58]

Co-operation and exchange. It is difficult to determine the extent to which the informal arrangement between Canaris and Adlercreutz regarding possible areas of co-operation between their respective counter-espionage branches, was implemented in practice.[59] Nevertheless the following items illustrate one side of the matter.

1. When the involvement of Blackman and his associates in possible sabotage preparations was brought to the attention of the German intelligence service, the matter was turned over to the Swedes for further action.[60]

2. In September 1941, an attempt was made to 'spring' William Kincaid Millar, a member of Munthe's team, then languishing in jail. The organiser of this attempt (Captain Marks), however, made the error of enlisting the help of a petty crook, who scenting financial benefit for himself, immediately got in touch with the German Legation about what was afoot. Dr Wagner then passed the information to Adlercreutz and the escape bid was duly foiled.[61]

3. During the lengthy investigation of the Soviet-sponsored, Rom group, the Security Chief asked the Domestic Section of the Defence Staff's Intelligence branch to contact Wagner. This was done and (after receiving the go-ahead from Süderblom at the Ministry for Foreign Affairs) Wagner was briefed about developments in the case. As a result, the true identity of the main participant in the group – which had up till then remained unclear – was quickly established.[62]

Two further studies in counter-espionage

Ascher's path to Rome.[63]   At the end of September 1939, Dr Josef Müller arrived in Rome for secret talks with Father Leiber, the principal personal aide and confidant of Pius XII.[64] A Bavarian and a good son of the church, Müller had many influential friends and acquaintances in the Vatican and was well qualified to serve as the special emissary of an anti-Hitler oppositional group formed round General Beck and Colonel Oster. His mission was in essence to persuade the Pope to act as intermediary in a dialogue with the British government. On 18 October, Müller returned with the encouraging news that the Pope had agreed. Thereby a potential line of communication had been opened up between Müller on the one hand and d'Arcy Osborne, the British Ambassador to the Vatican on the other via the Pontiff and his confidant.

Although – due partly as a result of heightened British suspicions of German peace feelers after the Venlo incident in November 1939 – nothing was to come of these discreet overtures, Müller's links with the Vatican risked being thrust into dangerous prominence later in

1940 when two telegrams sent to Brussels by the Belgian Ambassador to the Holy See, accurately giving in advance the date and time of the Western offensive, were intercepted by Goering's 'black chamber', the innocently named Research Office. Among those who set out to unveil the source who had betrayed this vital information, was Colonel Rohleder (Axel), the head of *Abwehr*'s Section III F. In 1941, he dispatched a V-man to Rome to undertake an on-the-spot investigation. The V-man's name was Siegfried Ascher.

Ascher, who had a background in banking and journalism, had converted to Catholicism in 1935. In November of the following year, he went to Rome and soon seems to have acquired a number of influential acquaintances, among them Father Muckermann who trustingly took him under his wing. When the latter in December 1937[65] went to Austria, Ascher followed, serving as one of the members of Muckerman's secretariat. After the annexation of Austria, Ascher was forced to move on, first to Switzerland and then back to Rome where he stayed for four months as the Vatican correspondent of *Basler Nachrichten*. Fearing the introduction of Aryanisation laws in Italy, Ascher decided to leave and after a brief interlude in Brussels, he set off for Sweden arriving there at the end of 1938.

Once established in Stockholm, he eked out a frugal existence, living on his small savings and on the income brought in by the occasional article for *Basler Nachrichten*. Thanks to the good offices of Muckermann, however, he obtained further journalistic work, writing articles for the *New Catholic Herald* in London. The payment for these articles came from Muckermann himself. After the outbreak of war, when it was no longer possible for Ascher to write for this paper, Muckermann nevertheless continued to send him 200 crowns per month, and these payments continued until the occupation of Holland, Muckermann's place of residence.

In October 1940, a new development took place when Ascher wrote letters to two persons, V and K, living in Berlin.[66] Although quite different in tone – one formal and the other familiar – the letters had a similar structure and contained a similar message. This was to the effect that the writer had recently, thanks to his excellent contacts, received reliable information that important circles in England wanted an end to the war.[67] Was it therefore possible for the recipient – or perhaps a reliable friend – to come to Stockholm?

How far these letters are to be taken at their face value is a matter of judgement. This was not Ascher's first attempt at freelance diplomacy. On balance, the evidence suggests that they may have been simply a way of activating some temporarily dormant contact with a control in Berlin, thus indicating that Ascher had had some previous involvement with the German intelligence service. Alternatively it might be argued that the actual letters – the product of Ascher's exaggerated view of himself as a peace-broker – were the immediate cause of his selection as an agent of the *Abwehr* which saw in him for the first time a man well suited to ferret out the secrets of the Vatican. Whatever the truth of the matter, it is clear that some time after the dispatch of these letters, Dr Wagner came knocking on Ascher's door.[68]

Ascher's own account of his dealings with Wagner which he dated – truly or falsely – from a meeting in January 1941, had all the marks of a man with something to hide. But the formal sequence of events can be reconstructed in another way. On 2 February 1941, Ascher wrote to the chief editor of *Basler Nachrichten*, informing him that important decisions were about to be made in the Vatican where the desire had been expressed that he should be on the spot to cover events for the German-language press. The financial cost of the trip, he was at pains to emphasise, would be borne by the Holy See. Ascher wanted the editor to send him a letter to the effect that he (Ascher) was being sent to Rome as Vatican correspondent for *Basler Nachrichten* for a trial period of some weeks and that it was not certain that he could be kept there on a permanent basis. This letter could then be presented to the Swedish authorities and would ensure that he would be able to make the trip to Rome and return to Sweden without any difficulty.

Behind these fabrications, the truth was rather different. It can reasonably be concluded that by the beginning of February the financing of the trip had been agreed between Wagner and Ascher. It remained only to cloak the trip from the Swedish and Vatican authorities with a respectable cover: hence the appeal for the letter from the editor of *Basler Nachrichten*.

Armed with the Swiss letter of appointment, everything else fell into place. Ascher could now approach the Catholic Bishop in Stockholm, Johannes Erich Müller, with an ostensibly valid reason for his trip to Rome. On 27 February the Bishop wrote a letter of recommendation on behalf of Ascher, to the German Legation, requesting that the journalist should be given a visa to travel through

Germany to Italy 'as Vatican correspondent for a Swiss newspaper'. The ruse of the *Abwehr* appeared to have been entirely successful: the editor of *Basler Nachrichten* had been duped into believing that the Vatican was sponsoring Ascher's trip while the Vatican, represented by Bishop Müller, had been duped into believing that Ascher's sponsor was *Basler Nachrichten*. In addition, the Swedish authorities could now be presented with two documents from persons of good repute, testifying to the reasonable nature of Ascher's mission. In point of fact, both documents had been obtained by false pretences.

On 18 March, Ascher was embroidering still another version of his forthcoming journey to a refugee friend now in America. At the beginning of April, he announced, he was going to Switzerland on behalf of *Dagens Nyheter*, Sweden's largest daily newspaper. At the same time, the Vatican was intervening on his behalf with the German and Italian governments to allow him to go to Rome where important things were about to take place.

On 29 April 1941, Ascher flew from Stockholm to Berlin. At Tempelhof airport, Dr Wagner, who had travelled on ahead, was there to meet him. He was also received in due course by the Apostolic Nuncio in Berlin, Archbishop Orsenigo, who provided a letter of recommendation to Mgr Giovanni Battista Montini, the Undersecretary at the Vatican. Then on 3 May, it was time to fly to Rome. There he duly did the rounds, speaking with Montini, Father Leiber and Mgr Kaas among others. But there were those in Rome who were not a little suspicious of his motives. How was it at all possible, Dom Cyrill von Korvin-Krasinski wondered, for a Jew to fly from Stockholm to Rome? The German Minister in Stockholm (said Ascher) had been very decent.

These suspicions would prove well founded. At the beginning of June, Ascher flew back to Berlin, to report his findings to the *Abwehr*. In his view, the man who had passed over the information about the date of the offensive in Rome, had been none other than Josef Müller.

Rohleder now passed Ascher's report to Canaris. Müller was questioned about the matter and he, Oster and Dohnanyi, another member of the oppositional group, challenged its veracity. According to Müller, the people named in the report only wanted to undermine his standing in the Vatican. And here the matter was allowed to rest. The report was not passed on to the Gestapo or the SD. Instead it was filed away, only to emerge when the Gestapo, in the wake of the attempt on Hitler's life on 20 July 1944, finally discovered it in the archives at the Army HQ at Zossen.

Ascher returned to Stockholm on 18 June. The same day he sent off a letter to the editor of *Basler Nachrichten*, summing up his impressions from Rome and listing the various people with whom he had spoken. The Germans, wrote Ascher, had succeeded in creating an atmosphere of panic. Clerics who had lived there for years were accusing one another of being Gestapo agents. A leading part in this campaign of libel was played by the Jesuits, who were able to command great influence through Father Leiber, the Pope's confidential secretary. The letter then zoomed in on Ascher's own precarious state. He had grounds for believing that the Jesuits were even trying to remove him from the columns of *Basler Nachrichten*, replacing him with a certain Baron Raitz von Frentz. Would the editor be kind enough to think over his proposal about Portugal? An appointment there as correspondent would entail no extra financial risk, since if he were *Basler Nachrichten*'s man, he would also be able to represent a Swedish newspaper. Reading between the lines, it is clear that Ascher had realised that Leiber had seen through the masquerade. This was true. On 26 June, the Pope's secretary had written to Montini, warning him about what had happened:

> In May a certain Ascher was here in Rome, coming from Stockholm. In his trip by way of Berlin, he was received by the Apostolic Nuncio, Archbishop Orsenigo. Here he made visits to the Secretariat of State, to Monsignor Kaas and also to me. From Berlin I have been informed of things he reported to the Central Office of the Gestapo about conversations he had with Mgr Kaas and with me, as also with Your Excellency. What concerns me, is that it is all invented and falsified from the first word to the last, and the same for Mgr Kaas. But these are dangerous inventions. Ascher is an extremely dangerous agent of the Gestapo.[69]

The Swedish Legation in Rome was evidently also appraised of Ascher's visit. On 19 September 1941, the Swedish Envoy, Beck-Friis sent a highly confidential letter to Söderblom at the Ministry for Foreign Affairs in Stockholm:

> With respect to your letter of the 11th concerning a certain Jewish journalist, I would like to stress – in support of what I relayed by word of mouth during my visit to Stockholm – that I have been warned by my previously mentioned informant about the person

in question, who is known to be an agent of the Gestapo. The mere fact that he was permitted to travel through Germany, says a great deal but my informant has also seen other proof.[70]

In Stockholm, unbeknown to himself, Ascher had been under the surveillance of the Security Service for some time. Now after his return from Italy, his movements were watched closely. Gradually a pattern of clandestine meetings in small cafés and parks with members of KO Sweden, emerged.[71] On 28 April 1942, the police finally decided to take him in for questioning. Interest was naturally fixed on his contacts with Wagner and the trip to Rome.

Ascher did not deny these: he was in no position to do so. Instead he presented them in a new light. According to him – with a deft inversion of the facts – the editor of *Basler Nachrichten* had in January 1941 suggested that he should go to Rome as the newspaper's correspondent. Following up this suggestion, Ascher had then visited the German Legation to enquire about a transit visa to Italy. When informed that this was unobtainable for non-Aryans, he had written to his friend V in Berlin, asking him to intercede on his behalf. In due course, a German arrived with a letter of introduction, declaring him to be an old friend of V: later it would transpire that his caller was Dr Wagner of the German Legation. Wagner explained that he was prepared to help with the matter of the transit visa and indeed to finance his trip, if Ascher was prepared to provide him with a comprehensive description of the state of the Italian economy. That was all there was to his trip. Apart from his plane tickets, he had also received a credit of 5,000 lire which he could draw upon in Italy and a further 1,000 crowns upon his return to Stockholm.

Afterwards, no formal charge was preferred against Ascher, a fact which Dr Wagner did not hesitate to ascribe to his influence in high places. Instead on 9 May 1942, Ascher was held in detention while a formal application was made for his expulsion from Sweden. Eleven days later, however, with – so it was said – his mental condition causing concern, the one-time Vatican observer was transferred to a hospital where he was to remain until the beginning of 1945.

Lönnegren and Paulson. In 1938, the Scandinavian Telegram Bureau (STB) was established in Stockholm. Formally it was a subsidiary of a Swiss press agency in Zürich: in reality both the Swedish and Swiss agencies were indirectly steered from Berlin both as regards the news they distributed and their financing. Placed in charge of it from 1938 to January 1941 was John Lönnegren. After a doctorate at Greifswald, he had a somewhat chequered career as journalist and businessman. In December 1944, he was held by the police and later confessed to having delivered information to Dr Wagner and Captain Utermark. His main source, he claimed, had been Robert Paulsson, a key official attached to the Control Section of the Aliens' Bureau. These revelations and the resulting trial of both men generated a great deal of publicity and led eventually to the appointment of a governmental commission of enquiry under the chairmanship of Rickard Sandler, to look into the wartime treatment of refugees and the activities of the general security service. Its findings were subsequently published in three post-war reports.

At some time in 1942, suspicions about Lönnegren's activities appear to have arisen and Paulsson, who was known to be an acquaintance of Lönnegren and who was also by virtue of his career, background and current position a man enjoying the confidence of the security service, was asked to look into these. No new facts emerged. In November 1943, however, on the basis of information received from the Defence Staff, the surveillance of Lönnegren was intensified. His telphone calls were monitored and his movements shadowed. In connection with the timing of the Defence Staff's intervention, it is perhaps worth noting that in September of the same year, a certain Grace Buchanan-Dineen had been indicted in the United States on charges of violating the War Espionage Act. An investigation showed that she had been in postal contact with at least four addresses in Stockholm, which on good grounds could be supposed to be used by the German Intelligence Service. One of these addresses belonged to Dr John Lönnegren.[72]

By the late autumn of 1944, an alternative way of checking Dr Wagner's sources became available to the Swedes via the Finnish counter-espionage man Kumenius. He had managed to ingratiate himself with Cellarius in Finland and had been sent to assist Wagner in Stockholm. In this way, a trap could be set up which would allow the authorities to determine if and how information was being leaked from the the Alien's Bureau to Bureau Wagner.[73] When on 6 December 1944, a conversation between Paulsson and Lönnegren was monitored in which stress was laid on informing Dr Wagner about a certain report, the police waited a few days and then brought Lönnegren in for questioning.

In his confession, Lönnegren admitted to meeting Wagner first in the autumn of 1941. During their association, he had provided information about 100 persons. Of more interest than this figure, however, is the type of person about whom information was collected. Thus he was asked to make enquiries about Sidney Smith and Victor Hampton, Wilfred Latham, Jerzy Dunkel, Maciej Konar, and Pjotr Iwanow, all associated with Allied intelligence services.[74] In 1943, he had been asked by Wagner to establish if two members of Tass in Stockholm, were engaged in espionage and whether they ran a number of agents. When a member of Bureau Wagner defected in the autumn of 1944, he made enquiries into her whereabouts. Around the same time, he told Captain Utermark about his suspicion that Kumenius was a plant. In other words, Lönnegren's activities did not simply consist in providing information of a routine nature to the German Legation about German refugees in Sweden or about foreign diplomats in general; it consisted of more qualified counter-espionage work than appeared at first sight.

Where, then, had this information come from? Lönnegren was quite explicit: it came from Paulsson. Although the latter had the means, the motive and the opportunity, he none the less refused to admit that he had unlawfully handed over privileged information, arguing that he had only maintained contact with Lönnegren as a way of keeping an eye on him. The judicial evidence against Paulsson remained more circumstantial. Lönnegren was sentenced to two years' hard labour while Paulsson received a sentence of one year and ten months which was subsequently considerably reduced after appeal.[75]

Intelligence collection

While the centre of gravity of Bureau Wagner lay in the area of counter-espionage, the *Abwehr* also made use of Swedish nationality and Swedish territory in its efforts to gain knowledge about enemy intentions.

The missions of Summer.[76] 'Summer' was the son of a Swedish parson. After a spell in Canada and an unsuccessful attempt at running a silver fox farm in Sweden, he drifted into journalism and in 1937, took up residence in Hamburg, where he worked on the newspaper *Hamburger Tageblatt*. At the beginning of December 1938, he received a visit from an individual, who presented himself as

174

Lieutenant Timmermann. Timmermann was keen to hear if Summer was willing to undertake a trip to England. There he was to take note of the mood of the people and in addition register any signs of preparations for war. As a Swede who spoke fluent English, Timmerman said, Summer was better placed to carry out this task than a German. Shortly after the meeting with Timmerman, Summer was introduced to a Dr Haupt, an army major with a small office at Jungfernstieg 7 in Hamburg. Haupt explained that Summer was to visit the cities of Birmingham and Coventry. The first thing he had to do was to acquire a new Swedish passport since his own revealed that he had spent some time in Germany and it would naturally be better if this was concealed. Arrangements for communications were then discussed. Summer received two cover addresses in Germany to which he was to dispatch his reports. For his upkeep in England, he would be sent £15 a month from Sweden. These would appear to come from a person called Åkerman but this would simply be a codename which Haupt would use in his correspondence with Summer.

Summer set off for Birmingham where he stayed at the YMCA. After making a tour of inspection of various factories in Birmingham and Coventry, he sent off his reports to the agreed addresses in Germany. At the beginning of February 1939, he received a letter from Åkerman instructing him to return to Germany.

Back in Hamburg, Haupt told him that his reports were inadequate. He had to try to get inside the factories to see for himself. Summer, after agreeing to try again, was given the names and addresses of various factories which German intelligence was particularly interested in and then headed back to Birmingham via Sweden and Denmark.

Summer, once more based in the YMCA, set about systematically collecting information and managed to send monthly reports with his observations right up to the outbreak of war, when postal correspondence between England and Germany ceased. The *Abwehr*, however, had failed to make any contingency plan for communication with Summer and for a time, he was allowed to drift. After a spell as a farm labourer, he finally managed on 3 December 1939 to find a ship and worked his passage home to Sweden.

Upon arrival, Summer wrote to Dr Haupt and intimated that as he was intending volunteering for service in Finland, he wanted to discontinue his intelligence work. However, his controllers in Hamburg took a different view. There were meetings in Copenhagen and later in Hamburg to take stock of his most recent observations about the situation in England and to discuss various future possibilities. Summer turned down a proposal to send him to Iceland but eventually agreed to continue working in England. It was decided that he should try to obtain a position in a British port. He was to sign on as a crew member on a Swedish vessel bound for England and when he arrived there, he was to jump ship. Summer was provided with a bottle of invisible ink to write his reports. These would be sent invisibly concealed in letters apparently about innocent subjects, to a certain export company in Copenhagen. This plan, however, misfired in a somewhat ironic fashion. The vessel on which Summer had signed up was sunk by German aircraft off Norway after having loaded up with iron ore in Narvik. The crew managed to survive and Summer found himself once more back in Sweden.

His contacts with German military intelligence were not yet over. In July 1940, a Swedish merchant vessel on which he was serving docked in Lübeck. There he received a visit from a certain Dr Schmidt whom he recognised as a colleague of Haupt and soon he was being whisked away to meet his controller in Hamburg. Haupt explained that the Germans were preparing for an invasion of Britain. It was therefore desirable to have agents in the country who could transmit weather reports by W/T. Summer was sent on courses in W/T and meteorology to equip him for his new mission. By 30 August 1941, all was ready and he was given a transmitter, £200 in one-pound notes and a special code for his communications. The same day, he boarded a Dornier at an airfield near Rennes in Brittany. The plane flew over Bristol but on account of bad weather and the heavy flak, Summer's drop was cancelled and the aircraft was forced to return to Rennes, the mission unaccomplished.

In Brittany, the mist kept them grounded for some days and it was finally decided to try instead from Brussels. In the Belgian capital, Summer met Major Ritter, head of *Abwehr* I's Air Section in Hamburg. His transmitter was now swapped for a transceiver and an insurance agreement was signed. It was hoped to invade Britain in the middle of September, Ritter told him, and all Summer had to do was to last out until then.

On the night 6/7 September 1940, the Dornier took off once more for England. This time in the vicinity of Northampton, Summer parachuted out at 4,000 metres. But his luck had run out. On landing, he was knocked unconscious and lay there until 18.00 the next day when he was found by a member of the Home Guard and taken to the police station in Northampton. From there, he was transferred to the interrogation centre at Ham Common where efforts were made to persuade him to work for the British.

After about a month's detention, Summer complied and in fact transmitted three – quite correct – weather reports from Aylsborough until apparently regretting his participation in the double-cross of his former employers, he tried to take his own life and was transferred to a hospital. After he had recovered, he agreed once more to transmit messages to Germany and for this purpose, he was moved to a villa outside Cambridge. On 13 January 1941, he overpowered his guard, stole his motor cycle and escaped, heading for King's Lynn. His flight was discovered and road blocks were set up and Summer eventually turned himself in to the police at Newmarket. He refused to take part in any further double-crossing and remained imprisoned in Britain until 1 September 1945 when he was repatriated to Sweden.

The Summer case shows how *Abwehr* I chose a Swedish agent for infiltration in Britain because it calculated that the agent's neutral nationality opened doors more easily in the territory of a potential enemy and offered an excellent mask. The examples which follow deal with *Abwehr* I's use of Swedish territory.

The activities of Dr Krämer.[77]   In May 1941, Dr Karl-Heinz Krämer, a member of Major Ritter's staff in Hamburg, was sent to Stockholm to investigate the posssibility of opening up intelligence activities in Sweden directed against Great Britain and the USA. Intelligence activities presuppose channels of communication and at that time, there were two direct official communication links between Sweden and Britain. One was the so-called 'Gothenburg radio link' which answered for telegram traffic between the countries. The other was the courier air service run by British Overseas Airways which carried post and personnel. The latter air link, with British encouragement, was later augmented by the courier service run by the Swedish company AB Aerotransport (ABA), with a first flight in mid-February 1942.[78]

Krämer's visit to Sweden in May 1941 was followed by several others and because of the value placed on his reports derived via Swedish channels, the Luftwaffe Operations Staff, which was responsible for the evaluation of airforce intelligence, asked *Abwehr* I's Air Intelligence Section, which looked after the collection of such intelligence by the deployment of agents in the field, to arrange for him to be placed there on a more permanent basis.[79] Because Krämer's previous official work made it impractical for him to be introduced as a private individual or businessman, it was suggested that he should be installed in the Legation under diplomatic cover. On 3 October, these questions were taken up by Major Busch of the *Abwehr* in a discussion with the Legation.[80] It was proposed that Krämer should be placed in the press attaché's department where he would be nominally involved in the evaluation of incoming British and American material. Internally, Krämer would be subordinate to Dr Wagner. The suggested cover post was the only possibility then available since a representative of the SD had only recently been assigned to the commercial attaché's department.

On 17 October the appointment was placed before Ribbentrop for decision. In the submission, it was noted that the number of *Abwehr* personnel enjoying diplomatic cover had more or less reached saturation point, but none the less it was felt that an exception should be made for Dr Krämer. Particular stress was again laid on Krämer's excellence as a reporter: his material provided the best basis for choosing which British factories should be targetted by the Luftwaffe.[81] He was in the habit of travelling to Stockholm from time to time to collect the letters and intelligence which came to the Swedish capital via the British courier aircraft. However, because the Luftwaffe Operations Staff was on the point of stepping up its activities against Britain, there was a need for target intelligence without delay and it was felt that the present arrangement regarding Krämer was inadequate. He should be on the spot all the time so that the incoming intelligence could be evaluated and transmitted as soon as it came in.

On 19 October, Ribbentrop gave his formal blessing to Krämer's incorporation in the Stockholm Legation under diplomatic cover. It did not take long before the new recruit was demanding special facilities. Although Krämer was prepared to be answerable to Dr Wagner in disciplinary matters, he none the less wanted direct access to the Legation's teleprinter for communications with Berlin without having to go via Wagner, a proposal which *Auswärtiges Amt* duly approved subject to certain reasonable conditions.[82] By November, Krämer was in place.

In the following years, he would acquire a controversial reputation among his colleagues because of his impressive flow of reports, attributed to sources veiled under such names as V-Mann 3579, Siegfried A, Siegfried B, Josephine, Hektor, Eisberg, Zuckerhut, Amor, Haifisch, Liang, Quelle 10, Pettersson-Hasso, etc. The reports themselves covered a wide range of topics from the output of various British factories to confidential discussions in British Ministries. The origin of some of this material could be established and seemed not altogether implausible. Thus by the end of 1940, German Intelligence had managed to set a useful reporting ring at Bromma airport which was used *inter alia* for the courier traffic with Britain. The latter was shared between two companies – British BOAC and Swedish ABA. Among those participating in the Bromma ring were Lufthansa's Swedish representative, Hans Schäfer and ABA's freight manager Swallving who had been recruited in October 1941 and duly registered as V-Mann 3579 of the Hamburg *Abwehr* station. Swallving was certainly in a position to provide information on Swedish supplies being routed to England and perhaps to make certain inferences based on them. But what of the reports specifically dealing with matters in England? Krämer's telegrams to Berlin prima facie offered certain clues. On 5 December 1942, Siegfried B was noting that the Swedish Legation in London was engaged in negotiations with the Foreign Office and the appropriate ministry about the supply of rubber.[83] Certain formulations seemed to suggest that Siegfried B had access to reports from the Legation. This access could naturally occur either in London or Stockholm or in theory at least, somewhere between these two endpoints. In an addendum to a Siegfried B report on 25 January 1943, Krämer refers to a report from the Swedish military/air attaché in London 'which landed here last Sunday' – a formulation which suggested a contact in Stockholm.[84] A telegram dispatched on 7 April 1943 was still more revealing. In it, Krämer took up a BOAC courier plane which had been reported missing and explained his interest as follows:

> The machine is probably of type Lockheed Hudson. Besides the crew, there were English, American and Swedish courier bags on board as well as some 10 Norwegian refugees. The number of the machine and its time of departure will be forwarded. Here we are interested in knowing if the aircraft was shot down by us. If yes, then where since the Swedish post contains letters and assignments for Siegfried.[85]

In a telegram in April 1944, 'Josephine' took up a reconnaissance carried out at Bristol by an unnamed agent, noting that 'internally it had been reported' that things had gone smoothly although great care was in order since aliens and diplomats were kept under the closest surveillance. None the less reconnaissance on the spot was still possible by making use of Norwegians who as a group were widely trusted in Britain.[86]

These clues taken together superficially suggested that Krämer had, one way or another, obtained access to reports reaching Stockholm from Swedish information-gathering sources, some of them covert, in England. But the particular alchemy of his espionage remained the professional secret of Dr Krämer alone. When in September 1944, doubts were being voiced about the authenticity of Josephine by certain intelligence analysts, the fundamental facts about Krämer's agent as they were known to the evaluating staff were recalled.[87] The source Josephine involved a neutral military attaché in an enemy capital. However this source could neither be directly steered as regards the information-gathering assignment nor were the reports emanating from the source directly available.

Dr Krämer continued to be highly valued as a confidential reporter at the highest level for some time. A rough measure of his standing in 1944 compared with that of other agents in the field valued by German intelligence such as 'Ostro', 'Garbo' and 'Brutus' is provided by the files of Colonel Krummacher, the *Abwehr* liaison officer with the OKW Operations Staff. It was Krummacher's job to filter out incoming messages of importance which were then passed upwards via Jodl to the Führer. Thus between 1 January and 6 June 1944, the two relevant files of Krummacher contain 65 messages from Josephine, 12 from Ostro and only one each from Garbo and Brutus. Even in the month immediately following D-Day, when Garbo and Brutus began to show more strongly with ten and nine messages in Krummacher's selection compared with Ostro's nine, Josephine still headed the field with 25 messages.

Krämer's reticence about his sources was interpreted variously by his colleagues in Stockholm. One school held that he had genuine contacts at the Ministry for Foreign Affairs who were able to supply him with information gleaned from incoming official Swedish reporting. Among the sceptics, a number of different explanations were advanced. Remembering Krämer's cover as a member of the Press Department charged with studying British and American open literature, there were those who believed that he simply made astute

180

deductions on the basis of this material and dressed it up as 'information from secret sources'. A different account of Krämer's inventiveness in rigging his reports was propounded with some fervour by Major Friedrich Busch, who had arrived in Stockholm in March 1943 to assist the air attaché, Colonel Reinhard von Heymann. Busch who had enjoyed an overview of *Abwehr* I Luft's incoming intelligence on Britain and America (including that from Krämer in Stockholm), had originally been well disposed to Krämer's reporting. This soon changed and Busch during his stay in Stockholm seems to have devoted more time checking up on Krämer than he did on trying to collect secret information of his own.

Particularly galling for Busch was the fact that his adversary had been allowed to have access to all centrally distributed intelligence evaluations and other secret material. This gave him the possibility of 'playing back' to the evaluators what was essentially their own information, perhaps with subtle variations. Busch was certain that this had in fact happened. On 19 March Krämer had sent four reports to Berlin about the strength of the RAF in Gibraltar, Corsica, Malta and North Africa. The relevant information about this had already been sent from Berlin to Stockholm three days before and a detailed comparison convinced Busch that this had simply been reproduced. A more exhaustive enquiry led him to the conclusion that more than 100 Josephine and Hektor reports were simply a rehash of intelligence already received.

Busch's criticism simply led in the end to his own downfall, for Dr Krämer was not short of influential backers. But it was a criticism that would also be echoed – equally to no avail – by certain junior intelligence evaluators. In charting the progress of Hektor, Josephine and Ostro (an Iberian source), they had come to the conclusion that all three were under enemy control and were simply serving the deception schemes of the enemy.[88] An analysis of Josephine's role in a specific deception scheme was set out in a retrospective memorandum of 6 January 1945:

Josephine's Reports on the First American Army Group (FUSAG)
1. FUSAG's existence was first notified on 9 January 1944, and was regularly mentioned with certainty up to 17 June. In the spring of 1944, it was increasingly reported by agents and by the Press.

2. In assessing Josephine's reports, the purport of all reports on FUSAG may be noted as follows:
   (a) The Allied Armies under FUSAG's command kept on changing. Finally it was stated that one English and one Allied airborne army were under the command of FUSAG, i.e. of an American Army Group.
   (b) Changes in the command of FUSAG were reported quite as frequently as changes in the formations subordinate to it.
   (c) When the invasion began, FUSAG was generally put down as being a second great group of forces, for a second landing operation north of the first.
   (d) After the continued withdrawal of divisions from the armies under FUSAG's command, to reinforce the invasion forces, reports were also received as to movements of FUSAG into Central and Northern England, in connection with landing operations against Jutland and Southern Norway, and later against the Heligoland Bight.

3. It may be seen from (2) that FUSAG was certainly used by the enemy as an 'army in being'. Technical adviser's personal impression is that FUSAG existed simply for this purpose.

4. During the second half of the year, reports from the agent Josephine conform to the enemy's decoy activities. Until the middle of October 1944, they did much to uphold the 'fiction' of FUSAG as a strong group of forces intended for further landings. The first reports came in very late – according to records on file, not until 6 August. Like other agents Josephine reported (German Security H.O. Mil (RSHA Mil) B/L 11102/8 of 8 August 1944):
   (a) 'FUSAG was originally to have been used for a second large-scale landing operation. As the timing of the Normandy invasion went completely wrong, it was decided not to undertake this second landing, which had been planned for the end of June; and formations from FUSAG were steadily transferred to France.'
   (b) As there was no longer any practical likelihood that FUSAG would be employed for a second landing, it was now mentioned in connection with a landing operation against Southern Norway and Denmark. (German Security H.O. Military B/L 13869 of 29 August 1944): 'Increased troop transports from Southern and Central England to

Northern England are being associated with movements of parts of FUSAG. Operations in Northern and Central Norway, starting from England, are not expected, but landings in Jutland and S. Norway.'

Replying to further enquiry he stated (German Security HQ (RSHA) 10031 of 1 September:

I was expecting your further enquiry(!), as my own suspicions had already been aroused at once. All sources however confirm that FUSAG formations have been stationed as far as the Humber. In addition there are individual reports about troop transports to Northern England/Scotland. As reported, these were not observed previously. Resumption of Swedish air traffic to England refused, although conceded at end of August. It is quite clear that either a large-scale decoy operation is planned to cover the employment of FUSAG in Belgium–Holland–Heligoland Bight, or that an operation against Denmark is actually intended.

(c) Later on, the idea of connecting FUSAG with the movements of troops to Northern England was withdrawn but the increasingly doubtful FUSAG was reported to be destined for a large-scale landing in the Heligoland Bight (GAF Ops. Staff Ic. Attaché Group 88087 of 15 September): 'FUSAG continues in Eastern England as far as Humber. Formations in Northern England and Scotland do not belong to FUSAG. Employment of FUSAG in Eastern Holland and Heligoland Bight after strong airborne landing has been carried out in Eastern and Northern Holland.'

5. In conclusion, it must be pointed out that Josephine was thus a participant in the enemy's decoy plans, which were aimed at holding down strong German forces for as long as possible at various points from Norway to France.[89]

However, if Krämer was perhaps an *indirect participant* in British deception plans, in the sense that he may have embroidered other agent reports to which he had access, he was certainly not an agent *controlled by* the British. His very independence made him a headache for the British deceivers, since the effect and scope of his embroideries always threatened to disturb the projected effect of their own schemes. His guesswork – if guesswork it was – was sometimes sufficiently near the target to be a continuing source of worry.[90]

The British authorities had in fact been able to monitor Krämer's reporting in a variety of ways.[91] Given his claims to have well-placed sources in Britain who were able to scoop up information from RAF officers and the internal meetings of the Ministry of Aircraft Production (MAP), Krämer became an obvious concern for MI5.[92] Their analysis showed, however, that Krämer's reports were a mixture of intelligent speculation and of refutable or uninteresting facts; his data about aircraft production was only occasionally accurate; his alleged source in MAP could not be identified and the timing of the reports appeared to exclude the use of the Swedish diplomatic bag or the Swedish airline; and finally the illicit use of radio was ruled out. MI5 therefore concluded that Krämer's network was fictitious. SIS, however, remained less certain.[93]

After the conclusion of hostilities, both the Allied and Swedish counter-espionage authorities expended some effort in trying to disentagle the various strands in the Stockholm-based *Abwehr* officer's activities. Krämer's own long interrogation yielded several new names and suggested various lines of enquiry. In addition to providing an account of his exchange of information with the Japanese military attaché, Onodera, who ran a veritable clearing house for intelligence, Krämer mentioned a number of his contacts in Stockholm. Among the more important, two key figures emerged. One was a journalist working for *Hamburger Fremdenblatt*.[94] According to Krämer, the journalist was an acute political observer, had excellent contacts with members of the Ministry for Foreign Affairs and had provided general evaluations, based on opinions current in Swedish official circles. Thus for example, he had stressed that these circles believed that all talk of an attack on Scandinavia in connection with the Allied invasion of Europe, was simply a device to mislead the German Supreme Command. The other informant was Grundböck, a businessman of Central European origin who was already on the books of AST Vienna and was also a close friend of Colonel Ujzazy, the Hungarian Chief of Intelligence.[95] When Krämer visited Stockholm in May 1941, he immediately looked up Grundböck and made preliminary plans for future co-operation.

Among the contacts of Grundböck was apparently a certain source (Fulep) in Spain. Information from this source now became available to Krämer, allegedly transmitted by Hungarian courier post to Stockholm.[96] It was to the Fulep organisation rather than to any more direct Swedish connection that Krämer attributed his intelligence on Britain, including certain of his more spectacular scoops.[97] His location in Sweden (he was to maintain) had been originally proposed by his businessman companion simply as a cloak for the vital communications link with Fulep in Madrid.[98] After these admissions, Krämer's long interrogation finally came to an end, his British inquisitors judging that he no longer had any reason to hide the truth.[99] Yet it can hardly be said that all doubts and obscurities had been dispelled. Had indeed every vital question been asked? In Sweden, various trails were followed up but apparently led nowhere.[100]

Yet however much he may have succeeded in hoodwinking both his own German superiors like Schellenberg and his British interrogators about his real sources and their relative importance in providing a basis for his conjectures, one thing was clear: irrespective of whether Krämer's sources were genuine or not, his reports had in many cases been found to be unreliable or conjectural when they had been confronted with the facts. It remained merely to speculate whether his assignment in Stockholm as a German intelligence officer, charged with collecting information about Britain, had provided him with a useful cover for work of another kind.[101]

Reports on Russia: Klaus. On 3 May 1919, the Swedish Ministry for Foreign Affairs received a report from its Legation in Berlin, which summarised a conversation with 'the secretary at the Danish Consulate in Riga, the German subject Herr Claus':

> As regards the situation in Riga, Herr Claus described these as particularly difficult and he stressed that the reports about this which had appeared in the press, were in no way exaggerated. When he had left the city on 14 April, the Bolshevik terror was in full swing. Before Herr Claus' departure, people had come to to the Swedish Consulate to search the premises on the grounds that it was known that money and securities belonging to members of the colony had been deposited there. Holmgren [the consul] who was not recognised by the Bolsheviks to have any official position, telephoned to the Danish Consulate and asked for their support. The Danes immediately contacted the people involved and explained that if a search of the Swedish Consulate were to take place, all the remaining consuls in Riga would as a

185

consequence break off relations with those in power in Riga. This resulted in the search being called off.

The above Herr Claus managed to flee from Riga after being assured safe conduct by the Bolsheviks because he would be submitting a report in Copenhagen about the activities of the Red Cross. Claus told me that he could have arranged so that Holmgren was allowed to accompany him but the latter however declined on the grounds that he did not see how he could leave as long as the remaining members of the Swedish colony were not given the same opportunity.

I then took up the question of sending a Swedish rescue party by sea to Riga to relieve Consul Holmgren and the colony. Herr Claus is against this, given the present situation, since it is certain that the Bolsheviks who had at their disposal a number of smaller warships, berthed in the harbour at Riga, would try to commandeer the vessel and not permit the Swedes to depart.

In his view, one possible way of saving the city, would be if the British and Americans were interested in a rescue party. He said that the British had capital investments in Riga of around 200 million roubles and the Americans, some 20 million roubles. Herr Claus is departing for Copenhagen to work towards this. He has conferred with the Danish Minister here, who has promised to do everything in his power in stressing for the Danish government the need for doing something so that Riga could be delivered from the current reign of terror.[102]

This was probably the first occasion that Herr Klaus came to the notice of the Swedish authorities; years later they would be interested in him for somewhat different reasons.

After an interwar career as a businessman in Germany and elsewhere, the outbreak of the Second World War found Klaus back in the Baltic Countries, ostensibly engaged in the film distribution business but also apparently reporting to German Intelligence in Kaunas.[103] This film cover would be used again in Sweden where he surfaced on 22 May 1941 as a representative of *Tobis* in Berlin. Contacts with the *Abwehr* could then be maintained through Werner Boening, a member of the Cultural Department with special responsibilities for film, and payments for services rendered could be correspondingly disguised. This arrangement, however, had not been cleared with the Minister.

Klaus claimed to have good contacts with Soviet Legation circles in Stockholm; whether this claim was justified and if so how it was to be interpreted, would later be thrown into question. But it is evident that the *Abwehr* took him at his word and believed that these contacts could be exploited for its own use. Klaus was duly installed in the Carlton Hotel in Stockholm and set to work cultivating a wide range of acquaintances.

Despite the *Abwehr*'s attempts to screen their agent's activities, many clues about his intelligence affiliation were forthcoming from routine police surveillance and the monitoring of communications. Thus in November 1941, it became known that Klaus was in receipt of a regular monthly payment sanctioned by *Auswärtiges Amt* in Berlin. Furthermore it could eventually be reasonably concluded that a series of teleprinter reports from Stockholm to *Abwehr* I Army (East) and attributed to the source Schönemann, in fact originated from Klaus. When in 1942, it became known that an officer from *Abwehr* I Army (East) von Lossow, was coming to Stockholm for 'an urgent conference with the Military Attaché', a watch was kept and it was verified that a meeting between von Lossow, Boening and Klaus had taken place at the German Legation on 3 May.

Shortly afterwards Klaus's residence permit expired and the *Abwehr*, which had evidently kept the Legation largely in the dark about cover arrangements regarding their agent, ran into difficulties when the Ministry of Social Affairs – with the Ministry for Foreign Affairs pressing in the background – refused to grant him an extension. As far as Klaus himself was concerned, the Swedish decision had come about because the German Legation had failed to back him up, presumably because of certain charges that had been made against him. As early as June 1941, it had been brought to the attention of the Legation that a certain Herr Klaus had been criticising Germany and at the same time had been claiming to be on intimate terms with the Legation and the Minister personally. In March 1942, the German Chamber of Commerce in Sweden had received a complaint about the man at the Carlton who 'mixed a great deal with Jews and half Jews' and who had apparently even boasted of becoming German Minister in Stockholm. Klaus was considered by some to be a swindler or a Soviet spy and had been duly reported to the Swedish authorities.

No doubt it was this last circumstance which particularly disturbed the diplomats at the German Legation in Stockholm: the

Abwehr's endorsement of Klaus was one thing but they had no wish to see the Legation compromised and their own efforts sabotaged by the unorthodox activities of a stringer for the intelligence service. Part of the trouble was Klaus: another source of irritation was Boening, Klaus's link man. The Minister had already raised objections about him in March. Now Boening was guilty of a further indiscretion by going behind the Legation's back in supplying an unauthorised recommendation on behalf of Klaus in support of the latter's application for an extension of his residence permit. In his submissions to the Ministry of Health and Social Affairs, Boening had explained that Klaus assisted him with propaganda for German films. As far as the Legation was concerned, this was not true. Boening had exceeded his instructions. He was entitled to forward certain letters on behalf of the *Abwehr*, that was all. In future, Klaus was to operate exclusively via Dr Wagner. This would ensure that Boening and hence the Legation would not be compromised.

Intense efforts were now made to stave off Klaus's expulsion. In August, Kramarz, the *Abwehr* liaison man at *Auswärtiges Amt*, was sent north to make a last-minute special appeal;[104] high-level Swedish contacts were activated. On 12 August, 'Swedish Friend A' had been asked to intervene on Schönemann's behalf and soon reported that he had been successful in his attempt only to discover that at twelve noon Klaus had been put on the train for Trelleborg/Sassnitz by the police.[105] A's intervention had come too late. For the time being, there was no alternative but to let the affair run its course. However, A was urged to continue his work behind the scenes and on 25 August, Dr Wagner reported that the matter had been resolved satisfactorily. Klaus – now in Germany – had been granted the necessary re-entry visa. As an apparent *quid pro quo*, A had requested that Schönemann's results could, at least in part, be placed at the disposal of the Swedish intelligence service. One other point was emphasised: Boening ('Berger') was to be dropped and in future Klaus was to work directly through Wagner. Once restored to the familiar surroundings of the Carlton Hotel in Stockholm, Klaus was able to resume those information-gathering activities on which Colonel Piekenbrock had placed such hopes.

Among the more extravagant rumours which had winged their way from Stockholm to Berlin via the Berger-Schönemann channel had been one intimating the imminent defection of Kollontay, the Soviet Minister in Stockholm, to Germany. On 20 July 1941, it was reported, incredibly, that Canaris had passed this on to the Führer who had ordered that everything was to be done to make her welcome. A more critical intelligence service would have quickly spotted this danger signal and demanded a critical examination of what Klaus was up to in Stockholm, but scepticism was perhaps hardly to be expected in the euphoria following the initial success of Barbarossa. Schönemann's reports to his trusting *Abwehr* superiors continued unabated. Some examples follow.

On 30 May 1942, a Schönemann report announced that in the second half of June, De Gaulle's troops, with strong British aerial support, would mount an attack on the French Atlantic coast from England. After the landing, large quantities of arms would be distributed to the civilian population with the intention of bringing about an uprising against the forces of occupation. A simultaneous landing in Norway was only intended to distract German attention.

On 10 August 1942 – two days before he was packed off to Germany – Schönemann reported the departure of a convoy of four ships from the Firth of Forth. On 15 October, once more in Stockholm, he was announcing an impending British bomb raid on the Berlin–Leipzig railway line. In January 1943, he was claiming to have heard of certain utterances of the British MA about further raids and in the same month there were also Schönemann telegrams dealing with Soviet troop deployments.

It is, however, one thing to relay information in a telegram marked 'Secret', it is quite another if this information is accurate and still another if it is useful. In the case of Klaus, there were several pointers which showed that his information should have been taken with a large pinch of salt. On 3 November 1942, he was asked to find out the starting point of certain Soviet submarines operating in the Baltic. Six days later, he came back with certain co-ordinates characteristically stressing, however, that the base was well hidden from the air.

The rationale behind this prudent reservation soon became evident when on 24 November Wagner was told that aerial reconnaissance had shown that Schönemann's co-ordinates had been innacurate. The same telegram also drew attention to another instance of Schönemann disinformation. He had apparently supplied a code allegedly used for some kind of Rumanian–Russian exchange of intelligence but according to the competent German authorities, the code had simply been cooked up. The conclusion drawn at the time was that Klaus had been duped. But who in fact was the deceiver? Was it perhaps the Soviet Intelligence Service which was sluicing its fabrications through Klaus? Or was it instead the ingenious Herr Klaus himself who for personal gain and after diligent study of open sources of various kinds, was able to peddle wares which to a large extent he had manufactured himself? Was it perhaps both? Walter Schellenberg when later questioned about this matter, did not hesitate to dismiss as useless the information delivered by Klaus. In his estimation, Schönemann was a bluff, in all probability under the control of the Soviet secret service.[106]

The *Abwehr* on the other hand continued to rely on him and even at the end of May 1943 when the Swedes once more raised difficulties over his presence, Canaris was personally agitating that everything should be done to retain him there. It was to be made clear to the Swedes that Schönemann worked exclusively against Russia and that great value was attached to having him in Sweden because of the importance of his reports. As it happened, the days of Schönemann as an *Abwehr* reporter were numbered. But as one door closed, another conveniently opened. In the shadow world of secret diplomacy, Dr Klaus would soon be busy with another alluring project.

Activities other than those of Bureau Wagner

It is important to realise, as the following examples show, that not every *Abwehr* operation mounted in Sweden was directed by Bureau Wagner.[107]

1.   In 1940, a commercial traveller with a colourful past was recruited by Klamroth, a representative of AST Copenhagen.[108] To begin with, he was deployed locally to keep an eye on Communists and those suspected of being pro-British. Then, in October, Klamroth sent him on a mission to Sweden and Finland. Once again, his general task was to make enquiries about Communist and pro-British persons but in addition, he was instructed to make contact with the British Legation and try to win the confidence of certain of its members. The *Abwehr* was also interested in finding out more about the air courier service between Stockholm and Britain.

The commercial traveller went north where he succeeded in making contact with Captain Munthe at the British Legation, who duly supplied him with a set of questions regarding German dispositions in Denmark. Upon his return to Copenhagen, the commercial traveller handed over Munthe's questionnaire to Klamroth, who then took him for a trip through the Danish countryside during which the *Abwehr* officer pricked in the supposed location of German airfields on a map, in a plausible blend of truth and falsity.

On 14 January 1941, the commercial traveller arrived back in the Swedish capital where he gave Munthe the map along with a list said to consist of the names of certain senior German officers serving in Denmark. At the same time, he employed his time in making enquiries about various persons in Stockholm of interest to the *Abwehr*.

Although Munthe provided him with the new assignment of distributing various propaganda items in Denmark, the traveller left with the impression that the British Legation was now suspicious of him. This was doubtless quite correct. On his way back, he was arrested in Malmö and evidence of his clandestine mission was discovered.[109]

2.   Another agent dispatched by AST Copenhagen to Sweden was Walter E. On 17 August 1941, he was sent to Gothenburg under commercial cover with the task of making contact with a certain Swedish businessman in that town.[110] This meeting took place and the Swede was instructed to carry out certain observations regarding the much contended Norwegian ships then berthed in the port. However, this amateur observer was spotted in the act by a Swedish officer and duly arrested. In cross examination, he made a statement implicating his German control. Walter E was picked up and later on 2 October 1941, received a sentence of ten months' hard labour for his part in the affair.

3.   A V-man reporting to Captain Loeschner of the AST Prague travelled regularly to Stockholm where he had a Russian contact who supplied him with information about Soviet armaments production and so on. Up to the beginning of 1944 the V-man, who was a businessman in Prague, had experienced no difficulty in obtaining a Swedish entry visa. Suddenly it was no longer so easy. It was therefore decided to establish a company in Stockholm of which the V-man would be a part-owner, thereby providing a more substantial reason for his visits to Sweden. Officially the firm would be fronted by a Swede known to the *Abwehr*. Approval for this operation was sought from the Central Financial Department of the *Abwehr* and eventually

permission was given for the transfer of 30,000 crowns for this purpose.[111]

4. At the end of 1941, Baron Waldemar von Oppenheim of the banking house Pferdmenges, visited Sweden to arrange with the co-operation of the Wallenbergs, with whom he had had previous financial dealings, for the construction of 50 fishing boats at a Swedish yard for the firm of Hugo Stinnes in Mülheim.[112] His trip was undertaken, however, on behalf of the German Supreme Naval Command. Plans were made for Oppenheim to make another trip in February 1942, having been furnished with an exit visa for this purpose by the *Abwehr* in Bremen. Because the *Abwehr* wished to conceal the true purpose of Oppenheim's visit, his trip was presented as a purely personal matter connected with his daughter's projected holiday the following month as a guest of the family Wallenberg. In April 1942, Oppenheim travelled to Stockholm again. In addition to discussing the fishing boat deal, Oppenheim had been instructed to ferret out details about American and British production statistics and he subsequently supplied the *Abwehr* with data about US production of tanks, aircraft, ships and other matters. Oppenheim's April visit resulted in some inconvenient publicity which was to lead to a German security enquiry. None the less in October 1942, he was sent to Stockholm again on behalf of the *Abwehr* to speak with a Swede, who had recently visited the USA. In his request that a visa should be granted to Oppenheim, Colonel Piekenbrock stressed that the *Abwehr* set great store by this meeting.

Sabotage

Sabotage, counter-sabotage, subversion and insurrection were among the responsibilities of *Abwehr* II under Colonel Erwin von Lahousen and some insight into the *Abwehr*'s contingency plans for sabotage and counter-sabotage in Sweden can be obtained from the latter's War Diary.[113]

The first relevant entry is a request at the end of 1939 from the Naval War Staff, for *Abwehr* II to disturb the railway traffic on the line Sundswall–Östersund–Trondheim which was said to be of vital importance for the transit traffic to England. The first quarter of 1940 also contains several references to an operation Eisberg. As the trend in French and British strategic thinking became increasingly obvious, some thought was given to ways of protecting those industrial regions in northern Sweden and Norway which were of key importance to the German war effort. The initial plan (Eisberg) had, however, been discontinued on 20 February on Hitler's express order, only to be reactivated about a month later – subject to the prior establishment of a radio link ensuring a clear chain of command from Berlin – in an extended form (Eisberg 2) which embraced sabotage activities and was intended to be implemented in the event of an enemy landing on the Norwegian coast. A principal object of the plan was to secure the safety of the northern Swedish iron orefields, the ore railway and the power station at Porjus which supplied electricity both to the railway and the mines. However opinions remained divided in the German camp about the proper division of responsibilities. While *Auswärtiges Amt* were happy with the idea that the *Abwehr* should take charge of all these arrangements in Sweden, the latter organ – pointing to the practical difficulties involved – refused this enlarged assignment and instead argued for the matter to be left in the hands of the Swedes.

In connection with Eisberg 2, a consignment of sabotage material had evidently been sent to Stockholm where it reposed in safety at the German Legation. But by the end of April, the *Abwehr* – perhaps forewarned of the spotlight of adverse publicity about to be focused on Rickman and his friends – had begun to question either the wisdom or necessity of such an explosive store and accordingly dispatched Lieutenant Herzner on 1 May 1940 to bring it back out of harm's way.

By the autumn of 1940, the power balance had moved decisively in Germany's favour. With new priorities, new tasks emerged also for *Abwehr* special operations. With the British repulsed from the European mainland, pressure was now applied to clip off their remaining contacts. On 21 September, the Luftwaffe Operations Staff was asking *Abwehr* II to target the courier air link between Britain and Sweden. The *Abwehr* had in turn referred the matter to the Chief of the Armed Forces High Command for decision. It was felt that such an action would merely serve to jeopardise the good political relations which had been established between Sweden and Germany. The Chief of the Armed Forces High Command therefore decided against the proposal.

None the less as events would prove, the idea was by no means dead as far as the Luftwaffe was concerned. On 12 August 1941, its Operations Staff appealed once more for the implementation of the sabotage plan (now codenamed Eskimo) against the British courier traffic from Stockholm. An expert in the appropriate black arts, a man known among the members of the German Legation in Stockholm as 'Stink Bomb' Müller, was already in place, prepared to set to work at a given signal.[114]

With all systems apparently poised for action, the German air attaché in Stockholm, Petersen, suddenly appeared in Berlin, urging the greatest restraint. If such an operation were to be executed, the Swedes would not have the slightest doubt about who was responsible. The positions of the local *Abwehr* Head and the air attaché would become impossible. Müller was to do nothing before Petersen had returned to Stockholm and had had a chance to confer with him. Above all, the destruction of a courier plane in Swedish territory had to be avoided. There should be an investigation to see if a device could be brought aboard the plane so that it would explode some time after take-off. However, Petersen was highly sceptical about such a possibility.

Three days later on 15 August, a telegram from the Military Attaché in Stockholm further emphasised the practical difficulties to be encountered by would-be saboteurs. As a result, Müller was instructed to bide his time until Petersen got back so that they could together discuss the possibility of implementing Eskimo on a later occasion. With this solution, the plan seems to have been effectively squashed and it is noteworthy that Petersen himself was to be instrumental in backing at the end of 1941 the proposal to extend the courier traffic between Britain and Sweden by allowing the Swedish company ABA to initiate a supplementary service. The wisdom of encouraging air links with Britain would be sold to the German intelligence service in another way.[115]

For a time, a ban was imposed on German sabotage activities in Sweden. However, in January 1943, a new situation arose which resulted in this prohibition being lifted. In Berlin, the Swedish naval attaché had relayed to his hosts that the Norwegian ships, *Lionel* and *Dicto*, would be free to leave Gothenburg on the 15th of that month.[116] At the same time, the German Naval War Staff reported that because of a shortage of watch vessels at its disposal, it could not be certain of preventing the Norwegian ships from successfully breaking out. A meeting was convened between representatives of Naval War Staff and members of the *Abwehr*'s sabotage section to discuss counter-measures, including a proposal for members of the special Brandenburg commando to mount a raid on Gothenburg harbour in speedboats, in an attempt to destroy or damage the Norwegian ships.

The latter proposal was, however, dropped and instead the Naval War Staff advocated immediate steps to organise broadly based sabotage activities in Sweden. This was essential not simply because of *Lionel* or *Dicto* but also because of other enemy ships present or under construction in that country. These vessels could be prevented from sailing by sabotage actions mounted from the land.

As a result of this discussion, the *Abwehr* decided (a) to lift the ban on sabotage activities in Sweden (b) to place a sabotage expert and assistant at the disposal of Bureau Wagner and (c) to dispatch special detonators, explosives and mines by courier to Sweden.

On 15 January 1943, Lahousen recorded that Lieutenant-Commander Müller of AST Oslo been engaged in discussions about the release of certain communist prisoners for a special task. By 1 April, Müller was reporting that a sabotage operation against 'English ships' in Gothenburg had been set in motion. Whatever the exact sequence of events that followed, the operation failed to achieve its objective. The idea, however, was to linger on for a while. In December 1943, prompted by a successful Danish action, the head of *Abwehr*'s Section II was asked whether an analogous German attempt against *Lionel* and *Dicto* could be made.[117] The reply was hardly encouraging.[118] The two cases were said to be quite different. In particular, it was stressed, the Danes could rely on support from the local population. Certainly a German sabotage action was theoretically possible but for it to be carried out, a considerable quantity of explosives had to be introduced into the country – an observation of some interest in the light of the decision taken at the beginning of the year.

The introduction of this sabotage material (the *Abwehr* went on to maintain) was not without dangers. It had to be brought in via the diplomatic bag. The possibility of acquiring it in Sweden was out of the question. Moreover transporting it over the closely guarded Norwegian–Swedish border was also impossible. As far as recruiting saboteurs was concerned, this too was possible but in view of the political climate not without risks, etc. Confronted with this litany of despair, the idea was dropped.

GERMAN SECURITY SERVICE ACTIVITIES

In contrast to the *Abwehr*, the *Sicherheitsdienst* (SD) – or security service – was by origin ideologically inspired, designed in effect to be the intelligence service of the NSDAP, supplying it with warnings of possible threats. Hitler's assumption of power swiftly removed the distinction between party and state and the security *apparat* emerged from the totalitarian revolution with its position consolidated and indeed enhanced. On 27 September 1939, the Reich Security Main Office (RSHA) was set up under the leadership of Reinhard Heydrich who enjoyed the title Chief of the Security Police and SD. Department IV of RSHA was the Gestapo while Department VI (formerly Branch III (*Ausland*) of the SD) was responsible for Foreign Intelligence. As a jealous competitor of the *Abwehr*, the SD was finally to gain the upper hand over its rival in the reorganisation of German intelligence which took place in accordance with the Führer's order of 12 February 1944.

Early Days

An important source of information about German security service activities in Sweden was provided by the post-war interrogation of *Sturmbannführer* Arthur Grönheim. In the summer of 1936, Grönheim had joined the *Ausland* branch of the SD, dealing with questions relating to Sweden and Norway. Four years later, he was to become head of the Scandinavian Section (D3) of Department VI of RSHA.

During the period from 1937 to the end of 1940, Grönheim visited Sweden a number of times on fact-finding missions. In 1937, he had had discussions with Sven-Olof Lindholm, the leader of one of Sweden's National Socialist factions and according to Grönheim, the only such faction worth supporting. Lindholm had provided information about membership numbers and had discussed the difficulties faced by his movement in Sweden but the question of financial support was not then taken up. Himmler was, however, keen to support the National Socialist groups in Sweden and in the autumn of 1939, Grönheim was given instructions to transfer certain funds from Germany to the SD representative in Sweden for channelling to Lindholm. According to Grönheim, these funds came entirely from party membership fees of Swedes living in Germany, which were then collected by the local group leader in Berlin.[119] In the period 1939–43, Grönheim claimed to have superintended some five or six transfers amounting in all to around 12,000 Reichsmarks.

Another one of his early contacts had been Carl Ernfrid Carlberg, one of the linchpins of National Socialism in Sweden.

Carlberg, who was a wealthy man, had been a member of the winning Swedish gymnastics team at the Stockholm Olympics in 1912. In 1928, he founded a gymnastics association and began publishing a magazine *Gymn*, dedicated to 'Health, Character and Beauty'. It was Carlberg's thesis that mechanisation and competition had removed the educative, aesthetic and moral value of sport and physical exercise and that it was necessary to restore these if the Western world was not to degenerate. These views were soon to be supplemented by others of a different colour. One of the first to contribute to Carlberg's magazine, was 'an expert in race-biology', Hermann Lundborg.[120] By degrees, the ideological programme of *Gymn* crystallised and by 1931, it was endorsing the view that established culture risked being overthrown by Jewish–Asiatic Bolshevism. The same year witnessed a growth of a provincial network of gymnastics clubs throughout the country, aimed at disseminating the appropriate cultural and racial values. In this way, National Socialist ideas could be introduced to a younger audience.

After press criticism, *Gymn* ceased publication in 1932 and the kindred association was dissolved only to be replaced by a new creation of Carlberg. This was the society *Manhem*, which was *inter alia* dedicated to preserving the Nordic race, opposing injurious foreign influences in Swedish cultural life, protecting Swedish small businesses from the depredations of monopolies and saving the trade unions from the snares of Marxism. It soon became a clearing centre for the ideas of diverse intellectual or upper-class elements from the Swedish extreme right, a role that it was to retain throughout the Second World War. Apart from sponsoring a series of lectures and debates, *Manhem* also arranged during the war for the private showing of German films which were publicly prohibited under the censorship regulations. Still another component in Carlberg's empire was the publishing company *Svea Rike* which provided Swedish translations of German-inspired and other National Socialist literature. During the war, in order that it could be published in compliance with Swedish government regulations, the popular German illustrated weekly *Signal*, which was under OKW's control and committed to instilling respect in neutral and occupied countries by charting the victorious progress of German arms, arranged for Carlberg to function as its responsible Swedish editor.

At the outbreak of the war, the SD *Ausland*'s man on the spot in Stockholm was Hans Georg Wagener, the representative for *Völkischer*

Beobachter.[121] Wagener had been involved with the SD from 1934. He knew Sweden well and had close contacts with National Socialist circles there but was apparently disliked at the Legation. Perhaps for this reason but also because it was suspected that his SD affiliation was an open secret, Wagener was eventually dropped. Instead, in March 1942, when the question of having a so-called Police Attaché permanently installed in Stockholm to take charge of SD matters, came up before Ribbentrop, Dr August Finke was proposed for the post.

Dr Finke and the SD staff

A lawyer by profession, Finke had begun working for the SD in 1935 and four years later he was assigned to *Amt* VI's HQ where he soon took over as Head of section A2. In May 1942, having been briefed by Grönheim, he travelled to Stockholm to take up his camouflaged position as 'assistant commercial attaché'.

Dr Finke enjoyed certain advantages over his *Abwehr* colleague, Dr Wagner. He was not to the same extent answerable to the minister; instead, he had his own special cipher and had the right to send encrypted reports dealing with political questions to which the minister had no access, to VI D3 – the Scandinavian Section of the SD – in Berlin.[122] A typical report coming into VI D3 from Finke might be attributed to 142/36 i.e. V-Mann 36 in country 142 (Sweden). Finke himself appears to have disposed over a group of some 30 V-men. Among his sources, were members of various Swedish National Socialist groups, several German journalists based in Sweden, the representative of a German shipping company, the director of a haulage company, and other miscellaneous business contacts in Sweden. One of his most interesting confidants concerning the Soviet Union was Sergius Dmitriewsky.[123]

Dmitriewsky was a man with many contacts. During the war, he sought out or was sought out by representatives of the Japanese, Soviet, British and German intelligence services. It is unlikely that he was entirely trusted by any of them. Born in Cholm in Russia in 1893, Dmitriewsky had joined the Folk Socialists and had been a member of the editorial committee of *Narodnoye Slovo*. But in 1919, he joined the Communist Party and began to carve out a career in the *Apparat*. Spells as Political Commissar in the Army and as a Chief Administrator in the Communications Department were followed in 1922 by an appointment with the Soviet Trade Delegation in Berlin, a brief period as First Secretary in Athens and three years in the Ministry of Foreign Affairs in Moscow. In 1927, he arrived in Stockholm as Counsellor at the Soviet Legation. But his career in the Soviet service was to end dramatically with his defection in Sweden in April 1930. Thereafter Dmitriewsky lived in the shadow of his past, eking out an existence as a writer on things Russian and as a commentator on Soviet Policy. He was taken under the wing of Ivar Kreuger but the days of that financial wizard were numbered. In due course, Dmitriewsky found a new patron in the shape of C. E. Carlberg, and in 1934 he was off to Erfurt for conversations with Lieutenant Colonel Fleischhauer of *Welt-Dienst*.[124] Dmitriewsky's relations with the new Germany were to become increasingly intimate. He was soon on good terms with successive representatives of the SD in Sweden, first Wagener and later Finke, supplying them with the gossip that came his way and his 'insider's view' of Soviet political strategy and tactics.

At the end of 1943, Dr Krüger, a member of the Swedish Institute at the University of Greifswald who was deemed to be well informed about the Swedish situation, was transferred to *Amt* VI of the SD and sent to Stockholm to assist Finke in his work and the SD presence at the Legation was further strengthened by the appointment of two other 'watchmen'.[125] In keeping with the SD's more conscious ideological profile, continuous attention was given to fostering ties both with Swedish ultra right-wing groups and politically committed members of the local German community. In this kind of liaison work, Finke had the co-operation of certain other members of the Legation who acted essentially as stringers for the SD. Among them were Baron von Gossler and Dr Bauersfeld.

Baron von Gossler had been appointed head of the German Tourist Office in Stockholm in the summer of 1938, a position which he held until his expulsion from Sweden at the end of 1944. During the war, the Tourist Office became an important centre for propaganda, with an annual budget of 10,000 crowns for this purpose and the work was carried out energetically and systematically. One aspect was the distribution of pamphlets and other printed materials which developed rapidly as the following annual statistics[126] show:

TABLE 6

Year	1940	1941	1942	1943
Publications distributed	21,805	56,553	46,740	13,376

Summing up the success of 1941, von Gossler had this to say:

During 1941 – in comparison with 1940 – the distribution of current publications by our information office has nearly trebled and altogether 56,553 current publications of all kinds have been distributed, for example the German White Papers, speeches of the Führer and other German statesmen. The immense increase in these figures alone seems to us to be a striking proof of the steadily increasing importance of our current information work. The largest portion of the material has been placed at our disposal by the Legation for free distribution and through personal contacts with the public we have been able to place in the right hands. In this way, the mass distribution of items has been avoided, most of which end up in the waste paper basket unread.[127]

Another method for spreading the word favoured by the Tourist Office was the hiring of display windows and one of von Gossler's secretaries was dispatched to various cities to arrange for the display of photographs and other propaganda material. The biggest such display was naturally at the Tourist Office in Stockholm. In addition to these efforts, von Gossler also keenly followed developments in the enemy camp, reporting for example on American and British films being shown in Stockholm and noting carefully the public's reaction. At the same time, he kept a critical eye on other aspects of the German Legation's information and cultural activities.

Dr Bauersfeld succeeded Dr Albrecht as the head of the German Academic Exchange Service in Stockholm in the autumn of 1941. Bauersfeld's work was nominally straightforward enough, dealing with stipendia, making contacts with Swedish universities and arranging for Swedish students to visit Germany and for German students to visit Sweden. But the latter visits were also able to serve other purposes. Thus German students visiting Sweden were called to a briefing at VI D3 to pick their brains about which Swedish academics they had found to be pro-German and why they were so. In this way, likely supporters could be identified and approaches could be made.

As regards the value of Finke's reporting, expert German opinions remained divided. Thus Kaltenbrunner declared to his interrogators that Finke continued to supply good material to the very end while *Obersturmbannführer* Theodor Paeffken described him more ambiguously as one of the most highly regarded agents of the SD and one of Schellenberg's special sources. At the same time, Paeffken was personally critical of certain aspects of Finke's work. Thus above all he had failed to gain access to British and American sources. Grönheim was still more critical; Finke was a good administrator but a bad intelligence man and his reports had been largely worthless. Among the exceptions had been one dealing with a reduction in iron ore supplies to Germany, another on the import of the Swedish–American negotiations on the exports of ball bearings to Germany and a third on the suspension of the war risks insurance on Swedish merchant vessels, plying German ports, which had more or less led that traffic to come to a standstill.

Soon after Finke's arrival, the Swedish security service became interested in him. An important clue about his true function at the Legation, became available in April 1943 via the Defence Staff, when it was learned that von Gossler was to have luncheon with his intelligence chief on a certain date. Surveillance revealed that the chief in question was none other than Finke. Thereafter he was closely watched. It was known that a certain Norwegian editor, belonged to his circle of acquaintances. Later during the autumn the editor had several conspiratorial meetings with Finke's secretary and also with Finke's associate, Dr. Krüger. In March 1944, the editor was arrested and on interrogation confessed that during a trip to Oslo in July 1943, he had been recruited by the German intelligence service. Thereafter until his arrest, he had supplied his control in Oslo with information about opposition in Catholic circles to government policy in England and America, about American forces in Iceland, about the attitudes of Polish refugees to the Soviet government, about certain Polish Red Cross activities in Stockholm and about convoys to Murmansk. At the beginning of August 1943, he received a letter from a person calling himself Fleischer who asked to meet him at a certain spot. The meeting duly took place and Fleischer (alias Dr Finke) explained that he wished the editor in future to deposit at the German Consulate in Stockholm a copy of the information collected on behalf of German Intelligence in Norway. At the same time, the Norwegian was encouraged to collect information about the journalist Edmond Demaitre whom Finke described as 'one of the major figures in the British intelligence service'. A new meeting was set up between the two men. However Dr Finke chose to send his secretary instead to collect the information gleaned by the editor about Demaitre. From September onwards, the editor was in the habit of depositing reports intended for Finke with Dr Krüger. On 29 March 1943, Finke's Norwegian informant was sentenced to five months' hard labour for offences under Chapter 8, Section 14a.

Further clues continued to flow in about Finke's role in the German intelligence network in Sweden. His contacts with Schellenberg during the latter's visit in November 1943 were noted and in the same month an incautious telephone caller from Berlin, asked the operator at the German Legation to put them on to 'Police Attaché Finke'.

In August 1944 a visitor, V, whose father-in-law was employed at Bofors, was notified that he had been given the task of obtaining drawings relating to a new cannon. On arrival, he was told to get in touch with Dr Bauersfeld who in turn referred him to Dr Krüger. A meeting between V and Krüger took place in Finke's apartment. V was told that when he had got hold of the drawings, a meeting would be set up at a hotel in the town of Örebro. V would come with the drawings and a man would be there to photograph them. The meeting took place on 18 August 1944 under police surveillance and Pioch, one of Finke's staff, was caught in the act of photographing the drawings.

As a result of these and other indiscretions, the Swedish government by the end of the year was ready to proceed with a demand for Dr Finke's recall and he finally left the country on 28 February 1945.

German police liaison officers

Finke's appointment as the resident Stockholm SD representative with diplomatic immunity took place in May 1942. His tasks, whether acquiring information or supplying financial support, were covert and presupposed *inter alia* that they remained hidden from the Swedish security service. But before that, the RSHA had made efforts to establish explicit contacts with the Swedish security services by means of a different link. To a large extent the pre-war investigations into the sabotage activities of Wollweber provided the necessary foot in the door. These investigations had involved the co-operation of the police forces of Denmark, Holland, Norway, Sweden and Germany whose representatives had attended a conference on the subject in Hamburg in September 1938. The exchange of information about these sabotage activities between the Swedish and other police forces concerned, including the German police, continued throughout 1939 and were maintained after the outbreak of war. They were to be given new actuality when Wollweber was arrested in Sweden in May 1940. In January 1941, the first of a series of German requests to have him extradited was received – an extradition claim that would be circumvented – and a month later an invitation arrived from Heydrich suggesting that Martin Lundqvist and two of his colleagues should visit Berlin as his guests for an exchange of ideas. Heydrich's invitation was put before Gustaf Möller whose Ministry took care of Security Service matters and Möller gave his approval for the visit to go ahead. At the same time, Lundqvist approached the Swedish Ministry for Foreign Affairs, to obtain guidelines about what could or could not be discussed in Berlin. The formula agreed was that all information offered by the Germans could be received and that the Swedes in return were empowered to hand over information about the Wollweber affair and also about Rickman's sabotage activities. No information concerning espionage cases in Sweden was to be provided, apart from material that had already appeared in the the press and no assurances regarding future co-operation were to be given. If the question of future co-operation was broached, Lundquist was instructed to reply that no answer could be given without having first consulted the relevant Swedish authorities.

The visit by the three Swedish police officials began on 10 April 1941 and ended on 14 April. The main topic on the agenda appears to have been Wollweber but two British matters, Rickman's activities and a case of commercial espionage which had figured in the newspapers, were also discussed. From their German hosts the visitors obtained a list of various German Communists said to be resident in Sweden and some information about supposed places for Communist rendezvous in Sweden. Finally, hints were dropped by the Germans that a special police liaison officer would be attached to their Legation in Stockholm.

Attempts were made to follow up this suggestion at the end of the year. In the interval, there was renewed German pressure for the Swedes to take more resolute measures against Communist organisations on their territory. To some extent, events were to unfold favourably. Information about Wollweber's and other Communist covert sabotage groups had accumulated and at the end of May, a meeting of the various Swedish authorities concerned was held in Stockholm to plan a concerted action. On 4 June 1941, the Swedish police carried out a series of raids thoughout the country in which numerous Communist functionaries were held and questioned and the premises of the Communist Party in Stockholm was searched. Partly as a result of this raid, a number of people were later tried and sentenced for sabotage-related offences.

The Security authorities in Berlin saw these developments in a wider perspective; in a report to *Auswärtiges Amt*, they noted that they had been agitating for ages for the Swedes to take active measures. Now finally after the launching of Barbarossa, their pressure had borne fruit. Just as neutral Holland and Belgium had in 1938 and 1939 been regaled with tales of the devious British Intelligence Service's involvement in espionage and sabotage, so now in neutral Sweden as the great campaign in the East got under way, some of the selfsame sabotage incidents could be attributed to the Communists.[128] But if Swedish indignation over Communist saboteurs could be viewed with some satisfaction, the political windfall was also perhaps less than might have been desired. The coverage of the trial of the 'Wollweber men' in the press, as the German Minister noted, helped to whip up anti-Communist sentiments in the country.[129] Several papers laid stress on the fact that the party itself, and not merely certain clandestine groups, had been compromised. In the end, however, calls for a ban on the Communist Party were to be unsuccessful.

Meanwhile somewhat earlier, at the end of July 1941, two members of the Gestapo, Horst Kopkow and Erich Mittmann, had arrived in Stockholm to confer about the Wollweber sabotage organisation. Their visit lasted about a week. In November, it was time for a new duo from German security, Neumann and Müller, to put in an appearance. They were to stay until 11 February 1942. In addition to information about sabotage activities, Neumann was also briefed about various cases of Soviet espionage that had come to light. A gradual extension of the terms of co-operation was exactly what Neumann's superiors in Berlin were calculating on.

> In this way the Swedes could be given the opportunity, unofficially and without endangering their neutrality, in covert ways to make a contribution to anti-Comintern work.[130]

But how far were the Swedes prepared to go along that particular road? Already on 10 November 1941, in a submission to the Security Chief, Martin Lundqvist had taken up the whole question of the rules governing contacts between the Swedish and German police. According to the suggestion of the Ministry for Foreign Affairs, these rules should be roughly along the following lines:

> As regards Communist sabotage activity carried out in Sweden, there were no objections to co-operation with the German police authorities where the Swedish police requested that the German police details concerning German or former German subjects involved and the German police were kept abreast of the results of the investigation. This rule ought to be subject to certain exceptions which depended in part on Sweden's friendly relations with states other than Germany (e.g. co-operation should not take place in cases of British-linked sabotage activities) or in part on an improper use by the German side of the information given by Sweden, during the co-operation. If, for example, it turned out that the Germans on insufficient grounds were to demand the extradition of an alien living in Sweden, about whom information had been given, this ought to lead to restrictions in the co-operation. The same was the case if the information provided by the Swedish police was used in Germany for propaganda purposes that were inappropriate from the Swedish point of view.

> As regards other types of subversive activity, in particular espionage, the governing principle was that no information was to be provided other than such as had been published in the press. Exceptions could only be made in cases where the Ministry for Foreign Affairs had given its explicit permission.

> There were no objections to the German police supplying the Swedish police with information available in Germany, about subversive activities in Sweden no matter what kind it might be. The question to what extent continued co-operation should take place, was to be judged in accordance with the rules already given.[131]

The Ministry for Foreign Affairs – no doubt well aware that it was handling a hot potato – concluded by adroitly suggesting that since the matter involved not simply foreign but also domestic policy, it should at the same time be placed before the head of the Ministry of Social Affairs.

Lundqvist had requested that Security Chief Hallgren should approve the guidelines. However, Hallgren had no wish to rush ahead. For the time being, Lundqvist was told simply to avoid giving answers to any questions put by Neumann and company. The head of the Ministry of Social Affairs was not asked for an opinion on the matter.

On 20 December 1941, Lundqvist reported to Hallgren on a new request by Neumann to extend the co-operation between the services. He was asking for information about all the criminal activities directed against Germany of refugees other than Norwegians, as well as about 'NKVD directed espionage' against Germany.

> With regard to the second request, Neumann had maintained that Sweden because of its position and because of the relative freedom still accorded to the Communist Party and its supporters in Sweden, could be assumed to constitute an important base for Russian inspired espionage or sabotage activities directed against Germany. Even in those cases of illegal activities that had come to the attention of the police and which were not explicitly directly aimed against Germany, there was reason to suppose that the major figures involved simultaneously had a leading position in activities directed against Germany, which had hitherto not come to the notice of the police. In such cases, therefore, the German police authorities wished to know the names of the most important agents, especially those who belonged to the Russian Trade Delegation in Stockholm, which could be suspected of being the centre of Russian espionage in Sweden. In exchange for any information Germany might thereby obtain from Sweden, the German police authorities would make available material about persons of a similar character, about whom Sweden desired information.[132]

Were there political objections to agreeing to this proposal? Lundqvist once more pressed for guidelines from his chief. Hallgren in turn passed the question to the Foreign Minister. On 8 January 1942, he wrote again to the minister, reminding him of his previous letter and at the same time pointing out that the Germans had got hold of an Estonian who, during the Soviet occupation of that country, had been instructed to organise in various Swedish ports an espionage network reporting on Swedish military establishments. However the Germans were not prepared to hand over the information about this network until they knew what decision the Swedes had come to regarding co-operation. Could the exchange of information go ahead?

The matter was remitted to the Cabinet Office. On 17 January 1942, Staffan Söderblom at the Ministry for Foreign Affairs informed the Security Chief that in general no information about refugees was to be handed over to the Germans. However, in certain particular cases, involving purely criminal activities – and only after examination – information could be passed. As regards Soviet espionage in Sweden directed against Germany, it was to be stated that the Swedes had no knowledge of any such espionage apart from that which dealt with the German transit traffic. On the other hand, the role of the Soviet-controlled radio transmitters in reporting this traffic could be presented in some detail for the Germans. Information which the Germans had claimed to hold about the Soviet espionage against Swedish targets, should be requested but no binding assurance should be given about future Swedish–German police co-operation. The question of future co-operation could be circumvented by some statement to the effect that the Swedish police hoped in the future to be able to provide further information.

Several days before, the Counsellor at the German Legation had approached Söderblom about the renewal of Neumann's visa. Söderblom was prepared to extend this by four weeks, but told Dankwort at the same time that the Swedes did not wish Neumann to be permanently stationed in Stockholm.

> Co-operation with the German police was to some extent desirable and took place to mutual satisfaction. But this did not however require that some German policeman was permanently based in Stockholm. If it became known that this was the case, a less desirable reaction could be expected from the Swedish public which it lay both in Swedish and German interest to avoid. Dankwort promised to report along these lines to Berlin.[133]

Neumann and Müller sucked up what information they could during their stay. After their departure, Neumann maintained contacts with Lundquist and visited Sweden on a number of occasions thereafter.[134]

SD special assignments

Apart from the more routine intelligence received from the resident organisation in Sweden, the SD's flow of information was also supplemented by reports obtained from special visitors.[135] The visits of Dr Weissauer and Alexander Meller-Zakomelsky help to illustrate this point.

Dr Weissauer.[136]   During the Phoney War, several attempts at peace-broking between Germany and Britain had been made through Swedish channels, most conspicuously through the businessman

Birger Dahlerus. By midsummer 1940, with Hitler master of the continent of Europe, it is fair to say that Britain had been largely written off in Sweden; it was felt that the wisest policy for Britain would be to reach some reasonable settlement with Germany while there was still a chance to do so. No doubt these sentiments were inspired by Sweden's own predicament and its consequent desire for an end to the conflict. They were also encouraged by a message that had reached Stockholm from London. On the night between 17 and 18 June, the Swedish Minister had sent a telegram to the Ministry for Foreign Affairs about a conversation with Butler at the Foreign Office. According to Prytz, Butler had said that 'no opportunity would be neglected for concluding a compromise peace if the chance was offered on reasonable terms' and that 'the so-called diehards would not be allowed to stand in the way of negotiations'. At this point in the conversation, Butler had been called away to Lord Halifax. When he returned, Butler passed on a greeting from Halifax to Prytz that 'common sense not bravado would dictate the British Government's policy'. Halifax added, however, that this greeting was not be interpreted to mean peace at any price. In Stockholm – despite the initial qualification and the clarifications that were to follow shortly – the phrase 'common sense not bravado' stuck; it was perhaps exactly the slogan the Swedes were looking for to underwrite their own policy.[137]

Hopes of a negotiated peace lingered on in Stockholm. Wafted to Berlin by the Swedish Minister Richert, who informed Weizsäcker at *Auswärtiges Amt* of the content of the Prytz telegram, they gave rise to speculations about possible factions within the British cabinet who might favour a more conciliatory policy. Weizsäcker's reactions were subsequently relayed by Marcus Wallenberg to Mallet who told his banker friend that all the signs indicated that the British government was resolutely determined to continue the war. At the end of June, it was time for the familiar duo of Goering and Dahlerus to enter the game again. In a conversation with the Swedish businessman, Goering emphasised the importance for the whole of Europe that the war should be brought to an end. The only person who was competent to act as a peace-broker between Germany and England, was the King of Sweden.

This flattering suggestion fell on fertile ground in Stockholm. On 1 August, the Swedish ministers in Berlin and London were conveying a message from Gustav V offering his good offices in the event that both powers wished through such a contact to investigate the possibilities for peace. For the British, the message was accompanied by an assurance that the monarch had acted entirely on his own initiative, inspired only by the conviction that he ought to spare Europe further bloodshed.

On 6 August, the Führer answered. Negotiations with the present rulers in London were as impossible as they were meaningless. The war had to go on until they were destroyed, even if it meant that the British Empire itself would be destroyed. This prima-facie negative but revealing answer was followed ten days later by the British reply: before any meeting of the type proposed could fruitfully take place, Germany had to demonstrate by its actions that any peace reached guaranteed the freedom of France, Poland and other countries which had fallen to German arms and the security of Britain and its empire.

The royal offer of mediation had led nowhere but the peace trail was not quite dead. At the beginning of September, Dr Ludwig Weissauer arrived in the Swedish capital. To his Scandinavian acquaintances, Weissauer appeared sympathetic but a trifle mysterious. It was widely believed that he acted as one of Ribbentrop's special emissaries which may well have been true. But it was certainly the case that Weissauer was a trusted confidential agent of the SD and reported to that organisation. His contacts in Sweden had come about through his Finnish connections, which had been sedulously cultivated from the time that Kivimäki had arrived in Berlin at the beginning of June 1940 as Finnish envoy. In July Weissauer had been dispatched to Finland where he had conversations with Mannerheim and Prime Minister Ryti. At the same time, he availed himself of the opportunity presented in passing through Sweden to talk to Birger Ekeberg, a senior figure in the Swedish judiciary, to whom he had a letter of introduction from Kivimäki. Among the subjects broached during these July discussions with Ekeberg was the question of the ways in which Sweden might be able to support Finland, if the latter country were to be attacked by the Soviet Union.

When Weissauer appeared in Stockholm in September, he had been given the task of testing a rumour that Mallet had confided quite unambiguously to a very select circle that the British government was prepared to explore unofficially Germany's willingness for peace negotiations. The German emissary now asked Ekeberg to take the matter up with Mallet himself and at the same time he stressed his own interest in meeting the British minister in conditions of the greatest secrecy to discuss peace. Ekeberg was given to understand that his visitor reported directly to Hitler and that only the British government and the German leader would be privy to what was discussed. In Weissauer's view, earlier attempts at mediation by kings and the pope had failed because they had been too public.

Ekeberg visited Mallet on 5 September and passed on Weissauer's message. From the subsequent discussion between the two men, Ekeberg apparently emerged with the opinion that there were two views within the British government about a negotiated peace. Some cabinet members believed that it was worth while sounding out the Germans while Churchill on the other hand was resolved to continue the war until the following spring. Mallet said that there was no point in meeting Weissauer but he agreed to consider the matter before reaching a final decision and he telegraphed London for instructions.

There the news of Weissauer's peace ploys were viewed with some suspicion.[138] Were they not simply part of a tactical scheme to cast doubt on British resolve? Mallet was told not to take up the offer of a meeting with Weissauer to avoid any danger of misconstruction. He was to tell Ekeberg that such a meeting would be useless because he could not enter into any discussion and was only in a position to receive a message which it was always open to Ekeberg to deliver himself. Ekeberg, after having conferred again with Weissauer, returned to Mallet in great excitement with a proposal that fell into four parts. (i) The world to be divided into two economic spheres, one continental, organised by Germany; the other maritime and colonial, organised by the British Empire. (ii) The political independence of the European countries occupied by Germany to be restored, including 'a Polish State' but not including Czechoslovakia. The economic division of Europe, however, was to be brought to an end. (iii) The British Empire to retain all its colonies and such mandates as were needed for its political and military interests; Germany possibly receiving compensation elsewhere. (iv) Questions concerning the Mediterranean, Egypt and the French, Belgian and Dutch colonies to be open to discussion. This was the 'last chance' and the only alternative was a continuation of the war which for Britain would mean the probable loss of Egypt, the Middle East and ultimately India.

The British answer to this alluring offer was simply to reiterate in somewhat briefer form what it had previously said to the King of Sweden. When this reply in due course reached Weissauer, he wrote to Ekeberg saying that he treated the British answer as negative but perhaps not definitive. As far as he was concerned, the channel of communication remained open and he was ready to come to Stockholm as soon as he got the word. The word never came. Dr Weissauer, however, continued behind the scenes with his peace offensive. On 19 November he called on Kivimäki in Berlin. Germany, he explained, would be most grateful if Finland could help to ensure that Ekeberg's mediation efforts were made known in non-governmental circles in England. A Finn travelling to Britain, for example, would be in a position to sound out 'economic circles' about the possibilities for peace. This latter suggestion was in fact subsequently followed up but the visit simply reinforced the view that no fundamental change in the previously stated British position was to be expected.

Weissauer popped up in Scandinavia on several other occasions during the war. On 8 May 1941, he called upon Ryti in Finland and informed him that a war between Germany and the Soviet Union would under no circumstances break out before the spring of 1942, a 'confidential leak' doubtless part of the conscious deception scheme designed to hide the preparations for Barbarossa.

Schellenberg, whose high opinion of Weissauer's abilities was tempered by certain doubts about his trustworthiness, noted another aspect of Weissauer's trips to Finland. The sum of 50,000 dollars had been made available to the emissary to allow him to see all the reports sent to the Finnish Ministry of Foreign Affairs from Finnish Missions abroad.[139]

Alexander Meller-Zakomelsky. Another high-level agent used by the SD in Sweden, was Alexander Meller-Zakomelsky, an emigré Russian aristocrat, who was apparently on familiar terms with members of the Royal Household.[140] On 18 December 1939, he arrived in Sweden from Berlin on a seven-day visa and during his stay travelled to Finland 'on a special mission to the HQ' in circumstances of great secrecy.[141] In September 1940, he was back again in Stockholm and made use of his social connections to take stock of the political climate of opinion both in the Swedish capital and elsewhere in the country. In the course of his visit, he was able to speak to the King and other members of the Royal Household as well as to the

Foreign Minister. His impressions were subsequently summarised in a seventeen page report to the SD[142]

On 25 September, he had been invited to breakfast with the Crown Prince and Princess at their summer residence at Ulriksdal. Next day it was time to call on Foreign Minister Günther, who received him very cordially. Casting an eye backwards to the Spring when Meller-Zakomelsky had evidently experienced some difficulty in obtaining an entry visa to the country, the Foreign Minister described it as a very anxious time. With the present situation on the other hand, he professed himself to be entirely happy. However at the same time, he emphasised for his visitor that it was important to take things very gently and not to try to force the pace. The trouble with the Germans was that they paid too much attention to unfriendly remarks in insignificant newspapers. In fact, great efforts had been made to suppress such opinions but it was no easy task in a country which enjoyed the freedom of the press.

Having ruled out any impending government shuffle, the Foreign Minister asked his visitor how the Germans viewed Sweden. As a Nordic–Germanic brother people, said Meller-Zakomelsky. The King was held in high regard and there was nothing but approval for Günther himself. On the other hand the Social Democratic press was disliked and still more, Günther's predecessor, Rickard Sandler. The conversation finally turned to Sweden's reaction to the challenge of the New Order in Europe. Meller-Zakomelsky explained that he would be asked about this on his return to Berlin: now he wished to hear what the Foreign Minister thought.

Günther restated his original point. 'If the Germans do not force us to rush things, all will be well.'[143] This was not diplomacy or a tactical manoeuvre, as the Germans appeared to suspect.

I am being entirely honest and am profoundly convinced that we will succeed in further leading Swedish domestic and foreign policy to the complete satisfaction of Germany. Any attempts to accelerate this development by force, could only have very grave and quite unforeseen consequences.[144]

On 27 September, it was time to see the King, whom Meller-Zakomelsky had first got to know some fifteen years earlier and whom he had met on several occasions on the Riviera.[145] Their conversation started with the subject of Finland, the monarch noting that he had been much criticised for his lack of support for an active Swedish involvement during the Winter War. Meller-Zakomelsky nudged the conversation back to present matters. What would happen if the Soviet Union in the late autumn were to attack Finland once more? The King ruled this out; Germany would never permit it. They moved on to the British position, which seemed quite incomprehensible to the elderly monarch. The British were quite mad: they still spoke a lot of nonsense about victory but in the end they would lose everything. At best, their obstinacy would drag out the war and that would spell the triumph of Bolshevism which he had always feared. Was Germany perhaps planning to begin a great offensive against England that autumn? Meller-Zakomelsky did not know. How could he, he mused, when only the Führer and two or three of his closest colleagues were privy to the secret. The Germans knew how to keep quiet, said the King; that was their great strength. But he still rather hoped that Hitler would succeed in making the British see reason before the winter.

The King now took up the question of German attitudes to Sweden. He had heard that there were two factions in Berlin, one to which Goering belonged and which was basically pro-Swedish and another to which Ribbentrop, Goebbels and probably Rosenberg belonged. This latter faction wished to accelerate the pace of Sweden's internal political development and to resolve the problems that the Swedes had to face, by force. This way of thinking greatly disturbed the King. He could not simply do what he wanted but had to abide by the constitution. Taking his leave of the King, Meller-Zakomelsky noted that the monarch seemed unusually cast down. He was an old man, who felt the approach of death and worried over the question of the succession.

Summing up some general conclusions from his visit, Meller-Zakomelsky began by reviewing the Swedish situation in the light of the recent election. The Social Democrats had consolidated their position. The bourgeois parties, because of their reactionary social policies, had failed to win the support of the broad masses and in particular that of the industrial workers. The Social Democrats, although theoretically indebted to Karl Marx, had in practice borrowed a great deal from National Socialism. As good Swedish citizens and patriots they had managed by virtue of their successful social legislation to win considerable support outside the ranks of organised labour. The leader of the Social Democrats and present Prime Minister, Per Albin Hansson, was a very accomplished and experienced parliamentarian and a gifted political tactician. It was to him that the Social Democratic Party owed the policy of 'intelligent adaptation' – a phrase much in use – which consisted in taking over the best ideas of National Socialism while naturally suppressing where these new ideas came from. At the same time, the Social Democrats had managed effectively to discredit all opposition and criticism of their policies on the part of the right-wing parties by accusing them of 'Hitlerism'. The coalition government had provided the Social Democratic Prime Minister with a way of unloading responsibilty for various ills on to his bourgeois colleagues and thus of distancing himself from the criticism.

Meller-Zakomelsky then went on very briefly to consider various other political groupings. The opposition from the left to Social Democracy came from Flyg's Socialist Party and the Communist Party, which belonged to the Scandinavian section of the Comintern. Recently Flyg's party had lost many supporters and its influence on developments was insignificant. The Communists had lost two seats in the election but had strengthened their position in Stockholm. They had received considerable amounts of money from Moscow for their election propaganda, a fact that had been pointed out to him by the Swedish Foreign Minister.

As far as fringe extreme right groups such as the National Bund under the leadership of Sandström or the Swedish Socialist Front under Sven Olof Lindholm were concerned, these were unable to assert themselves against the Social Democrats and numerically were insignificant. However, it would be false from a German point of view to under-estimate the propaganda activities of these groups. They were, however, handicapped in their struggle with the Social Democrats by the fact that the latter had carried through a domestic policy that (leaving aside the Jewish question which was of little importance in Sweden) was much more National Socialist than it was Marxist.

Because of the success of the Social Democrats in the recent election to the *Riksdag*, no government shuffle was to be expected in the near future. The Agrarian Party had wished to leave the coalition as a result of the election but the King – as the monarch had himself made clear – had persuaded them not to do so lest they should precipitate a government crisis.

With an eye to future German policy towards Sweden, Meller-Zakomelsky summed up the prevailing political situation as follows:

The position of the Social Democratic Party is unshakeable. A decisive success for the right-wing oppositional groups lies at present outside the range of possiblities. From the German point of view, the correct policy would be to demand 'the intelligent adaptation' – which has already begun – of Social Democracy to the new situation that has arisen in Europe and to accelerate the realignment of the foreign policy of the Social Democratic Party in favour of National Socialist Germany.[146]

Meller-Zakomelsky left for Berlin on 28 September. Shortly afterwards, a secret defence staff source reported that Meller-Zakomelsky was the leader of the Russian National Socialist movement based in Berlin and was possibly also the leader of the White Russians who had fought in the Spanish Civil War on Franco's side.[147] As a result of this information, when the aristocrat returned to Sweden on 10 February 1941, he was placed under surveillance by the security service and certain contacts, with C. E. Carlberg, Arthur Grönheim and Dmitriewsky among others, were later noted. In a letter of 7 May 1941 to a certain Colonel von Skalon in Dresden, Meller-Zakomelsky observed that 'We will now certainly have a great deal to do in organising the Russian emigrants in the Balkans.' A week later, he travelled to Berlin and first reappeared in Sweden again in the middle of October.[148]

This October visit resulted in yet another SD situation report on Sweden, a report the contents of which were in due course presented to Hitler.[149] In composition, it formed a natural successor to the survey of December the previous year.

Meller-Zakomelsky flew back to Berlin on 20 December 1941 and there is no record that he appeared in Sweden again during the rest of the war.

CERTAIN OTHER GERMAN INFORMATION ACTIVITIES

High-level channels

The establishment of confidential channels of information was a task which could not reasonably be left solely to the representatives of the covert services. Diplomats and service attachés, secure from any reproach of espionage, were obviously well placed to forge those personal bonds of trust which were the prerequisite for the transmission and receipt of delicate information. Thus the German military attaché, von Uthmann, who was perceived by his Swedish colleagues as a General Staff officer of the old school, competent and professional in his chosen métier, patriotic but untainted by the ideology of Nazism, initiated a useful exchange of military information about the Soviet Union with Adlercreutz, on condition that the reports which he supplied to the Swedish intelligence chief, were passed solely to the Swedish Supreme Commander, General Thürnell.[150] This arrangement seems to have worked smoothly until the late summer of 1942 when Adlercreutz went on holiday. Uthmann had previously enquired whether his confidential reports about the Soviet Union could be entrusted to Adlercreutz's deputy, Björnstjerna, and was told that it was perfectly safe to do so. However at the beginning of September, von Uthmann was informed by Berlin that an important leakage had occurred. According to a reliable source, the American military attaché had sent a communication to London, giving information about the proposed siege of Stalingrad and about German dispositions in the Caucasus, which was said to emanate from the German military attaché in Stockholm.[151] In his reply to his superiors, von Uthmann denied that he had made any statement regarding preparations for the siege of Stalingrad. Regarding the other matter, he explained that in an effort to refute potentially injurious enemy rumours in circulation, he had – on the basis of the fruitful exchange of intelligence which already existed between Adlercreutz and himself and the Head of *Abwehr* in Sweden – provided the Swede on a purely personal basis with certain select items of information, which however, gave no insight into operational intentions. It appeared that this information had got into the hands of some unauthorised person at the Swedish Defence Staff who had subsequently passed it on to an enemy intelligence service.

Shortly after this, the shuffle in the leadership of Swedish intelligence took place and it is unclear to what extent von Uthmann was able to establish the same rapport with Adlercreutz's successors. None the less as late as 21 August 1944, Lieutenant-Colonel Ogilvie, the head of the Swedish Desk at *Fremde Heere West*, still managed to enthuse over the excellent relations existing between von Uthmann and Kellgren, who was formally responsible at the Defence Staff for contacts with foreign military attachés.[152]

The exchange of information about the Soviet Union which was a prominent feature of the confidential channel existing between

Adlercreutz and von Uthmann had, as it happened, a non-military parallel. On 11 July 1941, the German Ministry of Foreign Affairs notified its Legation in Stockholm, of the great importance of being kept regularly informed about conditions in Moscow and in the Soviet Union in general. In addition to military information, information was needed about what was happening in the government and party, and about the mood of the people and particularly its attitude towards the government and the supply situation. The Legation was urged to persuade the Swedish government to mobilise its mission in Moscow for this purpose and to turn over the results to Germany. Four days later, the Counsellor at the German Legation, Below, reported on his conversation with Söderblom, the head of the Political Section at the Swedish Ministry for Foreign Affairs. Söderblom had begun by emphasising that the German proposal would have to be very carefully examined. At the same time, and in the greatest confidence, he insisted that the Swedish government had very little incoming information on the Soviet Union.[153] However there was a report (dated 14 July) from the Swedish Minister in Moscow and the information in it was now duly passed on. Söderblom ended by saying that without becoming involved in a discussion of the principle at issue, he was prepared to supply the Legation confidentially with relevant information from the source mentioned.

It is unclear how long these various under-the-table arrangements about Russia lasted or how really fruitful (from the German viewpoint) they were as channels of information. But certain statements made in connection with the official enquiry into the Wennerström affair in 1964 confirm that military information about the Soviet Union was being passed with official Swedish sanction to the German air attaché in Stockholm in February 1943.[154]

At the end of the same year, the Swedes were asked to recall their minister and military attaché from the Soviet Union on the grounds that they had supplied the German Supreme Command with secret information about the Soviet Army. Was this move simply a pretext to underline general Soviet displeasure with Swedish policy in other areas or did it rest on the fact that the Soviet security organs had finally got wind of the leakage of information that had being going on via Stockholm?[155]

OTHER ORGANISATIONS AND THEIR COVERT LINKS
While the *Abwehr* and the SD remained the principal German covert

services outside Germany, Ribbentrop had his own special information service – the so-called Information post III (INF III) – which came into being in April 1941, with the career official Andor Hencke as its first head. Its secrecy was less a matter of conspiratorial technique than an administrative device to ensure the quick relay of information from its chosen reporters. INF III was expressly forbidden to indulge in active espionage likely to disturb diplomatic relations. The normal resident was given diplomatic cover and the main agents were selected from the ranks of German journalists and businessmen in the country. In Sweden, INF III's resident was the German press attaché, Paul Grassmann. There is little doubt that Dr Grassmann was well informed about Sweden and enjoyed a wide range of contacts there. Soon after Hitler's assumption of power, he had undertaken an analysis of British influence in Sweden and proposed various counter-measures. Among his recommendations, was the proposal that in future German advertising should go to those papers sympathetic to, or at least not critical of, the new German régime. He also advocated measures to redirect the inflow of information in Swedish newspapers away from England and back to Berlin. After the outbreak of war in 1939, Grassmann did what he could to mobilise his old friend Sven Hedin for the cause of keeping America out of the war, an activity which resulted *inter alia* in a thinly disguised propaganda work allegedly written by the ageing explorer.[156] In addition to acting as an adviser on German press policy, including covert support for selected newspapers, Grassmann kept his acute ear to the ground, picking up whispers from confidential Swedish governmental press briefings and secret sessions of the *Riksdag*. Nor was perhaps Grassmann the only INF III resident with important sources of information in Sweden. According to an unconfirmed post-war Soviet article, the same was also true of the INF III resident in Denmark.[157]

Among Grassmann's contacts was the German-born businessman, Herbert Lickfett, the local representative of IGEFA (I. G. Farben).[158] This company was to function in effect as an important arm of the German state in collecting economic information about foreign countries and competitors and worked closely with the commercial section of the *Abwehr*. In 1936–37, Lickfett had employed a Swedish intermediary to establish what organisations – whether state-run or private – existed in Scandinavia to further cultural, commercial or military co-operation between the

Scandinavian countries in peacetime and in the event of war. In addition the intermediary was instructed to examine what countries outside the region through their friendly ties would be involved in supplying the Scandinavian countries with raw materials, spare parts and finished goods. Throughout the war, Lickfett would remain one of the more important non-diplomatic representatives of German interests in Sweden and an experienced observer of the industrial and economic scene.[159]

The activities of the German National Socialist Party's Foreign Organisation (the AO) which in Sweden was headed by *Landes-gruppenleiter* Friedrich Wilhelm Stengel, remained an important force for concerting the efforts of committed German supporters of the New Order living abroad.[160] Although somewhat vocal and conspicuous, its members did not hesitate on occasion to be involved in more conspiratorial activities. Thus in reviewing the record of the Local Group Leader in Gothenburg, a Swedish post-war report, after listing certain cases of espionage in which the man had been clearly involved, observed that the foregoing cases in no way did justice to the true extent of his subversive activity.

> For the person, whose job it has been to keep a watch on the man's activities, it has been clear that he has played an exceptionally important role in the organisation and execution of the German intelligence service in Western Sweden.[161]

Lastly it remains to note that the Gestapo independently of the SD had its informers planted here and there, furnishing reports about potentially unreliable members of the German community in Sweden but sometimes also with a wider brief.[162]

COVERT PROPAGANDA

In his study of propaganda in the First World War, Harold Lasswell noted:

> One of the most subtle and effective forms of indirect propaganda is the encouragement of everything which draws the neutral into some form of *de facto* cooperation with the belligerent.[163]

In the battle of ideologies which characterised the Second World

219

War, it was hardly to be expected that the role of propaganda in neutral countries would diminish.

> Propaganda was one of National Socialist Germany's foremost weapons in its struggle for hegemony in Europe. The German Reich's Ministry of Propaganda under the leadership of the Reich Propaganda Minister Joseph Goebbels, had at its disposal all the resources of a totalitarian régime, which were exploited to the uttermost.
>
> During the war years, Sweden was subjected to methodical and especially active German propaganda.[164]

In addition to undisguised information and propaganda activities carried on through their various official agencies in the country, the German organs also made use of covert methods in this domain in the furtherance of their policies in Sweden. Black propaganda brochures and books, purporting to come from British, American or French sources and as often as not intended to sow discord within the Grand Alliance, were produced[165]; the suggestions of individual Swedes sympathetic to the National Socialist cause who were prepared to masquerade as neutral commentators, were vetted and encouraged[166]; and secret measures were taken to strengthen the voice of the new Germany in the Swedish press. One way of accomplishing the latter objective was by the provision of covert financial support for newspapers. Among those papers enjoying such support were *Dagsposten* and *Folkets Dagblad*.

Dagsposten became the principal organ of SNF, (*Sveriges Nationella Förbund*) during the war. SNF was the outgrowth of what had been a conservative youth association, founded in 1915. During the 1930s, however, this association began to take on more and more the aspect of an extreme right-wing movement and already in April 1933, it had its own paramilitary corps, kitted out in steel-grey shirts and blue armbands bearing the association's insignia. In general, it appealed to the higher social classes but efforts were made to widen its support. On 7 December 1935, it was able to announce that the former Communist, Allan Ekberg-Hedqvist, had joined the movement and early in 1936, another conversion – this time of the Social Democratic member of the *Riksdag*, Sigrid Gillner – took place.

On 20 December 1938 the German Minister, Wied, reported that he had been visited by a group of people belonging to SNF who had decided to publish a daily paper in Stockholm from 1 October 1939.

The paper would put forward 'a purely Swedish, national policy' as a counterweight to other newspapers in the capital, which represented 'unSwedish interests'. Wied enthusiastically endorsed the project and called for its support on the grounds that it had every chance of being a succesful instrument for German propaganda in reaching

> a readership which has special importance for the future moulding of German–Swedish relations, namely young academics, younger members of the armed forces and the national circles spread throughout the country who today do not have any daily newspaper which represents their point of view.[167]

An initial scheme to order printing machinery from Germany fell through but contacts with the Legation were maintained and on 13 September 1939, Wied was suggesting that the proposed newspaper should receive financial support by enlisting the help of a reliable Swede to place a regular subscription for a substantial number of copies which could later be distributed free to members of the *Riksdag* and other influential people. *Auswärtiges Amt*, however, did not like the suggestion and for the time being nothing was done. In December, the question of financial support for *Dagsposten* (as the paper was to be called) was raised again. An additional sum in the region of 250,000 crowns was needed. An unidentified group of Conservatives had offered to provide this but their offer had been rejected because it would bind the paper to a definite political line. On the other hand, the gentlemen behind *Dagsposten* were prepared to accept the money from the Germans since the paper would be fundamentally pro-German in outlook. At the same time, the German interest in the newspaper would be known to only a small inner circle. The relevant German organ responsible for supplying the covert funds would in effect become a shareholder in the newspaper, the shares however, being held on their behalf by certain Swedish front men who would be bound over by a secret agreement. Some such arrangement appears to have been adopted and the newspaper began publication at the beginning of December 1941, with O. T. Telander as Chief Editor and Rutger Essén as Foreign Editor.[168]

It did not take long before the newspaper ran into financial difficulties and was looking for a fresh injection of funds. On 5 February 1942, a telegram sent, interestingly enough, to the Army High Command, summed up the situation:

Since 1 December, the Swedish daily newspaper *Dagsposten* has been published with the help of covert German support, In its attitude towards Germany, the newspaper constitutes an outstandingly successful organ of propaganda. The military commentaries and foreign policy leaders in the paper unambiguously and consistently give expression to German ideas – better than both *Aftonbladet* and *Stockholms Tidningen*. The paper has held its own and would, if it continues to appear, be of great service to the German cause. It has at its disposal, however, only particularly modest means with the result that it would not be able to come out in five or six weeks, if adequate monthly support was not forthcoming. The Military Attaché has already in Berlin applied to the representatives Colonel von Wedel and Lieutenant Colonel I. G. Kratzer for financial support for the newspaper. Because the paper's situation is becoming steadily more difficult and because within the last days it has published leaders which are well disposed to Germany, essays and individual reports which form a counter-balance to the recently publicised information about great Russian successes and other material which is disadvantageous to Germany, I would like once more with the full approval of the Legation to request earnestly for financial support as soon as possible. The newspaper could in time become a particularly effective organ of German propaganda.[169]

In a telegram to *Auswärtiges Amt* the following day, Wied, apart from asking for additional financial support, also revealed the method of covert financing hitherto employed:

Given the newspaper's known attitude to Germany, continued financial help in the form of share subscription via Swedish representatives is now an urgent necessity. Because of its skilful and consistent pro-Axis attitude, it constitutes the most important and valuable support for German policy in Sweden. Would therefore be grateful if subvention measures in this area were now concentrated to *Dagsposten* and that the Legation was empowered by telegram to supply the company in the way hitherto employed with 100,000 (one hundred thousand) crowns. At the same time, preparations have been made for support by appeal to potential, large interested parties.[170]

Dagsposten provided Berlin with another channel for getting across its message and sowing the seeds of dissension in the enemy camp. Thus on 6 March 1943, *Auswärtiges Amt* requested an item to the effect that Sikorski had requested that the Polish Goverment in Exile should be moved to Washington as a protest against the soft line taken against the Russians; on 22 March, it asked for prominence to be given to an article by Ilya Ehrenburg demanding the opening of a front in France; on 25 April, *Dagsposten* was requested to include a piece about the Katyn massacre; and on 7 May 1943, an item to be attributed to 'the London correspondent' was to be placed in the newspaper, noting that 6,000 blacks had been arrested in Johannesburg during Communist-inspired civil unrest.

There were also occasions when Berlin found it opportune to advise *Dagsposten* not to take up a particular issue. Thus on 18 September 1943, the newspaper had dealt with the possibility of a German–Soviet separate peace. A telegram three days later from Braun von Stumm in the Press Department at *Auswärtiges Amt*, asked that the editors should be informed 'in a suitable way that a discussion of this topic is not desirable'.

In October 1938, when the *Dagsposten* project had first come to his attention, the German minister had noted that such a paper would be a useful propaganda organ among the junior members of the Swedish armed forces. Ironically, it was to be this aspect of its circulation which was to lead to a lawsuit against the newspaper's editors. On 20 July 1944, the Supreme Commander of the Swedish Army, General Helge Jung issued a command which excluded *Dagsposten* and *Folkets Dagblad* from Officers' messes and other meeting places used by military personnel, on the grounds that these newspapers had received foreign financial support and had placed themselves at the disposal of foreign interests. Essén and Telander thereupon brought an action for defamation against Jung. The case came before a special military court and in his defence, the defendant produced intercepted and decrypted German telegrams which proved that his contention was entirely justified. The plaintiffs withdrew their charges and the case was dismissed. The intercepted telegrams and the statements contained therein led, however, to a new case being brought against certain of those associated with the newspaper (including Essén and Telander) for a possible offence under Chapter 8 for 'the unlawful receipt of foreign support'. As a result of this case, the German-born businessman Koux was sentenced to seven months' hard labour for having knowingly received from a German official a sum in excess of 100,000 crowns which he had subsequently handed over to the managing director of the newspaper.

It is now time to look at the other newspaper which fell under General Jung's 1944 prohibition. *Folkets Dagblad* was the organ of the Swedish Socialist Party, a group associated above all with Nils Flyg. Flyg had begun his political career as a Communist and during the years 1924–1929, he was Chairman of the Swedish Communist Party's Central Committee. In 1929, however, a split in the party occurred and brought into existence alongside the party loyal to Moscow and the Comintern, another independent faction, styling itself the Socialist Party. In due course, Flyg became its leader. The Socialist Party pursued a strongly anti-Stalinist line and a leader in *Folkets Dagblad* on 2 August 1939 roundly declared that

> it is obvious to everyone that the Stalinistic régime in Russia is completely totalitarian – as totalitarian as the Nazi and Fascist régimes in Germany and Italy.[171]

But while Flyg lost no opportunity to criticise the Soviet Union for its betrayal of the revolution, at the same time his distrust of and contempt for the 'capitalist countries' – Great Britain and France – and for 'the sham of the League of Nations' paved the way for a future accommodation with National Socialism. This marriage was accelerated by the Socialist Party's deteriorating economic position. In 1938, he approached the German Legation for the first time, about the possibility of obtaining financial support for *Folkets Dagblad*. Although the Legation was well pleased with that paper's campaign against the League of Nations and noted Flyg's role as a thorn in the side of the Social Democrats, no decision about financial support seems to have been taken and Flyg was to return several times before the outbreak of war in the hope of reaching some kind of agreement.

On 22 August 1940, *Folkets Dagblad* ceased publication. When it resumed on 4 July 1942, it was German-financed and openly National Socialist in its sympathy. A leader signed by Flyg which appeared on 25 July, offered the following reflection:

> A German victory entails certain great risks. This is especially true of people who – wholly or partly, openly or covertly – have helped Germany's enemies – people who have demonstrated that they do not have the capacity to understand the drama of our

time. Provided we are aware of this, we can act by carrying through a policy which will ensure that the war ends as far as Sweden is concerned, with a Swedish victory i.e. a meeting with a Europe that is being formed by a new age.[172]

Folkets Dagblad was able to add its voice to the agitation on behalf of Hitler's cause. On 22 August 1942, it had an article about the activities of the British Intelligence Service. On 3 September 1943, it called for 'Danish saboteurs' in Sweden to be watched. On 19 October 1943, Braun von Stumm of the Press Department, at *Auswärtiges Amt* in Berlin, enquired about an article which had appeared three days earlier in *Folkets Dagblad* about a Swedish organisation set up to rescue Jews from Denmark, only to be told that the article had been included with the object of sabotaging such rescue actions. Unwavering to the end, the paper carried on 7 May 1945 a tribute to the Führer declaring him to be one of humanity's greatest men, yielding place only to Jesus Christ.

It was estimated that between the middle of January 1943 and mid-May 1945, the paper had received 429,000 crowns. Flyg himself died in January 1943 and the main responsibility for the paper was assumed by his closest colleague, Herman Johansson. The arrangement for the actual transfer of funds to the paper and party representatives, was later entrusted to Dr Finke. Apart from any propaganda value the paper might have, the Socialist Party provided the SD with a useful link to a section of the labour movement which could be exploited for intelligence purposes. Thus in 1943, two young party members with aspirations to join the *Waffen-SS* were told by Herman Johansson that they had been selected for a course in Germany.[173] When they had difficulty in obtaining the requisite visas from the Swedish authorities to allow them to go to Germany, arrangements were made for them to travel to Arvika from where a contact man would smuggle them over the border into Norway. Once there, they could then proceed to Germany without difficulty. In due course, after this Norwegian detour, the two men arrived in Berlin where they were put up at the Hotel Manegold. On arrival, they were met by Grönheim, the principal SD field officer for Scandinavia who presented them with false identity papers. 'Anker' and 'Westerman' – as they now became – embarked on a training course which covered radio techniques, ciphering and weapon skills.

After their return to Sweden, they were contacted in January

1944, by Dr Finke's assistant Pioch, who suggested that they should acquire cottages on the outskirts of Stockholm. These could then be used as radio stations in the event that diplomatic relations between Sweden and Germany were broken. Pioch dropped out of the picture to be replaced by another of Finke's assistants, Schiller, and in the Spring of 1944, the scheme for setting up these contingency stations was put into effect with the renting of three cottages. Various trial transmissions appear to have taken place but no regular schedule for communication was established.

Much more potent than the influence exerted by *Dagsposten* and *Folkets Dagblad* – which largely preached to the converted and had a small readership – was that exercised by the mass-circulation papers, *Aftonbladet* and *Stockholms Tidningen*, both owned by Torsten Kreuger, the brother of the Swedish match king.[174] Here too, in the mainstream press, the German information and propaganda organs were able to make inroads, by placing articles and co-ordinating policy. Thus on 14 July 1941, the head of the Press Department at *Auswärtiges Amt*, Dr Paul Schmidt, sent an urgent express telegram to the German Legation in Stockholm, asking the Legation by hook or by crook to persuade *Stockholms Tidningen* or *Aftonbladet* to include an announcement of the utmost importance. Two hours later, the Legation telegraphed

> *Aftonbladet* has stopped its presses so as to get in your announcement already today under large headlines. I have been assured that the telegram will appear on the front page under the headline: Roosevelt all set to ignite the powder keg. US Navy said to have received orders to 'order an intermezzo'.[175]

The article which appeared under this heading the same day in *Aftonbladet*, read as follows:

> New York, Monday (AB).
> From circles close to President Roosevelt, it is rumoured that he intends as soon as possible to declare war on Germany in order to stand by England's side before the German campaign in the East has ended in victory.
> For this purpose, units of the US Navy have been given orders to fire without warning at every German submarine, aeroplane and warship.
> Should a German unit which is exposed to such a surprise attack,

nevertheless report the American aggression to Germany, the American government intends to deny it and present the matter as the result of a confusion with British battle forces. On the other hand, if such an American aggression brings about a German counterattack, Roosevelt plans to announce a German attack and declare war without asking the Congress.[176]

Kreuger's role behind the scenes can be glimpsed in other ways as well. In the spring of 1941, the Germans toyed with various schemes for buying a newspaper in Gothenburg – Sweden's second city on the west coast – to offset the influence of the liberal *Göteborgs Handels och Sjöfarts Tidning* which was one of the most outspoken and uncompromising critics of Hitler Germany in Sweden. On 8 July 1941, the Legation informed Berlin that in accordance with the instructions of Dr Paul Schmidt, it was working closely with Kreuger who had been highly co-operative, especially as regards the political stance adopted by *Aftonbladet*. In discussions between the Legation and Kreuger, it had emerged that the Swedish newspaper owner had plans to start a new newspaper in Gothenburg to counteract the anti-German press there. It would be closely tied to *Aftonbladet*, express similar political opinions and cater to the broad masses. To start such a paper, one million crowns was needed. The Legation stressed the need to organise matters in such a way that the financing appeared to have been supplied by Swedes and noted that suitable front men (including a member of the *Riksdag*) were available to carry out the transaction. Complete secrecy was necessary both to cloak German interests and to prevent counter-measures from commercial competitors.[177]

Newspapers formed an obvious vehicle for the efforts of the propagandists. The agencies which supplied the papers with their news, formed another. The Stockholm scene included a number of such bureaux which, while pretending to be neutral or independent, in fact to a greater or lesser degree were controlled by Berlin. One was the *Scandinavian Telegram Bureau* (STB) which has already been mentioned; so too *Bull's Press Service* which was originally a Norwegian firm, but which during 1940 gradually became more closely tied to German interests, through an arrangement with STB's Copenhagen office, brought about by the active intervention of the German press attaché in Stockholm. Still another was the short-lived *Radio Mundial*, which none the less provides an interesting illustration of a cloaking operation.

In 1941, the German Foreign Office gave its blessing to a scheme to set up a special news agency, specialising in items for and from the new medium of radio. The official German sponsorship of this agency, however, was to be carefully concealed. In order to disguise its origins, it was decided to set it up in a neutral country and because of the tighter controls imposed in Switzerland and Sweden, the final choice fell on Portugal. The Portuguese authorities were to be presented with the following cover story: a number of foreign journalists, dissatisfied with the fact that in Europe news agencies were either in the control of one belligerent or another, had decided on a fresh alternative. Under the leadership of Dr O. H. W. Lentz and Maximiliano Stahlschmidt, they wished to set up a new agency in Lisbon. Portugal had been chosen because it was one of the few free countries in Europe and because it also formed a springboard to the South American continent and Portugal's colony in Africa.

In the summer of 1941, a legal adviser attached to *Auswärtiges Amt* accompanied by Dr Lentz whose passport gave his place of residence as Oslo and the Brazilian Stahlschmidt travelled to Lisbon to get things moving. On 14 July, the agency *Radio Mundial SA* was finally officially registered as a Portuguese company with a capital of one million escudos; the shares, despite appearances to the contrary, were entirely in the control of the German Foreign Office.

Once established in Lisbon, steps were now taken to expand elsewhere.[178] After certain tentative discussions,[179] Axel Wolff Lenshoeck, who was in charge of the general administration of *Radio Mundial* in Berlin, arrived in Stockholm in August 1941 to discuss the possibilities of opening a branch of the bureau in the Swedish capital. The Swedish authorities to whom Lenshoeck was introduced, were less than enthusiastic. However, *Radio Mundial* had apparently acquired some useful and influential friends[180] and a preliminary deal was struck with the *Belgo-Baltic* company[181] of Stockholm whereby the latter agreed to act for *Radio-Mundial* in a number of ways, in return for a fixed monthly sum and a share of the profits in Sweden.

By the end of October 1941, Lentz was giving the impression that things were prospering. The Stockholm office was said to be co-operating well with both *Stockholms Tidningen* and *Aftonbladet*. A new office was opened in Helsinki with Swedish help and one of the Stockholm staff was dispatched to Ankara to investigate the possibilities of setting up an agency there.[182]

In Allied circles, these developments had not passed unnoticed.[183]

In mid September 1941, a counter-response got under way when Ralph Hewins, the Daily Mail's correspondent in Stockholm, attacked *Radio Mundial's* pretensions to independence, in an article which dismissed the organisation as a new German-directed propaganda enterprise with branches all over America and Europe.[184] At the same time, pressure was applied on *Belgo-Baltic* to distance itself from its deal with the news agency.[185]

Perhaps because of this and other reasons,[186] in April 1942, further plans for *Radio Mundial* were laid aside.

CONTACTS WITH THE ENEMY: PEACE FEELERS

With the reversal of German military fortune, there was a marked upswing in attempts to make discreet diplomatic contact with the enemy, whether to the West or to the East. These attempted contacts raised obvious problems of interpretation for Allied intelligence analysts. What were the credentials of the intermediary making contact? On whose authority was he acting? What possible motives lay behind the extended hand? What policy should be adopted in regard to contacts with intermediaries? From 1943 onwards, Sweden became a popular venue for separate peace-broking and rumours of separate peace-broking. Among the intermediaries to be found in Stockholm was Dr Felix Kersten.

After training as a masseur, Kersten had embarked on a success-ful career in his chosen métier and eventually acquired Himmler as a patient. Through his encounters with the *SS Reichsführer*, Kersten was to become privy to some of his powerful patient's musings and was also able to intercede on behalf of prisoners of the régime. As Sweden's wartime Foreign Minister was to recall:

> There can be no doubt that Dr Kersten during the closing stage of the war, saved the lives of thousands of people. As far as Sweden is concerned, among much else special mention may be made of his decisive initiative on behalf of the Warsaw Swedes and the planning of the rescue work in Germany at the beginning of 1945 which was entrusted to the Red Cross and carried out under the leadership of Count Bernadotte.[187]

The courier work of the Warsaw Swedes on behalf of the Polish resistance has already been mentioned. After their arrest in July 1942, the Swedish government did what it could on their behalf, with all the means at its disposal. Behind the scenes, Colonel Adlercreutz reasoned with the *Abwehr* – in his own judgement – to crucial effect. But half a year went by and the fate of the Swedes was still unresolved. The Germans had evidently decided on a waiting game. On 25 January 1943, *Abwehr* and SD representatives met to discuss tactics, aimed at extracting the most out of the situation that had arisen. It was generally agreed that there was no obstacle to initiating proper trial proceedings. The two Swedes, whose burden of guilt was the least, should be handed over to their fellow countrymen, if possible before the trial got under way. After it had begun but before it had reached the main stage, negotiations should take place about the remaining people and counterclaims discussed. Above all there was no wish to see the death sentence which was likely to be imposed, actually carried out.

The waiting game continued. The Swedes sat in prison where they enjoyed relatively speaking privileged treatment; the Poles who had been arrested, were not so fortunate. The names of Kersten and Schellenberg began to figure more prominently as useful influential behind-the-scene contacts for the Swedish authorities in ameliorating the position of their imprisoned countrymen.[188]

The trial of the Warsaw Swedes finally took place at the end of June 1943. According to the verdict of the court, four of the accused – Herslow, Häggberg, Widén and Berglind – were sentenced to death, the first for collaboration and espionage on behalf of the Polish government in London and the other three for intelligence work on behalf of the British government; a fifth man (Gerge) was sentenced to life imprisonment for intelligence work on behalf of Sweden; and two others (Grönberg and Lagerberg) were acquitted but were not released from the custody of the Gestapo.

On 2 July 1943, King Gustav appealed to Hitler, asking for mercy to be shown to those condemned to death. In the period that ensued, there were contacts between Kersten and Schellenberg on the one hand and Möller and Brandin of the Swedish Match company on the other, who were anxious to make a plea on behalf of their threatened colleagues directly to Himmler himself and particularly because no answer had been given to the King's appeal.[189] On 27/28 August 1943, they were finally received by the *Reichsführer* at his HQ in East Prussia. Himmler promised that the two men who had been acquitted, would be given exit visas and they finally left at the end of the month.

The fate of the remaining five Swedes was to remain in the balance for some time.

Kersten himself travelled to Stockholm at the end of September. There is little doubt that by this time both he and Schellenberg had built up a certain amount of goodwill at the Ministry for Foreign Affairs for their co-operation in the matter of the Warsaw Swedes. Their services – in different ways – would be increasingly used thereafter in acting as forces of moderation and in trying to extract concessions from a wavering Himmler.

Another recent arrival in Stockholm was Mr Abram Stevens Hewitt, an American businessman doubling as a representative of the US government. On 3 October, Kersten and Hewitt were brought together by a Swedish businessman, Holger Graffman. It was to be the first of several meetings. Later when the State Department drew up an *aide-mémoire* for circulation to its British and Soviet Allies regarding the talks that had taken place in Stockholm between Hewitt and Kersten, it summed up the latter's message as follows:

> Himmler, he said, knows that the war is lost and is anxious to arrive at an arrangement with the Americans and British which would leave something of Germany. The Doctor declared further that, realising it would be impossible for the Americans and the British to deal with Hitler, Himmler was now quite prepared to bring about his overthrow.[190]

Four times thereafter, Kersten urged Hewitt to go to Germany to confer with Himmler but in vain. With this possibility apparently ruled out, Kersten now wrote to the *SS Reichsführer* asking him to send Schellenberg to Stockholm to negotiate with the American on the basis of a seven-point proposal.[191]

On 1 November, Schellenberg arrived in Stockholm and a late-night meeting took place between Finke, Kersten and Himmler's personal emissary. It was not the first visit of the Head of SD Foreign Intelligence to the Swedish capital. He had been there at the beginning of 1942 and as recently as June 1943. All in all he would visit Stockholm on ten occasions, sometimes under his own name, often under the thinly concealed pseudonym of 'Schellenkampf'. Early next day, he and Kersten visited the Hotel Plaza for their first meeting with the American. Kersten confided to his diary that he had introduced Schellenberg to Hewitt and that the two men got on well together: 'It's my sincere wish that this contact will lead to peace.'

231

The talks between Schellenberg and Hewitt in Stockholm led nowhere. Once more an invitation was extended to the American to go to Germany to continue discussions there. When this was declined, Schellenberg suggested a further meeting in Lisbon. Meanwhile in Germany, according to Kersten, the *Reichsführer* had in any case begun to have second thoughts: would not removing Hitler and abolishing the party mean in effect cutting the ground from under his own feet?[192]

Two other more or less concurrent episodes, perhaps linked to one another and ostensibly concerned with bringing about some kind of dialogue between elements in the Nazi hierarchy and the Western Allies, deserve to be mentioned.

In March 1943, the British assistant naval attaché had bumped into a Swedish representative of the Skoda engineering and armaments concern on the ice at Lake Silja.[193] This encounter gave rise to a number of subsequent meetings at which the representative was wont to ask what Skoda had to do to be 'exempt from bombing'. The British answer was straightforward: before this question could in any way be considered, the company had first to provide all key statistics and in addition produce concrete plans for actively reducing the production of armaments and other war materials.

Nothing of any great significance appears to have transpired but in the autumn of 1943, the representative suddenly announced that a director of the company was coming to Stockholm. Would the British be prepared to speak to him? This was not at first ruled out. But when later it was intimated that another purpose of the meeting was to discuss peace between the Western Allies and Germany, whereby Germany would withdraw from occupied Western Europe in return for the Allies joining it in the campaign against Bolshevik Russia, the representative was told that the policy of the Allies was total surrender. After the Foreign Office in London had been appraised of developments, instructions were received to break off all negotiations.

The other episode involved the Swede, James Dickson.[194] Dickson had evidently met Dr Hans Febrans, a director of the Prague firm Omnipol, during the latter's visit to Sweden in the middle of 1943. According to the German side of the story, Dickson had informed Febrans that there was interest in certain British circles for an understanding with Germany. In September, when Dickson travelled to Czechoslovakia, he met Febrans again and filled out what he had said before by mentioning that David MacEwen, alluringly described as 'directly answerable to the British Prime Minister', was very keen to have a chat with Febrans in Stockholm. Later Dickson had also met State Secretary Karl Herman Frank and Dr Bertsch, the Minister of Economics. According to the account which Dickson subsequently relayed to the British Legation in Stockholm, Frank had suggested that a peace settlement should be offered to the West in return for 'a free hand in the East'; Great Britain would be invited to enlarge its empire at the expense of Italy while at the same time Europe would be saved from Bolshevism.

In the final weeks of the war, German efforts to reach accommodation with the Western Allies were pursued with renewed intensity through Swedish channels. In February 1945, Fritz Hesse arrived in Stockholm on a futile quest for suitable talking partners.[195] More significantly the duo of the agile and polished Schellenberg and the wavering Himmler once more appeared upon the scene, most prominently in connection with Count Folke Bernadotte's intervention on behalf of Norwegian and Danish prisoners in German concentration camps.[196] Prodded and supported by his younger intelligence chief, the *SS-Reichsführer* finally proposed to his Swedish visitor on the night of 22/23 April that the Count should ensure that the following proposal was conveyed by the Swedish government to the Western Allies: he, Himmler, was prepared to capitulate in the West – not in the East. The Western Allies, however, refused to bite: it was all or nothing.

Schemes for dialogue in Stockholm were not confined to projected meetings between German and Western Allied representatives. In some quarters, interest also focused on bringing about a dialogue between Germany and the Soviet Union. Prominently involved in one such protracted escapade was the trio Kleist, Klaus and Boening.

In the course of his duties in the Political Department of the *Ostministerium*, Kleist had become involved with the fate of the so-called Estonian Swedes – that small group of fisherfolk and farmers whose forefathers had for many centuries inhabited the coast and islands of Estonia, while still preserving the Swedish language and other tokens of their national identity. As reports of their precarious situation reached Stockholm, a committee was formed to look after their interests and to work towards bringing them over safely to Sweden. Negotiations about this question enabled Kleist to visit

Stockholm fairly regularly. Passing through the Swedish capital from Helsinki in December 1942, Kleist met his former acquaintance Boening and through him, Edgar Klaus. The idea of initiating a dialogue with the Soviet side was now mooted and Klaus, who was thought to enjoy close contacts with the Soviet Legation, was cast in the role of prospective go-between.[197] Their efforts were to run on late into 1944.

In the first half of 1943, flirting with the Russians markedly increased. Early that year, Sergius Dmitriewsky was consulted about the choice of a suitable contact at the Soviet Legation in Stockholm; Klaus claimed that he had been approached by Dr Wagner at the end of February of that year with a request to arrange a meeting with Madame Kollontay; in the spring (according to information reaching the British Legation from Major Petersén) the Soviet Counsellor, Boris Jartsev had actually met a German official in secret. The Finnish military attaché in Stockholm reported that around 10 May, three high dignitaries of the SS had arrived in Stockholm to discuss the possibility of a German–Soviet separate peace and that a meeting attended by the German Minister and Mikhail Vetrov of the Soviet Legation had taken place. In June, it was time for Kleist, Klaus and Boening to reappear on stage in connection with a rumour that Alexandrov, the head of the Central European Division of *Narkomindel*, was currently in Sweden and was interested in speaking with a German counterpart. Hitler was duly informed and in a fit of rage, dismissed the whole episode as a mere provocation.

Wary of incurring the wrath of his leader but doubtless keen at the same time to relive the triumph of 23 August 1939, Ribbentrop continued to sniff the air for winds of change in Soviet policy. At the beginning of August 1943, he dispatched his special associate Rudolf Likus to the Swedish capital to take stock of the situation in the light of the latest developments. There Likus conferred with Dr Werner von Knorre. Von Knorre who headed the official German news agency DNB in Sweden, had arrived in Stockholm from Riga in August 1940. He spoke fluent Russian, was deemed knowledgeable about Soviet affairs and more importantly was employed as a contact to Sergius Dmitriewsky. Yet the message which Likus brought back from Stockholm gave no encouragement to the notion that Stalin was in any way now open to negotiations with Berlin.

In November 1943, Molotov provided his Western Allies with a written statement that showed that the old team of Kleist and Klaus was still at work. According to this statement, the Soviet Legation in Stockholm had in mid-October received a letter in which the writer said that he was ready to place at the disposal of the Soviet government information which might prove useful for the ending of the war in 1943. The writer of the letter did not give his name but explained how he could be reached. Although (said Molotov) the Legation did not attach much importance to the letter, one of the Legation staff was instructed to meet the writer and find out what he had to say. The writer turned out to be a German businessman named Edgar Klaus. He had maintained that a group of German industrialists headed by Kleist – said to be chairman of the Stumm concern – who was in close contact with Ribbentrop, favoured a separate peace with the Soviet Union. Earlier in the autumn, representatives of the group had come to Stockholm but had failed to establish contact with the Soviet side. Klaus had been instructed to say that the Germans were ready to agree to every Soviet demand and were even prepared to accept the frontiers of 1914. It was clear to the Germans that they had lost the war, that the morale of the population was deteriorating in a catastrophic manner and that there were not enough troops to continue the war. Government circles were also disturbed by the Moscow conference and by the retreat of the German armies on the Eastern front. Klaus had then asked whether contact could be established between the people who had sent him and Soviet representatives and whether any Soviet representatives wished to meet Ribbentrop. On the instructions of the Soviet *chargé d'affaires*, he was told that there could be no question of any negotiations or contact with the Germans and that further meetings with him were impossible.[198]

Despite the Soviet statement apparently ruling out any further contacts with Klaus and Kleist, the latter continued with their efforts. On 19 July 1944, a new rumour about German–Soviet peace negotiations found its way into the newspapers. According to the *Daily Telegraph's* man in Stockholm – in a story that was taken up by the Swedish evening newspaper *Aftonbladet* – one of Ribbentrop's agents, Bruno Peter Kleist, had recently arrived in Stockholm to try to arrive at an agreement with the Soviet Union. Stalin was to be allowed to take over Eastern Europe while Germany would continue the war in the West. Contact with the Soviet Legation had been arranged through an intermediary. However, the Soviet reaction had been crushingly negative. Not surprisingly, this set off a buzz of gossip. A week later, the Swedish Minister in Helsinki was reporting home

> that in diplomatic circles here, it is considered incontrovertible that Kleist has met Semjonov in Stockholm, probably even on several occasions. On the other hand, no one seems to be in a position to say what it was all about and the speculations I have heard, do not appear to be of any great interest. A Balkan colleague took the view that the Germans were trying to scare the Anglo-Saxons and Hynninen maintained that the mere fact that the meeting had taken place at all, showed that the Russians were following their own policy, quite independently of the West.[199]

Not long afterwards, Kleist himself had brought the matter up quite spontaneously during a conversation with a member of the Swedish Legation in Berlin. It was all quite without foundation, he assured the Swede: he had not met any Russians and he did not know a soul at the Soviet Legation in Stockholm. Nevertheless the evidence collected by the authorities in Sweden suggested that Klaus and Kleist were still involved in some intricate scheme. On 16 June 1944, Kleist had arrived in Stockholm on one of his many visits. There now followed a curious sequence of events. On Friday the 23rd, Klaus made a telephone call to the Soviet Legation, asking when Semjonov – the Soviet *chargé d'affaires* – was likely to be available. An appointment was made for Klaus to see him on Monday. Klaus, however, asked for the appointment to be made not in his own name but in that of 'Zmein'. Despite this arrangement, Klaus phoned the Legation again on both Saturday and Sunday asking to speak to Semjonov. He was told that the latter was not available and was instructed to ring again on Monday at 11.00 a.m. He duly phoned. At 11.20 the insistent 'Zmein', the ambiguous merchant of Riga, finally disappeared into the Legation only, however, to re-emerge swiftly. Had he, in the ten minutes allowed to him, accomplished his purpose? Was it now time for Kleist to enter the dance? The jungle telegraph hummed with rumours. On Wednesday the 28th, according to one source described by the Swedes as 'reliable', a meeting was said to have taken place between the man from Berlin and two members of the Soviet Legation – Semjonov and Nikitouchev, the Soviet MA. That same evening, Klaus phoned Kleist at his hotel, but his partner had not returned. He phoned again the next day and arranged a meeting between the pair of them which subsequently took place at Kleist's hotel.

In London, the Foreign Office instructed the British ambassador in Moscow to find out what was going on:

> We have received a report through a German journalist referred to in my telegram No. 2346 (of 2 August) that Ribbentrop recently sent an emissary named Bruno von Kleist to Stockholm in order to enter into negotiations for concluding peace with USSR.
>
> Would it in your opinion be possible without arousing undesirable resentment to ask Molotov unofficially whether there is any truth in this report. You could if necessary say that confirmation or denial would help us in assessing the value of the source, whose reports have hitherto proved worth serious attention.[200]

On 7 September, Clark-Kerr was able to report:

> Soviet reply states that this summer their Legation at Stockholm received several anonymous letters communicating 'designs of a certain Dr Kleist' to contact Soviet representatives. The Soviet Legation at first ignored these letters but finally asked the Swedish authorities to save them from being pestered in this way. The United States minister had told the Soviet Minister that they had also received such letters. Otherwise the Soviet authorities had no information about Dr Kleist.[201]

Looking back at this trail of abortive meetings between German and Allied representatives,[202] certain concluding reflections are in order.

There is little doubt that this type of backstairs diplomacy tended to encourage suspicions affecting adversely co-operation between the Western and Soviet Allies. Indeed it was widely assumed that the enemy was prepared to sanction peace feelers – here, now there – precisely for this purpose. But a complicating feature was that the Germans were perhaps not the only player in the game of 'Eternal Triangle'.[203]

A formal step forward in dissipating the anxieties precipitated by rumour, speculation and shadowy meetings was achieved at the Foreign Ministers' Conference in Moscow in October 1943, when the governments of the United Kingdom, the United States and the Soviet Union agreed to inform each other immediately of any peace feeler which they received from the government of, or from any group of individuals in, a country with which any one of the three countries was at war. They further agreed to consult together with a view to concerting their actions in regard to such approaches. How far these undertakings were honoured to the letter by the Eastern and Western sides, remains however unclear. Suspicion remained the order of the day.

In practical terms the British, for example, appear wherever possible to have transferred to SIS and SOE the responsibility for contacts with enemy emissaries, a device which conveniently loosened the bonds of official accountability. The background of some of the enemy emissaries themselves – intelligence officials like Schellenberg who by his role in the Venlo incident had shown himself to be quite capable of using peace overtures merely as a trick – invited extreme caution and inevitably led to an adoption of the philosophy that 'he who sups with the Devil needs a long spoon'.

The use of the Special Services also opened the way to the exploitation of such contacts for the furtherance of other aims, whether tactical or humanitarian. The fact that the contacts could be used for other than their nominal purpose was in turn a reason why these furtive meetings were to some extent also encouraged by the various Allied partners.

It remains to note one final consequence of the entreaties of Schellenberg and the rest of those compromised by past actions and loyalties. They inevitably tended to drown out or contaminate the signals sent by men like Trott and his associates and made the terms of these opposition circles, already contentious for political and strategic reasons, all the more difficult to accept.

NON-GERMAN SERVICES AND THEIR LINKS

For the Japanese, Scandinavia and the Baltic States served as a convenient rear window from which to spy on Russia, nor was this anything new. During the Russo-Japanese War, Colonel Akashi in Stockholm had maintained contacts with the Russian Revolutionary Socialist party and other anti-Tsarist groups and did what he could to collect intelligence about the enemy and to disrupt its war effort.[204] There is also an interesting record of a covert Japanese intelligence enterprise in Scandinavia at the close of the First World War.[205] On 24 September 1917, Henry Klepatski – his father a Pole and his mother a Mongol – had arrived in Copenhagen from Petrograd. Claiming to be a newspaper correspondent for a Tokyo and Osaka newspaper, he was in fact a political agent for the Japanese Foreign Office and Ministry of War. His immediate superiors were said to be Majors Kasuki and Okono of the Stockholm Legation. The activities of all three, however, were directed by a certain Furuia, also resident in the Swedish capital.

Klepatski was described as a man of 60 with great experience behind him, who had travelled over the whole world and was particularly well informed about Russia and China. His special mission in Copenhagen consisted *inter alia* in getting hold of men travelling to Russia and the Baltic countries who could be relied upon to give sober and truthful accounts of what they learned on their journeys. The general instructions given to these travellers were as follows:

1. to collect all available information regarding the Bolshevik movement, its causes and its leading personalities;
2. to collect information concerning Russian currency and Russian commercial policy;
3. to collect information about *entente* activities in Russia and the political position of the *entente* towards Bolshevism;
4. to discover how the British and American secret services operated in Russia in the commercial, political and military spheres;
5. to study the dislocations and difficulties encountered by the *entente* armies and fleet in Russia, the sizes of forces involved and the corresponding movements of the Red Army and its principal officers.

In addition to these general questions, certain auxiliary secret instructions were to be given to specially trusted agents. These were:

6. to determine the attitude of the Russian population towards Bolshevism and the Bolshevik government's policy, particularly the attitudes of the intelligentsia;
7. to determine if there was a manifest distrust of the *entente* among the Russians and whether there was a basis outside Bolshevism for anti-*entente* agitation;
8. to seek connections with influential Russians outside the ranks of Bolshevism who might conceivably be able to form a nationalist government, enjoying popular support and prepared – under the pretence of hindering financial bankruptcy – to disregard the loans incurred in the *entente* countries by the former régime and the Kerenski government.

239

In such a way, it was hoped by peaceful means to win significant Japanese influence in important economic sectors in Russia.

During the Second World War, Scandinavia remained an important centre for Japanese intelligence activities in Europe.[206] The direction of these activities was in the hands of the military attaché in Stockholm, first Lieutenant-Colonel Toshio Nishimura and later (from the beginning of 1941) Lieutenant-General Makoto Onodera whose multifarious dealings were soon to become legendary.[207] Onodera, while indulging in a brisk exchange with his German colleague von Uthmann and the *Abwehr* men Wagner and Krämer,[208] at the same time cultivated contacts with the Polish intelligence service which had traditionally proved one of Japan's most valuable sources of information about Russia.[209] Apparently also greatly prized were the contacts made with a former head of the Second Section of the Estonian General Staff.[210] The list of Onodera's talking partners included in addition sundry representatives of the Swedish,[211] Hungarian[212] and Finnish intelligence services.

During the Winter War, the Finns had enjoyed wide sympathy and support in Sweden. Although their progressively closer involvement with Germany, which culminated in Finland joining in the assault on Russia in Barbarossa and carrying the fight beyond its former borders, led in some degree to a cooling in the relationship, the Finns could continue to count on Swedish co-operation and support, particularly in military circles. In part, this was due to ties of sentiment and history. More important, Finland remained for Sweden an important buffer state whose fate was intimately bound up with its own. Conversely for Finland, Sweden provided a neutral antechamber – a window to the West – which, when the time came to detach itself from Germany and reach an accommodation with the Soviet Union, offered a natural venue for peace feelers.

In the course of the Second World War the Finnish Intelligence Service achieved a number of important successes, particularly in the realm of Sigint.[213] Sometimes these successes were due in part to co-operation with other services. Thus in the summer of 1940, the Finns received from the Japanese intercepts of Soviet radio traffic between Vladivostok and Chabarovsk. This traffic, however, still awaited decryption. By January/February 1941, cryptanalyis had advanced as far as the amount of available material permitted. However, at the beginning of Barbarossa, new material became available when the Germans intercepted telegrams sent by Soviet forces in the Baltic states. It turned out that the underlying cryptosystem was the same as that which been employed in the Far East. Indeed the same system was also to be employed on the Finnish front and when the Finnish army began its offensive in July of 1941, triggering off a burst of signal traffic from the Soviet forces, no less than 70 per cent of these signals could be read.

Important breaks were also made in the diplomatic traffic of various countries. After the occupation of Norway and Denmark in April 1940, the transit of goods between Sweden and the West was switched to the port of Petsamo in Northern Finland and as a result there was a consequent increase in signal traffic from the British Consulate at this port. The basic cryptosystem used for these consular signals was based on a five digit code and superencryption. Partly due to carelessness in the use of the cryptosystem and partly due to the acquisition of a code book by the Germans during the Norwegian campaign, the Finns were able to read this traffic and also that of British Consuls in Sweden (e.g., in Gothenburg) who employed a similar system.[214]

More important as a general source of information was the Turkish and above all certain American diplomatic traffic. In their work on the Turkish traffic, the Finns co-operated not only with German but also with Hungarian Signal Intelligence which despite slender means had also chalked up a number of important successes in the field.[215] The main break in the so-called American strip system occurred in the spring of 1942 and thereafter the American missions at Helsinki, Moscow/Kuibysjev, Stockholm, Madrid, Cairo, Teheran, Lisbon, the Vatican, Ankara and Rio de Janeiro were closely monitored.

In Sweden, co-operation between the host intelligence service and its Finnish counterpart was close. The Finnish military attaché, Colonel Martin Stewen enjoyed for long a particular position of trust, more or less coming and going as he pleased in the offices of the Swedish Defence Staff. In the resulting exchange of information, Stewen was provided with information about the Soviet Union, Hungary, Rumania, Bulgaria and Turkey.[216] In return, Stewen provided information about Soviet operations and other matters connected with the northern section of the Eastern Front. The information thus obtained was judged to be of crucial importance by the Swedish Defence Staff in its assessment of the situation.

These relations at military attaché level were paralleled in turn by the trust accorded by C-Bureau to Finnish liaison officers.[217] The Swedish Secret Service had after all come into being largely because of the emergency occasioned by the Winter War. The head of the Swedish service, Carl Petersén, was an old friend of Finland and enjoyed the highest contacts, among them Mannerheim himself. C-Bureau had received technical assistance from Colonel Hallamaa's Signals Intelligence organisation.

As far as security matters were concerned, the Finnish and Swedish services concerned with such matters had worked closely together prior to Barbarossa. A continuation of these contacts was deemed advantageous by the Swedes and information was exchanged primarily but not exclusively relating to the investigation of cases of Soviet espionage which had ramifications in both countries. Ironically, however, by far the most serious breach of Swedish wartime security – the tip-off to the Germans that their signal traffic was being read – was attributed to a leak through a Finnish official source who had been given the highest clearance.

Some idea of the complex interplay of the various intelligence services in Stockholm, can be obtained from the Eisberg/Zuckerhut scheme. Dr Krämer, the Stockholm representative of the Air Section of *Abwehr* I, had first met Onodera at a celebration in honour of the Emperor of Japan in April 1943. At the time, Krämer was well aware that Onodera was exchanging information with Dr Wagner, General von Uthmann and the Hungarian, Rumanian, Italian and Finnish military attachés but refrained from becoming involved in the trading since he was mainly interested in developing his own sources. In November 1943, he had again encountered Onodera, this time in Berlin. They discussed intelligence matters and agreed on a tentative exchange of information. Onodera had given some details about the disposition of British forces in India and the Middle East while Krämer had passed over items from official German intelligence summaries. The question of a full exchange with Onodera was now taken up with Krämer's superiors and he was given the formal go ahead.

At the beginning of 1944, the Air Section of *Abwehr* I suggested to Krämer that he should attempt to obtain official and genuine intelligence from the Swiss General Staff and the information deriving from its military attachés abroad. All reports relating to this special sector were to be sent to Berlin separately, under the cover designation Zuckerhut, with an additional number indicating the specific source (e.g., Zuckerhut 4 specified a report coming from the

Swiss Legation in Madrid). Zuckerhut did not denote an organisation of special agents: it simply signified official Swiss Intelligence views.[218]

The Zuckerhut material was obtained by a pooling of resources. Among those contributing to the scheme in addition to Krämer were said to be the Hungarian businessman Grundböck, mentioned earlier as one of Krämer's principal contacts; Okamoto, the Japanese MA in Berne; Onodera; Lieutenant Colonel Hallamaa, the Head of Finnish Signal Intelligence; Lieutenant-Colonel Kobor and Major Vöczköndy, the Hungarian military attaché in Stockholm and his deputy. Because of his illness and his subsequent death, Grundböck was not able to play any part in the scheme's practical implementation. None the less the inclusion of his name among all these official representatives as a prospective participant in a Finnish–Hungarian–Japanese–German intelligence syndicate, seems a trifle anomalous.

If Grundböck's exact status as an intelligence officer remains obscure, there were no such doubts about Major Vöczköndy, who arrived in Stockholm at the beginning of 1944 to do a stint as military attaché and made no secret of his Axis sympathies.[219] The German intelligence service soon made use of him as a convenient cutout/plug-in to other services and in this way reports from Finnish, Swiss and Swedish official sources were obtained.[220] When the Hungarian Intelligence Service in the autumn of 1944 wished – perhaps in connection with schemes for contacts with the Western powers – to dispatch a young intelligence officer to Stockholm, the proposal received SD backing in the expectation that Germany's own information-gathering capability in the Swedish capital would thereby be further enhanced.[221]

Glimpses from the final phase

In 1944, successive thrusts by the Red Army brought the Baltic States once more within Stalin's control. In September of the same year, an armistice was concluded between Finland and the Soviet Union. The Bear's shadow loomed large in Stockholm and anxieties about future developments led to increased contacts between the Western intelligence services and Baltic refugee organisations.[222] Before this – early in 1943 – Colonel Hallamaa had discussed with his superior, Aladar Paasonen, the Head of the Finnish Intelligence Service, the likely consequences of a Soviet victory and a contingency plan for transferring their activities to neighbouring Sweden was mooted. In the spring of 1944, Major Petersén, the head of C-Bureau was invited to Finland as Hallamaa's guest in order to talk over matters. Petersén was then entrusted with the task of trying to obtain the approval of the Swedish military authorities for the relocation plan, which was called Stella Polaris.[223]

On 20 September 1944, the evacuation got under way and eventually altogether some 750 persons travelled to Sweden, of which half belonged to the intelligence staff of military headquarters. Once the boats arrived in Sweden, the refugees were taken in hand by the Swedish authorities.

In the first half of November, a deputation of Finnish officers met Commander Torgil Thorén, the Head of the National Defence Radio Institute (FRA) to discuss the purchase of the Finnish equipment and archives brought over as part of Stella Polaris. The negotiations dragged on but eventually at the end of March an agreement was reached whereby for a purchase price of 252,875 crowns, the Swedes took over certain of the Finnish material, including seven boxes containing Soviet ciphers and codes which were handed over to FRA. Under a previous agreement, other records of the Finnish Defence Forces were deposited at Rottneros and Hörningsholm castles.

More or less at the same time that the sale of the Stella Polalris material was being discussed with the Swedes, Colonel Hallamaa and his friends looked round for other buyers and backers in Stockholm. These were not slow in coming forward and a brisk black market in the fruits of Finnish intelligence soon developed.

In November 1944, a representative of the American OSS in Stockholm was offered numerous Soviet military documents as well as the key to the decoding method which the Finns had used to decipher them.[224] The matter was placed before the State Department and Secretary of State Stettinius ruled that such a transaction 'would be inadvisable and improper'. The OSS, nevertheless, went ahead and some 1,500 pages of Soviet material and associated cryptographic aids were purchased. When Stettinius found out what had happened, he went to the President to protest at the OSS action. Roosevelt told him 'to see that the Russians were informed on this matter at once', and to report back to the White House about what steps had been taken. At the same time, the OSS was instructed that the codes and documents were to be immediately handed over to the Soviet government. This was done and on 15 February 1945, the material was duly handed over to Gromyko.

Another person keenly interested in the Finnish material was General Onodera who was keen to assist Hallamaa in his efforts. The latter was paid 300,000 crowns which was intended for two interception stations, apparently to be located in Northern Sweden and for the equipping of a parachute force, able to function behind enemy lines as secret agents. Inside Finland itself, it was hoped to prepare several stay-at-home organisations to work against the Russians.[225]

The Finnish–Soviet Armistice had obvious repercussions for the various branches of the German intelligence service in Finland. In August 1944, Himmler had ordered Kaltenbrunner to organise underground communications networks, manned by pro-Nazi elements, in those areas likely to be occupied by Russia.[226] The idea was that such networks would form the nucleus of a German controlled partisan movement. To this end, the head of the SD in Finland, *SS-Sturmbannführer* Alarich Bross, had set up two clandestine radio stations just before Finland broke off relations with Germany. The original plan was for Bross to proceed to Stockholm from where he would direct his partisans but this scheme failed to get off the ground. Instead Bross and his *Abwehr* colleague, Alexander Cellarius, withdrew to Swinemunde where they continued their activities under the name of *Sonderkommando Nord*. This was said to have subsections in Denmark and Norway and agents in Stockholm.[227]

Another illustration of the changing fortunes of war was provided by the case of Dr Edmund Sala.[228] Sala was a German *Abwehr* officer who had been placed in Finland and had worked closely with Finnish intelligence at HQ and later at Rovaniemi. Sceptical about Germany's chances of victory, Sala had begun thinking about the likely constellation of forces in the post-war world. After the withdrawal of German forces from Finnish soil, he was transferred to Norway and was eventually stationed at the German HQ at Lillehammer. However although friends had become technically foes, Sala did not sever contacts with Finnish Sigint who in this way had access to a useful stream of information about both Soviet and German dispositions.[229] It is not improbable that the Swedes – and perhaps even the Western intelligence services? – were also indirect beneficiaries of this relationship. But in any case, the Swedes were in due course able to establish a direct contact with Sala through an officer of C-Bureau.[230] With Germany's surrender looming, Sala now began making preparations to move to Sweden. Some members of his entourage apparently succeeded in making the trip.[231] For Sala himself, however, things were less smooth. He was held in prison in Oslo by the Norwegians pending examination of his case while in the background there were arguments over his fate.[232]

In the Swedish capital, two other German intelligence officers were also concerned with developments in Finland. Before the Finnish–Soviet Armistice, Dr Krämer had been summoned to Berlin and contingency plans for the receipt of Finnish intelligence (mainly from the so-called Aulio organisation) were discussed. Because of the reluctance of the Finns to become involved with German contacts in Stockholm for fear of prejudicing their chances of getting out of the war, it was decided that one way out of the difficulty would be to use Onodera as an intermediary.

After Busch's recall to Berlin in the summer of 1944, Major Wenzlau was sent to Stockholm in September to take his place.[233] Wenzlau's assignment – apart from keeping an eye on Krämer – was explicitly to contact those Finnish refugees arriving in Sweden who had worked for German intelligence. Krämer therefore handed over his various Finnish contacts to Wenzlau and the latter assumed the main responsibility for the evaluation and transmission of intelligence concerning Finland, the Baltic States, Russia and Sweden. Major Wenzlau was soon working closely with Onodera as his communications to Berlin (sent under the codename Pandur) were to reveal.[234] Via the Japanese MA, the Germans were eventually to purchase an assortment of codebooks. On 25 March 1945, Wenzlau sent a report regarding the organisation of an intelligence net in the Soviet Union. According to this, Onodera (Agent 26) and Hallamaa had succeeded in setting up a network of Finnish and Estonian agents. The old net was said to be intact and Hallamaa claimed to be able to maintain contact with his agents in Leningrad and Moscow. Hallamaa reckoned on holding out in Finland for another two or three months. Thereafter he hoped to be able to continue his activities from Sweden although Onodera did not believe that the Swedes had agreed to this. If Swedish support fell through, the question arose as to how communications were to be maintained with the Finnish agent nets. There were also plans for extending the net in Estonia. According to Hallamaa, the Finnish–Estonian network which had been functioning for several years, would be in a position to continue its work. Its intelligence could be fed to the Americans who – it was said – were now greatly interested in information from the Soviet Union. At the same time, in Wenzlau's view, there was nothing to prevent the selfsame network from co-operating with the Germans and Japanese.

In the last months of the war in Europe, Onodera's intelligence activities continued unabated. A curious scheme for establishing an Estonian agent in the USA was mooted.[235] In another development, Dr Enomoto, a Japanese journalist who had co-operated with *Dienstelle Klatt* in the Balkans, suddenly popped up in Stockholm.[236] On behalf of the new arrival, Onodera now suggested to Wenzlau a joint German–Japanese operation to inaugurate a triangular intelligence communication net embracing agents in the USA, the Iberian Peninsula and Stockholm.[237] The Germans however – perhaps in part because of the Klatt connection – showed no great enthusiasm and in any case the march of events soon reduced this scheme to a curiosity in the history of secret service.

Appendix 1

A cryptological note

HAND CIPHERS

For agents in the field, a good cipher must combine a number of properties. It should be secure[1] (that is, if used properly, it should not yield to cryptanalysis); it should be simple in conception (not too difficult for the agent to understand and recall); it should not be too time-consuming in application; and it should involve the holding of as few compromising accessories as possible (spies should travel light). The practical implementation of these theoretical desiderata turned out to be not quite as simple as some people had imagined.

Between August 1941 and the date of his arrest, Vanek sent some 500 CX-telegrams to a telegraphic address, MINIMISE, in London. Each telegram was made up as usual of five-digit groups, among them four indicator groups containing special information needed by the receiver. The method of encipherment employed so-called double transposition.[2] Suppose for example, the message to be sent is COURIER ARRIVES MONDAY. We proceed to write it out beneath the 'scrambler' sequence of digits 34125 (the key), in rows:

```
3  4  1  2  5
C  O  U  R  I
E  R  A  R  R
I  V  E  S  M
O  N  D  A  Y
```

The letters are now read off, column by column, taking the columns in the normal numerical order, i.e., UAED RRSA CEIO ORVN IRMY. The procedure can be applied once more to this transposed message, using a different key, say 1243:

248

```
1   2   4   3
U   A   E   D
R   R   S   A
C   E   I   O
O   R   V   N
I   R   M   Y
```

Reading off by column, we get the sequence of groups URCOI ARERR ESIVM DAONY. If all one has is the cipher text, ingenuity is needed to find the original message. As soon as we know the keys, however, we can mechanically reverse the above procedures to arrive back at the plain text. The receiver therefore must be told which keys the sender has used. In the case of the Czech cipher, this was determined by two things, first, the date of encipherment; second, a book, possessed by both sender and receiver. In the case of Vanek, this was Masaryk's *Svetava Revoluce*. Armed with the date, he picked out from the book two text fragments in a unique manner and then converted them into numbers, according to a fixed procedure. The resulting two number sequences were then the desired keys.

Double transposition was also employed by German agents. Thus 'Anker', a Swedish agent recruited by the SD in 1943 to operate a radio link with Germany in case normal diplomatic communications were later disrupted, was provided with a modified double transposition cipher.

When Herbert Wehner was arrested in 1942, it was discovered that a report, written in invisible ink and in cipher, had been sent to the KPD leadership in Stockholm from a kindred group in Holland. The cipher employed was typical of those used by Comintern and Soviet agents. First of all, the letters making up the message to be transmitted, were replaced according to the following substitution table, in this case based on the keyword PERSIL:

	0	1	2	3	4	5	6	7	8	9
		P	E	R	S	I	L			
7	A	B	C	D	F	G	H	J	K	M
8	N	O	Q	T	U	V	W	X	Y	Z
9										

Thus E was replaced by 2, L by 6, A by 70, K by 78, X by 87 and so on. Furthermore certain entries in the table – which have not been filled in

– were used to represent not simple letters but words or sequences of letters. Modifying the method to be applicable to English rather than German, we can for example let $91 = IS$, $92 = SH$, $96 = AND$ and $98 = THE$.

Suppose now that the message we wished to send, began

THE FOOD SHORTAGE IN

Replacing the constituent letters one after the other, according to the substitution table, we get the sequence of numbers

$$98, 74, 81, 81, 73, 92, 81, 3, 83, 70, 75, 2, 5, 80$$

This was then rearranged in groups of five digits, retaining the order of the original sequence:

$$98748 \quad 18173 \quad 92813 \quad 83707 \quad 52580 \quad (\Sigma 1)$$

This first substitution of course offered no real cryptological protection. In order to make the message more secure, it was necessary to carry out a second process of concealment. Underneath the sequence ($\Sigma 1$), another sequence ($\Sigma 2$) was written and the two of them were added together – neglecting however, to 'carry ones' – to produce a new sequence ($\Sigma 3$). It was this latter sequence ($\Sigma 3$) which was then sent. Suppose, for example, we chose for our addition sequence

$$35435 \quad 43543 \quad 54354 \quad 35435 \quad 43543 \quad (\Sigma 2)$$

based on the 3 digit cycle, 354. When we add this to our original sequence ($\Sigma 1$) in the manner described, we get

$$23173 \quad 51616 \quad 46167 \quad 18132 \quad 95023 \quad (\Sigma 3)$$

Care had to be taken in the choice of the addition sequence ($\Sigma 2$). In the case of the Amsterdam–Stockholm communication, it was generated from two 'seeds' formed by two text fragments, each containing 25 letters, taken from the book *Kampf um Kautschuk* by Wolfgang Jünger. This yielded an addition sequence with a cycle of 1500 digits. In addition, the two seeds could be varied from message to message by including in the enciphered message an indicator group of digits specifying the page and line of the book (edition assumed known) from which the text fragments had been taken in accordance with some predetermined system, known to both sender and receiver.

A MACHINE CIPHER

Simultaneously with its invasion of Norway and Denmark on 9 April 1940, Germany presented Sweden with certain demands including that of making use of sections of the Swedish cable network for its telephone and telegram communications with Norway. Thereafter the German authorities rented lines for their links Oslo–Copenhagen–Berlin, Oslo–Trondheim, Oslo–Narvik and Oslo–Stockholm. Later there was also a link between Stockholm and Helsinki. In Stockholm, the German legation had cable contact with Berlin but the separately housed Air Attaché's office which was to become a central node of the German communications system in Sweden, also disposed over a number of lines.

Given the vulnerability of this German cable traffic (which embraced both military and diplomatic communications) to Swedish interception, its security ultimately depended on the assumption that the cipher systems underpinning it, could not be broken. The main component in ensuring German cryptosecurity was the *Geheimschreiber*.[3] This was a variant of the Siemens and Halske tele-typewriter and incorporated a special encryption mechanism consisting of ten wheels designed to effect certain subsitutions and transpositions on Baudot code. Technically sophisticated, it appeared to offer the desirable combination of high speed (up to 428 letters per minute) on-line communication and maximum security.

The *Geheimschreiber* was successively modified during the course of the war and at least five different models labelled A, B, C, D and E have been mentioned in the open literature on the subject. Types A, B and C were relatively similar whereas a new level of complexity emerged with types D (Dora) and E (Emil). The *Geheimschreiber* was employed in radio as well cable links and was known to the British as FISH.[4]

Already by the summer of 1940, the Swedes had succeeded in piercing the mystery of the earliest type of model. The decisive cryptanalytical breakthrough was due to Arne Beurling, a thirty-five-year-old professor of mathematics at the University of Uppsala. On the *sole* basis of one day's traffic (that of 25 May 1940) Beurling was able to reconstruct the basic principles involved in the German machine cipher system. This enabled the Swedes to build an electro-mechanical device designed to accelerate the decryption process. Some thirty such devices were produced in L. M. Ericsson's precision mechanics workshop and subsequently put into operation at the decryption centre at Karlaplan 4 in Stockholm.

General systems are one thing: specific keys are another. In order to proceed with the daily practical work of decryption, it was necessary first to determine the wheel setting being used. Here the Swedish cipher-breakers were assisted by recurring errors in German operating practice. Interference on the lines often necessitated the operator once more starting his transmission from the beginning. Instead of altering the wheel setting before repeating the transmission, as cryptosecurity required, operators often simply proceeded to retransmit the message, thus giving rise to parallel texts. Such parallel texts facilitated the solution of the setting being used. Another fatal short cut was to allow five of the wheels to have the same setting every day. Important clues about the encrypted traffic were also sometimes obtained from messages passed *en clair* by the teleprinter operator or from intercepted telephone calls.

When around the middle of 1942, the Germans discovered that the Swedes had succeeded in reading their traffic, various safety measures were put into effect. Modified versions of the *Geheimschreiber* were introduced, initially to no great effect since earlier cryptanalytical methods could be carried over without too much difficulty. More serious was the German decision to reroute their telegram traffic via cables outside Swedish territory, thus impeding physical interception. No such solution was of course possible for the traffic from the Legation and the Air Attaché's office in Stockholm. Certain of these lines apparently continued to be read – perhaps sporadically – by the Swedes into 1944 but the introduction of the Dora machine presented the Defence Radio Institute (FRA) with a new challenge.[5]

Appendix 2

The Security of Diplomatic Missions

EXAMPLE 1

In 1943, Mr Battley of Scotland Yard made a tour of inspection of the various British diplomatic and consular premises in Sweden with a view to assessing their level of security. As far as the Legation itself was concerned, he noted that the work of three Swedish cleaners who were employed there was quite unsupervised.

> One of them is entrusted with the key of the padlock to the grille outside the door of the room where the Naval Attaché's secret and confidential papers are kept. This padlock and key were purchased locally.[1]

Nor were the cleaners the only problem.

> Workman have been engaged here in carrying out extensive alterations to the premises for the past two or three years and it cannot be accepted that on many occasions their work has not been supervised. They have thus had some chance of installing microphones.[2]

Certain doubts were also entertained about the loyalty of a certain junior servant at the legation. Battley summed up as follows:

> It cannot be denied that the practice of using foreign Chancery servants has its dangers, particularly in wartime. These servants inevitably learn a great deal about the inner workings of the Legation and, as Swedish subjects, they may be called upon by their Government to pass on to the latter, as a patriotic duty, such information as they may obtain.[3]

253

EXAMPLE 2

Ironically enough, Battley's worries were later echoed by a member of the Swedish Legation in London who confided his impressions of security to the Swedish Defence Minister in February 1945:

> Only English watchmen: the military section's house is cleaned, looked after and inhabited by an English watchman and his wife. There are no Swedes there at night and the watchman has access to all parts of the premises.
> A check can very easily be kept by the English on all activities at the mission and on all visitors.
> The Cipher Room is locked with an English Yale key. It is unlikely that there is any great difficulty involved in entering the room at night.[4]

EXAMPLE 3

In Berlin, the Gestapo successfully managed to penetrate the Swedish legation by recruiting one of the secretaries. From the autumn of 1941 – perhaps even earlier – up to November 1943, this woman regularly delivered confidential material to her contact.[5] In this way, the German authorities were able to monitor not only official Swedish reporting from Berlin but also to some extent Swedish reporting in general in the shape of occasional special dispatches from Stockholm containing information gathered from other Swedish sources elsewhere and of potential relevance to the work of the legation in Berlin.[6]

As regards Swedish information-gathering activities in Germany, special interest focused on the reports of the military attaché, Juhlin-Dannfelt, an acute and experienced observer who was known to have a number of important, well placed contacts, among them Canaris himself.[7] The links between the Swede and Vladimir Kaulbars, the friend of Canaris, was to arouse in particular the suspicions of the German security service, suspicions which increased still more following their enquiries into the abortive coup attempt of 20 July 1944.[8] The German case against Juhlin-Dannfelt was further strengthened when the attaché's briefcase fell into the hands of Kaltenbrunner's men.[9] An opportunity to make use of some of the accumulated material later presented itself at a meeting at *Auswärtiges Amt*, when the recall of the *Abwehr* representatives in Stockholm was taken up by the Swedish Minister. Steengracht, the Secretary of State, countered with evidence against Juhlin-Dannfelt:

> He had before him two bound volumes containing copies of his [Juhlin-Dannfelt's] reports and read out several extracts from them dealing partly with the geographical location of various headquarters and of places where weapons were produced and partly of reports from Cologne, which indicated the regular agent activity of some German.[10]

However, by now the Swedes held most of the cards. The recall of the badly compromised German intelligence men from Stockholm was not negotiable. In addition, the Swedish minister was instructed by the Ministry for Foreign Affairs in Stockholm to point out that Juhlin-Dannfelt's recall would simply lead to a Swedish demand for the recall of von Uthmann, the German MA.

Appendix 3

A Mysterious Link

During the Second World War a communication link, Germany–Sweden–Argentina, making use of the ordinary commercial telecommunications net, attracted the attention of the Swedish authorities.[1] Beginning in the middle of September 1941, it was noted that a company director in Berlin had begun to phone to a subsidiary in southern Sweden. The person receiving the call then proceeded to telegraph Buenos Aires. The information transmitted was of a private rather than commercial character, between various firms and individuals abroad and their relatives in Germany. This traffic went on for three years and was largely unidirectional: while messages were transmitted from Berlin to Buenos Aires via Sweden there was no corresponding return flow of messages from Buenos Aires to Berlin via this Swedish route.[2]

In order to determine the nature of the traffic more closely, the Swedes experimented in editing the telegrams being sent in various ways. But these multifarious alterations produced a reaction from the receiver in only two cases. Eventually it was concluded that if the telegrams being sent constituted a concealed method of communication, then only the names (and not the text in general) were of importance.

The above traffic raised a number of questions: Why the detour via Sweden when there was no formal prohibition or practical obstacle to the direct dispatch of telegrams from Germany to Argentina? Why did German censorship authorities never intervene in the telephone calls between Berlin and the firm in Sweden, either in regard to what was said or regarding the length of the call? Why would a commercial company allow this expensive series of telegrams about essentially private, non-commercial matters to continue so long? Why was the traffic unidirectional? Why was care taken to cloak the individuals in

Buenos Aires to whom the telegrams were sent?[3] Why did the director in Berlin lay so much emphasis on the fact that the firm in Sweden should appear as the sender of the message? Although the proprietor of the Swedish firm was cross-examined and various other enquiries were made at the time, no clear conclusion was ever reached about the nature of this mysterious traffic.

Appendix 4

A note on Soviet and Comintern activities

Important representatives of Soviet State Security and Soviet Military Intelligence served under a variety of diplomatic covers on the staffs of the Legation and of the Trade Delegation in Stockholm during the war.[1]

In 1938, 'Jack', an intellectual who had attracted the favourable attention of State Security, was enlisted as a secret reporter in Sweden. During the Finnish Winter War, Jack functioned as a recruiter, looking out for suitable candidates for on-the-spot reporting from Finland. According to his own claims, some 30 agents were recruited in this way and their information routed back to the Soviet Legation in Stockholm for further transmission to Moscow.[2]

At the close of 1939, Anglo-French plans for intervention in Scandinavia were evidently being closely followed in the Kremlin. One small but interesting indicator of this fact was the dispatch of an agent to the iron ore district of Northern Sweden, charged explicitly with monitoring developments in the region in case Britain should attempt to establish bases there for operations against the Soviet Union.[3]

The ending of the Winter War removed an important pretext for – but not the driving thought behind – Allied plans for intervention in Scandinavia. Stalin's fears about a possible strong Anglo-French presence on his North-West flank were, however, dispelled by Hitler's swoop on Norway and Denmark. Quick to assure the German Ambassador in Moscow of Soviet sympathy and support for this action, Molotov was at pains a few days later to emphasise the Soviet interest in limiting the sphere of military operations and in maintaining Sweden as a neutral buffer.[4]

In the interim period between the summer of 1940 and the onslaught of Barbarossa, the Soviet organs in Sweden managed to keep a relatively low profile. Among the few interesting cases coming to light, was that involving a *Riksdag* stenographer (and expert on Soviet economic affairs) who was suspected of having been in contact with the Soviet covert services over a longer period of time. In October 1940, the stenographer had made under a false pretext a first attempt to persuade a journalist to go to Finland and there check certain rumours about the movements and disposition of German military personnel. In addition, the stenographer had presented his Soviet control with reports about events in Norway, the German transit of troops through Sweden and diverse other matters.[5]

Although Barbarossa presented the Soviet Union with a military threat of the first order, on the propaganda front (which was by no means irrelevant for the work of the Special Services abroad) it also provided an opportunity to recoup some of the broader based popular support which had been lost as a result of the Molotov–Ribbentrop Pact. In Sweden, however, the ideological counter-offensive had initially an uphill struggle. The summer and autumn of 1941 saw much press coverage being devoted to the so-called Wollweber men. The surveillance of known or suspected communists remained strict.[6]

Whatever the exact consequence this may have had on Soviet-sponsored covert activities, it is safe to assume none the less that these activities proceeded on a fairly broad front. Several 'pianists' in Soviet service were arrested after their radio traffic had been intercepted and pinpointed by the Swedish authorities.[7] A venal engineer was given a life sentence for selling the plans of an important Swedish fortification to Soviet representatives.[8] A military orderly attached to the Crypto Bureau photographed decrypts of German telegrams on behalf of his control, as well as revealing that certain Soviet ciphers were being read by the Swedes.[9] An émigré aristocrat with good contacts in both Swedish and Allied circles supplied a Soviet naval intelligence officer with sundry political, economic and military information.[10] A military intelligence officer with cover as an Aeroflot representative managed to recruit a former Tsarist naval attaché and a Swedish police officer as informants.[11]

Among the more important agents of State Security in Stockholm was 'Klara', a writer and journalist of central-European origin.[12] One of her initial tasks had been that of finding a number of suitable people who could be infiltrated into Germany, Austria and other parts of occupied Europe under the guise of having been converted to Nazism.

The use of Sweden as an outpost for maintaining contacts with underground circles in Germany had also been uppermost in the minds of the leaders of the German Communist Party (KPD). A number of Comintern instructors were successfully sent from Sweden into Germany but more ambitious plans for the establishment of an Inner German Operative Leadership in Berlin, drawn from experienced party members assembled in Stockholm, were scuppered in 1942 after the arrest of two of the principals, Herbert Wehner and Karl Mewis.[13] This reverse inevitably affected the work of the group as a whole. At a later stage of the war, a courier line between Berlin and Stockholm was established with the assistance of a chauffeur employed at the Swedish Legation in the German capital.[14]

Jack's group was also involved in trying to improve communications between Sweden and Germany although these endeavours did not always work out as planned. Thus a scheme to establish under a false flag a radio link between a POW camp in Germany and Stockholm, was betrayed to the SD and gave rise to a *Funkspiel* which lasted from the summer of 1942 until spring 1943.[15]

Another method of improving the flow of information from Germany itself was naturally to access – whether by agreement or by the suborning or infiltration of agents – the intelligence being collected there by non-Soviet services. In this way the plans and practices of the Western services could also be monitored.

In addition to trying to establish links with sources in mainland Europe, the Soviet Special Services in Stockholm were naturally involved in maintaining contacts with their own agents in neighbouring Scandinavian countries. Sweden provided a convenient back door to Finland. In Norway, among those in contact with a Soviet control in Sweden, was Asbjörn Sunde, whose partisan group was responsible for active measures such as sabotage as well as for the collection of intelligence.[16]

Like other powers, the Soviet Union also found Sweden a useful neutral platform for a discreet – direct or indirect – dialogue with enemy representatives. This was so in the case of Soviet–Finnish overtures but there were exercises in secret diplomacy involving other rather more far-flung countries as well.[17]

Notes

Full details of published sources referred to are given in the Bibliography.

The following abbreviations have been used:
AAA = Auswärtiges Amts Archiv
BA-MA = Bundesarchiv-Militärarchiv, Freiburg
IWM = Imperial War Museum, London
KrA = Krigsarkiv, Stockholm
NA = National Archives, Washington
PRO = Public Record Office, Kew
RA = Riksarkiv, Stockholm
RR5-YEAR [NUMBER], StA = Rådhusrättsarkiv 5: e avd., brottmål,
    hemliga mål, Stadsarkiv, Stockholm
SFS = Svensk Författningssamling
UDA = Utrikesdepartementets arkiv, Utrikesdepartementet, Stockholm
    (to be distinguished from UD:s arkiv, RA).

1 GAMEKEEPER'S PERSPECTIVE

1. Howard, pp. 235–37.
2. Polisbyråns korrespondens, Generalstabens arkiv, KrA.
3. Polisbyråns korrespondens, Generalstabens arkiv, KrA.
4. Polisbyråns korrespondens, Generalstabens arkiv, KrA.
5. See e.g., Andrew, *Secret Service*, pp. 182–4.
6. Dossier, A239, Statens Polisbyråns arkiv, RA.
7. Dossier A185, Statens Polisbyråns Arkiv, RA. Lockhart, op. cit., pp. 74–5.
8. See e.g., Andrew, *Secret Service*, pp. 107–9.
9. See the relevant documents in A. Scherer, and J. U. Grunewald, *L' Allemagne et les Problèmes de la Paix* (Paris, Vol. 1, 1962; Vol. 2, 1966).
10. For the possibilities of agitation against Russia, see Helphand's memorandum reprinted as appendix I in Zeman. Futtrell (and more recently Björkegren) deals with the activities of the Bolsheviks in Stockholm. For the mobilisation of nationalist groups, see Zetterberg's interesting essay on the Stockholm activities of the League of Alien Peoples.
11. Søhr, pp. 72–98.
12. See the appropriate texts in Schindler and Toman.
13. SFS 1937: 344.
14. SFS 1939: 28.
15. SFS 1939: 599 and 600.
16. SFS 1940: 231.

17. SFS 1940: 248, 287, 288 and 301.
18. SFS 1937: 913 and SFS 1940: 447.
19. Appropriate texts in Schindler and Toman, op. cit.
20. SFS 1940: 356.
21. SFS 1940: 356.
22. SFS 1940: 356.
23. SOU 1935: 8.
24. Riksdagens Protokoll 1936, FK 45.
25. SFS 1936: 327.
26. SFS 1939: 722.
27. SFS 1940: 356.
28. Riksdagens Protokoll 1940, FK 28.
29. SFS 1942: 103.
30. SFS 1942: 103.
31. SFS 1942: 103.
32. Riksdagens Protokoll 1942, FK 11.
33. Riksdagens Protokoll 1944, FK 17.
34. Riksdagens Protokoll 1944, FK 17.
35. SFS 1944: 314.
36. SFS 1939: 951.
37. SFS 1940: 197.
38. SFS 1940: 356.
39. SFS 1940: 117.
40. See, e.g., Nerman, 1942, p. 71.
41. SFS 1940: 197. An official account of the work of the Board is to be found in Fryschius' report of 31 July 1950 in Pressbyråns arkiv, UD:s arkiv, Vol. 176, RA. In September 1943, a small brochure *Svenskarna och propagandan* [The Swedes and Propaganda] appeared pseudonymously with the indirect authorisation of the Information Board and stimulated much controversy by its inclusion of a section which by implication disparaged and dismissed a number of widely respected Swedish publications as organs for 'propaganda on behalf of the Western Powers'. For the discussion in the *Riksdag*, see Riksdagens Protokoll 1944, FK 4:10 and FK 5:4.
42. SFS 1940: 995. In January 1940, a practical step towards increasing security at harbours, airfields, railways and other installations was taken by an agreement between the Security Service and the Confederation of Trades Unions, establishing a secret watch service made up of union representatives judged to be reliable.
43. SFS 1939: 614 and 615.
44. SFS 1939: 795 and 796.
45. SFS 1939: 724 and 725.
46. SFS 1940: 3–5.
47. SFS 1940: 503.
48. Leche to von Sydow, 23 March 1947, in F1:7, Sandler Kommissionens arkiv, RA, hereafter cited as Sandler, RA. See also E. Leche's article in *Effektivt försvar*, Nr. 7, 1963.
49. Leche to von Sydow, 23 March 1947. For Nothin's role as watchdog, see Nothin, pp. 262–3.
50. Ernst Leche, op. cit.
51. SOU 1948: 7, p. 12.
52. SOU 1948: 7, p. 15.
53. Falkenstam, pp. 289-90.
54. Report 7 April 1945 in F1:7, Sandler, RA.
55. Cf. SOU 1964: 15, p. 114.
56. Undated P. M. rörande civila myndigheters samarbete med Försvarsstabens Under-

rättelseavdelningen, Svenska sektion, in F1:10, Sandler, RA. See also Adlercreutz, *Kortfattad historik över underrättelse – och kontraspionageverksamheten*, in Adlercreutz vol. 27, KrA. Hereafter cited as Adlercreutz, *Historik*.

57. Th. Söderström, 27 November 1945 in F1:7, Sandler, RA.
58. SOU 1946: 36, p. 23.
59. SOU 1946: 36, p. 24.
60. For the *Geheimschreiber*, see Appendix 1.
61. This applied, for example, to confidential communications via official courier.
62. There were important breaks in Soviet military traffic but the diplomatic traffic remained unread. The Swedes also succeeded in breaking various British, American and French ciphers. The American and French breaks yielded more than the break into the British traffic.
63. Hellmuth Ternbergs Arkiv, Vol. 1, KrA.
64. Undated PM över C-byrån, p. 15, Hellmuth Ternbergs Arkiv, Vol. 1, KrA.
65. Undated PM, Hellmuth Ternbergs Arkiv, Vol. 1, KrA.
66. Utredning, pp. 47–55, C- Byråns arkiv, H1, KrA.
67. Undated PM över C-byrån, p. 16, Hellmuth Ternbergs Arkiv, Vol. 1, KrA. In his review of Carlgren's book on Swedish military intelligence, Lieutenant-Colonel Magnus af Petersen has drawn attention to C-Bureau's valuable exchange of information with both Switzerland and Hungary.
68. For the registration and surveillance of National Socialist individuals and organisations, see Lööw's dissertation.
69. For the censorship of telegrams, see Akt angående telegramkontrollen, in F1:9, Sandler, RA.
70. Palmstierna, p. 109.
71. Cf. SOU 1948: 7, p. 140.
72. Following Lööw, p. 415.
73. P.M. 9 February 1946, in F1:10, Sandler, RA.
74. See Denham, pp. 150–1. According to the file F0 850/9, PRO, the British had learned by January 1941 that microphones had been installed by the Germans in the Stockholm flats of the Fleet Assistant to the air attaché and others on the diplomatic list. While this may be true and is certainly not without interest, it is also naturally possible that the microphones were in reality installed by the Swedish security service for their own purposes. Von Platen has an amusing anecdote about a bungled Swedish attempt to 'bug' the German military attaché, see von Platen, pp. 39–40.
75. Riksdagens Protokoll 1943, FK 5:18.
76. Riksdagens Protokoll 1943, AK15:62 and 22:13; FK 15:18 and 22:14. Among the abuses brought up were the searching of a member of the Finnish *Riksdag*, A. Wirtanen and the detention of the Secretary of *Fighting Democracy* after a visit to the British Consulate in Gothenburg.
77. Riksdagens Protokoll 1943, AK 22:13.
78. SOU 1948: 7.
79. For the Tranmael case, see Adlercreutz, pp. 42–43 where the affair is recorded with unconcealed bitterness. Möller had also been active earlier when Inge Scheflo and Willy Brandt, had been held by the police as a result of the arrest of a Norwegian courier in August 1941. See Hammarlund pp. 54–5. For an insider's view of wartime Security Service issues, see Tage Erlander's memoirs.
80. Cf. Grimnes, p. 84 and Hammarlund, p. 57.
81. See p. 101.
82. Lindquist finished as Chief of the Home Section in September 1943. The Admiralty in London viewed him as one of their principal *bêtes noires*. 'On the other hand, in order to show their goodwill to us in security matters, the Swedish Government have just sent back to his regiment Major Lindquist, the objectionable personality in MI5

whose removal Director of Naval Intelligence personally pressed me to secure when I was in London in May.' Telegram, 15 September 43, Mallett to FO, FO 188/412, PRO.

2 POACHER'S PERSPECTIVE – 1

1. For IIC, see Wark, Ch. 7. For British economic warfare and Swedish iron ore during the Phoney War, Munch-Petersen's monograph provides a useful vade-mecum.
2. Consett, *The Triumph of Unarmed Forces*, pp. 79–80.
3. Cruickshank's *SOE in Scandinavia* provides an indispensable account of Rickman's activities based on British documents not yet available in the PRO. The present account supplements Cruickshank with information from private sources and from Swedish documents, *inter alia* the trial papers in RR5-1940 [6], StA.
4. This crane was to be the subject of a minute by Hugh Gaitskell at MEW on 19 February 1940. 'Mr. Roskill has also drawn my attention to the fact that just before the war the capacity of Oxelösund was doubled by the installation of an 18 ton bridge crane to meet German requirements. The strategic significance of this is obvious.' FO 837/802, Part 2. PRO.
5. See War Trade Agreement, Sweden, Report of Meeting of Sub-committee on Iron Ore held in Sir F. Leith-Ross's Room at the Ministry of Economic Warfare on 6 October 1939 in FO 837/802, PRO. The vague promises of obstruction to the German trade by various technical devices, however, appear to have been talk and little else.
6. Morton 26 October 39 in FO 837/802 Part 1, PRO.
7. Morton 4 October 39 in FO 837/24, PRO.
8. For Thyssen's contacts with the French, see Arnal.
9. Unsigned review of De Geer's article, dated 31 January 40 in FO 837/24, PRO. The significance of Swedish iron ore for the German War Economy has been much debated by economic historians. Interrogated after the war, Krupp, after noting that the shortage of raw materials never adversely affected German production, went on to remark 'Of course if our iron ore from Sweden had been cut off earlier that would have been a different matter.' FO1078/47, PRO.
10. Morton to Collier, 9 February 40, FO 837/24, PRO. In the original text, the amusing phrase 'certain *strange* friends of Mr Stephenson' has been corrected to read 'certain *Swedish* friends of Mr Stephenson'.
11. Thus the 'Freckles' mentioned in Cruickshank. p. 33. Wren played an important role in the marketing of the Aga cooker in Britain.
12. According to private information, we have the following timetable:

Early July 1939	W
30 June–3 July	S
6 August–23 August	F
31 August–2 September	F
1 October–8 October	S
3 November–6 November	F
24 November–28 November	F
14 December–23 December	S
21 January 1940–31 January	S
22 January–9 February	F

(W = Wren, S = Stephenson, F = Fraser)
13. See Berman Fischer's own account.
14. I am grateful to Walter Pöppel for information about SAP's illegal organisation in Prague. His own most interesting account, *Deutschlands verlorene Jahre 1933–1945*,

Betrachtungen aus der Emigration, should also be consulted.

15. Trial papers in RR5-1940 [6], StA.
16. Fraser's visit to Copenhagen is also interesting in the light of the following: 'The plan has already been studied by "D" for the blocking of Luleå harbour by sinking a ship filled with concrete in the channel. This scheme was regarded as difficult of achievement and was for all practical purposes put out of action by the German seizure of Denmark, since negotiations for chartering of a suitable ship and crew were being conducted in Copenhagen at the time of the German invasion.' Minute by Jebb, 11 May 1940, FO 371/24832.
17. I have been told that Holdsworth may have brought additional explosives with him.
18. There is no mention of the flight mechanics in Cruickshank.
19. Undersökningsprotokoll, 22 May 1940, pp. 1-2, RR5-1940 [6], StA.
20. Judging from their mode of operation, the author conjectures that the limpet mines belonged to the batch developed by Nobby Clarke after field trials in Bedford Public Baths. See Macrae.
21. Cruickshank's account of this matter in the official history *SOE in Scandinavia*, is incorrect.
22. The importance of the investigation of 'Kant' for the subsequent action against Rickman is quite clear from the Swedish documentation. See, e.g., Memorandum 7 February 46 folder Värdet av kontrollerna, in F1:10, Sandler, RA.
23. Report, 13 May 1940, pp. 1–2. Trial Papers in RR5–1940[4], StA.
24. Ibid. pp. 2–3.
25. 'Kant' was given an eight month sentence for his reporting activities. It was assumed on the basis of his confession that his reports about Rickman had gone to an agency of German intelligence. (In Adlercreutz, *Historik*, the first wartime head of Swedish intelligence, reviewing what had been written about the case by the journalist Berhardsson, put forward his view that Kant had worked for the Gestapo rather than the *Abwehr*.) In a submission to the Swedish authorities in January 1946, entitled *Meine einzige Straftat* Kant attempted to rescue his reputation as a liberal journalist by arguing (1) that Kutzner had been a cover for an oppositional group in Berlin and not for an agency of official German intelligence (2) that in 1940 he had been obliged to suppress the true identities of his Berlin contacts from the Swedish police in order to protect them and (3) that his letter in invisible ink about Rickman had been designed to bring about a dialogue between members of this group and British representatives.

    It is worth noting that this version of the facts is due to Kant and to Kant alone. The impression fostered by Kant that outside bodies such as the wartime German Labour Delegation in New York or individuals such as Fritz Tarnow, the respected former Social Democratic member of the *Reichstag*, then in exile in Sweden, were in a position to make a qualified, independent assessment of the relevant facts of the case in 1941–43, is an illusion. Thus while it is true that Tarnow in writing to Ragnar Casparsson on 24 June 1943 in an attempt to rehabilitate Kant concluded with the personal opinion that Kant was 'absolutely anti-Nazi and a decent and honourable man', he frankly admitted that as far as Kant's activities in Sweden were concerned, he had relied entirely on what Kant had told him.

    Passing to Kant's reinterpretation of the facts of his case, a number of comments are in order. *Re* (1) *Sturmbannführer* Grönheim who had detailed insight into the intelligence work of the *Sicherheitsdienst* in Sweden informed his Allied interrogators that Kant had worked for the SD and that his reports, dealing with economics and foreign affairs, had been sent to a Press Bureau in Berlin which functioned as a cover for that organisation. It is also known that the same address was used during the Phoney War by another German agent working in Denmark. *Re* (2) Kant withheld his 'true version' not only from the police but also from Hugo Lindberg, a man of the highest integrity who had been initially engaged to undertake his defence. Kant had the possibility when first apprehended of giving his subsequent explanation in general terms without naming his contacts in Berlin, at least to his counsel. Why did he not do so? *Re* (3) an examination of the reports to Berlin containing information about Rickman suggest that Kant was involved in routinely monitoring the Englishman and his circle rather than in trying to bring about a dialogue. This impression is reinforced by the fact that Kant although provided with invisible ink for sending messages *to* Berlin had no reagent to develop messages *from* Berlin.

For these reasons, Kant's reinterpretation fails to convince. Charity allows that Kant may not have known that he was working for the SD specifically. It is much harder to believe that a journalist of his experience had not twigged that his covert reports to Berlin were in all probability destined for *some* official German intelligence service. Indeed his complicity seems greater than this.

Kant's name occurs in a list (copy in FO 188/538, PRO) of October 1946 of persons said to be of German nationality and believed to be resident in Sweden, whom the British, American, Soviet and French Missions in Stockholm wished to see repatriated, presumably for interrogation about their wartime activities.

26. Kant's dossier, Socialstyrelsen/utlänningskommissions arkiv, RA.
27. Personal information.
28. It was naturally open to German interception. In contrast, German signal traffic from Sweden was carried by cable and was not directly accessible to British interception.
29. For a full account, see Tennant's volume of memoirs.
30. In the autumn of 1942, the Swedes learned of the existence of one such British-sponsored radio-telegraphy organisation in Norrköping and arrested several of those involved in the spring of the following year. Memorandum rörande brittiske press-attachén Peter Tennant, 14 July 1943 in P 53 Ba/81, UDA.
31. Cruickshank, *SOE in Scandinavia*, p. 64. In case of a German invasion of Sweden, a British contingency plan was devised for the transfer of certain leading Swedes, among them Gustav Möller, Rickard Sandler, Torgny Segerstedt and Östen Undén, to Britain.
32. Cruickshank mentions Threlfall's presence in Stockholm but has nothing whatsoever to say about what he was up to.
33. The telegram will be found among those featuring in the trial papers relating to Vanek, RR5-1942[5], StA.
34. PM angående brittiska marinattachén Henry Denham, 3 December 1943, P53 Ba/Denham 1940-, UDA.
35. Memorandum, 8 June 1942, Uppgifter om spioner i Sverige, R72 L, UDA.
36. PM angående brittiske marinattachén Henry Mangles Denham, 14 January 1943, P53 Ba/Denham, UDA.
37. This telegram was intercepted by the Swedish authorities. See the collection of intercepted telegrams in Curt Kempffs Tjänstearkiv, ÖVI: 3, KrA. For more about the general terms governing liaison between the *Abwehr's* Dr Wagner and Swedish security in combating sabotage, see Ch. 3.
38. An interesting remark about responsibility for the Threlfall débâcle will be found in Beevor, pp. 45–6.
39. For more about Binney, see Barker, Cruickshank, *SOE in Scandinavia*, Ch. 4 and Tennant, Ch. 14.
40. Cf. Ursula Powes-Lybbe, *The Eye of Intelligence*, 1983, pp. 57–8.
41. Specimen form in FO 837/797, PRO.
42. The Statutory and Proclaimed Lists were published lists, the first being issued on 13 September 1939. Whereas copies of the List were on sale in shops in Switzerland, this was not apparently the case in Sweden. More extensive lists of suspicious firms and individuals were retained by the relevant departments for internal use. Cf. Leifland, p. 210.

43. A discriminatory policy against commercial enterprises in Sweden was also adopted by the Germans. For the coal industry, see footnote 13, pp. 218–19, in Olsson's dissertation. See also PM. över iaktagelser vid censurväsendet under tiden 1 April–30 September 1944, Handelsrapport nr 2, 1944, in Hemligt Arkiv Vol. 7, Flyktkapitalbyråns arkiv, RA.

44. By comparison, the Swiss list numbered some 1,200 names and the Spanish list some 1,500 names.

45. The matter was taken up in the *Riksdag*. See Riksdagens Protokoll 1945: AK 9:69 and AK 12:25.

46. See the documentation in HP 1725, UD:s arkiv [1920 Dossier System], RA. The British reply was that listing was a necessary complement to the War Trade Agreement.

47. Notably SFS 1939: 951 and the relevant section of Ch. 8.

48. In an analysis of the 330 names on the Swedish Statutory List in November 1945, the Swedish Ministry for Foreign Affairs concluded that 170 had been included on grounds of being under German economic or financial control (Group 1), 33 because of their commercial relations with the Axis countries (Group 2) and 35 because of their political stance (Group 3). This left a total of 92 cases where the grounds of listing were unknown. Furthermore it was claimed (in November 1945) that the bureau set up by the Swedes to look into the cloaking of German assets (*Flyktkapitalbyrå* [FKB]) had found that in only 76 of the cases in Group 1 had the Allied charges been proved according to their own investigations. At the same time, FKB included in its own list 55 firms not appearing on the Allied lists.

49. On 22 November 1944, Martin Lundqvist of the Swedish Security Service when asked to comment on a British move to list a certain RR, replied that there was no reason to suspect him of espionage. A communication of the head of the German Security Police to AA, of 8 March 1943, in Inland II Geheim, Geheime Reichssachen, however, makes clear that the man in question had worked for the Gestapo for some time. His business address had already been used for accommodation purposes in 1939.

50. Memorandum from Commercial Counsellor, Stockholm to MEW (Black List Section), 12 April 1943, FO 837/885, PRO.

51. Memorandum from Commercial Counsellor, Stockholm to MEW (Black List Section), 12 April 1943, FO 837/885, PRO.

52. Mitcheson to Ståhle, 22 January 1942, in UD: arkiv [1920 Dossier System], HP 1726, Svarta Listan, UD:s arkiv, [1920 Dossier System] RA.

53. As a way of coping with this, the Swedes tightened the currency regulations (SFS 1944: 693) and placed restrictions on the import of gold and platinum into the country (SFS 1944: 694 and 695).

54. Hemliga arkivet, Handelsrapport nr 2 1944, 1 April–30 September 1944, FKB arkiv, RA.

55. Undated report (probably January 1945) in FO 837/1154, PRO. The story turned out to be unfounded. In the judgement of the British Legation in Stockholm there was no traffic in loot and when it was proposed to send an art expert to Sweden, the legation insisted that his services were not required. See British Legation to FO, 21 June 1945 in FO 837/1156, PRO.

56. See, e.g., the editions of 21 November 1944 and 1 December 1944. Schellenberg later alleged that Schmidt had moved a large sum of money to Sweden via his mistress. See P.M. angående samtal med Schellenberg, in HP 331, UD:s arkiv [1920 Dossier System], RA.

57. See the editions of 12 January 1945 and 20 January 1945.

58. Document 77 in the collection, Frågor i samband med Norska Regeringens vistelse utanför Norge 1940–1953, issued by the Swedish Ministry for Foreign Affairs, Stockholm, 1948.

59. Op. cit., Document 78.
60. Op. cit., Document 80.
61. Op. cit., Document 81.
62. Prytz to Ministry for Foreign Affairs, Stockholm, 27 December 1941, P53 An, Allmänt ang. norska beskickningen i Stockholm 1939–juni 1942, UDA.
63. Further examples are provided in Adlercreutz's *Historik*.
64. Trial papers in RR5-1940 [9], StA.
65. Trial papers in RR5-1942 [2], StA. According to the Swedish military expert consulted the information supplied was 'of considerable military value, is business-like and well-edited and to the extent that they can be checked, entirely correct'. The young Norwegian involved later served as a member of the SIS coast-watching net inside Norway.
66. For one illuminating incident, see Gidlund, pp. 64–73.
67. Cruickshank, *SOE in Scandinavia*, p. 61.
68. Hallgren to Günther, 28 January 1941, Uppgifter om spioner i Sverige, R72 L, UDA.
69. Boheman, 29 January 1941, Uppgifter om spioner i Sverige, R72 L, UDA. The Norwegian military attaché Colonel Strugstad was also under threat of expulsion because of his involvement in covert activities.
70. Cf. Cruickshank, *SOE in Scandinavia*, Ch. 9.
71. An attempt by Captain Marks to 'spring' Millar from prison, ended in failure. See Ch. 3.
72. Letter from Söderblom to Prytz, 24 April 1941 in P 53 Ba/99 (Munthe) UDA.
73. Ibid.
74. He had been declared *png* on 29 May 1941.
75. Söderblom to Richert, 18 July 1941 in P53 Ba/99, UDA.
76. GKOS an AST Norwegen, 19 July 1941 [intercepted telegram], Curt Kempffs Tjänstearkiv, Ö VI: 3, KrA. Section III dealt with counter-espionage.
77. Cf. Cruickshank, *SOE in Scandinavia*, Ch. 9.
78. As noted in Hammarlund, p. 41, there had already been contacts between Swedish and Norwegian officers regarding courier activities at the beginning of 1941. C-Bureau's active involvement dated from 1942.
79. Pp. 105–7, Utredning av vissa förhållanden vid försvarsstabens numera avvecklade s.k. C-Byrå in H1, C-Byrås Arkiv, KrA. The director had supplied the radios to the Norwegians at an early stage and C-Byrå had also been in contact with him in 1941 about the purchase of radio equipment.
80. Cf. Hammarlund, pp. 73–4.
81. Information about the Norwegian Legation in Stockholm derives from the excellent account in Grimnes.
82. Quoted in Haestrup, p. 77.
83. Quoted in Trommer, pp. 70–1.
84. Quoted by Cruickshank, *SOE in Scandinavia*, p. 134.
85. The work of the Contact Committee and Cuttings Office is dealt with in detail in Grundt Larsen's monograph.
86. Fuel of course was strictly rationed. Official Swedish permission was granted for 1,500 litres of petrol and there were hopes – with the police turning a blind eye – of buying other quantities on the black market.
87. For a detailed study of support for the Danes, see Torell's monograph.
88. The distribution was much criticised by activist groups who held that a dis-proportionately large share of the weapons went to the Danish Army's so-called O-groups.
89. Nevakivi, pp. 180–1.
90. A pioneer work about Polish underground activities in Sweden during the Second World War is Joseph Lewandowski's monograph and I am greatly obliged to him for

help in throwing light on Polish personalities.

91. PM angående polske medborgaren legationstjänsteman Tadeusz Rudnicki alias Tadeusz Vinci alias Mateucki, Uppgifter om spioner i Sverige, R72 L, UDA.

92. Trial papers, RR5-1940[11], StA.

93. Memorandum, 31 May 1941, in P53 Ep, UDA.

94. See Herslow's own account, *Moskva–Berlin–Warszawa*. According to Ternberg, Herslow collected intelligence on behalf of General Ivar 'Hickory' Holmquist who maintained 'a private intelligence service which had no contacts with C-Bureau'. Anteckningar vid samtal med H. Ternberg den 18/8/1970, Hellmuth Ternbergs Arkiv, Vol. 1, KrA.

95. Lewandowski, Item 5, p. 102. The passage occurs in summary report no. 101 of 17 January 1942 from C-in-C, Home Army to 6th Dept., Supreme Commander's HQ, London. This report was not delivered until 1 June 1942.

96. Lewandowski, Item 13, p. 104. The passage occurs in summary report no. 123 of 16 May 1942 from C-in-C, Home Army. It was dispatched by Swedish courier via Stockholm and reached London on 30 June 1942.

97. Personal information.

98. Anteckningar vid samtal med H. Ternberg den 18/8/1970, Hellmuth Ternbergs Arkiv, Vol. 1, KrA.

99. Axel to Wagner, 1 August 1942, [intercepted telegram], Curt Kempffs Tjänstearkiv, Ö VI: 3, KrA.

100. Söderblom to Gisle, 26 August 1942 in file P 53 Ep 26 [Potworowski], UDA.

101. See Novak, Ch. 8.

102. See Moravec.

103. Telegram included in Vanek trial papers, RR5-1942[5], StA.

104. Telegram included in Vanek trial papers.

105. Telegram included in Vanek trial papers.

106. Telegram included in Vanek trial papers.

107. Goerdeler was also intimately involved in the so-called 'Bosch affair'. After the war, it was revealed that Wallenberg's Enskilda Bank had acted as a cloak for the German industrial company Robert Bosch to prevent the seizure of certain of Bosch's foreign holdings by the Allied authorities. For two views of this matter, see Ulf Olfsson's book and the writings of Aalders and Wiebe.

108. Quoted in Lindgren's article, p. 288.

109. Ibid.

110. Ibid.

111. See Brodersen.

112. FO 371/30912, PRO. Cited in Lamb, p. 254.

113. Hågkomster p. 316, Juhlin-Dannfelts arkiv, KrA.

114. What, for example, was one to make of a man like Nebe, with whom the British were in contact, through Harry Söderman, the head of the Swedish Forensic Laboratory? As Fabian von Schlabrendorff frankly acknowledges 'Nebe's uniform was good reason for us to approach him with considerable caution'. (See *The Secret War against Hitler*, London, 1966, p. 173). If the need for caution was felt by Schlabrendorff who was in a much better position through his friends to test Nebe's sincerity, can it be wondered that the British experienced certain hesitations? In addition Nebe's detailed proposals seemed to have more than a touch of cloud-cuckoo land about them.

115. Boheman, p. 299.

116. In the first months of 1940, the British had tried to interest the Swedes in the exchange of military information but to no avail. See CAB 21/1003, PRO.

117. Official Swedish responses to British queries about the 'fishing boats' episode and the Oxenstierna affair [see my earlier essay on the Krämer affair] are illuminating in this respect. In both cases – and for good reason – the Swedes did not reveal all that

they knew.

118. See Boheman pp. 154–5. Boheman's recollection should be compared with the account given in the official history of British Intelligence. According to this, a Swedish estimate (substantially correct) of German intentions had been passed to the US Ambassador in Moscow on 24 March. On 7 June, the Swedes informed the Foreign Office that Germany would bring force to bear about 15 June. On 19 June their message to the FO was that they expected Germany *to issue an ultimatum*. For the oscillations in Cripps' own position, see Hinsley. It is interesting to note that the German naval attaché in Moscow was reporting to Berlin on 24 April that Cripps had announced that war was going to break out between Germany and Russia on 22 June, see document 399 in ADAP, Serie D, XII.2.

119. British Mil. Att. to FO, 4 November 1944 in FO 371/43509, PRO. Quoted in Leifland's essay in the Carlgren *Festschrift*.

120. CAB 119/109, PRO. Quoted in Leifland's essay in the Carlgren *Festschrift*.

121. Mil. Att., London to Kempff, 6 March 1945, Fstab, Utrikesavdelning Serie EII:4, Handbrev 1943–45, KrA.

122. PM rörande förbindelser med engelska underrättelseväsendet, 30 June 1945, folder Förbindelse med utländsk polis, Vol. F1:3, Sandler arkiv, RA. It is not inconceivable that before this, in less harmonious times the British Secret Service had succeeded in engaging an unauthorised source to report on Swedish security investigations of German espionage and related matters.

123. Parrot, Memorandum, 9 October 1941 in FO 371/29669, PRO.

124. Mallet, Memorandum, 16 October 1941 in FO 371/29669, PRO.

125. I am grateful to Mr. Herbert North for his recollections of the organisation of work in the Bureau.

126. Parrot, Memorandum, 9 October 1941 in FO 371/29669, PRO.

127. Mallet, Memorandum, 16 October 1941 in FO 371/29669, PRO.

128. Parrot to Scarlett, 15 April 1944, in FO 371/39279, PRO. When the Kallay Government in Hungary began to extend feelers to the Allies in 1942, Andor Gellert, the Berlin ex-representative of the Revisionist League, who had made friends with a number British and American diplomats, went to Stockholm where he made contact with Böhm. Subsequently Gellert was able to pass over 'the contents of many interesting and genuinely valuable Hungarian Foreign Ministry intelligence reports'. See Report from Stockholm dated 16 September 1944 in FO 371/93 39276, PRO. Prior to his stationing in Budapest, Raoul Wallenberg consulted Böhm about internal developments in Hungary.

129. Barman's comment on telegram from Mallet to Ministry of Information 12 February 1942 in FO 898/253, PRO.

130. M. Balfour to Lt.-Col. Hope, 1 December 1943 in FO 898/253, PRO. Among British journalists to attract the attention of the Swedish authorities in the earlier stage of the war was Ralph Hewins of the *Daily Mail* who was held in May 1940 on the grounds that he had tried under false pretences to obtain information about iron ore transports from Luleå.

131. The present exposition relies principally on Denham's War Narrative in the archive at Churchill College, Cambridge. I am also grateful to D. G. Harris for certain supplementary observations.

132. Quoted in Kramish, p. 109. The main importance to the Allies was in ensuring a flow of naval intelligence to Denham and not in preserving some link to Paul Rosbaud in Germany as Kramish maintains.

133. See Jacobsen, Ch. 6.

134. This was confirmed quickly by aerial reconnaissance. Denham's signal was the first of a series of operations which culminated in the sinking of the *Bismarck*. See Denham, pp. 84–6. Denham gave the information the rather low grade B3. Ullstein (Vol. 1, 136)

claims that Denham's doubt was due to the fact that he had earlier been given 'planted information' that turned out to be false.

135. On 21 May 1941, the *Abwehr* informed the Naval High Command that it had positive proof that the Admiralty had received such a report. See Hinsley *et al.*, Vol. 1, p. 346.
136. Personal information.
137. As late as 10 September 1941, Churchill was pleading for Roscher-Lund to be kept in Sweden. Ulstein (see Ulstein, Vol. 2, p. 186) suggests that the probable cause of Nygaardsvold's insistence was the shortage of competent people in London.
138. In Denham's mid-term assessment in 1942, Björnstierna scores highest among sources followed after a two point gap by Petersén.
139. According to Denham [See Denham, p. 99 and Carlgren's *Svensk underrättelsetjänst 1939-1945*, p. 100] Björnstjerna informed him that the Supreme Commander had fired him on the spot and threatened him with court martial. For more about the [German] detection of the leakage of information through Björnstjerna, see Ch. 3. As has been noted, German pressure successfully brought about greatly intensified surveillance of Denham from mid-June 1941.
140. Cf. Carlgren, *Svensk underrättelsetjänst 1939–1945*, pp. 141–3.
141. For the Walter affair, see Tennant [1] and [2], Ch. 15.
142. Hallgren to UD, 18 January 1943, in P53 Ba/Denham, UDA.
143. Warner to Mallet, 29 January 1943 in FO 188/425, PRO.
144. Ibid.
145. Ibid.
146. 10/3/43, Riksdagens Protokoll vid Lagtima Riksmötet År 1943, AK, Förste Bandet.
147. PM över iaktagelser vid censurväsendet under tiden 15/1–28/2/42. Handelsrapport nr. 2 1942. FKB arkiv, Secret Archive, Vol. 7, RA. The military significance of the fishing boats and the identity of the real customer is also made entirely clear in a telegram intercepted by the Swedes. This telegram (dated 13 December 1941, Censurpärmar, UDA) was however not distributed outside the Defence Staff. For Oppenheim's role in arranging the deal, see Ch. 3.
148. See note, p. 470, Medlicott, Vol. 2.
149. For O'Brien-Ffrench's escapade, see his own volume of reminiscences, *Delicate Mission*.
150. M. Lundqvist to Security Chief, 15 March 1940 in Uppgifter om spioner i Sverige, R72 L, UDA.
151. Presentation follows the facts as set out in the trial papers in RR5-1940[1], StA. This relevant aspect of the matter is nowhere mentioned in Cruickshank's book on *SOE in Scandinavia*.
152. See, e.g., *Volkischer Beobachter* of 14 February 1940.
153. A report from Section III of the *Abwehr* to *Auswärtiges Amt* of 6 August 1942 clearly identified Carr as a case officer for British intelligence in Finland and Martin as head of the Secret Service in Sweden.
154. Report from the Commander of the Security Police and SD in Denmark to Müller and Schellenberg, dated 1 October 1944. I am very grateful to Hans Christian Bjerg for allowing me to see this report. Hampton, who ran R34, was guilty of several very grave indiscretions. But this and the fact that several of his agents were undoubtedly con-men, does not detract from the general plausibility of R34's account. This latter statement was potentially a major breakthrough for the German security organs if there had been time to evaluate it and exploit it to the full.

For SOE agents inside Germany during the closing stage of the war, see Butler, *Amateur Agent*, Ch. 9.
155. A further insight into British covert attempts to gain information about the German armaments industry came to light in 1946 in the trial in Stockholm of a young Swedish engineer, who was charged and later convicted with having unlawfully passed over in

1943 to foreign legations in Stockholm certain military secrets. In the early part of the year, he had approached a British military attaché about the possibility of obtaining a position with Vickers-Armstrong in Britain. Instead, however, he was apparently persuaded to work as a British agent in Germany with a threefold task: (i) to investigate a new German recoil-less gun with conical barrel of Gerlich type, which was being developed at Rheinmetall-Borsig; (ii) to collect all possible information concerning the production of U-boats; (iii) to make contact and collect the names of persons involved in the German development of new weapons. The engineer was provided with one month's special training in Sweden to equip him for his task. In due course, he was installed as an engineer in the Maget firm in Berlin–Tegel and worked in various departments until 1 June 1944 when he was transferred to the Skoda works. He was employed partly in Prague and partly in Pilsen in the development department until the capitulation. At his trial, the engineer claimed that he had sent fortnightly messages in lettercode to his wife in Stockholm, providing the British with detailed information about a wide spectrum of German weapons, including V-rockets. See trial papers in RR5-1946[5], StA.

156. Interest seems to have been taken in the Swedish monarch's tennis partner, Baron Gottfried von Cramm. A report from the Press Reading Bureau to the Foreign Office about von Cramm's opinions, will be found in FO 371/39143, PRO.

157. This work also naturally involved liaison with opposite numbers in the counter-espionage branches of the Norwegian and Danish intelligence services.

158. Personal information, letter dated 12 March 1989.

159. Casey, p. 40.

160. Trial papers RR5-1939 [1], StA. See also SOU 1946: 36, pp. 67–73. I am most grateful to Staffan Lamm, Stockholm, for several useful exchanges and for generously providing me with information about Knüfken which he turned up in the course of making his excellent television programme about the man.

161. See Howe, p. 34.

162. An allusion to agent 101B will be found in the German document on the British intelligence service reproduced in the appendix to West. The information came from the interrogation of Stevens and Best.

163. Memorandum 18 September 1940 in Knüfken's file R 70 Ct, UDA.

164. Mallet to Hopkinson, 6 February 1941 in FO 371/29535, PRO. Hopkinson acidly noted 'The Swedish Govt are under no obligation to prevent activities against the Nazi Government; but they are going out of their way to do so.'

165. Letter to FO 10 July 1941 in FO 371/29695, PRO.

166. Trial papers in RR5-1940[3], StA.

167. Trial papers in RR5-1940[3], StA.

168. Trial papers in RR5-1940[3], StA.

169. It is not clear, however, that these latter rumours were correct.

170. For the Enderles see, e.g., Brandt, pp. 267–8 and Szende, pp. 20–2.

171. See Englich. I am grateful to Walter Pöppel for his recollections of Pulz and Englich. Pulz & Co were also involved in the purloining of Schellenberg's diary. See Butler, *Amateur Agent*, pp. 182–3.

172. See Tennant, p. 166.

173. For a full account, see Bjerg, on which the present section is heavily dependent.

174. In June 1941, Sneum had flown to Britain with valuable film which included shots of radar installations in Denmark. In September the same year, he was parachuted back into Denmark for the SIS along with a radio operator, Christoffersen. Although Sneum managed finally with the help of Duus Hansen to make radio contact with Britain, the mission for a variety of reasons went badly and Sneum, hunted by the police, was forced to flee to Sweden in March 1942.

175. Bjerg, Vol. 2, pp. 73–4.

176. Bjerg, Vol. 2, p. 80.
177. Quoted in Bjerg, Vol. 2, p. 94.
178. Quoted in Bjerg, Vol. 2, p. 104.
179. Ibid.
180. Quoted in Bjerg, Vol. 2, pp. 106–7.
181. This section relies upon the recent books by Rørholt, Nøkleby and Ulstein as well as upon the book by Grimnes. The latter volume, although not specifically about intelligence matters, contains a great many interesting facts.
182. Nøkleby, p. 32. FD/E took over and expanded the work of an earlier intelligence bureau UD/E which had been set up by the Norwegian Ministry of Foreign Affairs at the end of June 1940 under Sverre Midtskau. UD/E had been responsible for the initial contacts with the SIS.
183. Such a command had existed during the Norwegian campaign. Thereafter the individual services had reasserted themselves.
184. These internal dissensions are described in Grimnes.
185. Translated from the text quoted (in Norwegian) in Jacobsen, pp. 205–7. I have used FD/E instead of F.D.E for consistency's sake.
186. See the supplementary agreement quoted in Jacobsen, pp. 207–8.
187. In the enthusiasm for Sigint which followed the Enigma revelations, the fact that radio silence was routinely used to avoid detection and localisation, was often forgotten. It should also be noted that ships in port in Norway had access to land lines which could not be intercepted by the British. An order given over the radio could be countermanded by an order down the line. Lastly as pointed out in Rørholt, p. 414, whereas the interception of German communications was fundamentally passive in the sense that it yielded principally information which the Germans themselves let drop, agents on the ground were able to go beyond this, as active enquirers, to provide answers to other supplementary questions the Allies might be interested in.
188. Ulstein, Vol. 2, p. 45.
189. Condensed from the table on p. 166 of Nøkleby. It should be noted that apart from its role in facilitating these operations into Norway, Sweden was indispensable as a place to flee to when things went wrong.
190. Nøkleby provides the following example of a Scorpion message passed to FOII in London in February 1943: 'Thursday. The *Tirpitz* has been exercising today. A large mobile floating crane here ought to be sunk'.
191. Specimen intelligence received from Lyra on 6 February 44: '*Tirpitz* has not weighed anchor since she was damaged. As time goes on we will get the *Tirpitz* situation in hand. We have sketches of the camouflage and they will be sent from here on the 8th addressed to you. Details of camouflage will be sent in my next telegram'. Quoted in Nøkleby.
192. See Melberg's book *Doppeltspill*.
193. Ibid, pp. 89–90.
194. For more about Rosbaud, see Kramish. Kramish's main thesis that Rosbaud was the author of the Oslo report, has turned out to be false. See R. V. Jones, *Reflections on Intelligence* (London, 1990), Ch. 11.
195. Henriksen also supplied information to Denham. In 1942, he was pegging equal with Ebbe Munck as a source but following behind Major Dahl, the Norwegian M.A.
196. Grimnes, p. 184.
197. See Amort and Jedlicka, pp. 52–3 and p. 66. One of the cover addresses used for routeing A54 reports had been identified by the Swedish security authorities as early as October 1939.
198. Vanek trial papers, RR5-1942[5], StA.
199. Vanek trial papers, RR5-1942[5], StA.
200. Vanek trial papers, RR5-1942[5], StA.

201. Vanek trial papers, RR5-1942[5], StA.
202. For insight into the work of the Polish secret intelligence service in Sweden I have been much indebted to Vaclav Gilewicz and Michal Rybikowski. See also the books of Gondek and Strumph-Wojtkiewicz. I am grateful to Dr Josef Lewandowski for helping me to clarify the contents of these books.
203. Gilewicz retained his contacts with the Danes after moving to Stockholm. At the end of 1940, he met Lt-Col T. Ørum in the Swedish capital. Ørum was subsequently arrested in Berlin.
204. Later Prey's name would crop up in connection with the Wennerström affair.
205. In his War Narrative, Denham mentions intelligence from the Polish naval attaché Captain Morgenstern (and later from Plawski). It is unclear whether this intelligence originated from the networks described or whether the latter were responsible for supplying, e.g., SIS independently with information.
206. Smith had dealings with both Rudnicki and Gilewicz. The Swedes learned from a source at the Polish Legation that in the summer of 1941, Smith had handed over £20,000 to Rudnicki. See Memorandum on Rudnicki dated 22 August 1941 in Uppgifter om spioner i Sverige, R72 L, UDA.
207. A German report in October 1941 spoke of Kuncewicz being identical with 'Jakubianiec' who 'after his flight from Poland, was the leader of the intelligence service of the Polish Resistance in Lithuania'. According to the Germans, the courier postal service via Stockholm to London had the code name Daniel and in the reverse direction the names Rafael and Konrad.
208. There was also to be active Japanese–Polish intelligence co-operation in Bucharest.
209. Trial papers, RR5-1943[18], StA.
210. See trial papers, RR5-1944[11], StA, where Piotrowski appears under his pseudonym.
211. Cf. Corey Ford, pp. 283–4. Swedish documentation relating to this matter can be found in HD:s koncepter den 18 september 1944; HD:s koncepter den 21 september 1945; HD:s besvärs – och ansökningsmål den 21 september 1945 nr 1861, RA.
212. For Swedish attempts to circumvent Allied pressure to reduce export of ball-bearings to the Axis, see Fritz's essay *Swedish Ball-Bearings and The German War Economy*.
213. By means of Hinsley *et al.*, Vol. 3, Part 1, p. 360 and the German report relating to the interrogation of Andreasen mentioned in note 154.
214. See Kramish, p. 179.
215. Personal information. The Poles were provided with details relating to the call-signs, frequencies and transmission schedules of the stations of interest.
216. It is known from the Paulsson–Lönnegren investigation that the *Abwehr* duly noted Thornton's arrival and were interested in discovering what was behind it.
217. On 30 June 1944, Mallet asked the Foreign Office if Graffham 'may now be regarded as dead'. On 4 July, he was told that it was not and he would be informed of further steps for keeping it alive. See appropriate telegram exchange in FO 188/446, PRO.
218. Grafströms Dagbok, entry for 8 June 1944.
219. Ibid.
220. Ibid.
221. Cruickshank, *Deception in World War II*, provides on the whole a positive valuation. For much more critical viewpoints see Klaus-Jürgen Muller's essay on *A German Perspective on Allied Deception Operations in the Second World War* and Leifland's essay on Graffham.
222. Dr Wagner to the Head, OKW, Abwehr I, 7 May 1942, [intercepted telegram] in Curt Kempffs Tjänstearkiv, ÖVI: 3, KrA.
223. Citation for Medal of Freedom with Bronze Palm, Erik Erickson's Arkiv, Bunt 4, RA. A popular presentation of Erickson's activities is to be found in Klein. Erickson had been blacklisted by the British earlier in the war for his defiance of the British

economic blockade. His company Belgo-Baltic was also involved in providing introductions and backing for the German-sponsored news agency *Radio Mundial* when it opened an office in Stockholm in 1941. (See Ch. 3)

224. About the choice of Stockholm and a general description of the operation, see Denham's War Narrative, Churchill College, Cambridge. The Allies were eventually able to read the signal traffic of the Japanese military attachés in Europe in the latter part of the war. Michael Howard in Volume 5 of *British Intelligence in the Second World War*, p. 225 presents an example of another deception perpetrated on the Japanese making use of the Stockholm channel. See also note 42, Ch. 3.

3   POACHER'S PERSPECTIVE – 2

1. Höhne, *Der Krieg im Dunkeln*, p. 292.
2. Ibid.
3. Juhlin-Dannfelt, *Hågkomster* (typewritten recollections), p. 184, KrA. Cf. Adlercreutz, *Historik*, p. 6.
4. Adlercreutz, *Historik*, p. 6. Adlercreutz explicitly notes that the visit was cleared both with the Minister of Defence (Nilsson) and the Foreign Minister (Sandler). A marginal note in the manuscript observes that in the years 1938–39, there were also visits to France (Colonel Gauché) and Britain ('Major-General Anderson in Civil Security').
5. Ibid. For Major Th. Lindquist's service record, see entry 225 in Kungl. Svea livgardes historia, VI Biografiska uppgifter om regementsofficerskåren 1903–1981, Stockholm, 1983.
6. See Ch. 1 for the discussion of the laws relating to espionage against a third party.
7. Kersaudy, pp. 58–9.
8. Reile, pp. 60–2. January 1940 saw the arrival of Major Erich Pruck's team in Oslo.
9. Lunding, pp. 45–6.
10. Hammar, p. 239.
11. Hammar, pp. 294, 367–8.
12. Nørgaard, p. 109.
13. The problem of the so-called 'ghost aircraft' generated a good deal of public interest and was the subject of discussion in the *Riksdag*. See Riksdagens Protokoll 1937: AK 10:3 and AK 32:5. See also Sjöberg's book which sings much the same refrain as Pantenburg.
14. See illustration XXX facing p. 145 in Pantenburg.
15. A number of salient details can be found in RRA(5)-1940[2], StA.
16. See document 13, Kungl. Utrikesdepartementet, Förspelet till det tyska angreppet på Danmark och Norge den 9 April 1940, (1947).
17. Hallgren to Foreign Minister, 7 March 1940, P 53 Ct/ Steffan, UDA.
18. Bolte was also considered as a potentially useful candidate for Ribbentrop's own intelligence service, which was run independently of the *Abwehr* and SD. A memorandum prepared for Likus, Ribbentrop's confidant, speaks of him as knowing Sweden thoroughly, with 15 years' experience, and of being 'above all silent as the grave'. Bolte's role as an *Abwehr* agent, working closely with Steffan, is noted as is his earlier involvement with Pflug-Hartung. Meissner, Vermerk für SS-Oberführer Likus, 12 June 1939, Personb. Ausländer 1938–43, Dienststelle Ribbentrop/R. Likus, [Kopior ur AAA, Vol. 128, UD:s Arkiv], RA. For a British mention of Bolte, see Tennant's Memorandum on German Propaganda in Sweden, of 23 November 1939 in FO 371/23709, PRO.
19. Hallgren to Günther, 2 April 1940, Uppgifter om spioner i Sverige, R72 L, UDA.
20. War Diary of the German Naval Attaché, Stockholm. Only excerpts of this survive.

The original documents have been returned to Bundesarchiv-Militärarchiv, Freiburg. A microfilm of the diary is kept at the National Archives, Washington (PG 48859-PG 48862). The author has made use of a microfilm of the diary retained in London.

21. Ibid.

22. Court papers relating to the trial of Fleck, RR(5)-1940[5], StA.

23. Adlercreutz, *Historik*, p. 51, observes that the Fleck case was 'overadvertised'. This tendency to overestimate the importance of Fleck was continued in certain postwar books. Thus in Berhardsson's *Spionpolisen går på jakt* published in 1952 and largely based on Swedish trial papers, a photograph of the impressively studious-looking Fleck appears with a caption labelling him as 'one of Germany's most highly skilled agents in Sweden during the Second World War'. Typically Berhardsson devotes a great deal of space to Fleck and von Schoeler but says nothing at all about, e.g., Steffan or Krämer.

24. Submission from A. Ausland. Abw, 9 July 1940 in Handakten des Vertreter des AA:s bei OKH/Etzdorf, [Kopior ur AAA, Vol. 107, UD:s arkiv], RA.

25. Fleck appears to have been employed as an 'intelligence irregular' by the German Military Attaché's department in Stockholm. For the Ribbentrop intelligence bureau's interest in him as a potential reporter, see Vermerk für SS-Oberführer Likus, 12 June 1939, Personb. Ausländer 1938–43, Dienststelle Ribbentrop/R. Likus, [Kopior ur AAA, Vol. 128, UD:s arkiv], RA.

26. When he met Adlercreutz in Stockholm in September 1940, Canaris explicitly denied that the German agents jailed by the Swedes, had been carrying out an assignment for the *Abwehr*. See Canaris, Bericht über Reise nach Stockholm v. 12.-14.9.40, RW39/1, BA-MA. Among those then in custody were Kant (see Ch. 2), Fleck and von Schoeler. It is interesting however that the latter had been in contact with Bolte, Steffan's associate.

27. Court papers relating to trial of von Schoeler in RR(5)-1940 [7], StA. It is worth noting that von Schoeler's message agreed very well with the image that the Swedes themselves were trying to project at that time.

28. For the details concerning Wagner's appointment in Sweden, see *Abwehr Einbau*, Dr Hans Wagner, Inland II geheim, [Kopior ur AAA, Vol. 97, UD:s arkiv], RA.

29. Canaris, Bericht über Reise nach Stockholm, 14 September 1940, RW39/1, BA-MA.

30. On the subject of Wagner's appointment, Adlercreutz (*Historik*, pp. 18–19) has the following to relate: 'Neither the Ministry for Foreign Affairs, the Defence Ministry nor the Chief of Security had any objections against this in spite of the fact that I made clear that Wagner represented the *Abwehr*. It was considered within the Security Service better to know who it was thus facilitating surveillance. It was stated by the German military attaché that Wagner would be available to give advice relating to protection against sabotage. His advice was courteously received and he was informed that our security service had already been under development for several years.' Adlercreutz goes on to add that although Wagner was kept under surveillance by the Security service, it was first in March 1942 that it could be established (the Ascher case) that he had gone outside the gentlemen's agreement arranged with Canaris. 'It is a myth that the Security Service or the Defence Staff relied on any type of loyalty from Wagner, although in a number of cases he supplied information which was useful from a Swedish point of view.'

31. Canaris, Bericht über Reise nach Stockholm, 14 September 1940, RW39/1, BA-MA.

32. Ibid.

33. *Abwehr Einbau*, Dr Hans Wagner, Inland II geheim, [Kopior ur AAA, Vol. 97, UD:s arkiv], RA. It had been originally intended that Cellarius although responsible for Finland, would be resident in Stockholm. According to the War Diary of the German naval attaché in Stockholm, Cellarius first severed his formal connection with Stockholm on 10 June 1942.

34. See for example, Ritter 13 February 1942, Pol I M, *Abwehr Einbau*, Allgemeines [Kopior ur AAA, Vol. 74, UD:s arkiv], RA.

35. As of 15 August 1944, the distribution of *Abwehr* specialists among the respective neutral countries was: Switzerland (15), Sweden (6), Portugal (13) and Turkey (10). On 1 December 1943, Spain had no fewer than 28 such specialists.

36. P.M, 4 December 1944, in P 53 Ct, Allmänt ang. Tysklands beskickning Stockholm 1920–1944, UDA.

37. Ibid. Nigel West's remark (in his book on the wartime operations of MI6) that 'Wagner drove his staff hard' is contradicted by the judgements of those who knew Wagner well. 'He is credulous and goodnatured, lacks the ability to command and above all has a poor memory which often plays him nasty tricks. Thus having received a highly important report one day, the next day he may have no recollection at all of its contents. The general view is that it is very easy to deceive "Papi" because he is so credulous. He is thoroughly phlegmatic in nature: he prefers to eat well, drink well and work as little as possible. Moreover he has a weakness for anything in skirts.' Report, 4 December 1944 in P 53 Ct, UDA. 'Uncle Albert' (Utermark) was a very different kettle of fish. About the respective personalities of Wagner and Utermark, see also Kumenius.

38. P.M, 4 December 1944, in P 53 Ct, Allmänt ang. Tysklands beskickning Stockholm 1920–1944, UDA. In addition to this sum, there was an additional 5,000 dollars which largely went to Dr Krämer.

39. Ibid.

40. Wagner to OKW, Abwehr I, 28 July 1942, (intercepted telegram), Censurpärmar, UDA.

41. Aufzeichnung, Kramarz, 2 September 1942. Pol IM, [Kopior ur AAA, Vol. 74, UD:s arkiv], RA.

42. Himmler to Ribbentrop, 31 December 1942, Buro des Staatsekretärs, Schweden. [Kopior ur AAA, Vol. 74, UD:s arkiv], RA. At the meeting between Canaris and Adlercreutz in Stockholm in 1940, both the exchange of intelligence about Russia and co-operation in the field of counter-espionage were discussed. Some interest attaches to the question of how far the Swedes were able to limit the range of the exchange agreement in practice. On at least one occasion after the war, Captain Utermark, the Deputy Head of *Abwehr* in Sweden, claimed that he had enjoyed excellent contacts with Messrs Petersén and Ternberg of C-Bureau and had established a useful exchange with them, trading information about Russia for information about Britain and America. This claim is in itself certainly interesting and deserves to be noted. But even if it were true, more would obviously have to be known about the nature and relative quality of the material traded, before one could begin to speculate about the nature of Petersén and Ternberg's participation in such an exchange. According to personal information, Petersen's help was enlisted to pass certain British deception material, code-named 'Justice', to the Germans and the Japanese.

43. Wied to AA, 30 March 1942, Pol IM. The man in question was Boening, the contact of Edgar Klaus, [Kopior ur AAA, Vol. 74, UD:s arkiv], RA.

44. Wied to AA, 20 October 1942, *Abwehr Einbau*, Inland II geheim [Kopior ur AAA, Vol. 97, UD:s arkiv], RA.

45. Thomsen to AA, 14 February 1944, *Abwehr Einbau*, Inland II geheim [Kopior ur AAA, Vol. 97, UD:s arkiv], RA.

46. Thomsen to AA, 12 February 1944, *Abwehr* Schweden, Pol IM [Kopior ur AAA, Vol. 74, UD:s arkiv], RA.

47. Among those recommended for the chop were Busch (*Abwehr*) and Finke, Engel and von Gossler (SD).

48. Thomsen to AA, 14 July 1944, Pol I M. [Kopior ur AAA, Vol. 74, UD:s arkiv], RA. Reproduced in Mader, pp. 178–9. For the exploits of Günther, see RR(5)-1944[6], StA.

49. Thomsen to AA, 14 July 1944, Pol I M. [Kopior ur AAA, Vol. 74, UD:s arkiv], RA.
50. A Captain Abshagen had been temporarily attached to Bureau Wagner in February 1942. See P 90 OI3, UD: arkiv [1920 dossier system], RA.
51. For I. G. Farben's intelligence connection, see also section 5 of this chapter.
52. In October 1944, Schellenberg consulted *Auswärtiges Amt* about installing a radio and radar specialist (Dr Müller) in Stockholm with a view to soaking up information from Swedish technical experts, but this was turned down. Schellenberg to von Thadden, 9 October 1944, Abwehrakten, Inland II Geheim. [Kopior ur AAA, Vol. 99, UD:s arkiv], RA.
53. Although the relative tardiness to render Wagner *png* was undoubtedly inspired in part by a Swedish desire not to rub up the Germans the wrong way, there was also another important consideration to be taken into account. The counter-espionage authorities had achieved from an early point of the war onwards impressive results as regards insight into German intelligence organisation and agent activity in the country. Dr Wagner and his associates were known quantities. By keeping him and others at the helm and by inspiring in him and his colleagues a false sense of security, one effectively prevented the Germans from revitalising their espionage efforts.
54. P.M, 20 July 1943 in P 53 Ct, Allmänt ang. Tysklands beskickning Stockholm 1920–1944, UDA.
55. Axel to KO S, 9 July 1942 (intercepted telegram), Censurpärmar, UDA.
56. Telegram Axel to KO Schweden, 16 July 1942 (intercepted telegram) Curt Kempffs Tjänstearkiv, Curt Kempffs Tjänstearkiv, ÖVI: 3, KrA.
57. Telegram Axel to KO Schweden, 27 November 1942 (intercepted telegram), Curt Kempffs Tjänstearkiv, ÖVI: 3, KrA.
58. P.M, 20 July 1943 in P 53 Ct, Allmänt ang. Tysklands beskickning Stockholm 1920–1944, UDA.
59. C-Bureau seems also to have acted from time to time as a convenient covert channel of communication for counter-espionage matters, although counter-espionage lay strictly speaking outside its field of activity. See the communication Petersén to Juhlin-Dannfelt, 8 April 1942, Vol. 2, BII, C-Byrås arkiv, KrA, regarding the forwarding of 'a book' to Hauptmann Raven in Rohleder's department, Tirpitzufer and the exchange of information with the *Abwehr*, recorded in the same archive in February 1942, regarding a certain Estonian engineer related on his mother's side to Dzerzhinsky.
60. Telegram from KO Schweden to Axel, 30 July 1942 (intercepted telegram) Curt Kempffs Tjänstearkiv, ÖVI: 3, KrA.
61. Adlercreutz, *Historik*, p. 34.
62. Ibid, pp. 22–3.
63. I am much indebted to Father Robert Graham S.J. for allowing me to read his unpublished Ms. study of Nazi espionage in the Vatican (untitled). I shall refer to this manuscript hereafter simply as Graham. Through other personal sources, I have been able to fill in the picture of the elusive Ascher and his activities in some detail.
64. For general background, see Deutsch.
65. See Muckermann, p. 642.
66. Personal information.
67. Ascher claimed to have been in contact with Palairet, the British Minister in Athens. Palairet was a convert to Roman Catholicism and had served previously as minister in Stockholm (1935–37) and Vienna (1937–38).
68. Ascher was certainly vulnerable to the carrot and the stick. His money had run out, he had no job, he had a brother still in Berlin and he had perhaps been compromised in various ways through his private life.
69. Quoted in Graham where the source is given as the papers of the late Prof. Burkhart Schneider S.J., custodian of the Leiber papers, Gregorian University, Rome.

70. Copy of letter in a private archive.
71. See also Adlercreutz, *Historik*, p. 56.
72. US Legation to UD, 13 December 1944, Uppgifter om spioner i Sverige, R72 L, UDA.
73. Kumenius, pp. 209–10.
74. Trial papers in RR5-1945[1], StA. For Hampton, Sidney Smith and Iwanow, see Ch. 2. Wilfred Latham was a member of the Stockholm SOE group. Jerzy Dunkel was a Polish intelligence officer who had served in Finland and who had visited Sweden on a number of occasions. Konar had come to Sweden from Copenhagen. It is far from certain that the real significance of these people was made clear at the trial. Another person to attract the attention of Paulsson was the C-Bureau senior officer Hellmuth Ternberg whom Paulsson suspected of being an Allied agent.
75. In actual fact, the Swedish Security service had legitimate reason to investigate Paulsson at a much earlier stage. On 4 February 1942, the Swedish interception service read a telegram from the naval attaché in Helsinki urgently requesting his counterpart in Stockhom to contact Paulsson regarding the Norwegian ships in Gothenburg. Both Paulsson's home and office telephone number were given and 'sehr deutschfreundlicher Oberstleutnant Martin Ekström' was named as a reference. See the intercepted telegram in Curt Kempffs Tjänstearkiv, ÖVI: 3, KrA. It is rather interesting that this telegram does not seem to have figured in the investigation into Paulsson and it may well be that it was retained within the Defence Staff. Ekström's role as a doughty defender of the German cause and as a recruiter for the Waffen-SS was known but by dint of his earlier military exploits, he had acquired influential friends. See Esther Petersén's memoir *Från Land till Land*. AST Münster appears to have maintained covert contact with Paulsson via a Finnish agent, 'Nordstern'.
76. For Summer see, e.g., Masterman or more recently, *British Intelligence in the Second World War*, Vol. 4. I have made use of certain complementary Swedish documentation, namely a letter from the Swedish Consul-General in London of 18 August 1945 and an accompanying report of 5 September 1945, UDA.
77. The author's earlier essay should also be consulted. The present account, however, has been brought up to date in the light of *British Intelligence in the Second World War*, Vol. 4.
78. At the end of 1941, Florman, the head of ABA, had notified the Lufthansa manager at Bromma airport of his plan for a service to England. At the same time, he managed to win the tacit support of the German Air Attaché (Petersen) in Stockholm. By the middle of 1942, certain German organs began to have second thoughts. On 21/22 June, the plane *Gripen* was fired upon on its return flight from Scotland and on 7 July, Petersen was told that the German Foreign Office and the *Reichslufts-ministerium* were against the ABA service since it allowed the potential seepage of supplies to England. In his reply, Petersen pointed out that *Auswärtiges Amt* appeared to be unaware of the fact that the Luftwaffe Operations Staff Ic and the *Abwehr* were interested in this service. In any case, the service now existed *de facto* and the aim should be to use it to German advantage. On 28 July, he summarised for his superiors in Berlin a discussion with Söderblom at the Swedish Ministry for Foreign Affairs. Söderblom had underlined the Swedish desire for an independent link with the Swedish Legation in London. Such a link also had a value for the Germans in view of Sweden's diplomatic role as a protecting power for German, Hungarian and Finnish interests overseas. Söderblom then added: 'Moreover in this way an information service about prisoners of war, internees etc, could be maintained.' German telegrams in the Censurpärmar, UDA. It would be interesting to know if and how such an information service was organised.
79. Amt Ausland Abwehr to V.A.A, 23 September 1942 in Dr Karl-Heinz Krämer, Abwehr Einbau, Inland II Geheim, [Kopior ur AAA, Vol. 97, UD:s arkiv], RA. The stated reason for Krämer's positioning in Stockholm is interesting in view of Krämer's

later claim that he had been put there mainly for cover as a way of disguising his sources in Spain/Portugal.

80. Wied to AA, 3 October 1942, Krämer, Abwehr Einbau, Inland II Geheim [Kopior ur AAA, Vol. 97, UD:s arkiv], RA.
81. Ritter to RAM, 17 October 1942, Krämer, Abwehr Einbau, Inland II Geheim [Kopior ur AAA, Vol. 97, UD:s arkiv], RA.
82. von Grote, Aktenvermerk, 27 October 1942. Krämer, Abwehr Einbau, Inland II Geheim [Kopior ur AAA, Vol. 97, UD:s arkiv], RA. From June 1943, he was allowed to telegraph his reports via the air attaché's office thus speeding up the relay of purely military information.
83. Except where it is explicitly stated to the contrary, I have referred to the microfilmed collection of Krämer telegrams in rolls T 120, 98 and T120, 399, NA.
84. See note 83.
85. See note 83.
86. EDS AL 1828/1 PT2, IWM.
87. See the report from Amt Mil., RHSA of 16 September 1944, RH2/v.1513 (alt: H2/114), BM-MA.
88. The coupling of Ostro with Krämer is interesting in the light of his post-war interrogation where he emphasised the importance of the Fulep organisation. Did Fulep also pool information with Ostro?
89. Cited in the so-called Hesketh Report and made available to the present author through the kindness of T. L. Cubbage II.
90. In February 1944, Krämer had reported that the second front, owing to Allied disagreements, had been postponed until June; a telegram from Krämer (dated 16 September 1944) forecast an airborne landing in the Arnhem area. This arrived at OKW in Berlin after Operation Market Garden had begun on the 17th.
91. One aspect is touched upon in Ch. 2. *British Intelligence in the Second World War*, Vol. 4, p. 200, emphasises the importance of the documents received by OSS in Switzerland in the autumn of 1943. British knowledge and fears of Krämer's activities in Stockholm however predated the information passed on by OSS although the latter material may have given it a new dimension.
92. I have followed the account given in *British Intelligence in the Second World War*, Vol. 4 which remains the only reliable guide to documentation unlikely to be made public. For certain subsidiary aspects, the reader is referred to my earlier essay on Krämer.
93. SIS was aware that Krämer had certain *bona fide* sources in Stockholm. Thus his claims could not be written off completely.
94. The two had first met in London in 1939. The same journalist figured among the select list of confidants of the German AMA in Stockholm, von Watzdorf. At one stage in 1944, the British toyed with plans for 'listening in' on a meeting in Stockholm between Krämer, his boss in the *Abwehr* Air Intelligence Section, Kleyenstüber, and the journalist but nothing came of this.
95. Cf. *British Intelligence in the Second World War*, Vol. 4, p. 277. Grundböck is named as a Krämer source in, e.g., Kahn's 'Hitler's Spies'. Krämer had first met Grundböck in Budapest in August 1940.
96. The information was said to be sent in microfilm (not microdot), carried by Hungarian diplomatic bag via the air route Lisbon–Berlin, Berlin–Stockholm, with a transmission time of eight days and upwards. For some reason, the British Official History does not take up the possibility of *radio* contact although the early account of Reile, pp. 292–3, which obviously refers to Krämer's activities, explicitly mentions this. One oddity of Reile's account may be explained if it is assumed that this radio link was maintained not by the Germans themselves but by some other intelligence service or services who then supplied information to Krämer in Stockholm.

97. Notably his Arnhem scoop. British opinion, for technical reasons, remained sceptical and concluded that this particular scoop was 'an intelligent guess'.

98. According to Hinsley and Simkins, Krämer's association with Fulep was later independently confirmed when the press attaché at the Hungarian Legation in Madrid, Joseph Fullop, was interrogated and admitted to having been involved in a group supplying information to Krämer and the Japanese. This information had come from open sources: *Life, Fortune, Flight, The Aeroplane, Aero Digest, The Economist*.

99. *British Intelligence in the Second World War*, Vol. 4, p. 278.

100. When cross-examined by the Allies about his knowledge of Krämer's sources in Sweden, Schellenberg maintained that Krämer after much soul-searching had mentioned only one name, that of a diplomat, to whom he had paid out 8,000 crowns every month. This charge was subsequently investigated in Stockholm but was dismissed as unfounded by the Swedish Ministry for Foreign Affairs. Other investigations concerned female secretarial staff in key departments who had been known to have had contact with Krämer.

101. Busch asserted to his American captors that he knew that Krämer had been involved in channelling the capital of various Nazi potentates to a financial safe haven but the Americans dismissed this as entirely unfounded. Another hypothesis, toyed with by various German counter-espionage experts in the wake of the Rote Kapelle arrests at the end of 1942, was that Krämer was in touch with the Russians and was feeding them information from German intelligence reports in return for mediocre *spielmaterial*.

102. Swedish Legation in Berlin to UD, 3 May 1919, UD:s arkiv, Vol. 279 (1902 Dossier System), RA.

103. See Mader p. 223 where Cramer (KO Lithuania) is named as his case officer.

104. Kramarz's visit, which was evidently surrounded with a certain secrecy, causd an angry telegram to be sent from the German service attachés in Stockholm complaining that Kramarz, although the AA liaison to OKW, had failed to meet and consult them. On the other hand, he had had one or two meetings with Wagner. See the intercepted telegram dated 26 August 1942, Censurpärmar, UDA.

105. The author conjectures that A = Adlercreutz. Both he and Lindquist flew to Berlin on 23 September 1942 for discussions with the chief of OKW Ausland-Abwehr. Part of their mission was to try to extract some concession on the part of the imprisoned 'Warsaw Swedes'. The other subjects on the agenda remain unknown. In all probability, the British impression that the Chief of Swedish Intelligence (Landquist) had visited Berlin (and which resulted in an invitation to the latter to visit London) resulted from a scrambled vowel in the whisper that reached them.

106. It is tempting to see Klaus as a Swedish-based counterpart to 'Max'. However to Petrov, who had an insight into Soviet covert activities in Sweden, his various names and codenames said nothing.

107. Apart from secrecy and security considerations, external direction was a way of keeping Wagner's nose clean (thus honouring the agreement between Canaris and Adlercreutz) and satisfying the *Abwehr*'s requirements at the same time.

108. Officer in the Imperial Russian Army; instructor to the Persian Gendarmes; polo-trainer in Argentina and a member of the Argentinian secret police. Klamroth represented *Abwehr* IIIF, i.e. counter-espionage. See Bjerg, p. 214, Vol. 2.

109. He was sentenced to ten months' hard labour in accordance with Ch. 8 Paragraph 14 of the Penal Code. See trial papers in RR5-1941[3], StA.

110. Ausland Amt Abwehr to V.A.A., 23 October and 30 October 1941 in Pol I M, Abwehr Schweden, [Kopior ur AAA, Vol. 74, UD:s arkiv], RA. Walter E's association specifically with the *Abwehr* was not thought to be known to the Swedes.

111. This money was eventually paid over by a member of Bureau Wagner but the Bureau was kept in the dark about the reason for the payment.

112. See documentation concerning Frhr. Waldemar von Oppenheim (Baron Schroeder)

in Inland II Geheim [Kopior ur AAA, Vol. 100, UD:s arkiv], RA.
113. This is available in the files AL 1678/1, AL 1678/2, IWM.
114. For the nickname 'Stink Bomb' Müller, see RR(5)-1945[5].
115. See the previous section on Krämer.
116. Telegram to Air Attaché for Naval Attaché, Stockholm, 10 January 1943 (intercepted telegram), Censurpärmar, UDA.
117. von Grote to Chief, Abwehr II, 20 December 1943, Pol I M [Kopior ur AAA, Vol. 74, UD:s arkiv], RA.
118. Bürkner to V.A.A., 24 December 1943, Pol I M [Kopior ur AAA, Vol. 74, UD:s arkiv], RA.
119. Cf. the discussion in Lööw, Ch. 5.
120. Lundborg headed the Institute of Race Biology at the University of Uppsala.
121. For Wagener see correspondence in Spionageabwehr, Vertrauensmann und Agenten, Band 3 1940–1941, Inland II Geheim [Kopior ur AAA, Vol. 100, UD:s arkiv], RA.
122. An employee of the military attaché's office later testified to the fact that the telegrams received from Finke for forward dispatch were already encrypted. They were presumably then encrypted a second time before transmission from that office.
123. For Dmitriewsky as a source of insight into Soviet policy, see Rosenfeldt.
124. For the activities of Colonel Fleischhauer of *Welt-Dienst*, see, e.g., Wärenstam.
125. For a little more about Krüger, see Oldmarks.
126. SOU 1946:86, p. 108.
127. SOU 1946:86, p. 108.
128. This is clear from the German charges against Knüfken and Wollweber.
129. Wied to AA, 19 August 1941, C75, Nr. 789 (intercepted telegram) C-Papper, KrA.
130. Head of the Security Police to Luther, 15 January 1942, Inland II Geheim [Kopior ur AAA, Vol. 100, UD:s arkiv], RA.
131. SOU 1946:93, p. 88.
132. SOU 1946:93, p. 89.
133. Söderblom to Richert, 17 January 1942, HP 321, UD:s arkiv (1920 Dossier System), RA.
134. According to Bamler, Neumann told him that the SD had influential connections in Sweden which he often visited to concert its efforts there.
135. The most prominent special visitor was of course Schellenberg himself.
136. Based primarily upon Woodward Vol. II, pp. 192–6, the interesting essay of Manninen and upon certain supplementary private information.
137. A revealing insight into the state of Swedish morale in the second half of 1940 will be found in Grafström's diary. See in particular his entry for 19 November 1940 on Boheman's performance at the information dinner.
138. John Colville recorded in his diary on 19 September 1940 that the Germans had been making tentative peace-feelers through Stockholm, adding 'Needless to say, these are not even considered'.
139. Another German secret emissary who was allowed to study Finnish attaché reports from London was Goering's friend, the arms dealer Veltjens. In December 1940, it was reported that he had been allowed, through his military contacts, to see the reports of the Finnish air attaché in London about the effects of the German air raids. This information was said to be of great interest to the Luftwaffe and the German Foreign Office gave its Minister in Helsinki instructions to obtain further such reports via his military attaché. See Document 474, ADAP, Serie D, XI. 2.
140. For a mention of Meller-Zakomelsky, see J. J. Stephan, *The Russian Fascists*, London, 1978. See also Åke Thulstrup's article 'Gustav V:s roll under midsommarkrisen 1941', *Historisk Tidskrift*, pp. 72–9, where Meller-Zakomelsky's 1941 report is cited as evidence for the monarch's abdication threat. In Thulstrup's article, the name of the visitor is not given and he remains at best a shadowy figure.
141. He carried a letter from Eljas Erkko, the former Finnish Foreign Minister and later

Finnish *chargé d'affaires* in Stockholm, requesting that no record was to be made of his entry into Finland. A similar provision was made when he left.

142. Unsigned report dealing with the visit to Sweden from 9 to 28 September 1940, Auslandsmeldungen des SD Schweden, 1940–44, Inland II Geheim [Kopior ur AAA, Vol. 100, UD:s arkiv], RA.

143. Ibid.

144. Ibid.

145. Meller-Zakomelsky was not the only German agent to cultivate the ageing monarch. Another was Baron Gottfried von Cramm who partnered the King at tennis.

146. Unsigned report dealing with the visit to Sweden from 9 to 28 September 1940, Auslandsmeldungen des SD Schweden, 1940–44, Inland II Geheim [Kopior ur AAA, Vol. 100, UD:s arkiv], RA.

147. According to Stephan, op. cit., p. 132, Meller-Zakomelsky was the general secretary of ROND, the Russian National Socialists with an HQ at Bleibtreustrasse in Berlin. The leader of this movement was the adventurer Bermondt-Avalov, known from his exploits at Riga in 1919.

148. He entered Sweden on 17 October 1941 and flew back to Berlin on Saturday 20 December, 1941. See E7:2, Expedition för Utländska passärenden, UD:s arkiv (1920 Dossier System), RA. Apart from his conversations with members of the Swedish Royal House, Meller-Zakomelsky also records impressions gleaned from conversations with various Stockholm-based journalists for British newspapers – Ralph Hewins, Demaitre and Ossian Goulding – as well as with the British Council representative, the poet Ronald Bottrall, in whom he divined 'a typical and experienced I[ntelligence] S[ervice] man'.

149. ADAP, Serie E, Band I, Document 107 of 9 January 1942.

150. von Uthmann had of course other valuable contacts at the Defence Staff. Thus, to take only one example, in the autumn of 1943 a Swedish diplomat gave a confidential lecture to senior staff officers about his observations in the Soviet Union. von Uthmann was able via a Swedish officer friend to send a full report about the lecture the very next day.

151. Telegram to Mil. Att., Stockholm, Stockholm, 6 September 1942 (intercepted telegram) Censurpärmar, UDA. In his Naval War Diary, Denham blames an American attaché in Stockholm for carelessness which put the Björnstjerna connection at risk. According to von Uthmann, German knowledge of the American communication came from interception and cryptanalysis of the American traffic.

152. A short official report dealing with Kellgren's contacts with the German MA was published by the Ministry for Foreign Affairs in 1946. Kellgren's defence was essentially that he had acted in accordance with his instructions, the gist of which was 'Keep the bugger happy!'. In the eyes of at least one experienced observer, he certainly appears to have succeeded. Whereas to Major Vagi, the Hungarian military attaché, Colonel Björnstjerna was 'Western orientated and anglophile' and Colonel Adlercreutz appeared as an 'opaque personality whose attitude is decidedly in doubt', Colonel Kellgren struck him as 'decidedly pro-German and sympathetic to the Axis'. See entry for 16 June 1942, Diary of the German Naval Attaché, Stockholm. For an interesting example of Kellgren as opinion-moulder, see von Roenne, Notiz zur Feindlage, 12/4/44, Handakte Chef Abt., FHW, AL 1622, IWM.

153. On the difficulty of obtaining information in Russia, see Carlgren's *Svensk underrättelsetjänst 1939–1945*, pp. 162–3.

154. See p. 19 of SOU 1964:15.

155. One possibility was that it was simply a reprisal for the conviction and imprisonment of V. Sidorenko, the Stockholm Intourist representative, at the end of 1942. In addition, on the broader diplomatic front, the Russians at that time wished to put pressure on the Swedes to be more active in getting the Finns to conclude a peace.

156. Lahousen's diary (entry for 5 May 1941) reveals another service performed by Sven Hedin. When *Abwehr* II were investigating various schemes for stirring things up in the Far East, the explorer provided the Section with maps and other relevant material.

157. In an article presumably designed to embarrass Bonn, which appeared in *New Times* No. 13, 1965, Lev Bezymensky asserted on the basis of the Soviet interrogation of a former member of Inf III, that Duckwitz who was the Danish Inf III Resident had numbered among his sources two Swedish shipowners, one in Bergen in Norway and the other in Gothenburg, a young titled widow who moved in court circles in Stockholm and a member of the Swedish Royal Family. Duckwitz, who was officially a shipping expert at the German legation in Copenhagen, is better known as the man who tipped off the Danes about the imminent Gestapo action against the Jews in 1943, thus allowing them to make their escape to Sweden.

158. Grassmann supplied Lickfett with reports against payment from IGEFA.

159. In their book, Aalders and Wiebes give several examples of Lickfett's role as a German economic agent and indicate his involvement in the Bosch affair. As a naturalised Swede, he was particularly active in buying up small Swedish mines and was involved in acquiring the Hörken Gyttorp, Inglamåla and Sjangeli mines for German companies. The mine at Hörken produced wolfram and molybdenum. See the report on German infiltration in the Swedish mining industry in Vol. 7, Heml, FKB arkiv, RA.

160. AO i.e. *Auslandsorganisation*. Stengel later on in the course of the war moved to Switzerland.

161. P.M, 28 September 1945, Allmänt angående Tysklands beskickning i Stockholm, II, P53-Ct, UDA.

162. Thus, for example, among the informants of *Stapoleitstelle*, Hamburg, was a person representing a foreign consulate in Stockholm who supplied information regarding members of the diplomatic corps, their morale and their views as to the outcome of the war. The contact was maintained through a Hamburg businessman.

163. Lasswell, p. 137.

164. SOU 1946: 86, p. 9.

165. Some examples are given in SOU 1946:86, pp. 264–7.

166. Colonel Frey Rydeberg, a former Swedish military attaché in Finland, suggested to the German naval attaché in Stockholm, shortly before the outbreak of the war, that if the German Legation were prepared to help with the financial details, he would send letters to friends and other persons in England criticising British policy. A member of the legation much concerned with propaganda and information matters, Kurt Brunhoff, saw in this proposal an excellent opportunity for influencing public opinion in Britain via neutral channels. Brunhoff to Schlemann, 16 August 1939, Greuel und Lugenmeldungen [Kopior ur AAA, Vol. 125, UD:s arkiv], RA.

167. Wied to AA, 20 December 1938. Reproduced in Thulstrup, p. 197.

168. Schellenberg cited Rutger Essén as one of his Swedish contacts before 1942. See P.M. angående samtal med Schellenberg, in HP 331, UD:s arkiv (1920 Dossier System), RA.

169. Intercepted telegram quoted in Thulstrup, pp. 199–200.

170. Wied to AA, 6 February 1942. Reproduced in Thulstrup, p. 201.

171. Quoted in Wärenstam, p. 234.

172. Trial papers in RR5-1945[10], StA.

173. Trial papers in RR5-1945[7], StA.

174. Torsten Kreuger's exertions on behalf of the New Germany were not always as great as some of his more zealous employees would have wished. A German report records that in May 1941, his son was dispatched to Stockholm on the initiative of Gunnar Müllern, *Aftonbladet*'s Berlin correspondent, in the hope of persuading his father to ensure that his newspapers adopted a wholeheartedly pro-Axis position. According to Müllern, a purge of liberal pro-British elements was needed in Stockholm.

Vertrauliche Bericht, 9 May 1941, Dienstelle Ribbentrop/R. Likus [Kopior ur AAA, Vol. 128, UD:s arkiv], RA.

175. Quoted SOU 1946:86, p. 42.
176. Ibid, p. 43. On 13 August 1941, instructions were given for an announcement about Roosevelt's appointment of Colonel William Donovan as the co-ordinator of an information and propaganda ministry, to be channelled through *Aftonbladet* or *Stockholms-Tidningen*. See AA to Diplogerma, 13 August 1941, C75, Nr. 724, (Intercepted telegram) C-papper, KrA.
177. Nothing, however, came of these schemes.
178. Branch offices were eventually opened in Madrid, Vichy, Paris, Geneva, Stockholm and Berlin. Plans were also made to cover Bucharest, Sofia, Kiev, Ankara and Rio.
179. News of the plans for *Radio Mundial* appear to have reached various interested parties through the young Count von Rosen.
180. Among those were said to be two princes of the Royal House, T. Kreuger, Carl Florman of ABA and the editor Brilioth. Report by Lentz, 13 September 1941, Einrichtung einer Radio Mundial-Redaktion in Stockholm, Kulturpol. Abteilung, Rundfunk Abteilung, Radio Mundial [Kopior ur AAA, Vol. 94, UD:s arkiv], RA. It was undoubtedly the involvement of the princes in this matter which led to the American suspicions noted by Aalders and Wiebes, p. 189.
181. One of the driving forces behind *Belgo-Baltic*, was the Swedish-American business-man, Eric Siegfried Erickson, the so-called 'counterfeit traitor'.
182. This person was later arrested and sentenced for espionage.
183. Apart from *Radio Mundial*'s role as a covert organ of propaganda, it was suspected that it was also designed to act as a cover for intelligence collection, arrangements having been made for the forwarding of purely military intelligence to Lausanne. It is perhaps not without interest that one of Dr Krämer's earlier tasks in Sweden was that of winding up *Radio Mundial*'s affairs and that one of his informants was a Mexican diplomat who had been involved in the work of the news bureau.
184. Hewins' dispatch was specifically censored by the Swedish authorities regarding *Belgo-Baltic*'s involvement in the establishment of a Swedish subsidiary.
185. The Swedish authorities warned the Royal participants about their suspicions regarding *Radio Mundial*. At the same time, the British and American authorities decided to apply economic pressure. The latter threat made the *Belgo-Baltic* withdraw from its direct involvement. However *Radio Mundial* did not give up immediately. Instead with the help of a local lawyer and a recommendation from *Belgo-Baltic*, a new company *Radio Mundial A.B.* was set up with a capital of 5,000 crowns. All shares were controlled by *Radio Mundial* in Lisbon.
186. There were charges of financial mismanagement and also allegations that the agency had been infiltrated by foreign intelligence services.
187. Günther to Littorin [Kersten's lawyer], 28 November 1946, in HP 39 N/Spec, Felix Kersten, UD:s arkiv (1920 Dossier System), RA.
188. In comparison to certain of his more brutish companions, Schellenberg appeared a man of charm and reason both of which he used to good effect in impressing the Swedes.
189. The account which follows relies on Kerstin's account of 12 June 1945 in HP 39 N/Spec Felix Kersten and Walter Schellenberg's Trosa Memorandum in HP 1637, both files in UD:s arkiv (1920 Dossier System), RA.
190. *Aide-mémoire* from State Department, 24 January 1944 in FO 371/39085, PRO.
191. (a) The evacuation of all territories occupied by Germany and the restitution of their sovereignty; (b) the abolition of the Nazi Party and democratic elections under American and British supervision; (c) the abolition of Hitler's dictatorship; (d) the restitution of the 1914 German frontier; (e) the reduction of the German Army and Air Force to a size excluding the possibility of aggression; (f) the complete

control of the German armament industry by the Americans and British; (g) the removal of the leading Nazis and their appearance before a court charged with war-crimes.

192. Entry 4 December 1943, The Kersten Memoirs.
193. Letter to the author, 6 May 1987.
194. Dickson appears to have enjoyed intimate contacts with C-Bureau.
195. See Hesse's own account.
196. According to private information, Schellenberg had a personal meeting with Mallet in Stockholm, most probably in mid-January 1945. When Mallet reported to London about this direct encounter, he was taken to task by Churchill.
197. Storch, the representative of the Jewish Agency in Stockholm and an acquaintance of Klaus, gave a probably reliable picture of Klaus's 'contacts' to Sven Grafström after the war: 'He [Klaus] come to me and say: you speak good Russian you willing to earn much money easy deal fifteen minutes. I say I no do easy deal but let hear. He say German delegation come here contact the Russians. I no manage to make the connection. You play Russian negotiator. I tell Germans peace cost 200,000 crowns paid immediately to you. You take 100,000. I keep 100,000. I answer that deal no suit me.' *Grafströms Anteckningar*, Vol. 2, p. 878.
198. Various attempts were also made by the German Security Service during 1943 to establish contacts with Soviet representatives, using Swedish channels. The Berlin lawyer, Langbehn, who had also been involved in assisting the seven imprisoned Warsaw Swedes, was dispatched by the SD to Stockholm to ascertain from Soviet representatives there what Stalin's attitude was to separate peace. This mission was apparently designed merely to make the Western side more amenable to negotiation. At the end of the year, an abortive attempt was made through Section VI of the SD in Copenhagen to initiate a dialogue with the Tass correspondent Pavlov in Stockholm.
199. Beck-Friis to Grafström, 24 July 1944, HP 329, UD:s arkiv (1920 Dossier System), RA.
200. FO to Clark Kerr, Moscow, 20 August 44 in FO 371/39088, PRO.
201. Clark Kerr to FO, 7 September 1944, in FO 371/39088, PRO.
202. In addition to the Finns, the Hungarians and Romanians also made use of Stockholm in their efforts to extricate themselves from the war. For the Hungarian and Romanian exercises in secret diplomacy, see, e.g., the book of Juhasz and the essay of Nanno, respectively. In September 1944, the Japanese tried via the Swedish minister in Tokyo to engage the Swedes as go-betweens in a dialogue with the British government. The latter, having been apprised of this approach by Mallet in Stockholm, intimated (after consultation with the American government) that it was only prepared to deal with a direct request from the Japanese. A second Japanese attempt via the same channel took place in April 1945 and shortly afterwards in May 1945, Onodera tried to enlist the help of Eric S. Erickson, in contacting the British and American ministers in Stockholm. In the light of the earlier British response, the Swedes took no further action and gave instructions that Erickson should refrain from further involving himself in this matter. For Onodera–Erickson, see the Memorandum 10 May 1945 in HP 1637, UD: arkiv (1920 Dossier System), RA.
203. The activities of the Japanese in trying to bring about a German–Soviet Separate Peace provide an obvious example.
204. See Nish's essay on 'Japanese Intelligence and The Approach of the Russo-Japanese War' in Andrew and Dilks.
205. Henrik Brock and Hjalmar Ringberg to H. M. Minister, Copenhagen, 21 January 1918 in FO 211/491, PRO.
206. Among the few things in Sweden itself of direct intelligence interest for the Japanese

was presumably the Hagelin cipher machine in view of its later use by the Americans. In his book *Intercept, The Enigma War*, p. 124, Garlinski claims (quoting as his source Oskar Stürzinger, Zug) that during the war the Japanese were so anxious to obtain copies of certain Hagelin machines that they went as far as dispatching a submarine to the Baltic to pick them up. According to Allen, the Japanese, with the help of Swedish cipher machines similar to the one used by the Americans, managed to start breaking US machine ciphers in the summer of 1944.

207. Onodera, like Krämer, claimed to have agents in England. He also boasted on one occasion that he was able to read the reports which Captain Cheshire, the Head of SIS in Stockholm, sent to London, For the latter point, see SAIC /29, 28 May 1945, NA. See also the entry for 27 May 1942 in the diary of the German Naval Attaché, Stockholm. The Allies, who eventually had access to Onodera's reporting via Sigint, had in general a low opinion of the material which he was transmitting. See *British Intelligence in the Second World War*, Vol. 4, p. 276.

208. The German reporting reveals a fair sprinkling of telegrams with information from Oran(= Onodera) or Haifisch (Japanese Sources).

209. Cf Allen, p. 555.

210. The Estonian had contacts with the Swedish, German, Japanese and French intelligence services and probably with others as well.

211. C-Bureau maintained contact with Onodera through a cutout from the turn of the year 1942/43 until the end of 1944. The Swedes supplied information about Germany and Russia in return for summaries relating to the meetings of Japanese attachés. Onodera was also interested in open publications.

212. See SAIC/29, 28 May 1945, NA.

213. Mäkelä provides useful insights.

214. It would be interesting to know what use was made of the latter breaks.

215. Report dated 23 March 1945 in Uppgifter om spioner i Sverige, R72 L, UDA. According to this, the Finns were reading Turkish traffic exchanged between Ankara and foreign missions from at least June 1943. Regular information about keys was said to be obtained from Germany and Hungary. For the achievements of Hungarian signal intelligence and cryptanalysis, see Höttl, Ch. 13.

216. Ehrenswärd to K. I. Westman, 22 November 1945, Uppgifter om spioner i Sverige, R72 L, UDA.

217. According to the evidence collected in connection with the C-Bureau investigation of 1948, at least one observer thought that C-Bureau had been too trusting altogether in the way it had permitted Finnish liaison officers to come and go as they liked. See Serie H, C-Byråns Arkiv, KrA.

218. Once the scheme actually got under way, information became available from sources in Switzerland, other than the Swiss General Staff and the designation of the Swiss material was accordingly changed from Zuckerhut to Eisberg.

219. He had met Krämer in Hungary in 1940/41. An arrangement was made for the exchange of information between AST Hamburg and the Air Branch of the Hungarian Intelligence Service.

220. The Swiss reports apparently emanated from the Swiss military attaché, Colonel Kaech, and dealt with Britain and America: operational strength, the possibilities of the invasion of NW Europe. The Finnish reports dealt mainly with the Eastern Front. The Swedish reports dealt with various conversations between Colonel Kempff, (from the end of 1943, Head of the Foreign Section of Swedish Military Intelligence) and Hungarian officers.

221. See Höttl, p. 140.

222. Some details about these wartime contacts will be found in Bower, Ch. 2.

223. An official summary of the pertinent facts relating to Operation Stella Polaris by the Finnish Ministry of Interior will be found in FO 511/121, PRO. See also the essay by

Cederberg and Elegemyr.
224. Smith, pp. 353–5.
225. Letter to author, 10 December 1985.
226. Black, pp. 186–7.
227. British Legation, Helsinki to FO, 30 July 1946 in FO 511/121, PRO.
228. Bericht über die Abwehrtatigkeit des Lt. Edmund Sala, Kempff, Ö II, Vol. 2, KrA.
229. The flow of information was two-way. The Finns apparently supplied Sala with information about Soviet vessels in Finnish harbours while Sala provided details about Soviet land forces as well as about German dispositions in Lappland, Norway and East Prussia.
230. According to Kumenius, Bureau Wagner had learned of the contacts between Sala and C-Bureau. See Kumenius, p. 203.
231. Thirty-six made the trip.
232. Sala had apparently hoped to continue his intelligence operations against the Soviet Union by offering his services to the Swedes. In addition to monitoring Russian tactical communications, Sala's group (Meldelcopf Nordland) had also succeeded in breaking certain Swedish military ciphers.
233. Wenzlau had joined the *Abwehr* in Bremen in July 1939. One of his first foreign agents was a Swiss businessman who agreed to collect information in England. Before coming to Sweden, Wenzlau had served in Portugal, travelling under the name Dr Wessel and employing the codename Leander.
234. This material came into the hands of the Allied authorities via agents in Stockholm. Certain documents later appeared in the Swedish newspaper, *Expressen*. See in particular the edition for Tuesday, 12 February 1946, p. 6.
235. Cf Kumenius, pp. 227–30.
236. For Klatt and his Soviet connection, see *British Intelligence in the Second World War*, Vol. 4, pp. 198–9. Enomoto supplied information for the Moritz telegrams which dealt with the Near East. See also Leverkuehn, p. 174.
237. The suggestion seems to have been inspired by Klatt. Radio was envisaged as the means of communication.

APPENDIX 1

1. The adoption of OTP produced a major improvement in the overall security of networks.
2. These double transposition systems were far from adequate. The basic system, although simple in conception, was tortuous in application. Vanek, for example, complained about the amount of time ciphering matters took up. The modified double transposition system which made use of keys prepared in advance, although an improvement, was still likely to engender ciphering errors. More importantly, all double transposition systems were vulnerable to cryptanalytical attack.
3. See Kahn's article in *Cryptologia*.
4. For British success in reading Fish traffic, see Appendix 2 of Hinsley *et al.*, Vol. 3, Part 1.
5. In coming to grips with Dora, the Swedes were eventually obliged to break into the office of the German air attaché at Karlavägen.

APPENDIX 2

1. Battley's report on security at British installations in Stockholm will be found in FO 850/72, PRO.

2. Ibid.
3. Ibid.
4. Memorandum dated 8 March 1945, Angående säkerhetstjänst (muntligt meddelat försvarsminister 22/2/45), Fsstab, Utrikesavdelning, Serie EII: 4, Handbrev 1943–45, Vol. 1, KrA.
5. Trial papers RR5-1946[8], StA. Grönheim, a member of the SD who was supplied with the fruits of this operation, declared immediately after the war that he had seen copies of reports from the Swedish Legation as early as 1940.
6. As an example of the latter type of information, Grönheim recalled reports from the Swedish Minister in Moscow which came into his hands thanks to the penetration of the legation in Berlin.
7. Juhlin-Dannfelt's memoir (Hågkomster, typewritten manuscript, Juhlin-Dannfelts arkiv, KrA) contains some interesting remarks about Canaris. Among other things, he tells briefly how Canaris personally arranged for Madame Szymanski, the wife of the former Polish military attaché in Berlin, to pass secretly and in safe keeping from Poznan through Germany to Switzerland. 'The admiral greatly admired this strong-willed and fearless woman.' In Berlin, Szymanska was hidden for a day or two in Juhlin-Dannfelt's apartment before moving on to Berne where (according to Juhlin-Dannfelt) 'she entered the Western intelligence service'. Cf. West, p. 116. Another important informant of Juhlin-Dannfelt was Count von Albedyll who warned him three or four times about leaks in Stockholm. See von Post's Memorandum, 28 August 1945 in HP 330, UD:s arkiv (1920 dossier systemå, RA.
8. Kaltenbrunner appears to have believed that Juhlin-Dannfelt was passing on information from Canaris-Kaulbars to the Russians in Stockholm. Kaulbars served as Canaris' special adviser in Russian matters and after the launching of Barbarossa, had travelled to the Eastern front to report on developments on behalf of the *Abwehr*. On his return to Berlin, he usually looked up Juhlin-Dannfelt and recounted what he had witnessed. While the idea that Juhlin-Dannfelt passed on any information to the Russians may be discounted, it is possible that some account of his meetings with Kaulbars and Canaris reached the Western intelligence services. Cf. Denham, p. 161.
9. The contents were photographed and the case returned. According to Kaltenbrunner, there were reports about the Luftwaffe and experiments in nuclear fission.
10. Richert to von Post, Stockholm, 27 January 1945, P53 Ct III, UDA.

APPENDIX 3

1. See p. 112, Foreign Relations of the United States, 1942, Vol. 5, regarding the increased use of the Swedish route for cable communications to and from Argentina after the introduction of censorship in the USA.
2. There was some speculation whether there was a reverse flow through Switzerland.
3. The owner of the parent Argentinian firm involved in this telegram traffic was well known for his pro-Axis sympathies. However, when the Americans pressed for the blacklisting of his operations in Chile, they were told by MEW that the gentleman in question had been of assistance to an 'interested Department', that it was hoped to use him to watch the movements of Axis funds in Argentina and that these plans would be nullified by blacklisting. The British Minister in Santiago, on the other hand, had little faith in the new collaborator, believing that it played into his hands and simultaneously risked destroying Chilean confidence in the conduct of Allied economic warfare. Top Secret/GUARD telegram from MEW to Halifax, 4 December 1944; Orde to Halifax, 6 December 1944, both in Fo 115/1266, PRO.

APPENDIX 4

1. Among the senior State Security personnel to serve in Stockholm were Ivan Chichaev, later legal Resident in London, Andrei Graour later serving in London and subsequently proposed as liaison officer with the OSS in the United States and Boris Jartsev whose importance as a Soviet representative had become apparent in Helsinki in 1938.
2. Personal information.
3. See Adlercreutz, *Historik*, p. 23.
4. Documents 73 and 104, ADAP, Serie D, IX.
5. Trial papers RR(5)-1941 [7], StA.
6. For the surveillance of Communists, see Molin.
7. See, for example, the trial papers RR(5)-1942 [11] and RR(5)-1943 [17] StA.
8. Cf Adlercreutz, *Historik*, pp. 45–6.
9. Cf Adlercreutz, *Historik*, pp. 47–8.
10. Trial papers RR(5)-1943 [7], StA.
11. Trial papers RR(5)-1944 [18] and RR(5)-1945 [11], StA.
12. Cf. Petrov on Klara.
13. For KPD activities in Sweden, see Peters.
14. See Wilhelmus.
15. Private information.
16. Tofte, pp. 58–61.
17. See, e.g., Nano's article on Soviet–Rumanian discussions in Stockholm. The gradual opening of Russian wartime archives will provide a much more detailed picture of Soviet foreign policy-making and intelligence operations.

Bibliography

1 OFFICIAL PUBLICATIONS

Svensk Författningssamling
Riksdagens Protokoll
Protokoll vid riksdagens hemliga sammanträden 1942–1945 (Stockholm, 1976).

Aktstycken utgivna av Kungl. Utrikesdepartementet
Förbindelserna mellan chefen för lantförsvarets kommandoexpedition och tyske militär attachén i Stockholm (Stockholm, 1946).
Frågor i samband med norska regeringens vistelse utanför Norge 1940–1943 (Stockholm, 1948).
1945 års svenska hjälpexpedition till Tyskland, Förspel och förhandlingar (Stockholm, 1956å.
Förhandlingarna 1945 om svensk intervention i Norge och Denmark (Stockholm, 1957).

Statens Offentliga Utredningar

Justitiedepartementet. [SOU 1940:8] Betänkande med förslag till lag om ändrad lydelse av 8 kap. strafflagen m.m (Stockholm, 1940).
[SOU1964:15] Utl)tande av Juristkommissionen i Wennerströmaffären (Stockholm, 1964).
[SOU1964:17] Rapport av parlamentariska n)mnden i Wennertrömaffären (Stockholm, 1964).

Socialdepartementet. [SOU 1946:36]: Betänkande angående flyktingars behandling (Stockholm, 1946).
[SOU 1946:86]: Den tyska propagandan i Sverige under krigsåren 1939–45 (Stockholm, 1946).

291

[SOU 1946:93]: Betänkande angående utlämnande av uppgifter om flyktingar (Stockholm, 1947).

Inrikesdepartementet. [SOU 1948:7]: Parlamentariska undersöknings-kommissionen angående säkerhetstjänstens verksamhet (Stockholm, 1947).

2 COLLECTIONS OF DOCUMENTS

Akten zur deutschen auswärtigen Politik, Serie D, E (Göttingen, 1969).
Spiegelbild einer Verschwörung, Die Opposition gegen Hitler under der Staatsstreich vom 20. Juli 1944 in der SD-Berichterstattung, (Herausgeben von H-A. Jacobsen) (Stuttgart, 1984).

3 OFFICIAL HISTORIES

Carlgren, Wilhelm, *Svensk utrikespolitik 1939–1945* (Stockholm, 1973).
Carlgren, Wilhelm, *Svensk underrättelsetjänst 1939–1945* (Stockholm, 1985).
Cruickshank, Charles, *SOE in Scandinavia* (Oxford, 1986).
Hinsley, F. H., Thomas, E. E., Ransom, C. F. G and Knight, R. C., *British Intelligence in the Second World War*, Vols 1–3 (London 1979–1984).
Hinsley, F. H. and Simkins, C. A. G., *British Intelligence in the Second World War*, Vol. 4 (London, 1990).
Howard, Michael, *British Intelligence in the Second World War*, Vol. 5 (London, 1990).
Medlicott, W. N., *The Economic Blockade*, I, II (London, 1952–59).
Woodward, Sir Llewellyn, *British Foreign Policy in the Second World War*, Vols 1 and 2 (London, 1970–1971).

4 OTHER PUBLISHED WORKS

Aalders, Gerard and Wiebes, Cees, *Affärer till varje pris, Wallenbergs hemliga stöd till nazisterna* (Falun, 1989).

Abshagen, Karl Heinz, *Canaris, Patriot und Weltbürger* (Stuttgart, 1949).

Amort, C. and Jedlicka, I. M., *The Canaris File* (London, 1970).

Anderson, Ivar, Från det nära förflutna, Människor och händelser 1940–1955 (Stockholm, 1969).

Andreen, Per G., *De mörka åren, Perspektiv på svensk neutralitetspolitik våren 1940–nyåret 1942* (Stockholm, 1971).

Andrew, Christopher, *Secret Service: The Making of the British Intelligence Community* (London, 1985).

Andrew, Christopher and Dilks, David, (ed.) *The Missing Dimension: Governments and Intelligence Communities in the Twentieth Century* (Southampton, 1984).

Assarsson, Vilhelm, *I skuggan av Stalin* (Stockholm, 1963).

Badh, Walle, *I statspolisens nät* (Stockholm, 1960).

Barker, Ralph, *The Blockadebusters* (London, 1976).

Bedarida, F., *La stratégie secrète de la drôle de guerre* (Paris, 1979).

Beevor, J. G., *SOE: Recollections and Reflections, 1940–45* (London, 1981).

Bermann Fischer, G., *Bedroht-Bewahrt* (Frankfurt, 1967).

Bernhardsson, Carl Olof, *Spionpolisen går på jakt* (Stockholm, 1952).

Birnbaum, I., *Achtzig Jahre Dabeigewesen* (Munich, 1974).

Björkegren, Hans, *Ryska Posten, De ryska revolutionärerna i Norden 1906–1917* (Kristianstad, 1985).

Björkman, Leif, *Operation Barbarossa, Svensk neutralitetspolitik 1940–1941* (Uddevalla, 1971).

Black, Peter R., *Ernst Kaltenbrunner, Ideological Soldier of the Third Reich* (Princeton, 1984).

Bludau, Kuno, *Gestapo (Geheim!), Widerstand und Verfolgung in Duisburg, 1933–1945* (Duisburg, 1973).

Boheman, Erik, *På vakt* (Stockholm, 1974).

Boldt-Christmas, G. E. F., *Voro vi neutrala?* (Stockholm, 1946).

Bower, Tom, *The Red Web* (Avon, 1989).

Brandt, Willy, *Att ta parti för friheten, Min väg 1930–1950* (Stockholm, 1983).

Bremer, Jörg, *Die Sozialistische Arbeiterpartei Deutschlands (SAP) Untergrund und Exil 1933–45* (Frankfurt, 1978).

Brodersen, Arvid, *Mellom Frontene* (Oslo, 1979).

Buchheit, Gert, *Der deutsche Geheimdienst, Geschichte der militärischen Abwehr* (Munich, 1966).

Burns, Frank (pseudonym), *Paradis för oss* (Stockholm, 1952).

Butler, Ewan, *Amateur Agent* (London, 1963).
Carlsson, Holger, *Nazismen i Sverige . . . ett varningsord* (Stockholm, 1942).
Casey, William, *The Secret War against Hitler* (London, 1989).
Christensen, Chr., *Det hemmelige Norge* (Oslo, 1983).
Cruickshank, Charles, *The Fourth Arm: Psychological Warfare 1938–1945* (Oxford, 1977).
Cruickshank, Charles, *Deception in World War II* (Oxford, 1979).
Dahlerus, Birger, *Sista försöket, London–Berlin sommaren 1939* (Stockholm, 1945).
Denham, Henry, *Inside the Nazi Ring: A Naval Attaché in Sweden 1940–1945* (London, 1984).
Deutsch, H. G., *The Conspiracy against Hitler in the Twilight War* (Minneapolis, 1968).
Englich, Kurt, *Den osynliga fronten, Spioncentral Stockholm* (Stockholm, 1985).
Erasmus, Johannes, *Der geheime Nachrichtendienst* (Göttingen, 1952).
Erlander, Tage, *1901–1939* (Stockholm, 1972).
Erlander, Tage, *1940–1949* (Stockholm, 1973).
Esters, Hans and Pelger, Hans, *Gewerkschafter im Widerstand* (Hannover, 1967).
Falkenstam, Curt, *Minan, En kriminalreporters minnen* (Stockholm, 1981).
Farago, L., *The Game of the Foxes* (London, 1972).
Fleischhauer, Ingeborg, *Die Chance des Sonderfriedens, Deutsch–Sowjetische Geheimgespräche 1941–1945* (Berlin, 1986).
Ford, Corey, *Donovan of OSS* (Boston, 1970).
Friberg, Göte, *Stormcentrum Öresund, Krigsåren 1940–45* (Borås, 1977).
Fritz, M., *German Steel and Swedish Iron Ore* (Gothenburg, 1974).
Futrell, Michael, *Northern Underground* (London, 1963).
Gidlund, Alfons, *Rörelsen* (Hedemora, 1989).
Gihl, Torsten, *Folkrätt under krig och neutralitet* (Stockholm, 1941).
Gilbert, Martin, *Finest Hour: Winston Churchill 1939–1941* (London, 1983).
Gjelsvik, Tore, *Hjemmefronten, Den civila motståndsrörelsen i Norge under den tyska ockupationen 1940–45* (Falköping, 1979).
Gondek, Leszek, *Na tropach tajemnic III rzeszy* (Warsaw, 1987).
Grafström, Sven, *Anteckningar 1938–1944* (Stockholm, 1987).
Grafström, Sven, *Anteckningar 1945–1954* (Stockholm, 1987).

Grimnes, Ole Kristian, *Et flyktingesamfunn vokser fram, Nordmenn i Sverige 1940–45* (Oslo, 1969).

Grundt Larsen, Jørgen, *Mostandsbevaegelsens Kontaktudvalg i Stockholm 1944–45* (Odense, 1976).

Haestrup, Jørgen, *Kontakt med England 1940–43* (Copenhagen, 1954).

Haestrup, Jørgen et al. (eds) *Besaettelsen 1940–45* (Copenhagen, 1979).

Hägglöf, Gunnar, *Svensk krigshandelspolitik under andra världskriget*, (Stockholm, 1958).

Hammar, Tomas, *Sverige åt svenskarna, Invandringspolitik, utlänningskontroll och asylrätt 1900–1932* (Stockholm, 1964).

Hammargren, Henning, *Vapenköp i krig* (Malmö, 1980).

Hammarlund, K. G., *På hemliga vägar, Svensk-norsk kurirtrafik 1940–45* (Stockholm, 1989).

Handel, Michael I., (ed.) *Strategic and Operational Deception in the Second World War* (London, 1987).

Heiskanen, Raimo, *Saadun Tiedon Mukaan . . . Päämajan johtama tiedustelu 1939–1945* (Helsinki, 1988).

Herslow, C., *Moskva, Berlin, Warszawa* (Stockholm, 1946).

Higham, Charles, *Trading with the Enemy* (London, 1983).

Hochmuth, Ursel and Meyer, Gertrud, *Streiflichter aus dem Hamburger Widerstand 1933–1945* (Frankfurt, 1969).

Höhne, Heinz, *Der Krieg im Dunkeln, Macht und Einfluß der deutschen und russischen Geheimdienste* (Munich, 1985).

Höttl, Wilhelm, *Hitler's Paper Weapon* (London, 1955).

Howard, Esme, *Theatre of Life: Life seen from the Stalls* (London, 1936).

Howe, Ellic, *The Black Game* (London, 1982).

Hyde, H. M., *The Quiet Canadian* (London, 1962).

Jacobsen, Alf R., *Muldvarpene, Norsk etterretning fra 1. verdenskrig til Arne Treholt* (Oslo, 1985).

Jarring, Gunnar, *Memoarer 1939–1952* (Stockholm, 1981).

Jones, R. V., *Most Secret War, British Scientific Intelligence 1939–1945*, (London, 1978).

Jones, R. V., *Reflections on Intelligence* (London, 1989).

Juhasz, Gyula, *Hungarian Foreign Policy, 1919–1945* (Budapest, 1979).

Kahn David, *The Codebreakers* (London, 1968).

Kahn David, *Hitler's Spies*, (London, 1978).

Karlsson, Rune, *Så stoppades tysktågen, Den tyska transiteringstrafiken i svensk politik 1942–1943* (Uddevalla, 1974).

Katkov, George, *Russia 1917: The February Revolution* (London, 1967).

Kellgren, Henry, *Sex krigsåren i Skölds skugga* (Stockholm, 1951).

Kersaudy, François, *Stratèges et Norvège 1940, Les Jeux de la Guerre et du Hasard* (Paris, 1977).

Koblik, Steven, *'Om vi teg, skulle stenarna ropa' Om Sverige och Judeproblemet 1933–1945* (Stockholm, 1987).

Kramish, Arnold, *The Griffin: The Greatest Untold Espionage Story of World War II* (Boston, 1986).

Kubu, Mert, *Gustav Möllers hemliga polis* (Stockholm, 1971).

Kumenius, Otto, *Kontraspion för fem nationer* (Stockholm, 1984).

Lamb, Richard, *The Ghosts of Peace 1935–1945* (Wilton, 1987).

Leifland, Leif, *Svartlistningen av Axel Wenner-gren, En bok om ett justitiemord* (Stockholm, 1989).

Leverkuehn, Paul, *German Military Intelligence* (Worcester, 1954).

Lewandowski, Josef, *Swedish Contribution to the Polish Resistance Movement during World War Two (1939–1942)* (Uppsala, 1979).

Lindberg, Hans, *Svensk flyktingspolitik under internationellt tryck 1936–1941* (Stockholm, 1973).

Lindley, Charles, *Memoarer* (Kristianstad, 1987).

Lööv, Heléne, *Hakkorset och Wasakärven, En studie av national-socialismen i Sverige 1924–1950* (Munkedal, 1990).

Lorain, Pierre (adapted by David Kahn), *Secret Warfare: The Arms and Techniques of the Resistance* (London, 1984).

Lunding, H. M., *Stemplet fortroligt* (Copenhagen, 1970).

Lützhöft, H-J, *Deutsche Militärpolitik und schwedische Neutralität 1939–42*, (Neumunster, 1981).

Macrae, R. S., *Winston Churchill's Toyshop* (Kineton, 1971).

Mader, Julius, *Hitlers Spionagegenerale sagen aus* (Berlin, 1970).

Mäkelä, Jukka L., *Hemligt krig* (Malmö, 1966).

Masterman, J. C., *The Double Cross System in the War of 1939 to 1945* (New Haven, 1972).

McLachlan, Donald, *Room 39* (London, 1968).

Meurling, Per, *Spionage och Sabotage i Sverige* (Stockholm, 1952).

Molin, Karl, *Hemmakriget* (Falköping, 1982).

Moravec, Frantisek, *Master of Spies* (London, 1975).

Muckermann, Friedrich, (edited and introduced by Nikolaus Junk), *Im Kampf Zwischen Zwei Epochen* (Mainz, 1973).

Munch-Peterson, T., *The Strategy of Phoney War* (Stockholm, 1981).

Munck, Ebbe, *Sibyllegatan 13* (Stockholm, 1967).

Munthe, Gustaf, *Tennsoldaten, Minnen från krigsåren* (Stockholm, 1960).

Munthe, Malcolm, *Sweet is War* (London, 1954).

Müssener, Helmut, *Exil in Schweden* (Munich, 1974).

Nerman, T., *Sverige i beredskap* (Stockholm, 1942).

Nerman, T., *Trots Allt!* (Stockholm, 1954).

Nevakivi, Jukka, *The Appeal that was Never Made: The Allies, Scandinavia and The Winter War 1939–1940* (London, 1976).

Nøkleby, Berit, *Pass godt på Tirpitz!, Norske radioagenter i Secret Intelligence Service 1940–1945* (Oslo, 1988).

Nørgaard, E., *Revolutionen der udeblev* (Copenhagen, 1975).

Nørgaard, E., *Den usynlige krig* (Copenhagen, 1975).

Nothin, Torsten, *Hågkomster* (Stockholm, 1966).

Nowak, Jan, *Courier from Warsaw* (London, 1982).

Nybom, Thorsten, *Motstånd-anpassning-uppslutning, Linjer i svensk debatt om utrikespolitik och internationell politik, 1940–1943* (Uddevalla, 1978).

Ohlmarks, Åke, *Efter mej syndafloden* (Köping, 1980).

Oldberg, U., *Attentat mot Norrskensflamman* (Stockholm, 1972).

Olsson, Ulf, *Bank, familj och företagande, Stockholms Enskilda Bank* (Stockholm, 1945).

Olsson, Sven-Olof, *German Coal and Swedish Fuel 1939–1945* (Gothenburg, 1975).

Ostelius, Hans, *Det var roligt nästan jämnt* (Malmö, 1975).

Palmstierna, Erik, *Orostid II, 1917–1919, Politiska dagboksanteckningar* (Stockholm, 1953).

Pantenburg, Vitalis, *Rußlands Griff um Nordeuropa* (Leipzig, 1938).

Peters, Jan, *Exilland Schweden* (Berlin, 1984).

Petersén, Esther, *Från land till land* (Stockholm, 1942).

Platen, Carl Henrik von, *Strängt förtroligt* (Stockholm, 1986).

Pöppel, Walter, *Deutschlands verlorene Jahre 1933–1945, Betrachtungen aus der Emigration* (Stockholm, 1986).

Posse, Amelie, *Åtskilligt kan nu sägas* (Stockholm, 1950).

Reile, Oscar, *Geheime Westfront, Die Abwehr 1935–1945* (Wels, 1962).

Rickman, A. R., *Swedish Iron Ore* (London, 1939).

Rørholt, Bjørn (with Bjarne W. Thorsen), *Usynlige soldater, Nordmenn i Secret Service forteller* (Larvik, 1990).

Rosenfeld, Niels Erik, *Knowledge and Power, The Role of Stalin's Secret Chancellery in the Soviet System of Government* (Copenhagen, 1978).

297

Salonen, Pekka (pseudonym) *Det spioneras i Helsingfors* (Stockholm, 1945).

Schellenberg, W., *Aufzeichnungen* (Wiesbaden–Munich, 1979).

Schindler, Dietrich and Toman, Jiri, *The Laws of Armed Conflict* (Leiden-Geneva, 1973).

Schlabrendorff, Fabian von, *The Secret War against Hitler* (London, 1966).

Singer, Kurt, *I spied and survived* (New York, 1980).

Sjöberg, Valentin, *Skuggan över Norden* (Stockholm, 1942).

Skodvin, Magne et al., *Mellom nøytrale og allierte* (Oslo, 1968).

Søhr, Joh., *Spioner og Bomber, Fra opdagelsepolitiets arbeide under verdenskrigen* (Oslo, 1938).

Söderman, Harry, *Skandinaviskt mellanspel* (Stockholm, 1945).

Stafford, David, *Britain and European Resistance 1940–1945: A Survey of the Special Operations Executive, with Documents* (London, 1980).

Strumph-Wojtkiewicz, S., *Tiergarten* (Warsaw, 1968).

Sykes, Christopher, *Troubled Loyalty: A Biography of Adam von Trott* (London, 1968).

Szende, Stefan, *Mellan våld och tolerans* (Stockholm, 1975).

Tanner, Väinö, *Finlands väg 1939–1940* (Helsingfors, 1950).

Tennant, Peter, *Vid sidan av kriget, Diplomat i Sverige 1939–1945* (Stockholm, 1989).

Thulstrup, Åke, *Med lock och pock, Tyska försök att påverka svensk opinion 1933–45* (Stockholm, 1962).

Thulstrup, Åke, *Svensk Utrikespolitik under andra världskriget* (Stockholm, 1950).

Torell, Ulf, *Hjälp till Danmark, Militära och politiska förbindelser 1943–1945* (Uddevalla, 1973).

Trommer, Aage, *Jernbanessabotagen i Danmark* (Odense, 1971).

Uhlin, Åke, *Februari krisen 1942* (Uddevalla, 1972).

Ulstein, Ragnar, *Etterretningstjenesten i Norge 1940–45*, Bind 1, Amatørenes Tid (Østerås, 1989).

Ulstein, Ragnar, *Etterretningstjenesten i Norge 1940–45*, Bind 2, Harde år, (Østerås, 1990).

Wagram, Walter (pseudonym) *I världskrigets skugga, Svenska spionerihistorier* (Stockholm, 1928).

Waldén, Thomas, *Den slutna världen, En redogörelse av de svenska säkerhetsorganisationerna* (Stockholm, 1970).

Wallenberg, J. A., *Fem år med Kreuger* (Stockholm, 1944).

BIBLIOGRAPHY

Wärenstam, Eric, *Fascismen och nazismen i Sverige* (Stockholm, 1972).
Wark, Wesley K., *The Ultimate Enemy: British Intelligence and Nazi Germany, 1933–1939* (London, 1985).
Wehner, Herbert, *Zeugnis* (Cologne, 1982).
West, Nigel (pseudonym), *MI6: British Secret Intelligence Service Operations 1909– 45* (London, 1983).
Wester, Sivert, *Martin Ekström-orädd frivillig i fem krig* (Uddevalla, 1986).
Westman, Karl Gustaf (ed. W. M. Carlgren), *Politiska anteckningar september 1939–mars 1943* (Stockholm, 1981).
Wheatley, Dennis, *The Deception Planners: My Secret War* (London, 1980).
Young, G., *Outposts of Peace* (London, 1945).
Zeman, Z. A. B., *Germany and the Revolution in Russia 1915–1918* (Oxford, 1958).
Zetterquist, Alvar, *Kriminalchefen berättar*, 2 vols. (Stockholm, 1957).

5 ARTICLES AND REVIEWS

Aalders, G. and Wiebes, C., 'Stockholms Enskilda Bank, German Bosch and IG Farben: A Short History of Cloaking', *Scandinavian Economic History Review*, Vol. XXXIII, No. 1 (1985), 25–50.
Allen, Louis, 'Japanese Intelligence Systems', *Journal of Contemporary History*, Vol. 22 (1987), pp. 547–62.
Arnal, Pierre, 'Fritz Thyssen et la route du fer', *Revue d'histoire diplomatique* (1962), pp. 147–57.
Barke, Gunnar, 'De sejlede Vandet tyndt i Øresund', *Aktuellt och Historiskt* (1968), 141–64.
Carlgren, Wilhelm, 'Die Meditationstätigkeit in der Aussenpolitik Schwedens waehrend des Zweiten Weltkrieges', in Bindschedler, R. L. (ed.) *Schwedische und schweizerische Neutralität im Zweiten Weltkrieg* (Basle and Frankfurt a. M., 1985).
Cederberg, Jörgen and Elvemyr, Göran, 'Operation Stella Polaris, Nordic Intelligence Cooperation in the Closing Stages of the Second World War' in *Clio goes spying*. Lund Studies in international history 17 (Malmö, 1983).
Fritz, Martin, 'Swedish Ball-Bearings and the German War Economy, *Scandinavian Economic History Review*, Vol. 15–35 (1973).

Kahn, David, 'The Geheimschreiber', *Cryptologia*, Vol. 3, No. 4 (1979), pp. 210–14.

Leche, Hakon, 'Huvuddragen av de militära insatser i säkerhetstjänstens område, in Carl-Axel Wangel (ed.) *Sveriges militära beredskap 1939–1945* (Köping, 1982).

Leifland, Leif, '"They must get in before the end" Churchill och Sverige 1944 och 1945', in *Utrikespolitik och Historia, Studier tillägnade Wilhelm M. Carlgren den 6 maj 1987* (Stockholm, 1987).

Leifland, Leif, 'Deception Plan Graffham and Sweden: Another View', *Intelligence and National Security*, Vol. 4, No. 2 (1989), pp. 295–315.

Lindgren, Hendrik, 'Adam van Trotts reisen nach Schweden 1942–1944', *Vierteljahreshefte für Zeitgeschichte*, 18 (1970), pp. 275–91.

Manninen, Ohto, 'Ludwig Weissauer i hemliga uppdrag 1940–1943', *Historisk Tidskrift för Finland* (1975), pp. 177–93.

McKay, C. G., 'Iron Ore and Section D: The Oxelösund Operation', *The Historical Journal*, 29, 4 (1986), pp. 975–78.

McKay, C. G. 'The Krämer Case, A Study in Three Dimensions', *Intelligence and National Security*, Vol. 4, No. 2 (1989), pp. 268–94.

Nano, F. C. 'The First Soviet Double Cross', *Journal of Central European Affairs*, 12 (1952), pp. 236–58.

Petersen, Magnus af, 'Svensk militär underrättelsetjänst under 2. världskriget', *Kungliga Krigsvetenskaps Akademiens Tidskrift*, 189 (1985), pp. 113–25.

Tennant, Peter, 'How we Failed to buy the Italian Navy', *Intelligence and National Security*, Vol. 3, No. 1 (1988), pp. 141–61.

Wäsström, Sven, 'Schweden als Arena der Nachrichtendienste während des Zweiten Weltkrieges', in Bindschedler, R. L., (ed.) *Schwedische und schweizerische Neutralität im Zweiten Weltkrieg*, (Basle and Frankfurt a. M., 1985).

Wäsström, Sven,' Den dolda fronten', in Nyström, B. O. and Skeppstedt, S, (eds), *Boden, Fästningen-Garnisonen-Samhället* (Västervik, 1990).

Wilhelmus, W., 'Märkliga Chaufförer', *Arbetarhistoria* (Stockholm), No. 35 (1985), pp. 2–11.

Zetterberg, Seppo, 'Die Tätigkeit der Liga der Fremdvölker Russlands in Stockholm während der Jahre 1916–1918', *Acta Balitica*, X, pp. 211–57.

BIBLIOGRAPHY

Postscript, March 1992: Jan Ottosson and Lars Magnusson's book *Hemliga Makter* (Stockholm: Tidens Förlag), which provides an interesting account of the Swedish Intelligence Service from 1905 to the Cold War, appeared after the completion of the present manuscript. Sir Peter Tennant's memoir of his wartime service in Sweden, *Touchlines of War*, was scheduled to be published by the University of Hull Press and Lampada Press in May 1992. The references in the present work are to the earlier Swedish edition of his book.

Index of Personal Names

(According to the Swedish convention, the letters Å/å,Ä/ä,Ö/ö come at the end of the alphabet. In the Index, an ordering which will appear more natural to English-speaking readers, has been preferred.)

302